Voice Over!
Seiyu Academy

3

Don't
Give u

D0465694

Vol.3
Story & Art by
Maki Minami

TECHNICAL ADVISORS
Yoichi Kato, Kaori Kagami, Ayumi Hashidate,
Ayako Harino and Touko Fujitani

Voice Over! Seiyu Academy

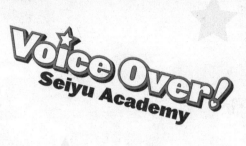

Vol. 3

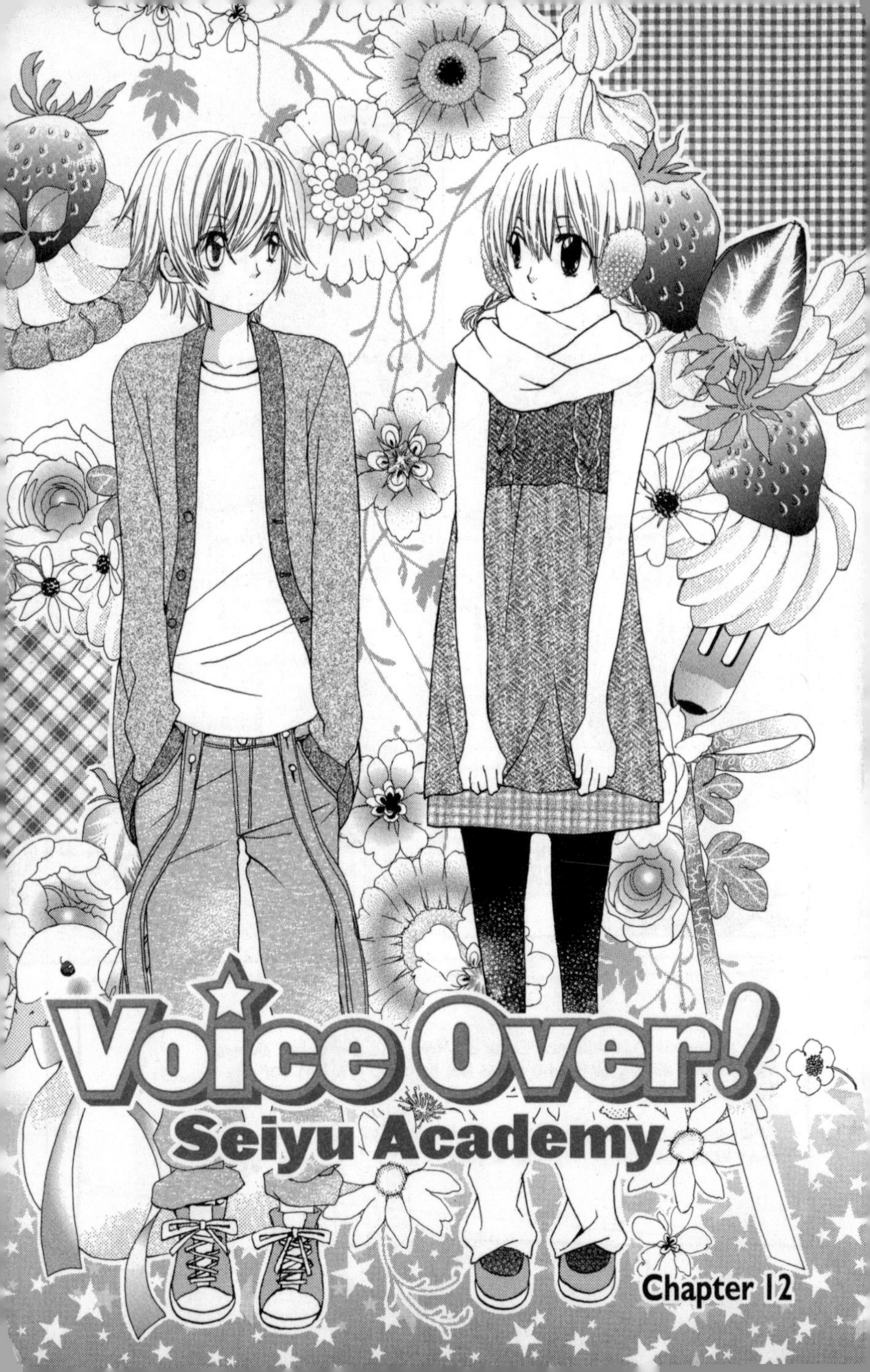
Voice Over!
Seiyu Academy
Chapter 12

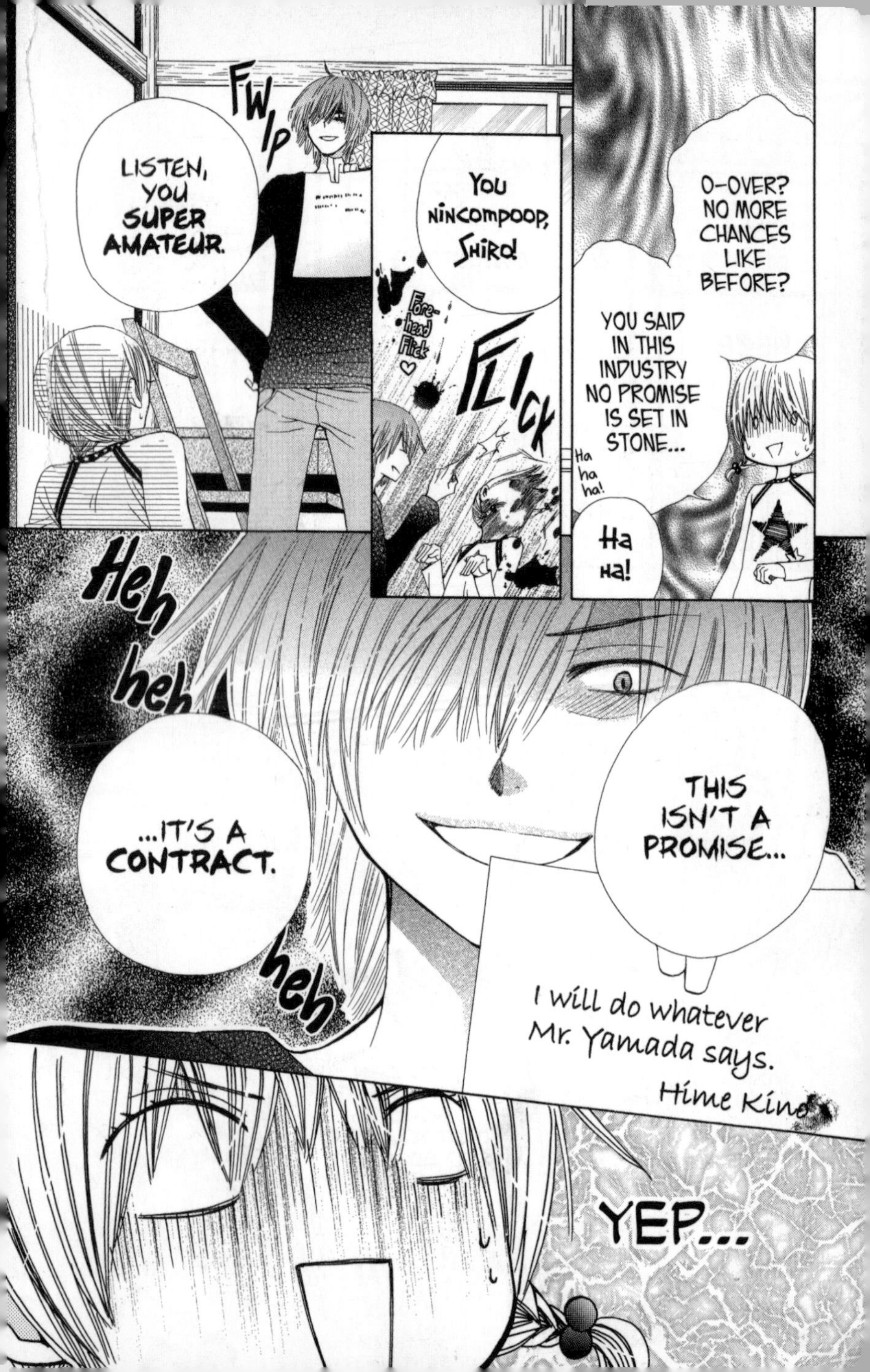
O-OVER? NO MORE CHANCES LIKE BEFORE?
YOU SAID IN THIS INDUSTRY NO PROMISE IS SET IN STONE...
Ha ha ha!
Ha ha!
YOU NINCOMPOOP, SHIRO!
Fore-head Flick ♡
FLICK
FWIP
LISTEN, YOU SUPER AMATEUR.
THIS ISN'T A PROMISE...
Heh heh
...IT'S A CONTRACT.
heh
I will do whatever Mr. Yamada says.
Hime Kino
YEP...

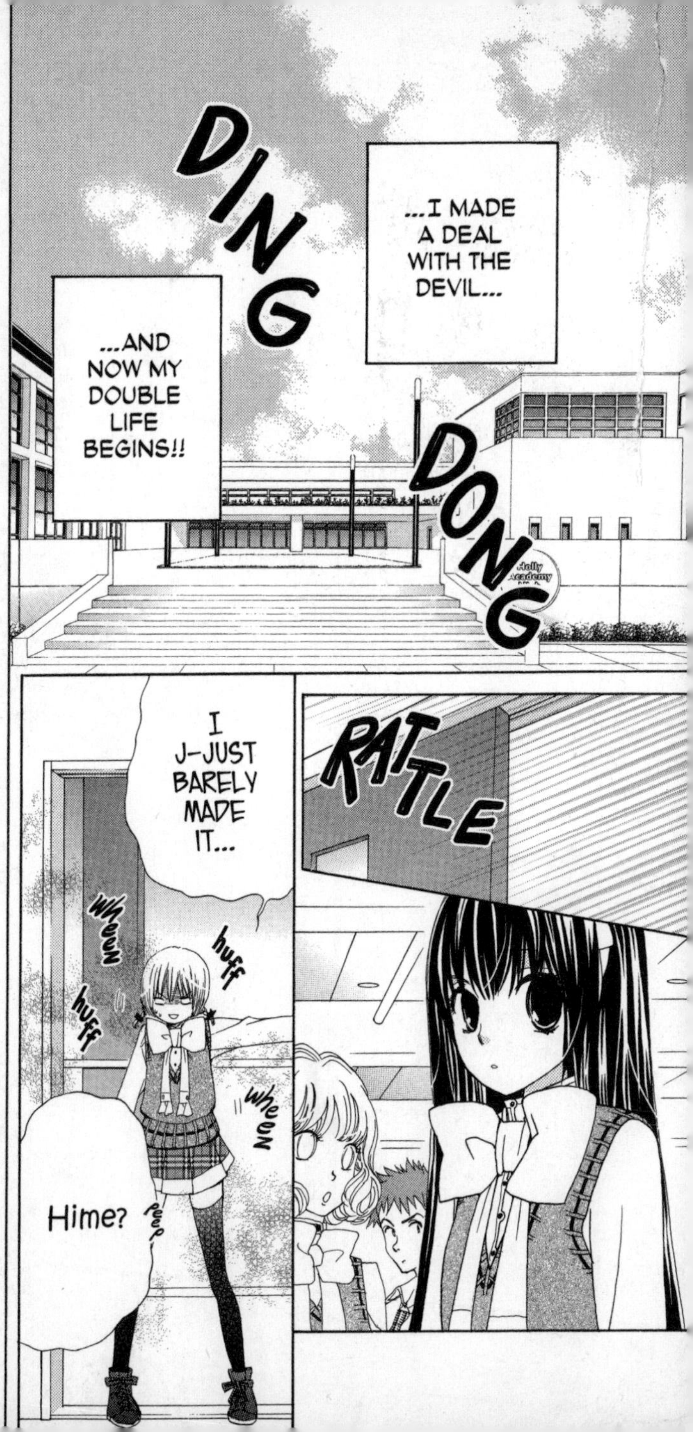
...I MADE A DEAL WITH THE DEVIL...
DING
DONG
...AND NOW MY DOUBLE LIFE BEGINS!!
Holly Academy
RATTLE
I J-JUST BARELY MADE IT...
huff
wheeze
huff
wheeze
peer
Hime?

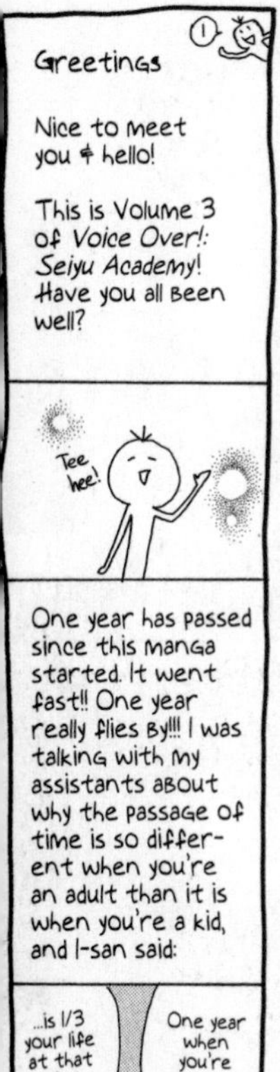
1
Greetings
Nice to meet you & hello!
This is Volume 3 of *Voice Over!: Seiyu Academy*! Have you all been well?
Tee hee!
One year has passed since this manga started. It went fast!! One year really flies by!!! I was talking with my assistants about why the passage of time is so different when you're an adult than it is when you're a kid, and I-san said:
One year when you're 3 years old...
...is 1/3 your life at that point, right?
One year when you're 60...
...is 1/60 of your life, so it feels faster!
Whoa...
It totally made sense.

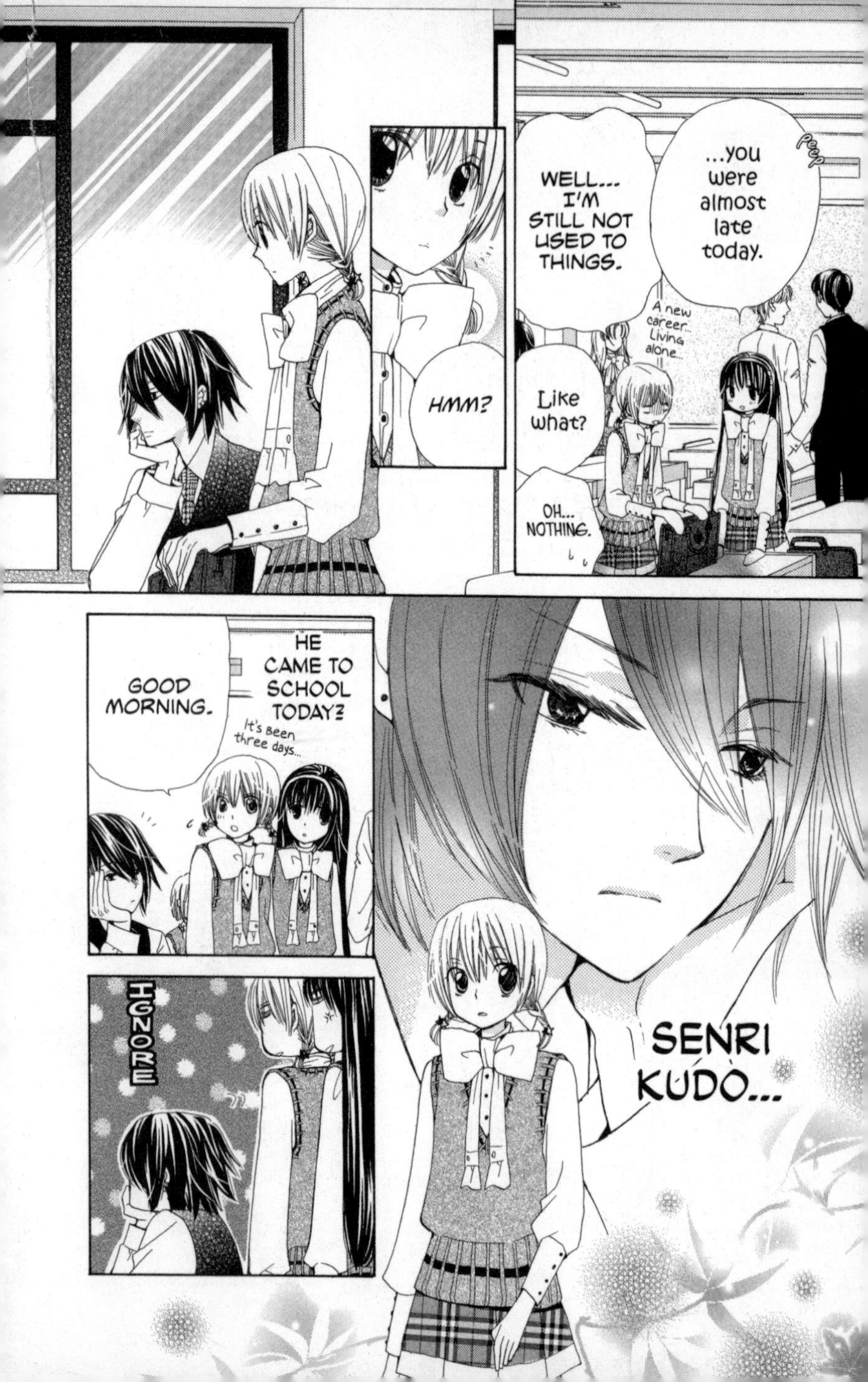
peep
...you were almost late today.
WELL... I'M STILL NOT USED TO THINGS.
A new career... Living alone...
Like what?
OH... NOTHING.
HMM?
SENRI KUDO...
HE CAME TO SCHOOL TODAY?
It's Been three days...
GOOD MORNING.
IGNORE

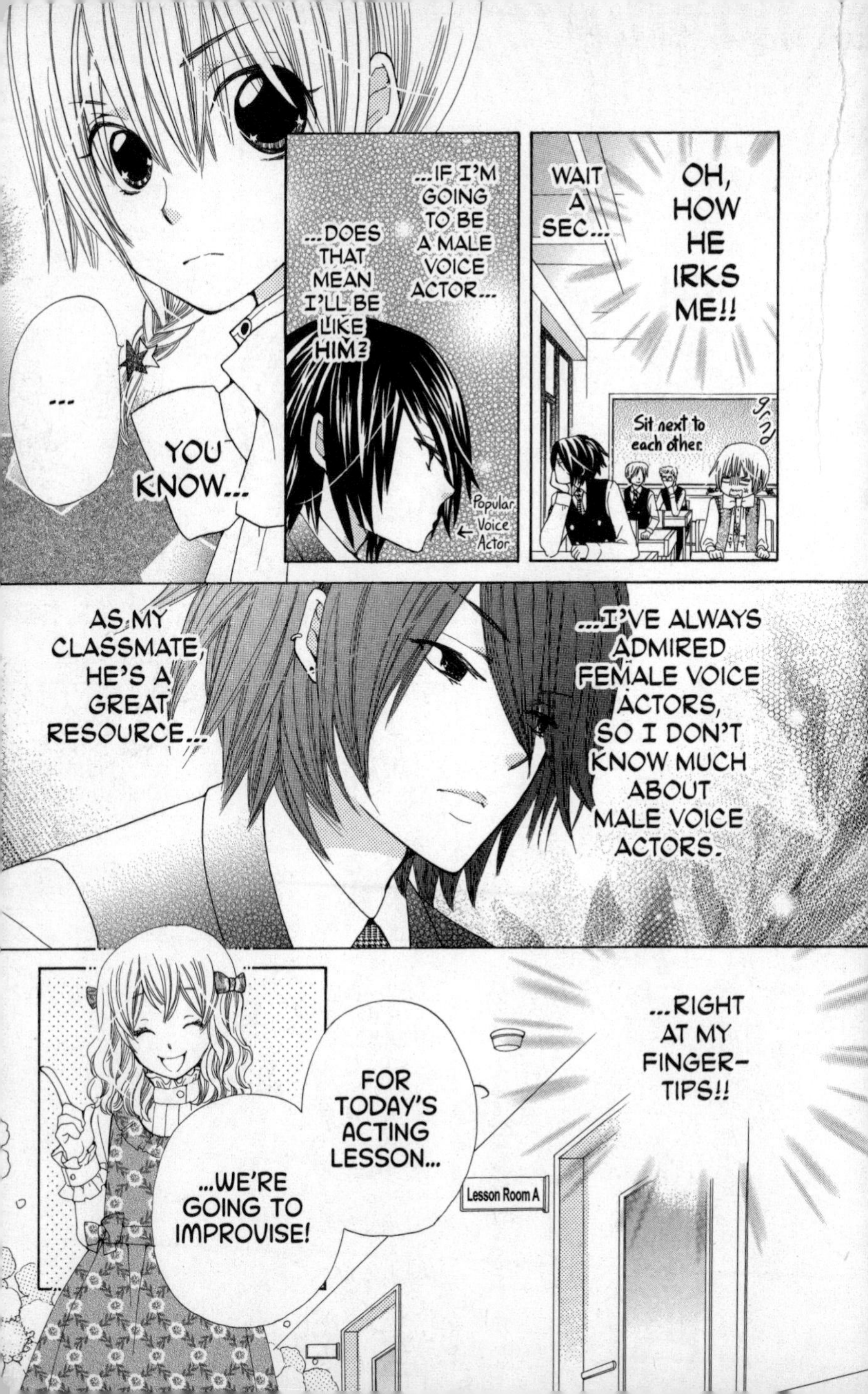
OH, HOW HE IRKS ME!!
WAIT A SEC...
grnd
Sit next to each other.
...IF I'M GOING TO BE A MALE VOICE ACTOR...
...DOES THAT MEAN I'LL BE LIKE HIM?
Popular Voice Actor
YOU KNOW...
...
...I'VE ALWAYS ADMIRED FEMALE VOICE ACTORS, SO I DON'T KNOW MUCH ABOUT MALE VOICE ACTORS.
AS MY CLASSMATE, HE'S A GREAT RESOURCE...
...RIGHT AT MY FINGER-TIPS!!
Lesson Room A
FOR TODAY'S ACTING LESSON...
...WE'RE GOING TO IMPROVISE!

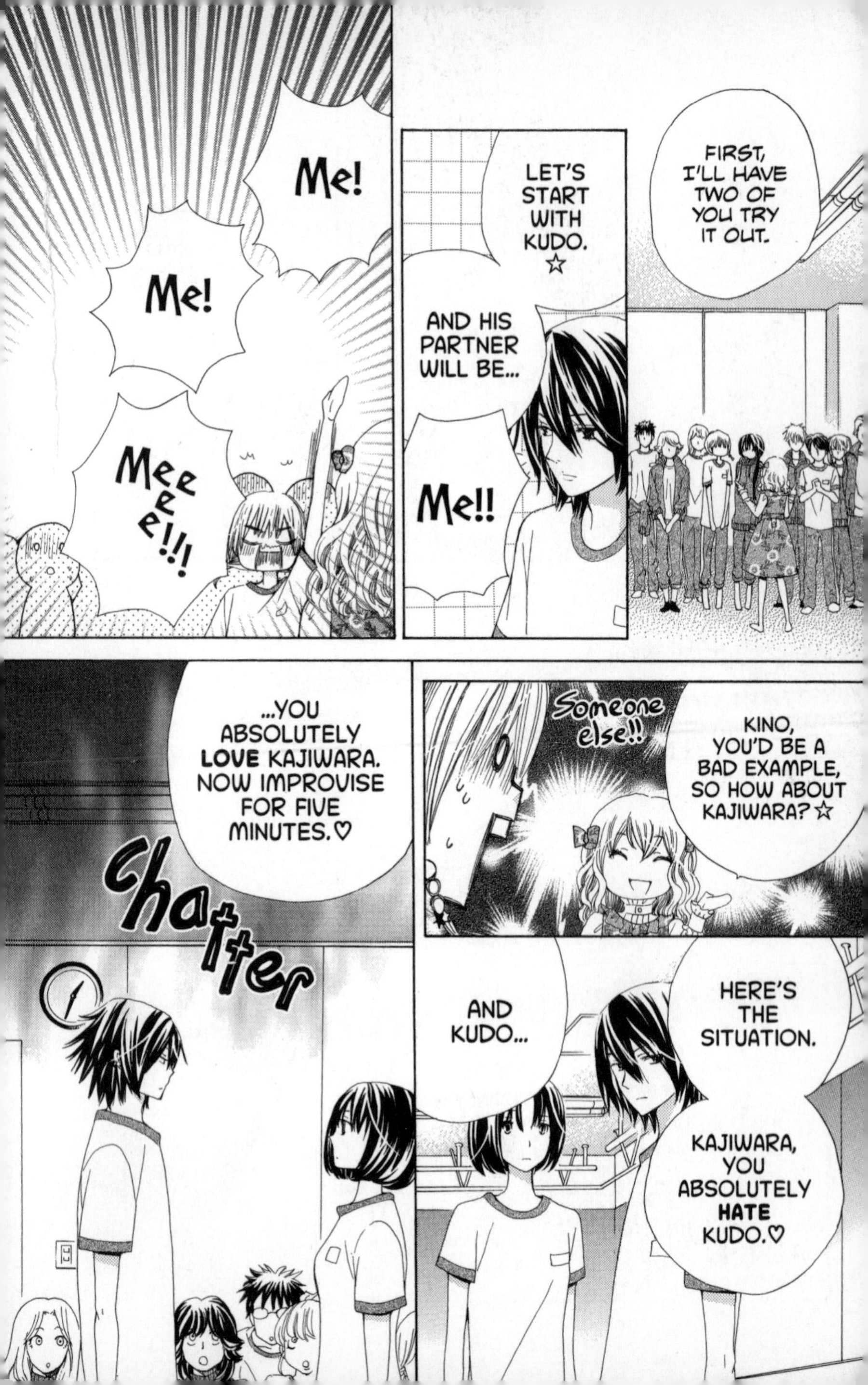
FIRST, I'LL HAVE TWO OF YOU TRY IT OUT.
LET'S START WITH KUDO. ☆
AND HIS PARTNER WILL BE...
Me!!
Me!
Me!
Meeee!!!
KINO, YOU'D BE A BAD EXAMPLE, SO HOW ABOUT KAJIWARA? ☆
Someone else!!
HERE'S THE SITUATION.
KAJIWARA, YOU ABSOLUTELY HATE KUDO. ♡
AND KUDO...
...YOU ABSOLUTELY LOVE KAJIWARA. NOW IMPROVISE FOR FIVE MINUTES. ♡
Chatter

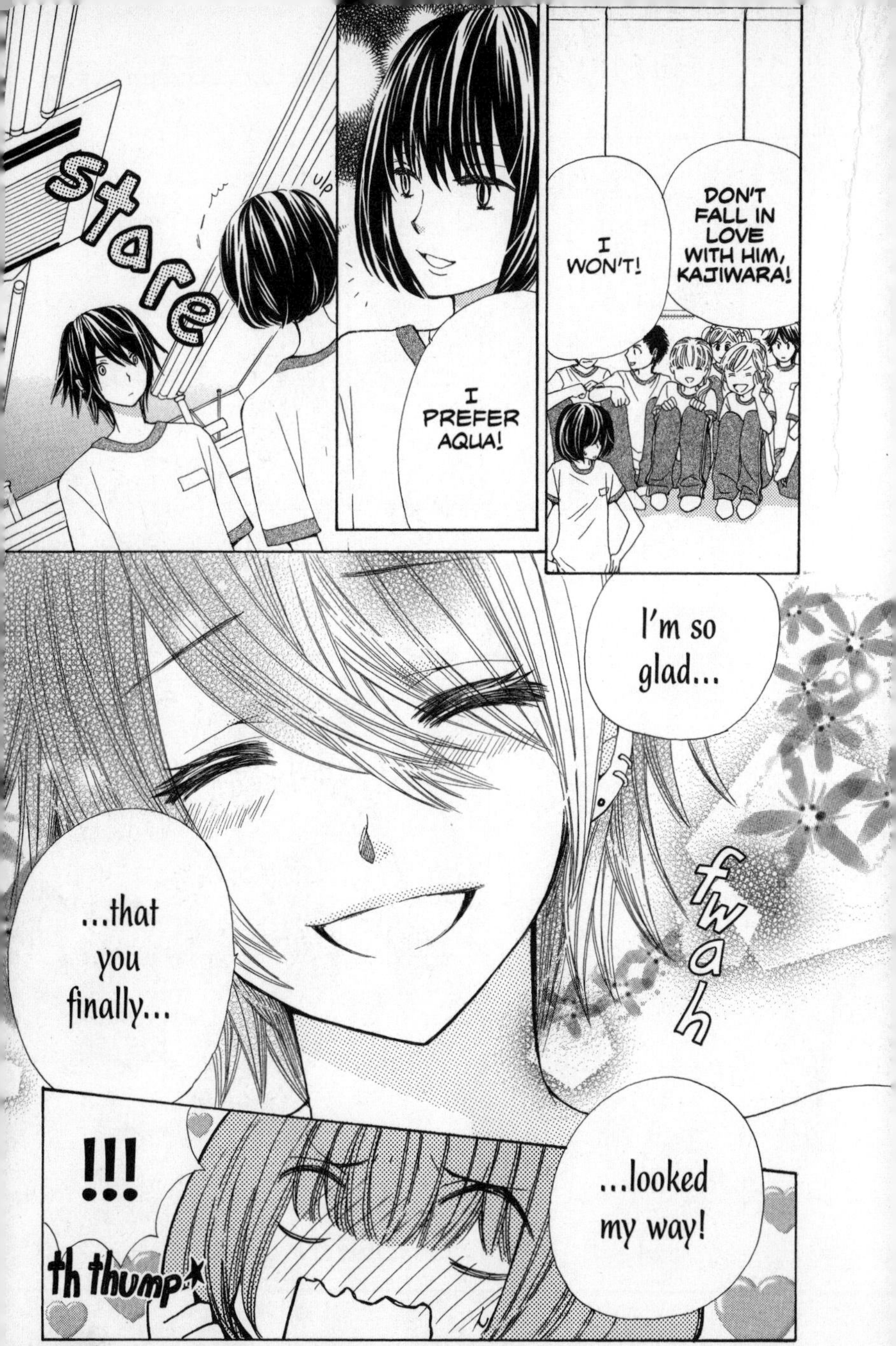
DON'T FALL IN LOVE WITH HIM, KAJIWARA!
I WON'T!
I PREFER AQUA!
stare
I'm so glad...
fwah
...that you finally...
...looked my way!
!!!
th thump★

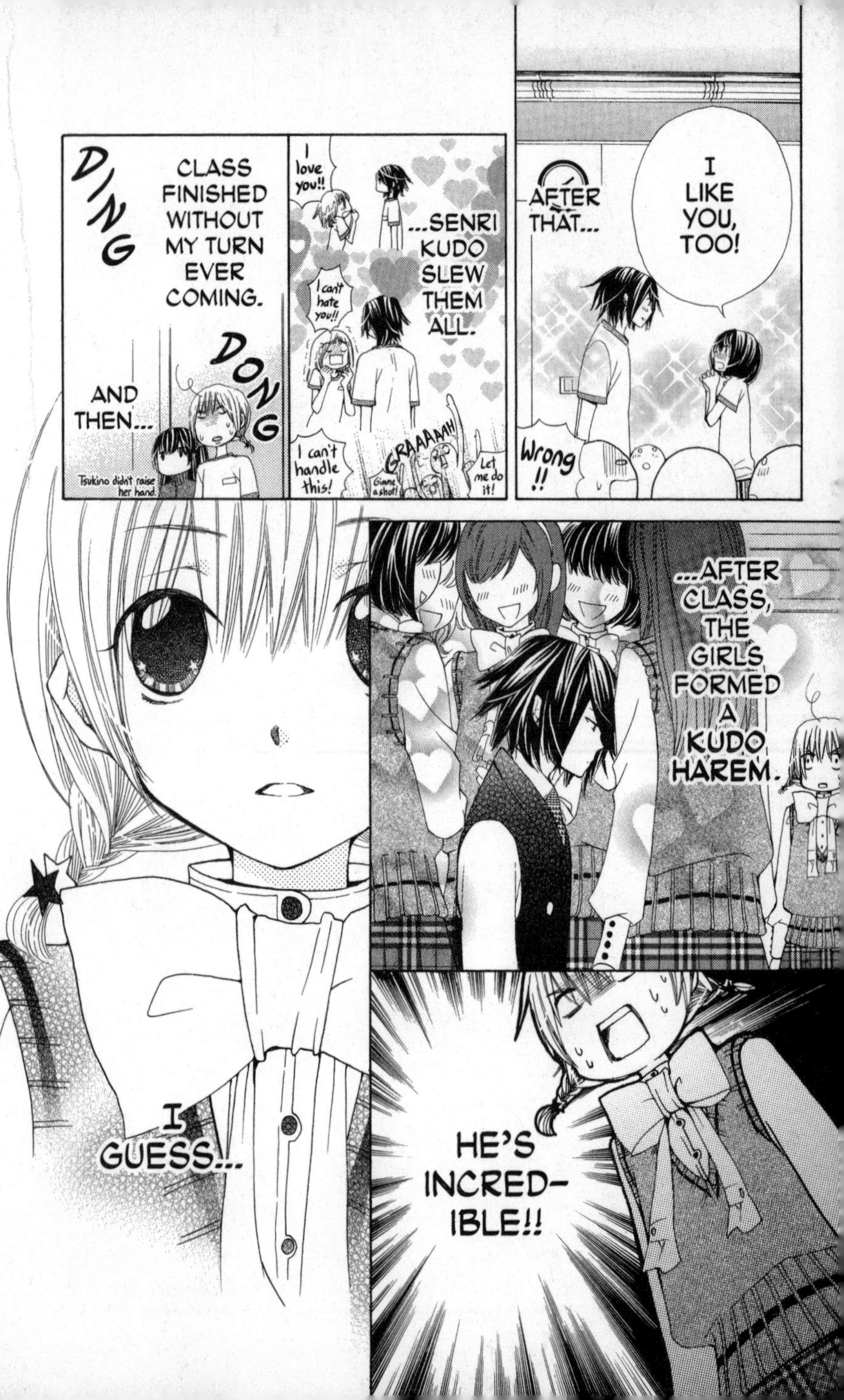
AFTER THAT...
I LIKE YOU, TOO!
Wrong!!
I love you!!
...SENRI KUDO SLEW THEM ALL.
I can't hate you!!
GRAAAAAH
Let me do it!
Gimme a shot!
I can't handle this!
CLASS FINISHED WITHOUT MY TURN EVER COMING.
DING
DONG
AND THEN...
Tsukino didn't raise her hand.
...AFTER CLASS, THE GIRLS FORMED A KUDO HAREM.
HE'S INCRED-IBLE!!
I GUESS...

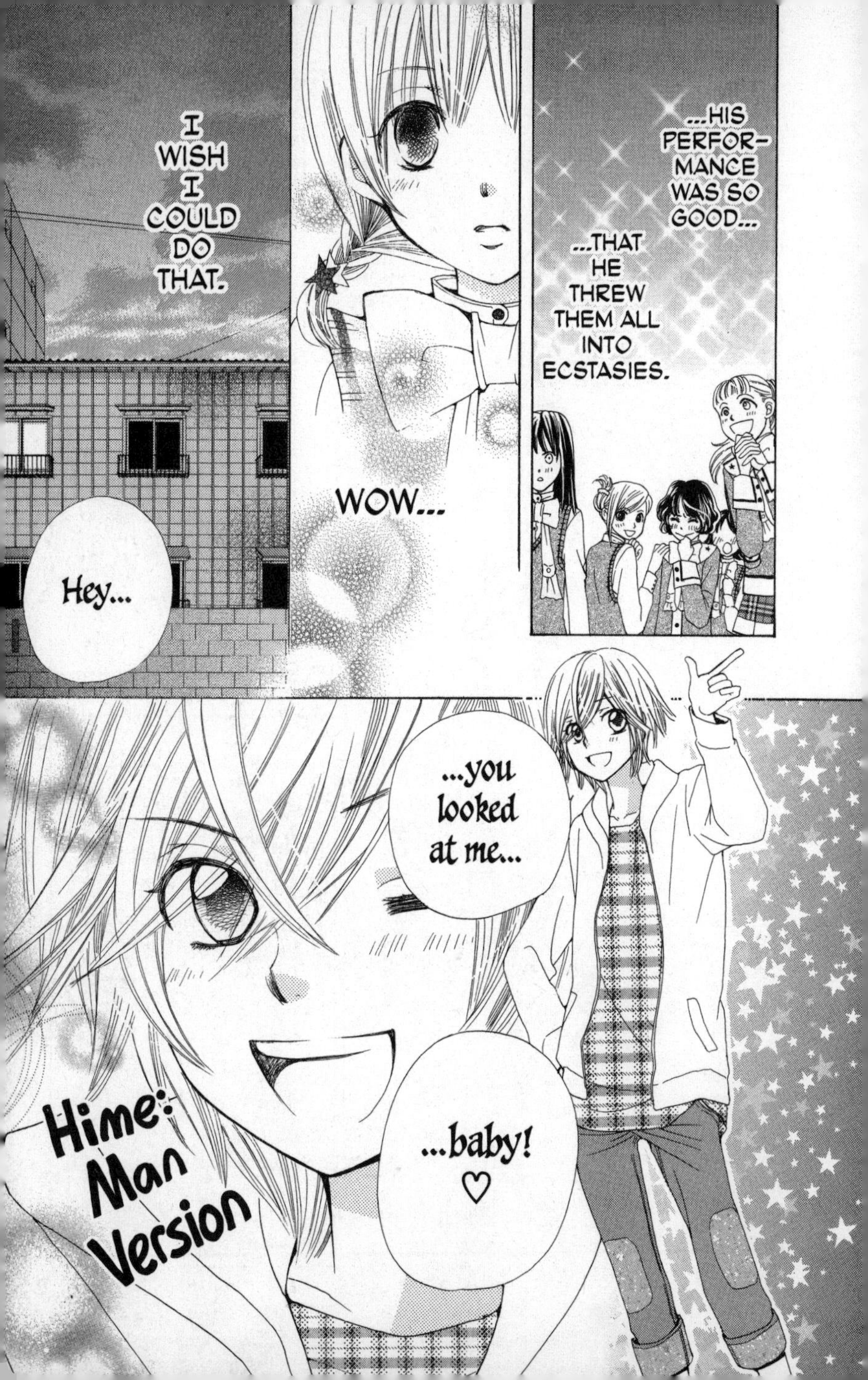
...HIS PERFORMANCE WAS SO GOOD...
...THAT HE THREW THEM ALL INTO ECSTASIES.
WOW...
I WISH I COULD DO THAT.
Hey...
...you looked at me...
...baby! ♡
Hime: Man Version

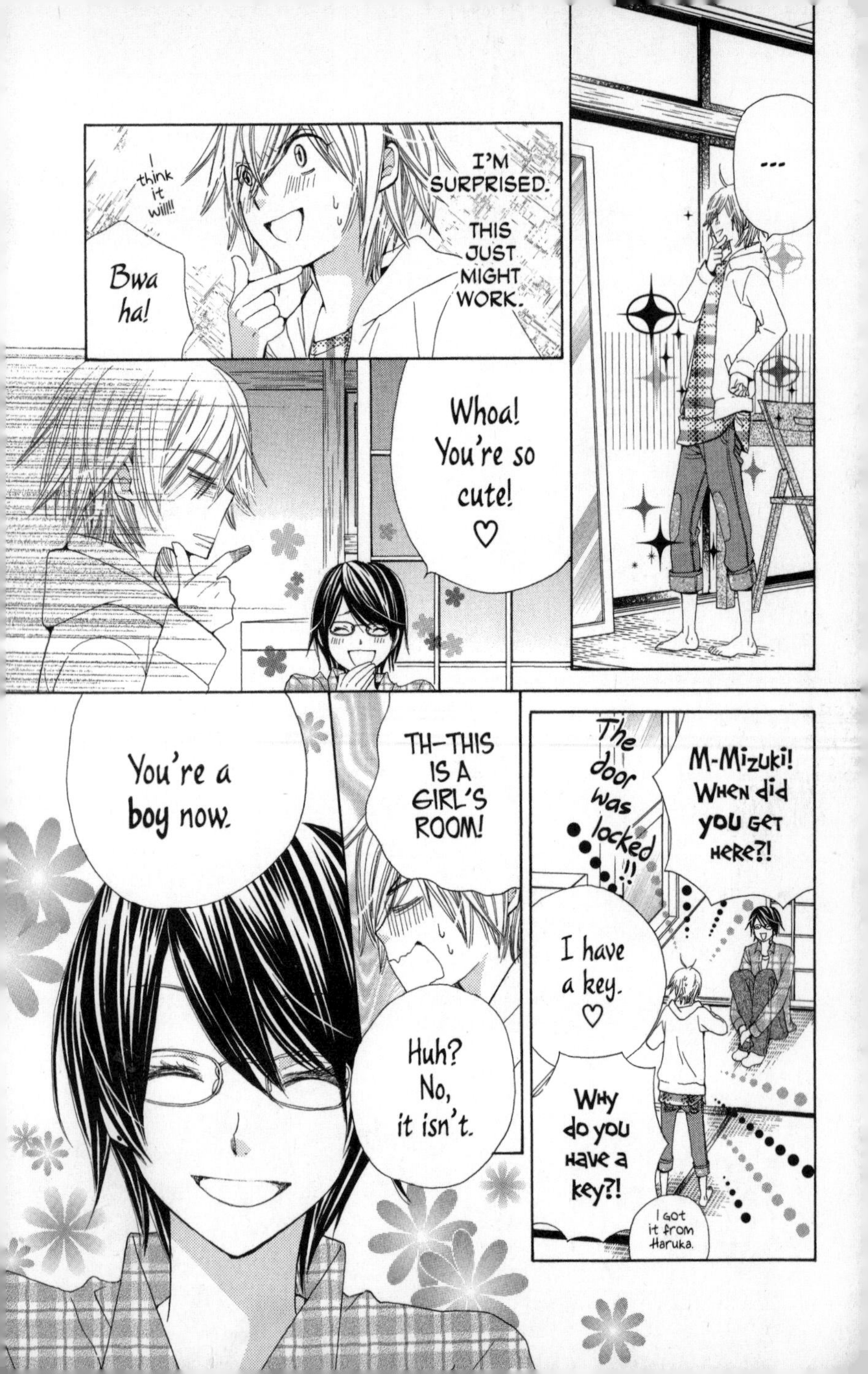
...
I'M SURPRISED.
THIS JUST MIGHT WORK.
I think it will!!!
Bwa ha!
Whoa! You're so cute! ♡
M-Mizuki! WHEN did YOU GET HERE?!
The door was locked!!
I have a key. ♡
WHY do YOU HAVE A KEY?!
I GOT it from Haruka.
TH-THIS IS A GIRL'S ROOM!
Huh? No, it isn't.
You're a boy now.

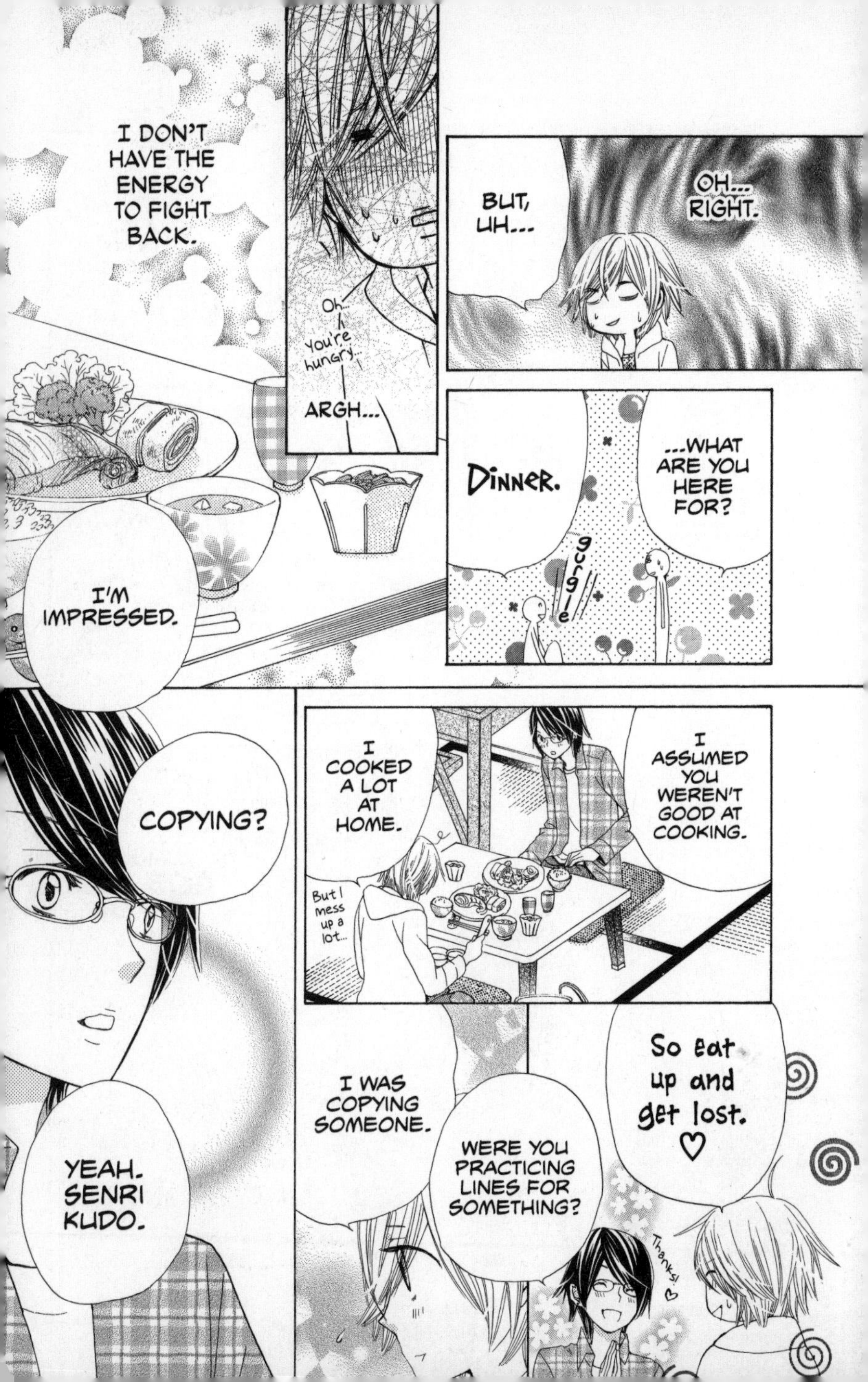

OH... RIGHT.
BUT, UH...
...WHAT ARE YOU HERE FOR?
gurgle
Dinner.
Oh... You're hungry...
ARGH...
I DON'T HAVE THE ENERGY TO FIGHT BACK.
I'M IMPRESSED.
I ASSUMED YOU WEREN'T GOOD AT COOKING.
I COOKED A LOT AT HOME.
But I mess up a lot...
So eat up and get lost. ♡
Thanks! ♡
WERE YOU PRACTICING LINES FOR SOMETHING?
I WAS COPYING SOMEONE.
COPYING?
YEAH. SENRI KUDO.

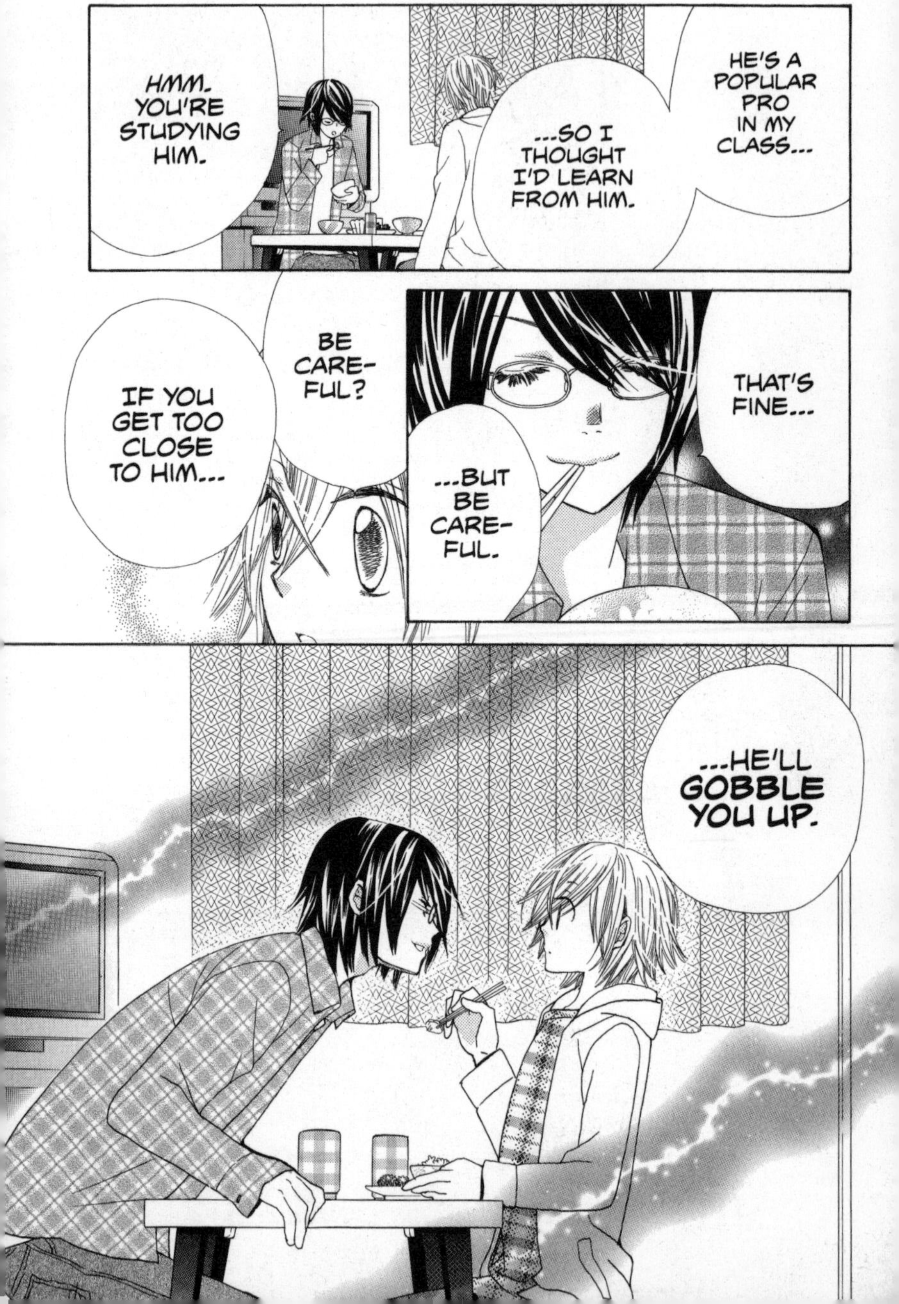
HE'S A POPULAR PRO IN MY CLASS...
...SO I THOUGHT I'D LEARN FROM HIM.
HMM. YOU'RE STUDYING HIM.
THAT'S FINE...
...BUT BE CAREFUL.
BE CAREFUL?
IF YOU GET TOO CLOSE TO HIM...
...HE'LL GOBBLE YOU UP.

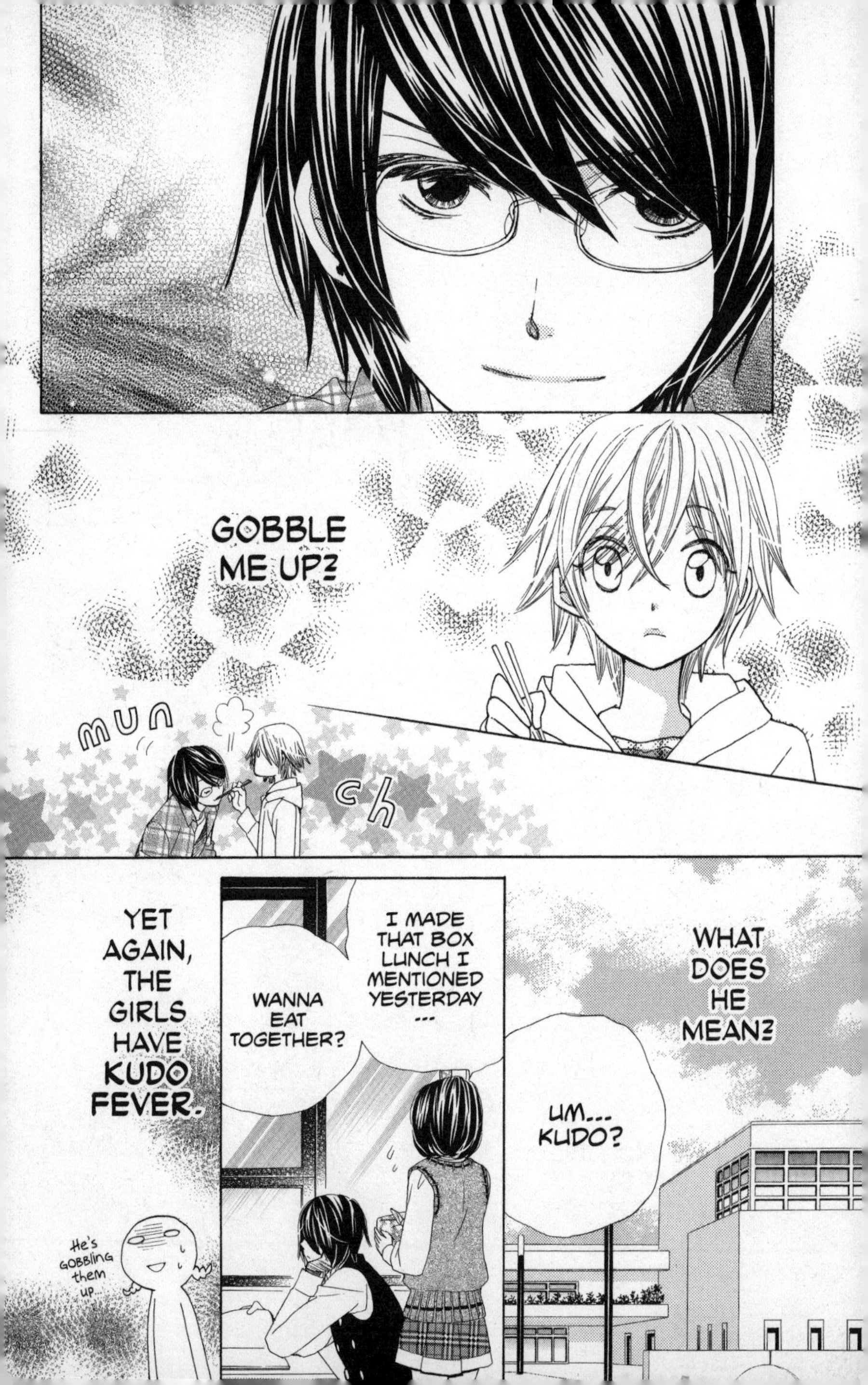
GOBBLE ME UP?
mun ch
WHAT DOES HE MEAN?
UM... KUDO?
I MADE THAT BOX LUNCH I MENTIONED YESTERDAY...
WANNA EAT TOGETHER?
YET AGAIN, THE GIRLS HAVE KUDO FEVER.
He's GOBBLING them up...

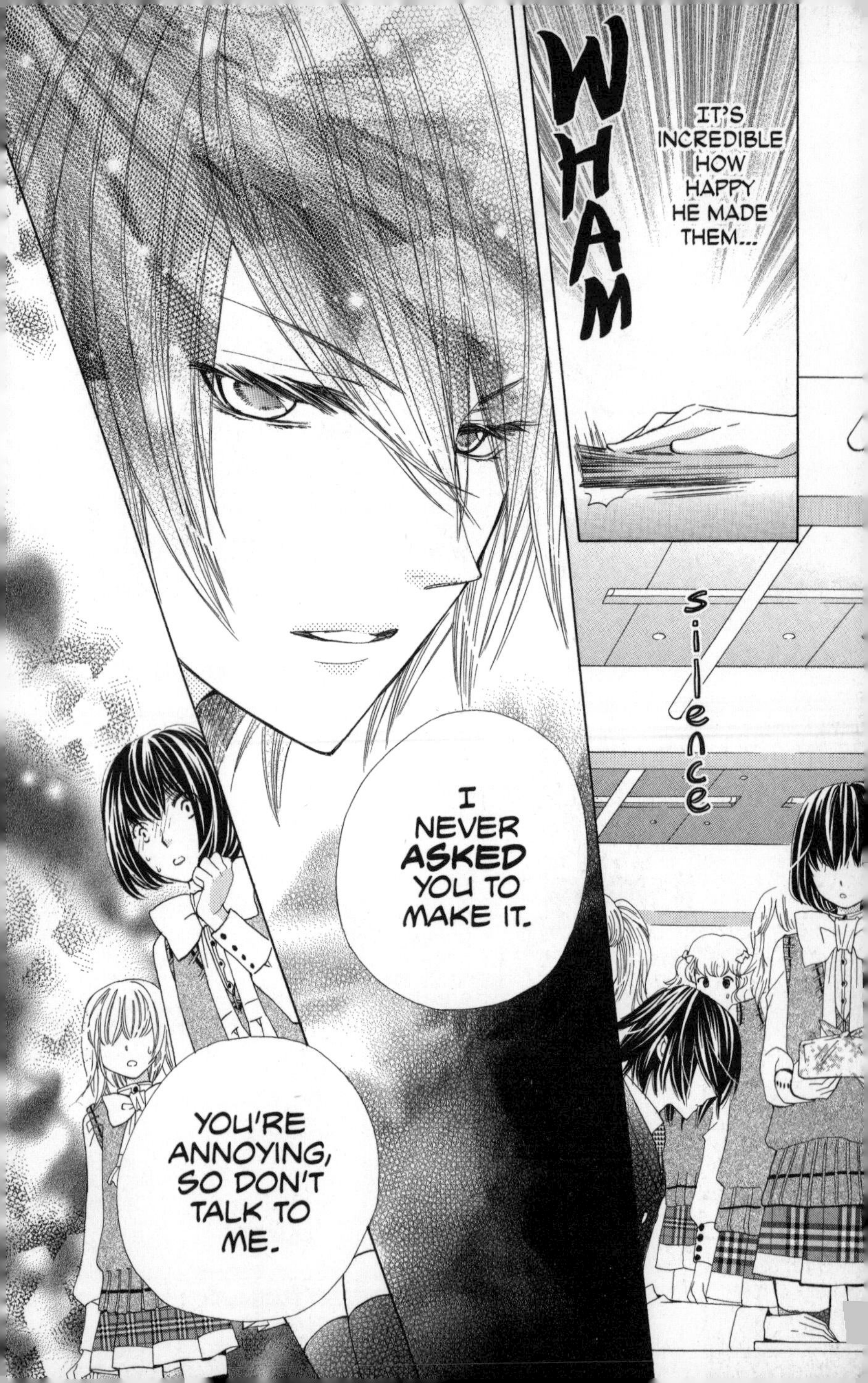
WHAM
IT'S INCREDIBLE HOW HAPPY HE MADE THEM...
silence
I NEVER ASKED YOU TO MAKE IT.
YOU'RE ANNOYING, SO DON'T TALK TO ME.

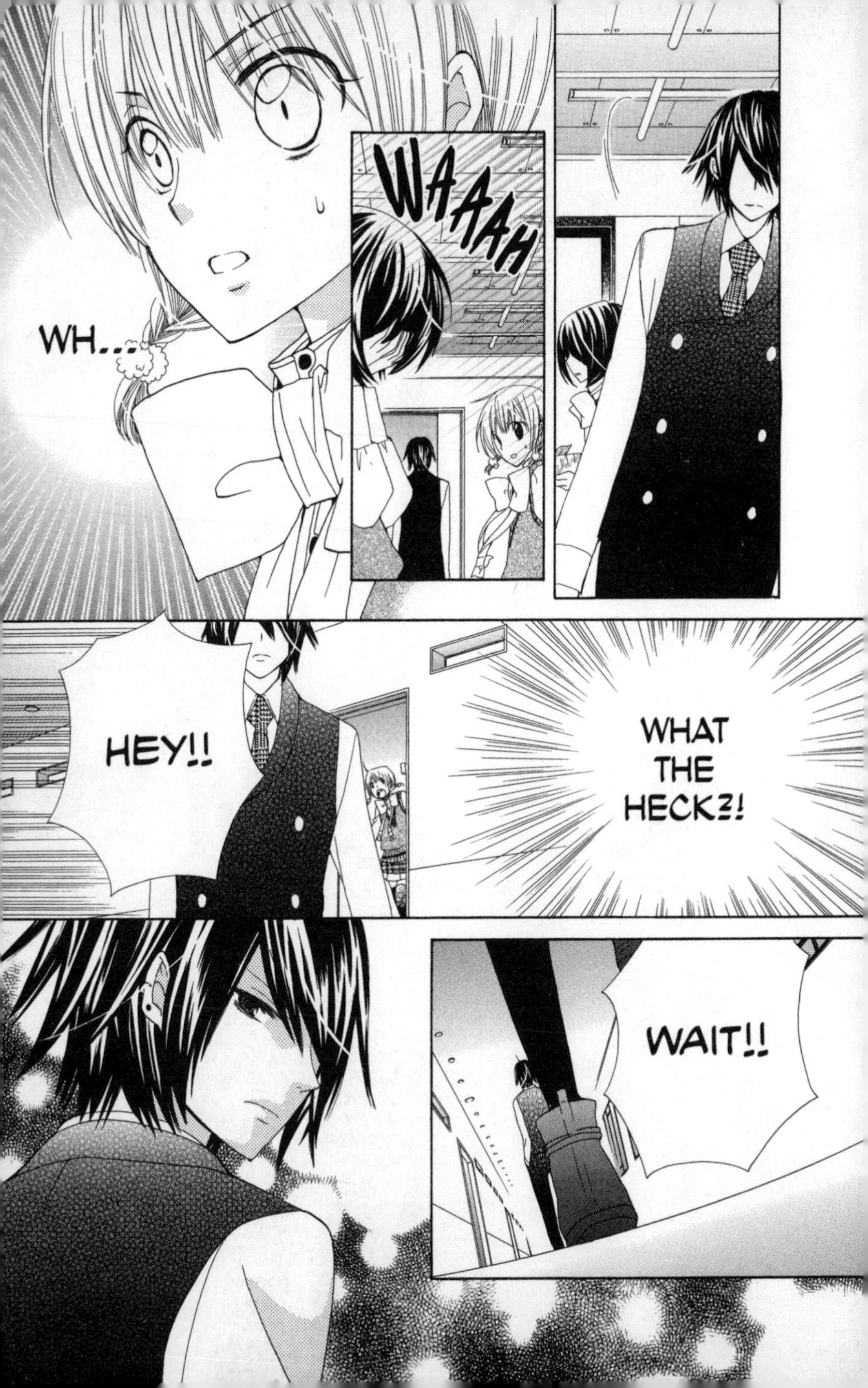

WAAAH
WH...
WHAT THE HECK?!
HEY!!
WAIT!!

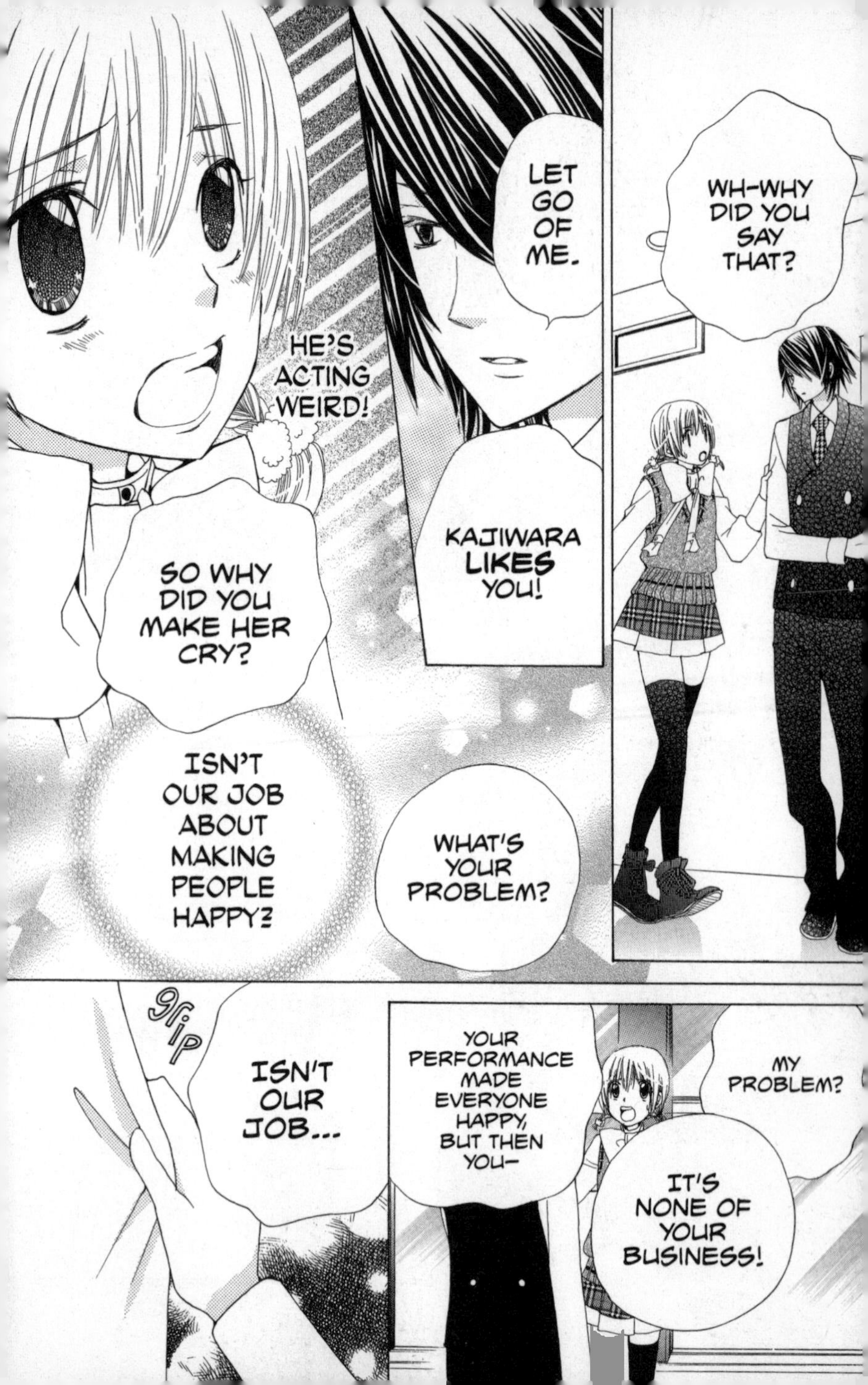
WH-WHY DID YOU SAY THAT?
LET GO OF ME.
KAJIWARA LIKES YOU!
HE'S ACTING WEIRD!
SO WHY DID YOU MAKE HER CRY?
WHAT'S YOUR PROBLEM?
ISN'T OUR JOB ABOUT MAKING PEOPLE HAPPY?
MY PROBLEM?
IT'S NONE OF YOUR BUSINESS!
YOUR PERFORMANCE MADE EVERYONE HAPPY, BUT THEN YOU–
grip
ISN'T OUR JOB...

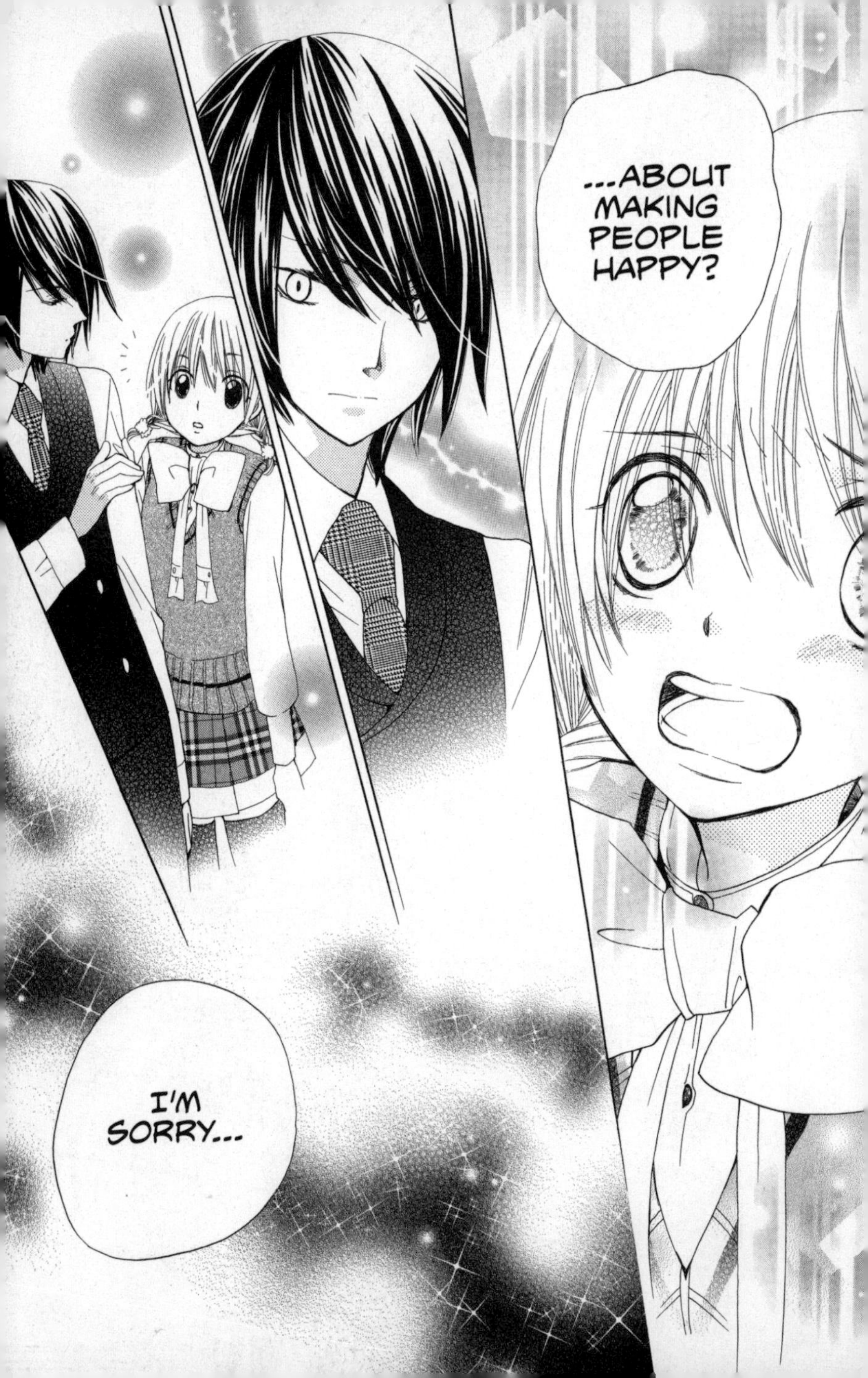
...ABOUT MAKING PEOPLE HAPPY?
I'M SORRY...

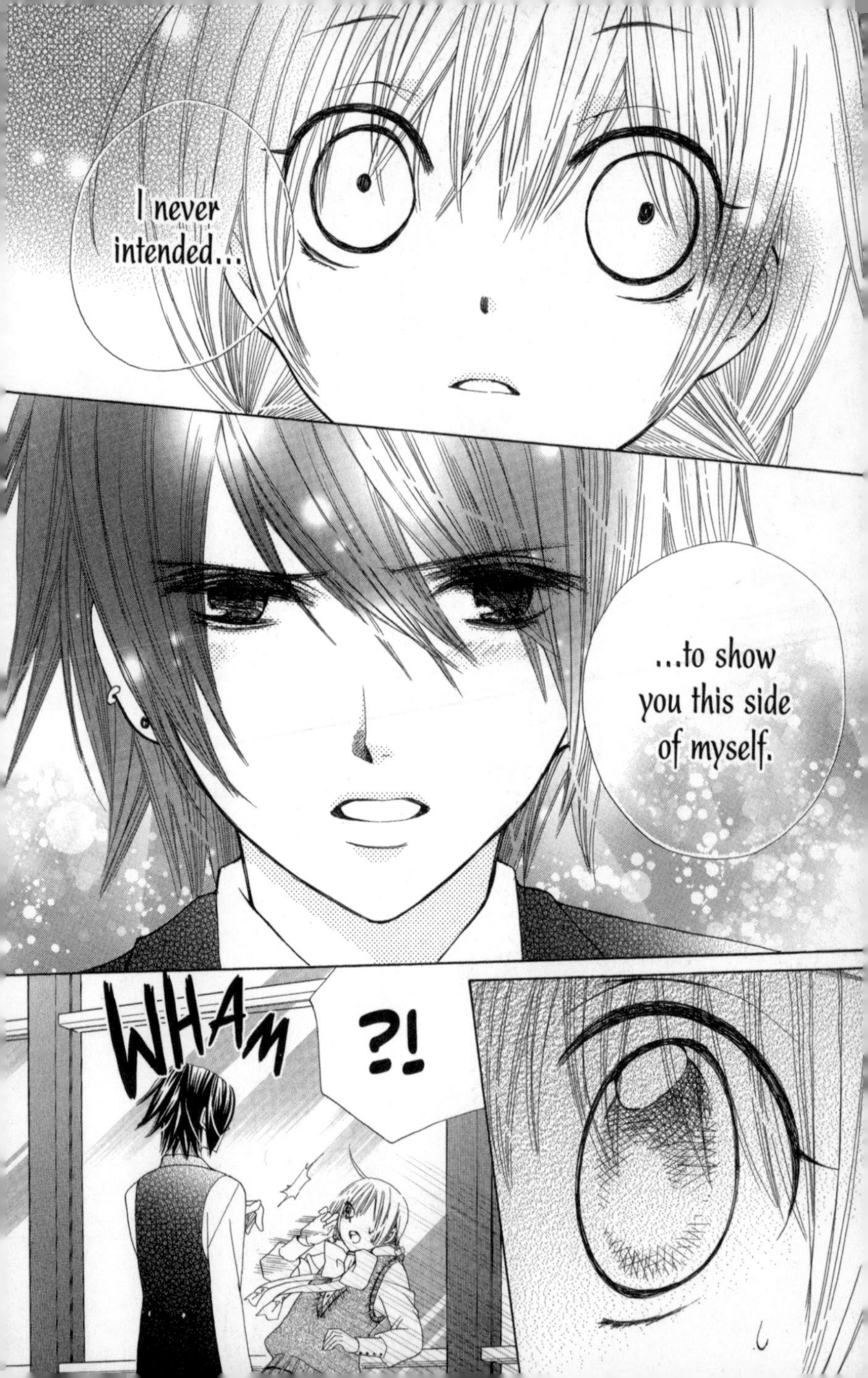
I never intended...
...to show you this side of myself.
?!
WHAM

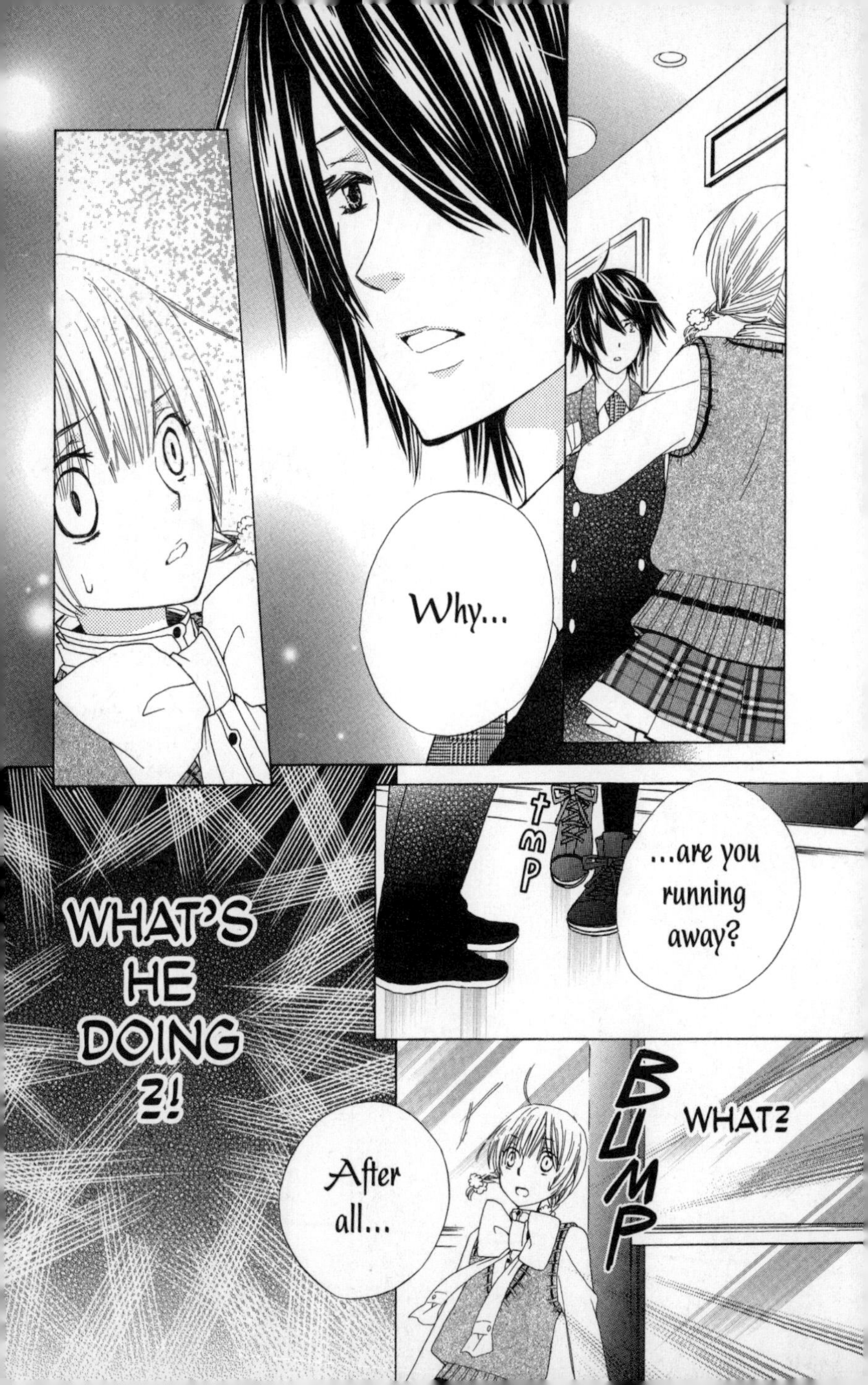
Why...
...are you running away?
TMP
WHAT?
BUMP
After all...
WHAT'S HE DOING?!

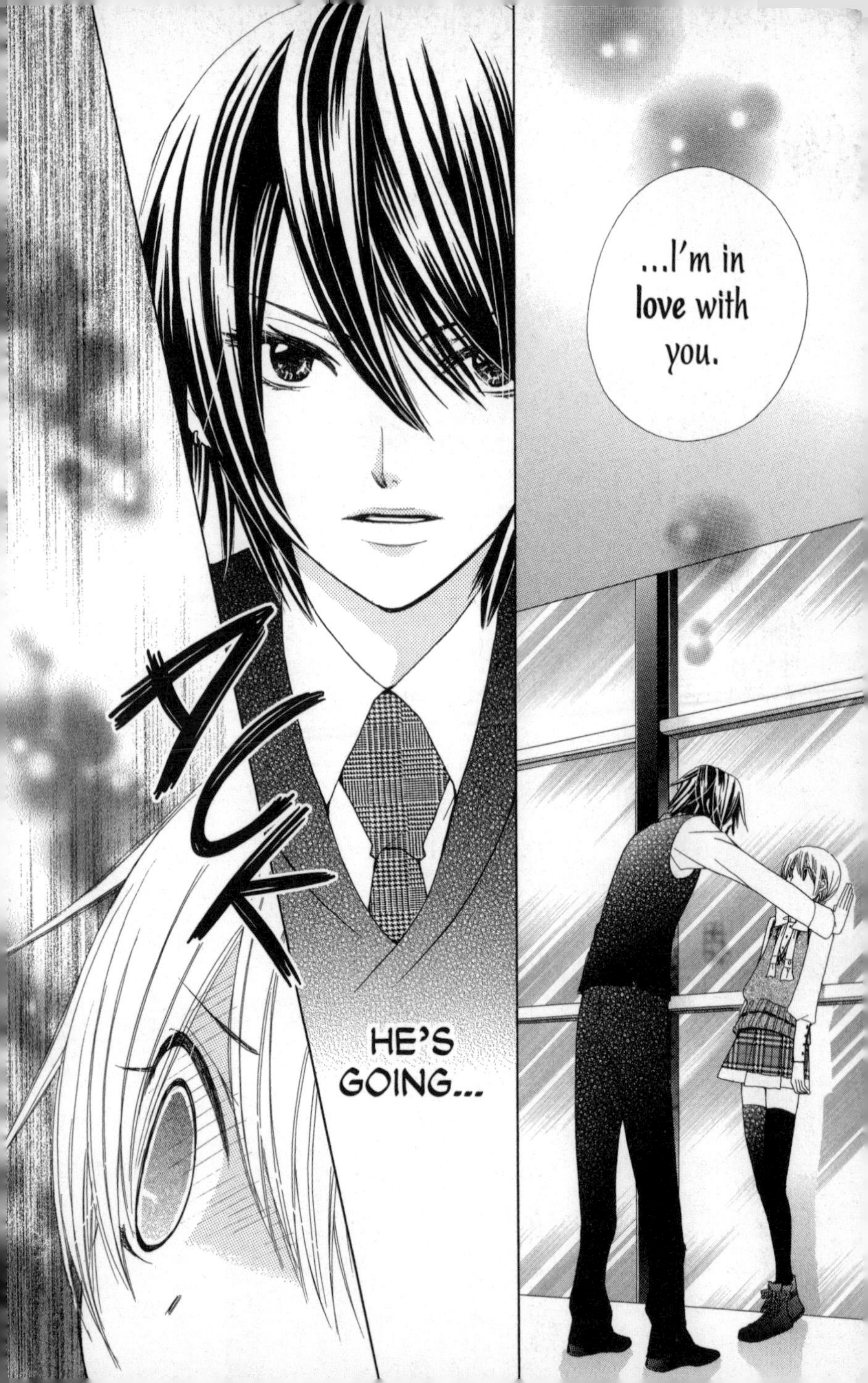
...I'm in love with you.
ACK
HE'S GOING...

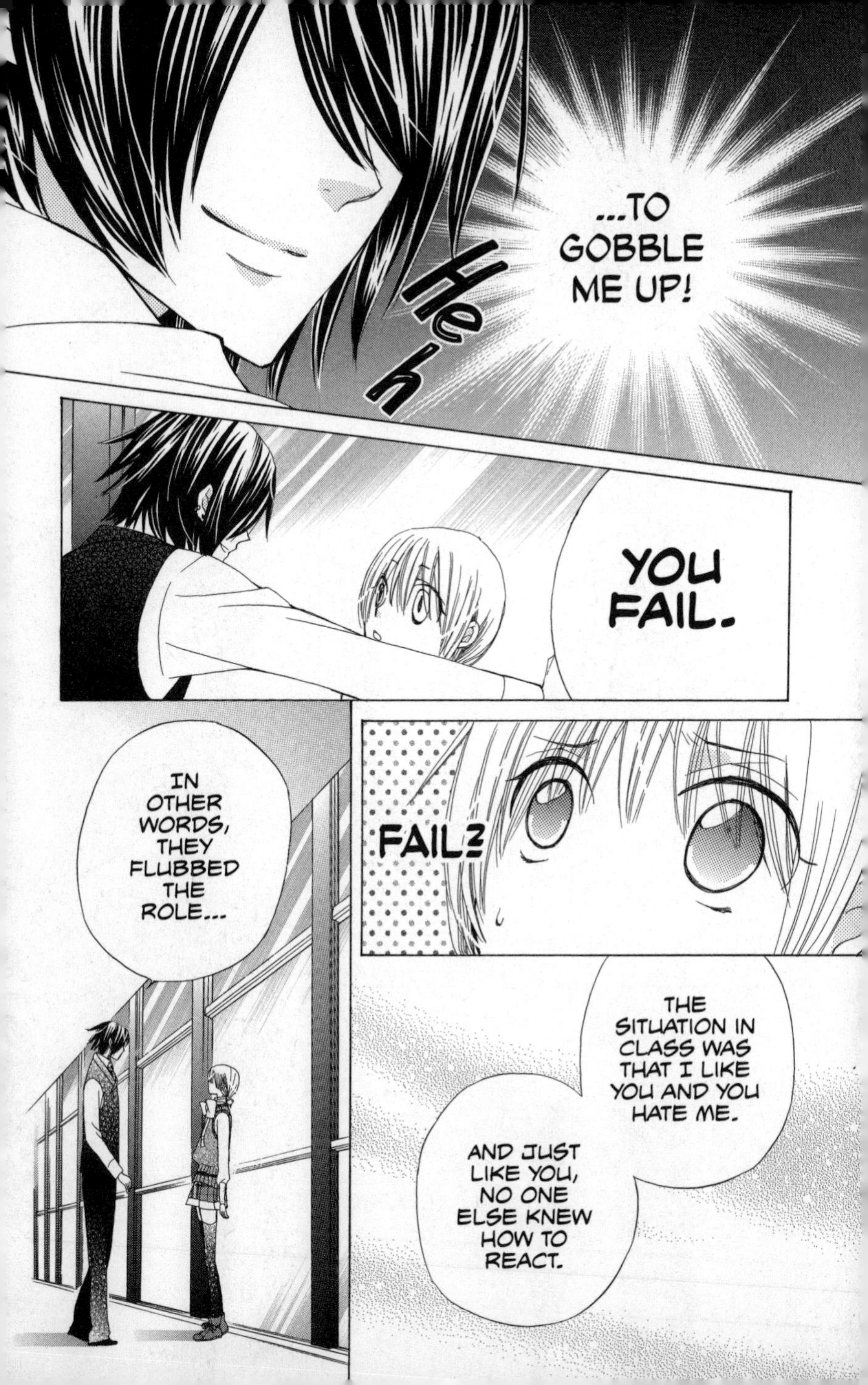
...TO GOBBLE ME UP!
Heh
YOU FAIL.
FAIL?
THE SITUATION IN CLASS WAS THAT I LIKE YOU AND YOU HATE ME.
AND JUST LIKE YOU, NO ONE ELSE KNEW HOW TO REACT.
IN OTHER WORDS, THEY FLUBBED THE ROLE...

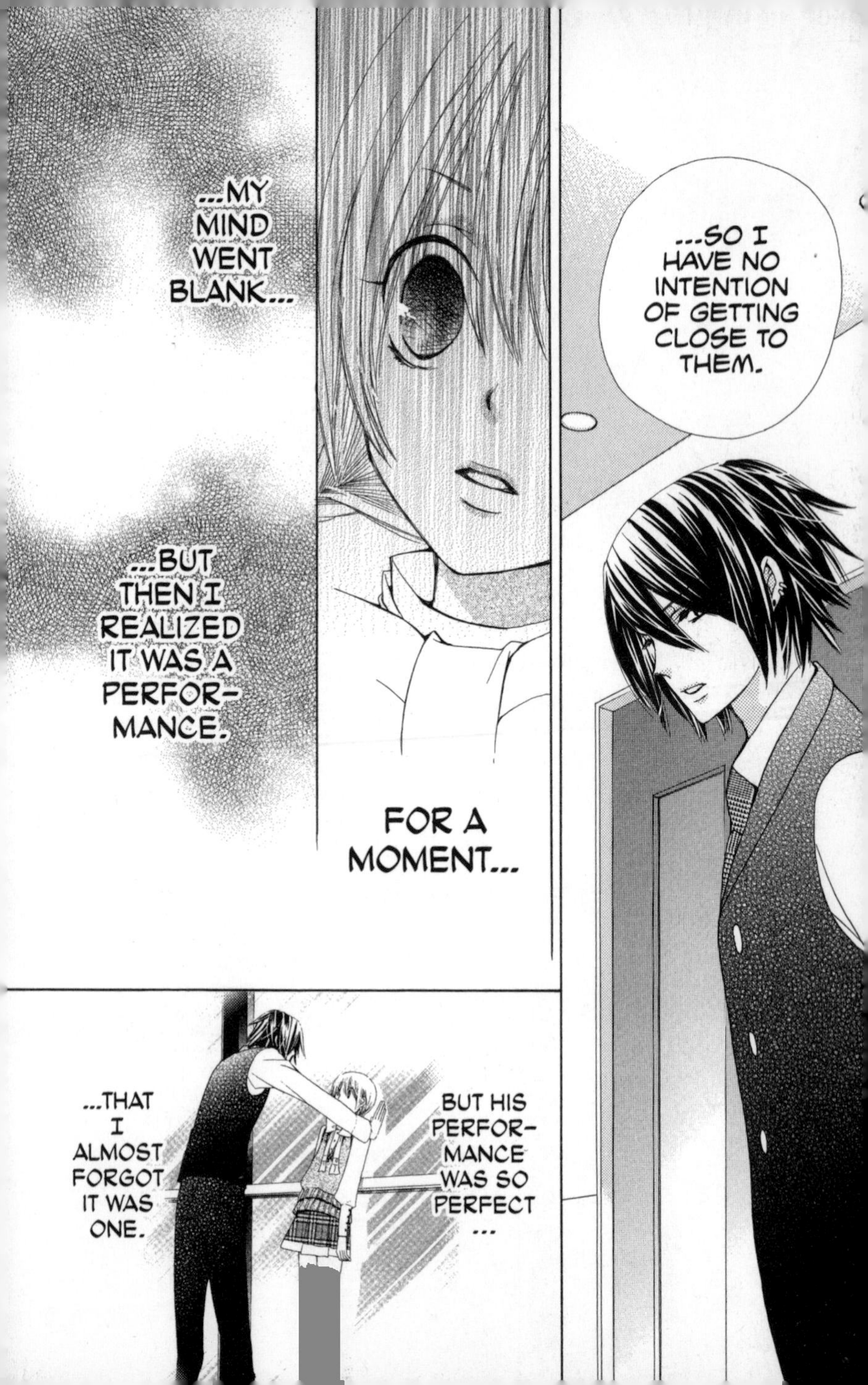
...SO I HAVE NO INTENTION OF GETTING CLOSE TO THEM.
FOR A MOMENT...
...MY MIND WENT BLANK...
...BUT THEN I REALIZED IT WAS A PERFOR-MANCE.
BUT HIS PERFOR-MANCE WAS SO PERFECT...
...THAT I ALMOST FORGOT IT WAS ONE.

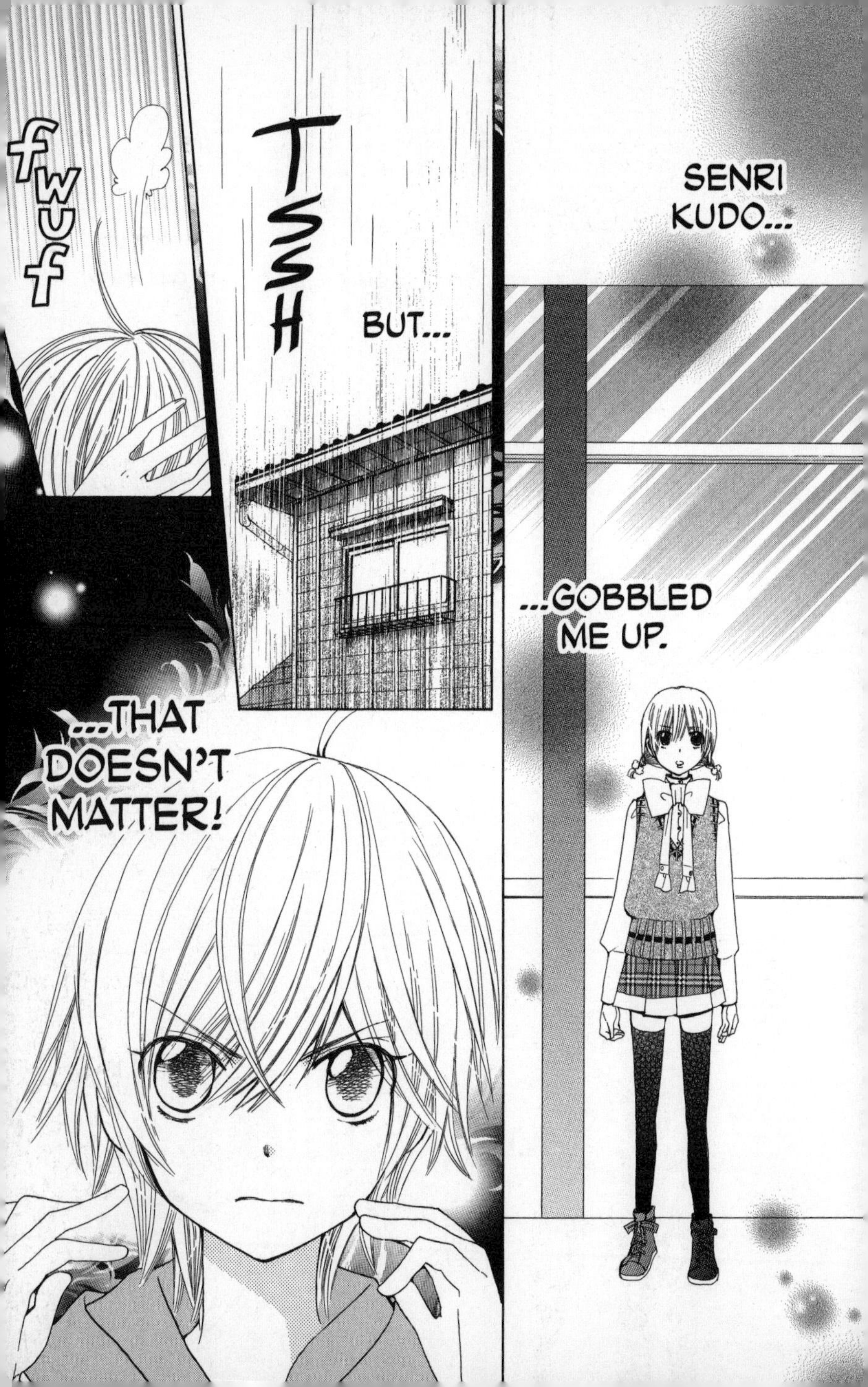
SENRI KUDO...
...GOBBLED ME UP.
TSSH
BUT...
fwuf
...THAT DOESN'T MATTER!

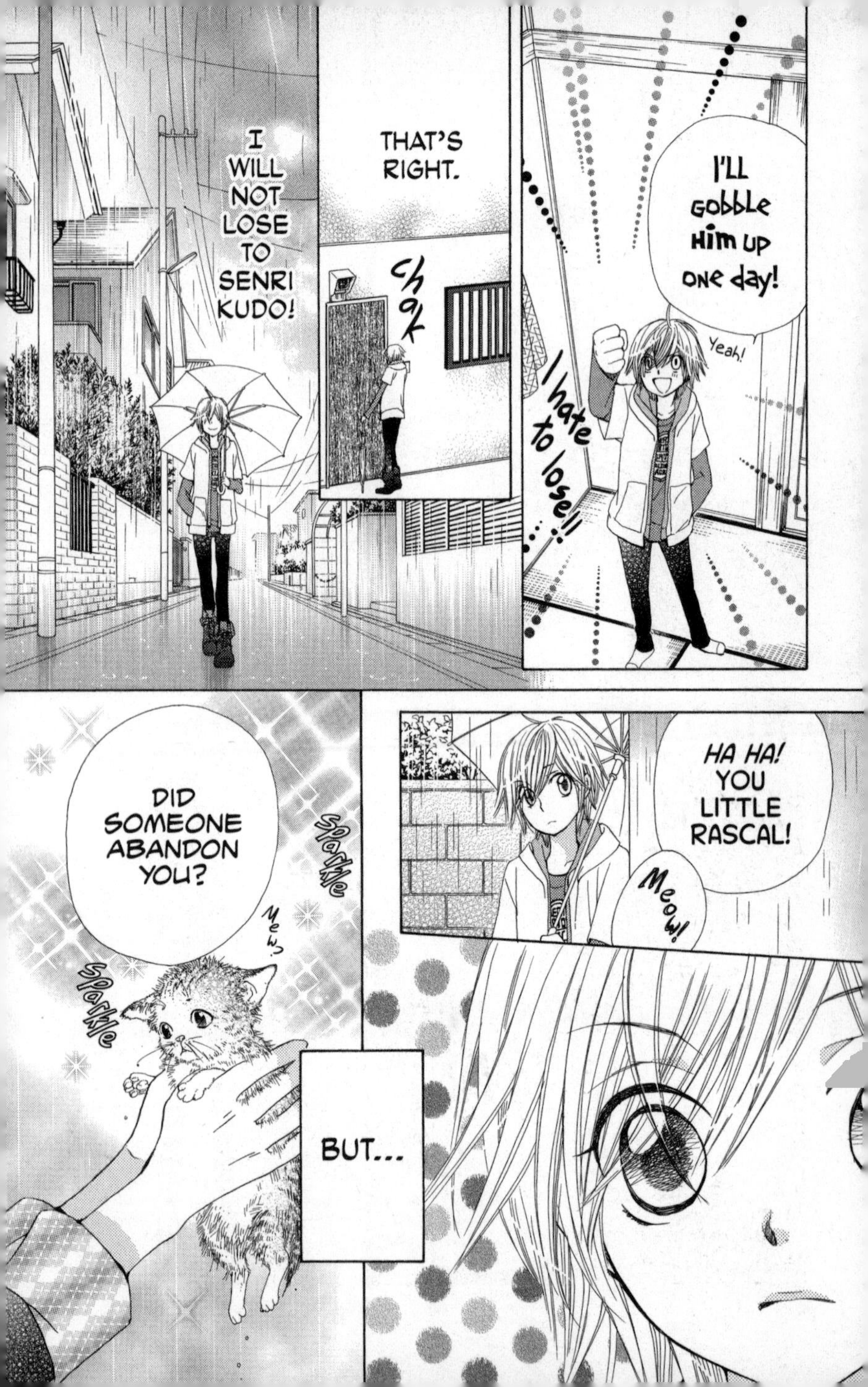

I'LL gobble Him up one day!
Yeah!
I hate to lose...!!
THAT'S RIGHT.
Chak
I WILL NOT LOSE TO SENRI KUDO!
HA HA! YOU LITTLE RASCAL!
Meow!
BUT...
DID SOMEONE ABANDON YOU?
Sparkle
Mew?
Sparkle

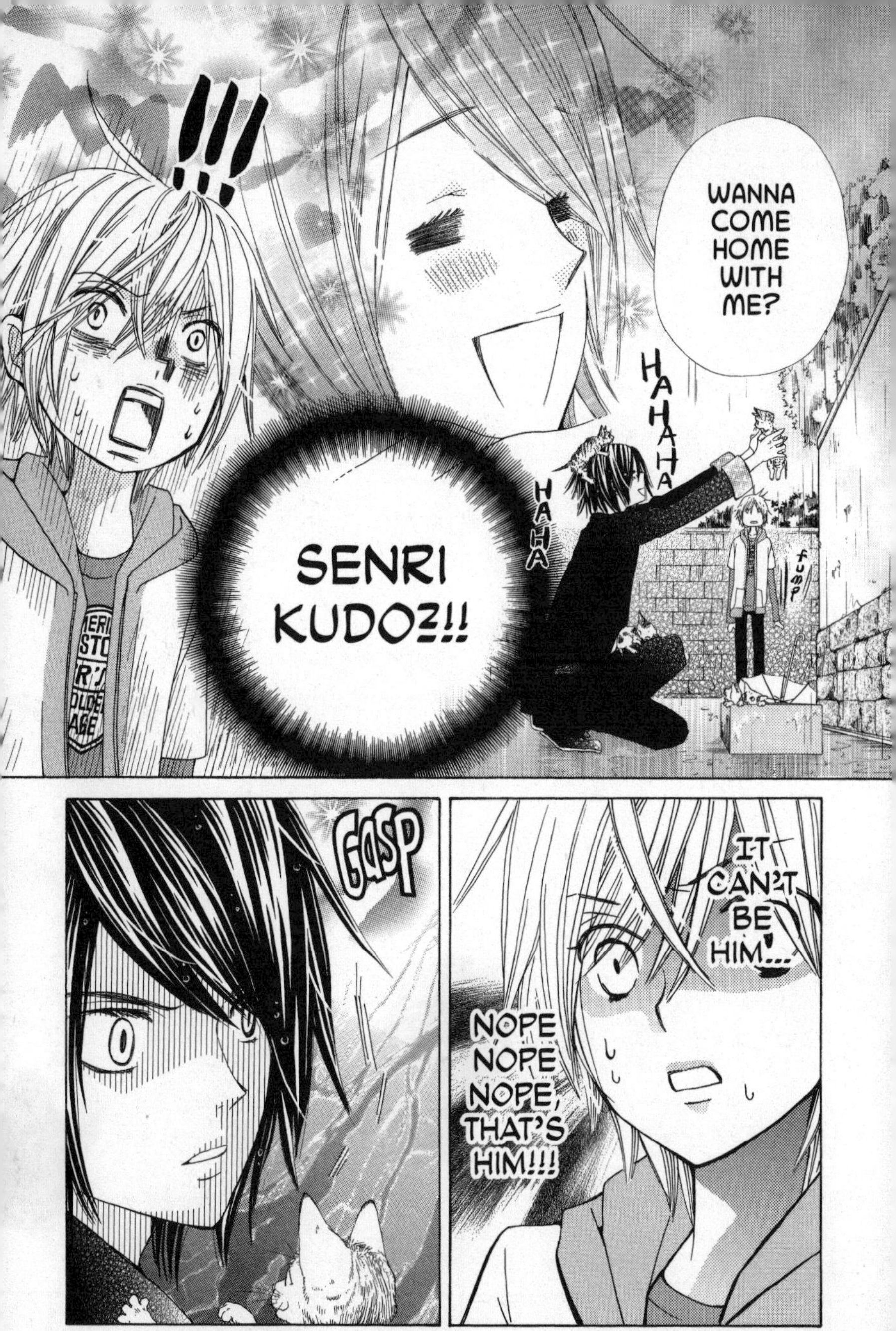
WANNA COME HOME WITH ME?
HAHAHAHA
FUMP
!!!
HAHA
SENRI KUDO?!!
IT CAN'T BE HIM...
NOPE NOPE NOPE, THAT'S HIM!!!
GASP

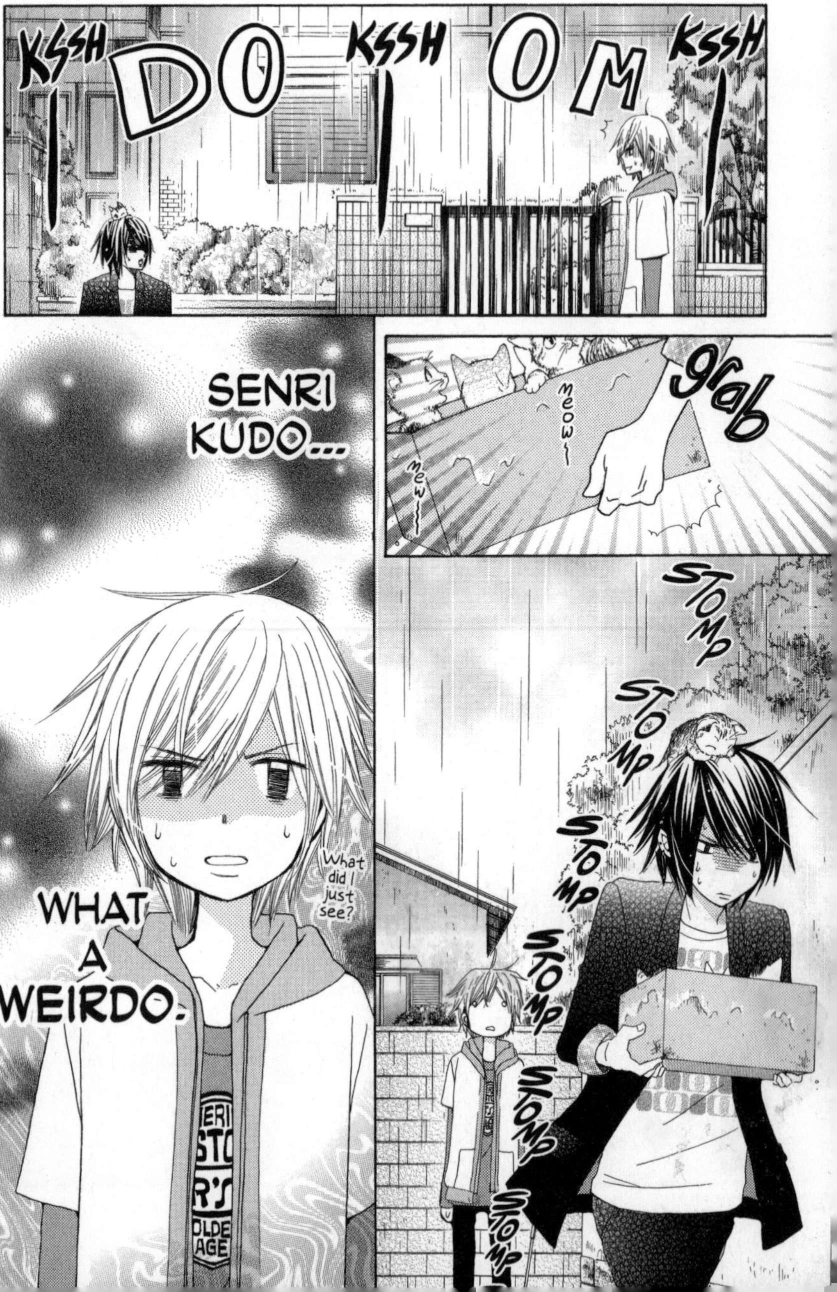
KSSH
KSSH
KSSH
DO OM
grab
meow~
mew~~
STOMP
STOMP
STOMP
STOMP
STOMP
STOMP
SENRI KUDO...
What did I just see?
WHAT A WEIRDO.

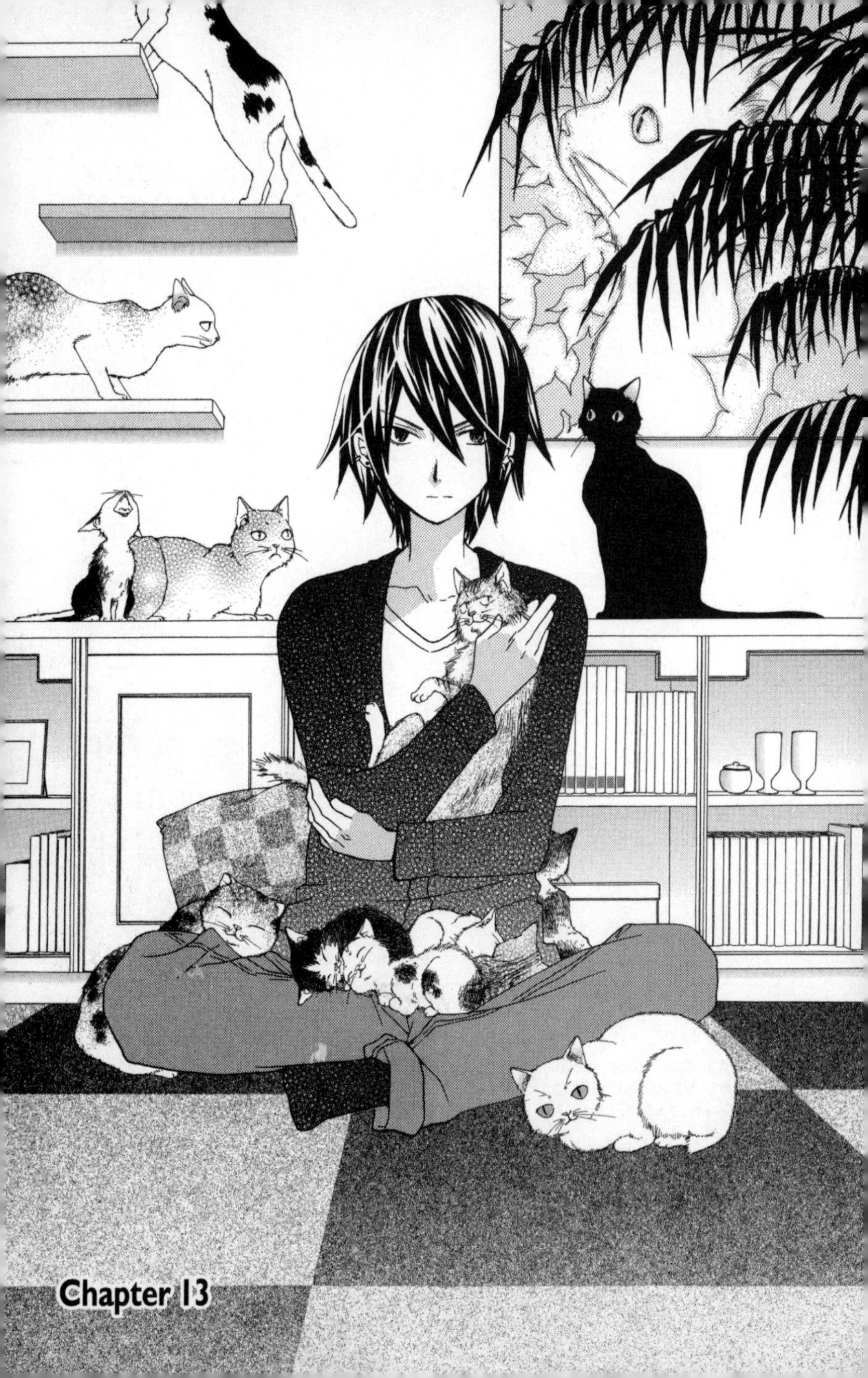
Chapter 13

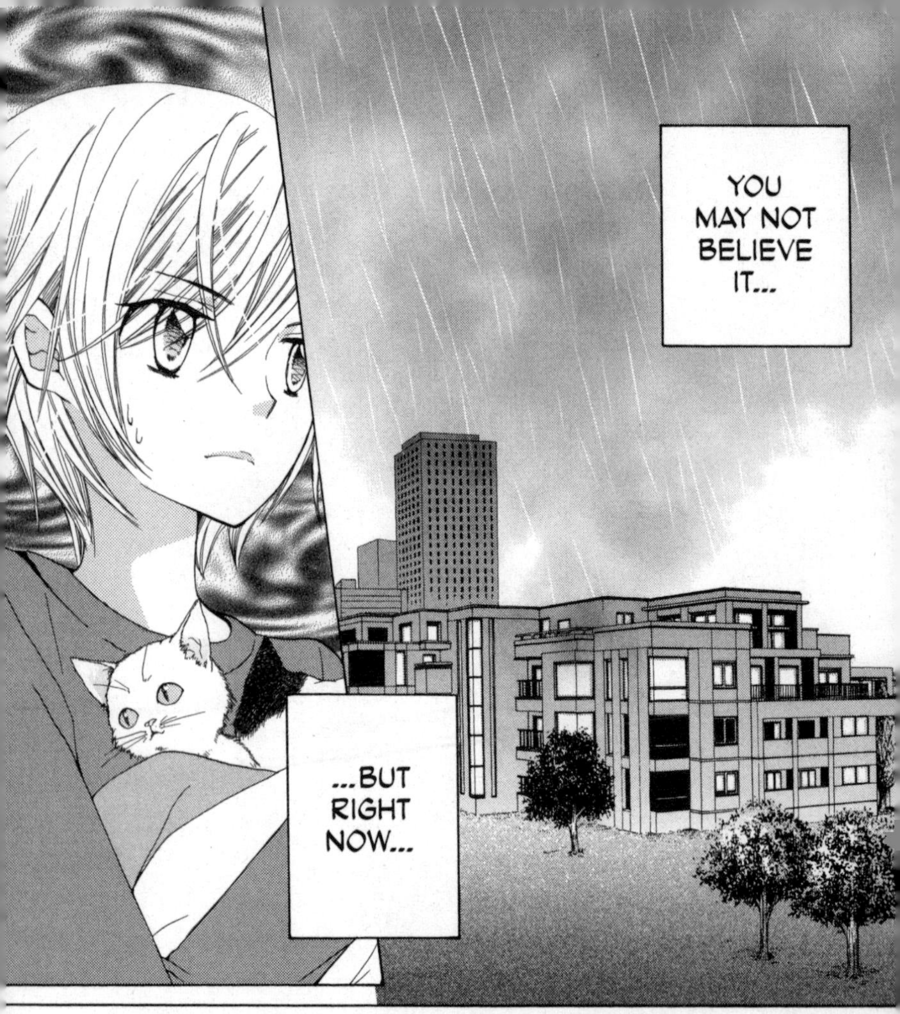
YOU MAY NOT BELIEVE IT...
...BUT RIGHT NOW...

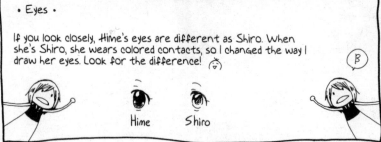

• Eyes •

If you look closely, Hime's eyes are different as Shiro. When she's Shiro, she wears colored contacts, so I changed the way I draw her eyes. Look for the difference!

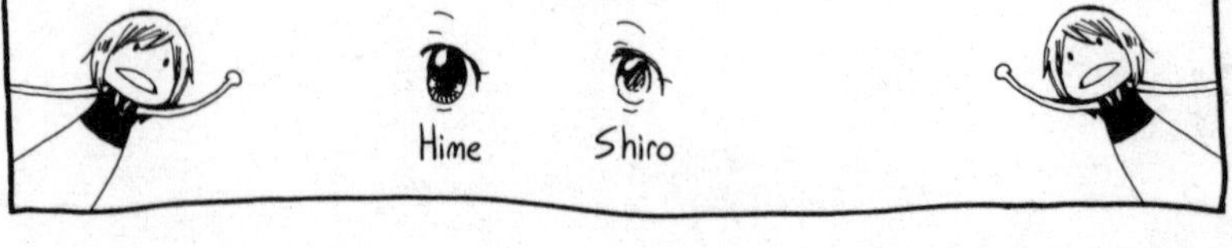
Hime
Shiro

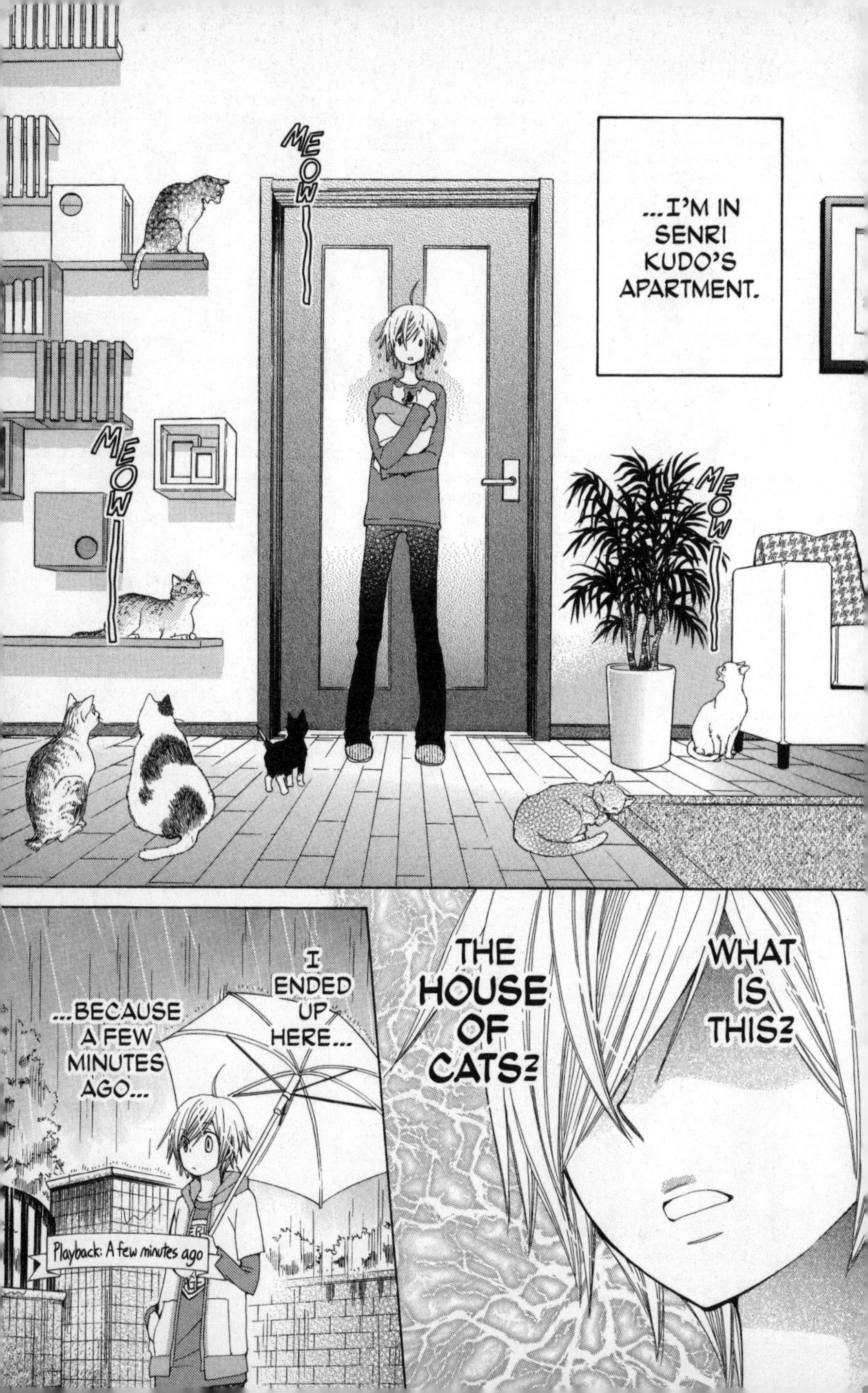
...I'M IN SENRI KUDO'S APARTMENT.
MEOW
MEOW
MEOW
WHAT IS THIS?
THE HOUSE OF CATS?
I ENDED UP HERE...
...BECAUSE A FEW MINUTES AGO...
Playback: A few minutes ago

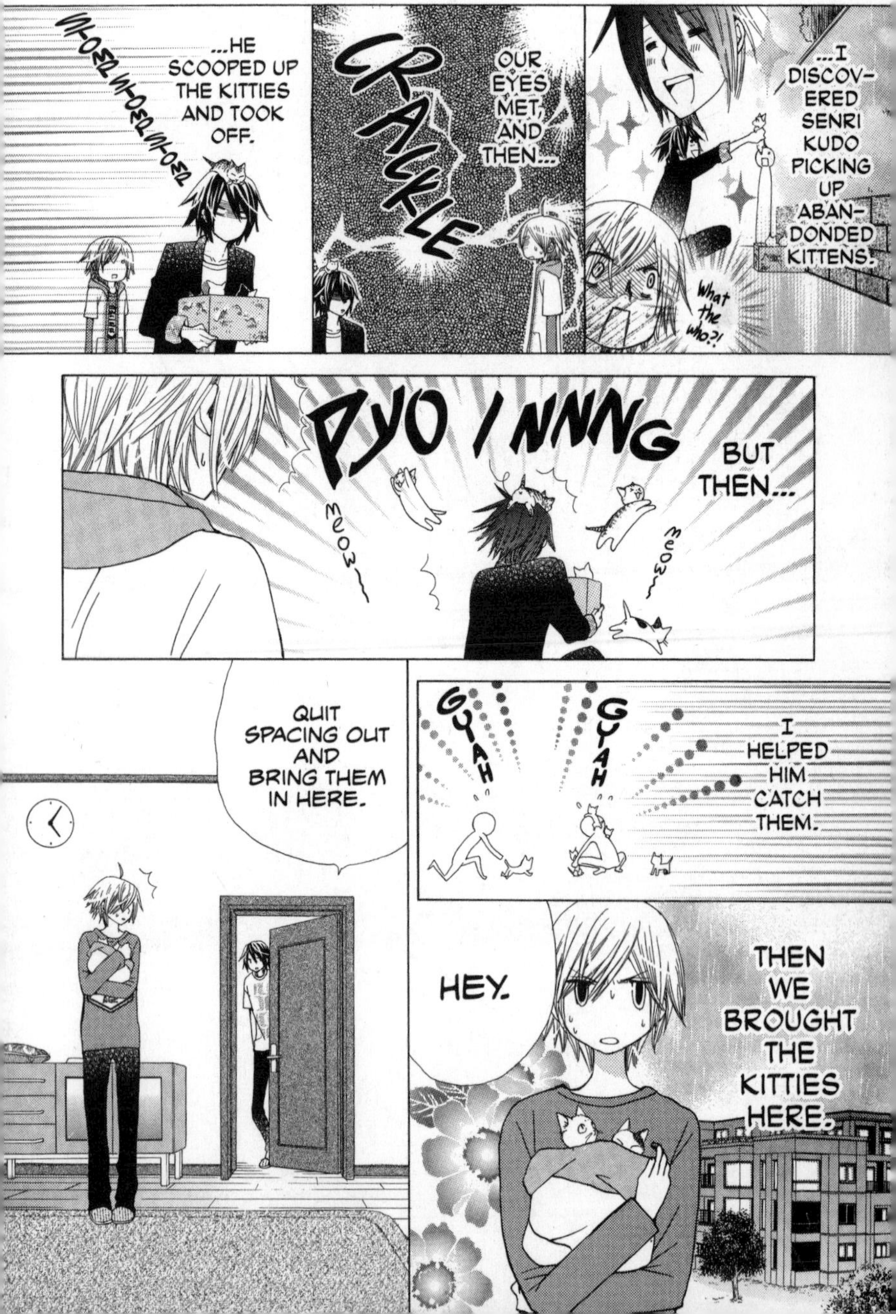
...I DISCOVERED SENRI KUDO PICKING UP ABANDONED KITTENS.
What the who?!
OUR EYES MET, AND THEN...
CRACKLE
...HE SCOOPED UP THE KITTIES AND TOOK OFF.
STOMP STOMP STOMP STOMP
BUT THEN...
PYO INNNG
meow~
meow~
I HELPED HIM CATCH THEM.
GYAH
GYAH
THEN WE BROUGHT THE KITTIES HERE.
HEY.
QUIT SPACING OUT AND BRING THEM IN HERE.

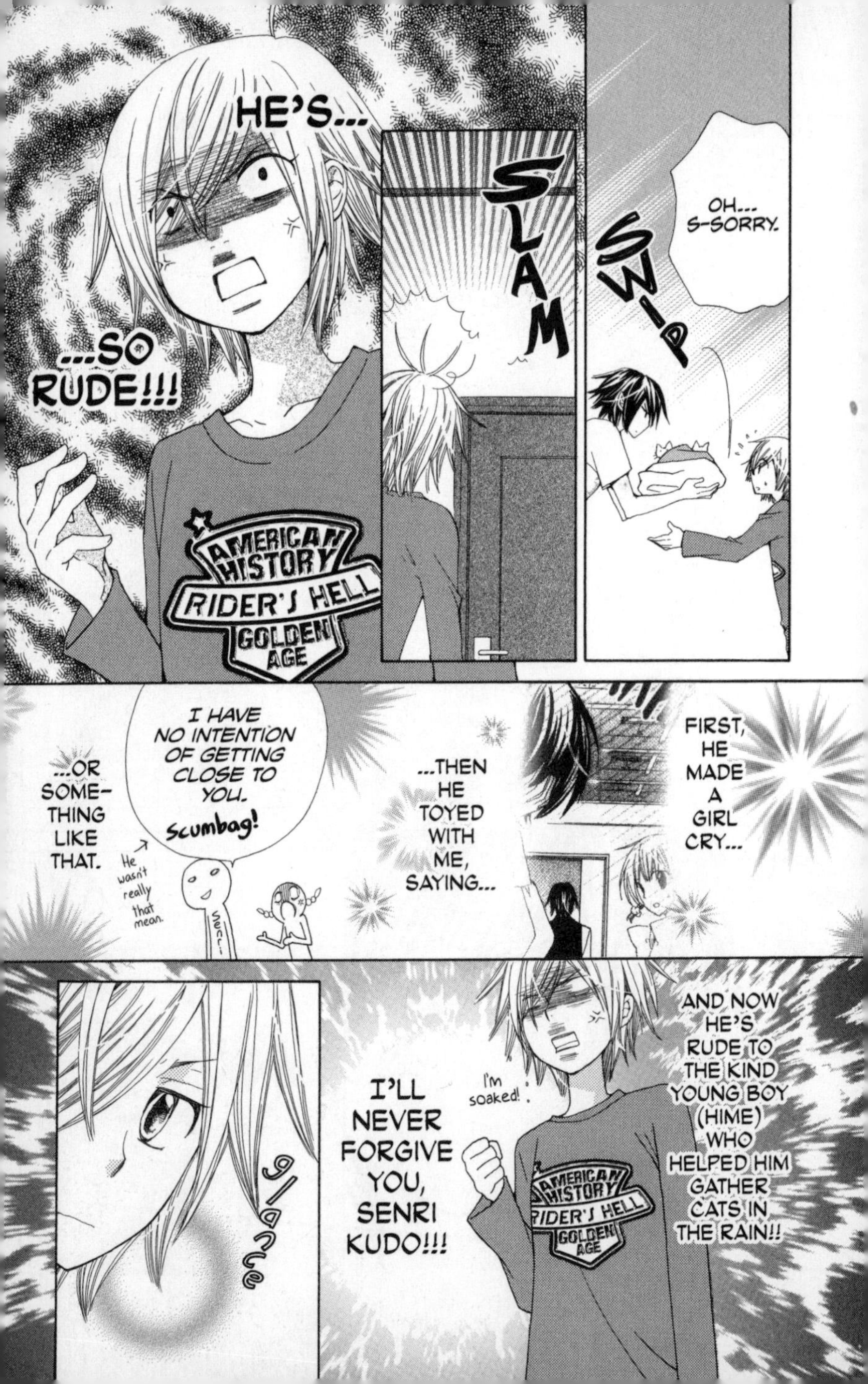
OH... S-SORRY.
SWIP
SLAM
HE'S...
...SO RUDE!!!
AMERICAN HISTORY RIDER'S HELL GOLDEN AGE
FIRST, HE MADE A GIRL CRY...
...THEN HE TOYED WITH ME, SAYING...
I HAVE NO INTENTION OF GETTING CLOSE TO YOU. Scumbag!
He wasn't really that mean.
Senri
...OR SOME-THING LIKE THAT.
AND NOW HE'S RUDE TO THE KIND YOUNG BOY (HIME) WHO HELPED HIM GATHER CATS IN THE RAIN!!
I'm soaked!
I'LL NEVER FORGIVE YOU, SENRI KUDO!!!
AMERICAN HISTORY RIDER'S HELL GOLDEN AGE
glance

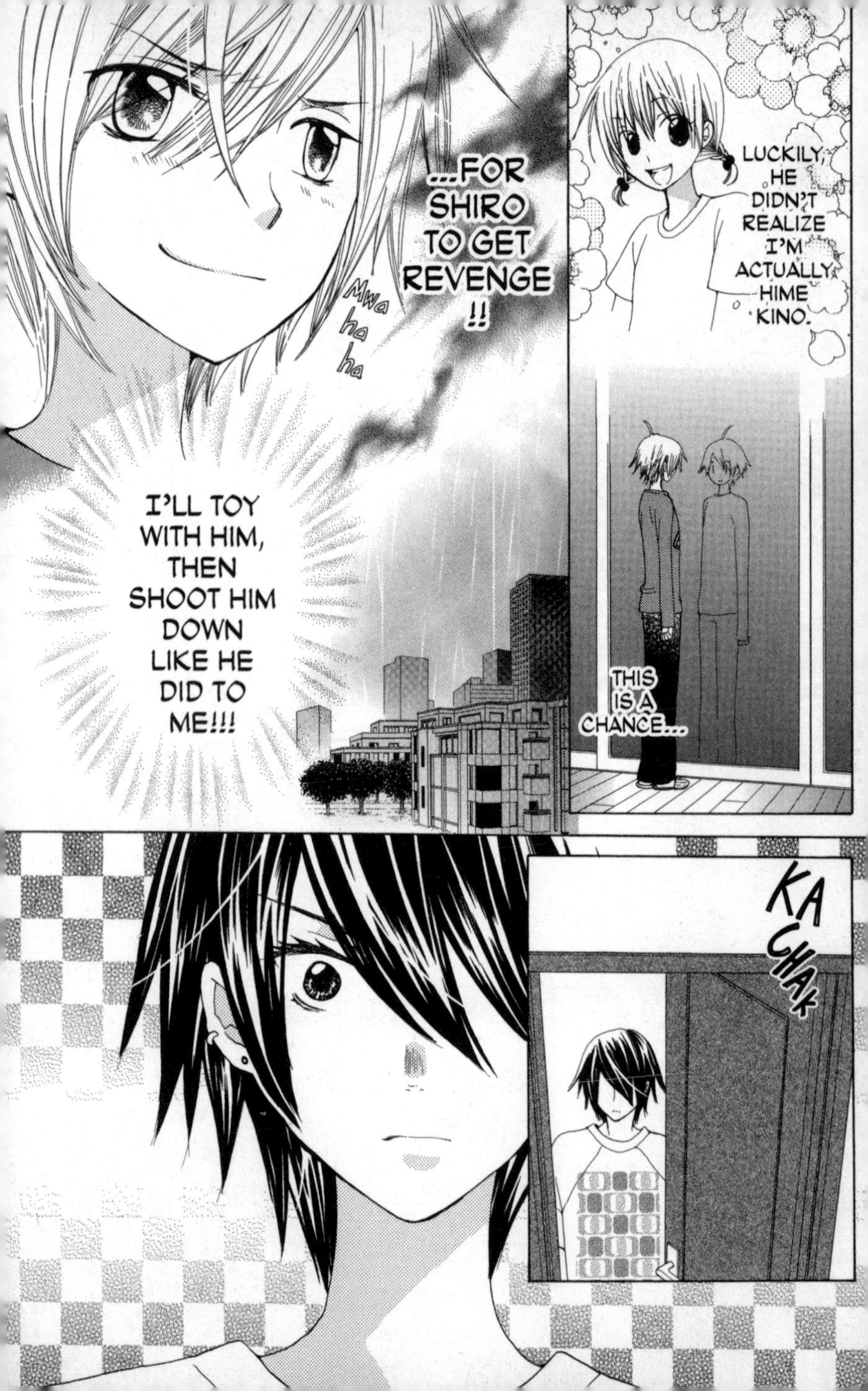
LUCKILY, HE DIDN'T REALIZE I'M ACTUALLY HIME KINO.
THIS IS A CHANCE...
...FOR SHIRO TO GET REVENGE!!
Mwa ha ha
I'LL TOY WITH HIM, THEN SHOOT HIM DOWN LIKE HE DID TO ME!!!
KA CHAK

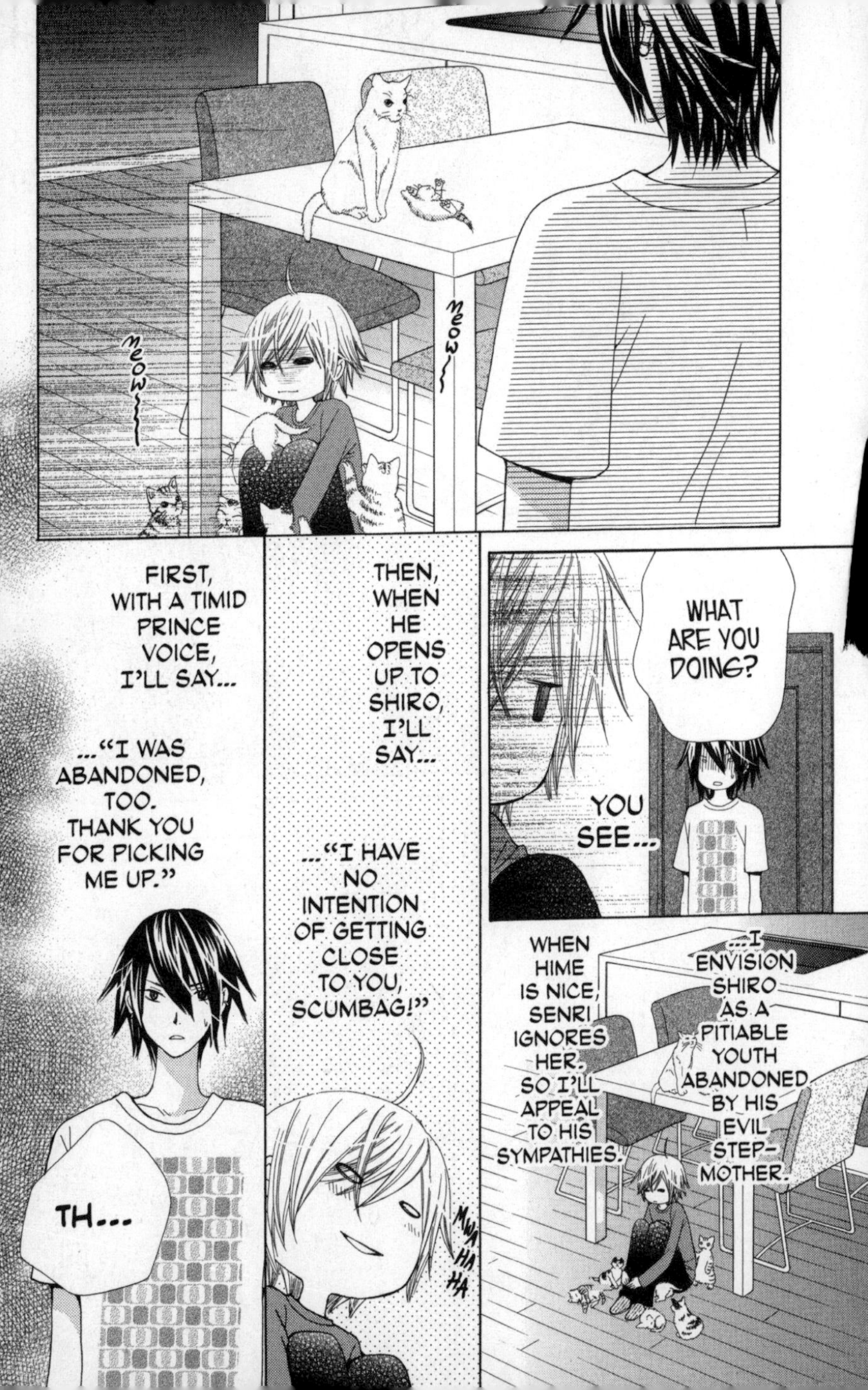
MEOW~~
MEOW~~~
WHAT ARE YOU DOING?
YOU SEE...
...I ENVISION SHIRO AS A PITIABLE YOUTH ABANDONED BY HIS EVIL STEP-MOTHER.
WHEN HIME IS NICE, SENRI IGNORES HER. SO I'LL APPEAL TO HIS SYMPATHIES.
THEN, WHEN HE OPENS UP TO SHIRO, I'LL SAY...
..."I HAVE NO INTENTION OF GETTING CLOSE TO YOU, SCUMBAG!"
MWA HA HA
FIRST, WITH A TIMID PRINCE VOICE, I'LL SAY...
..."I WAS ABANDONED, TOO. THANK YOU FOR PICKING ME UP."
TH...

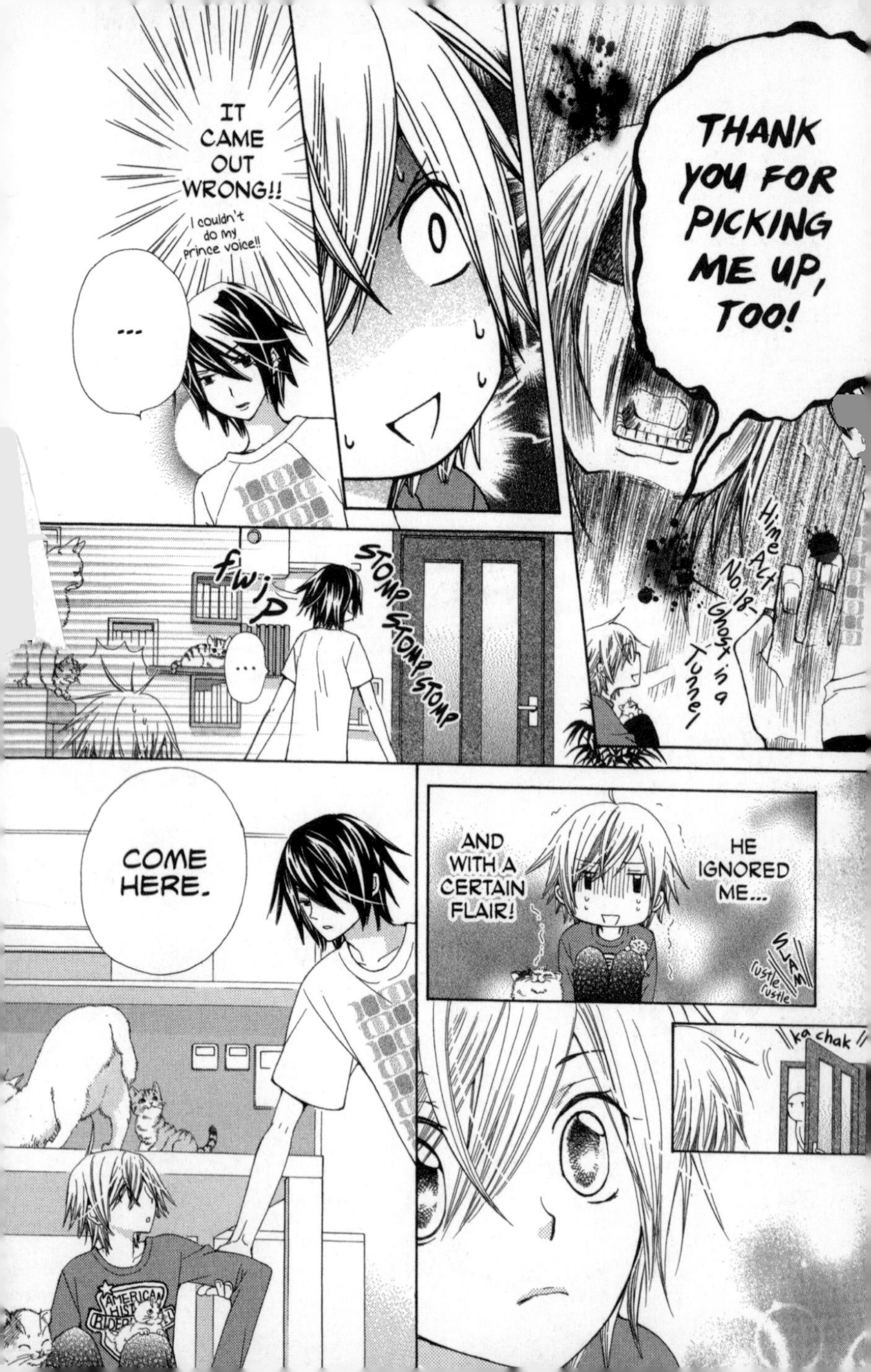
THANK YOU FOR PICKING ME UP, TOO!
Hime Act No. 18 - Ghost in a Tunnel
IT CAME OUT WRONG!!
I couldn't do my prince voice!!
...
STOMP STOMP STOMP STOMP
fwip
...
HE IGNORED ME...
AND WITH A CERTAIN FLAIR!
SLAM
rustle rustle
ka chak
COME HERE.

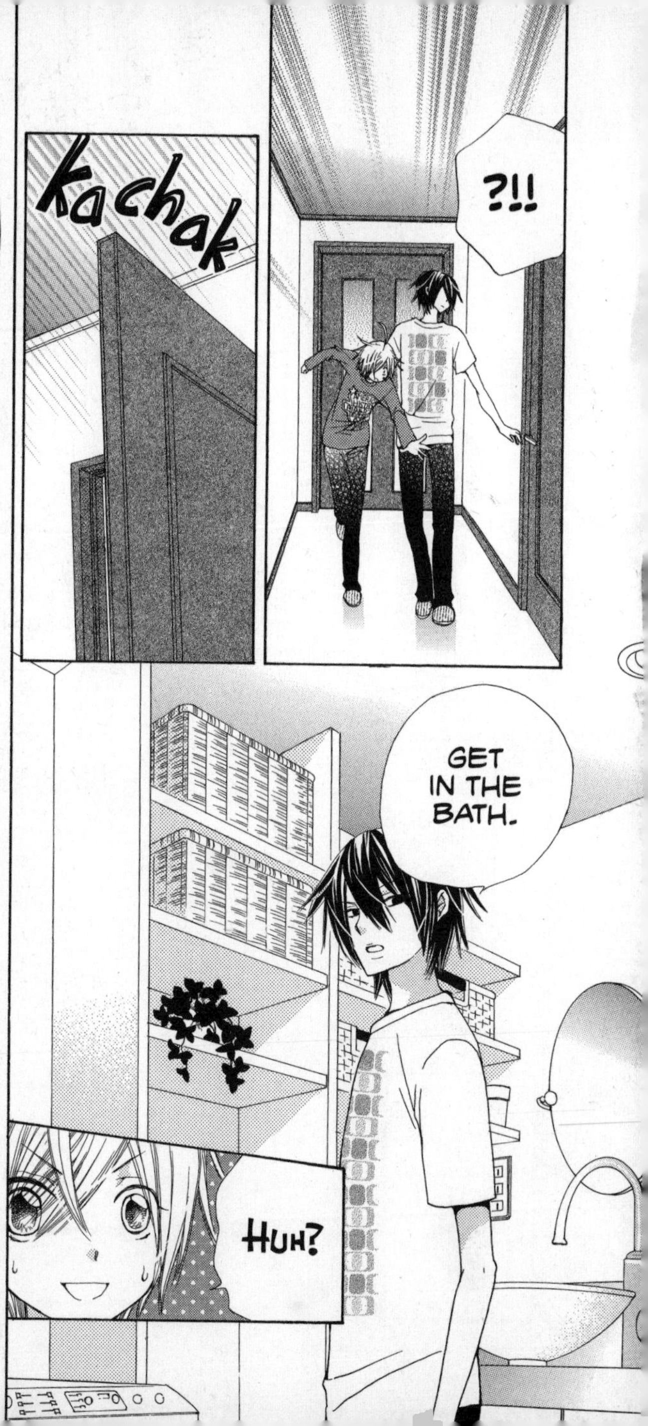
?!!
kachak
GET IN THE BATH.
HUH?

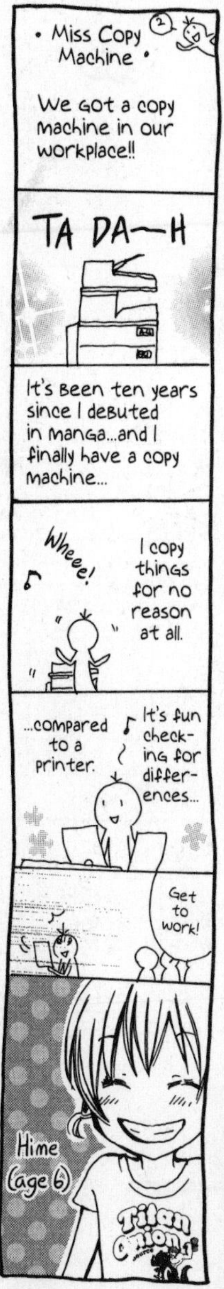
• Miss Copy Machine • ②
We got a copy machine in our workplace!!
TA DA—H
It's been ten years since I debuted in manga...and I finally have a copy machine...
Wheee!
I copy things for no reason at all.
It's fun checking for differences...
...compared to a printer.
Get to work!
Hime (age 6)
Titan Onion

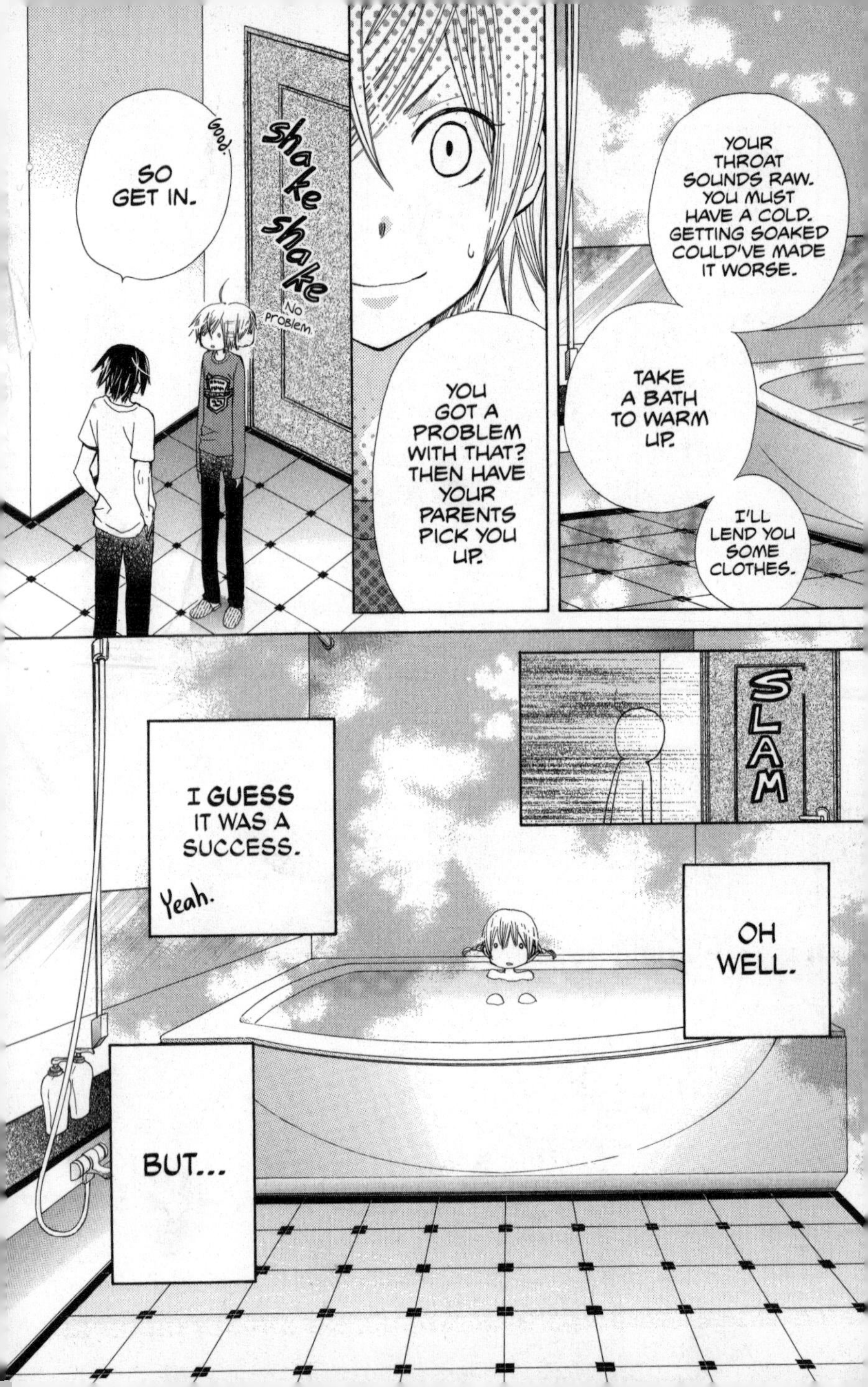
YOUR THROAT SOUNDS RAW. YOU MUST HAVE A COLD. GETTING SOAKED COULD'VE MADE IT WORSE.
TAKE A BATH TO WARM UP.
I'LL LEND YOU SOME CLOTHES.
YOU GOT A PROBLEM WITH THAT? THEN HAVE YOUR PARENTS PICK YOU UP.
shake shake
No problem.
Good.
SO GET IN.
SLAM
I GUESS IT WAS A SUCCESS.
Yeah.
OH WELL.
BUT...

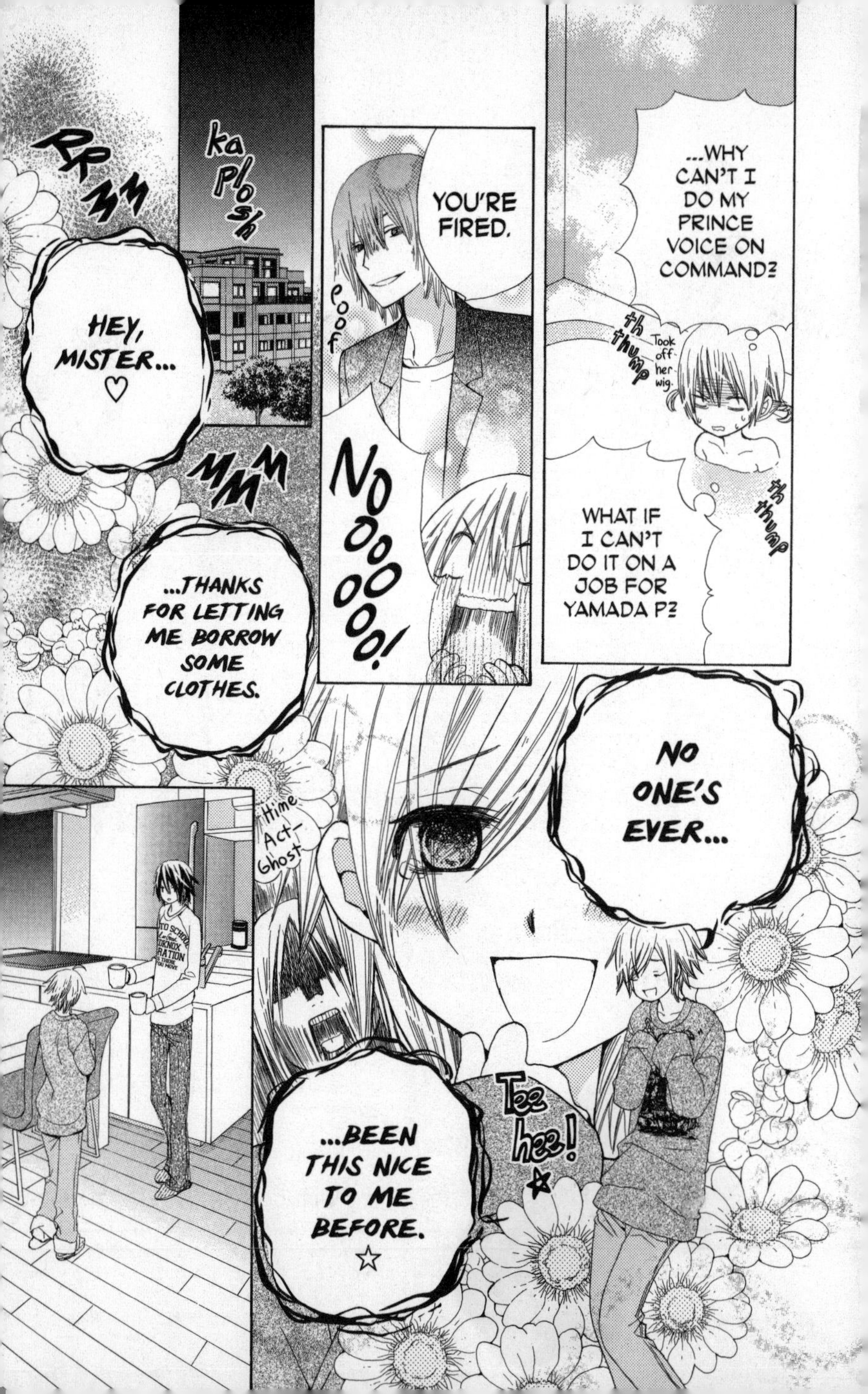
...WHY CAN'T I DO MY PRINCE VOICE ON COMMAND?
th thump
Took off her wig.
WHAT IF I CAN'T DO IT ON A JOB FOR YAMADA P?
th thump
YOU'RE FIRED.
poof
NOOOOOOOOO!
ka ploosh
RRMMM
HEY, MISTER... ♡
MMM
...THANKS FOR LETTING ME BORROW SOME CLOTHES.
NO ONE'S EVER...
...BEEN THIS NICE TO ME BEFORE. ☆
Tee hee! ☆
Hime Act-Ghost

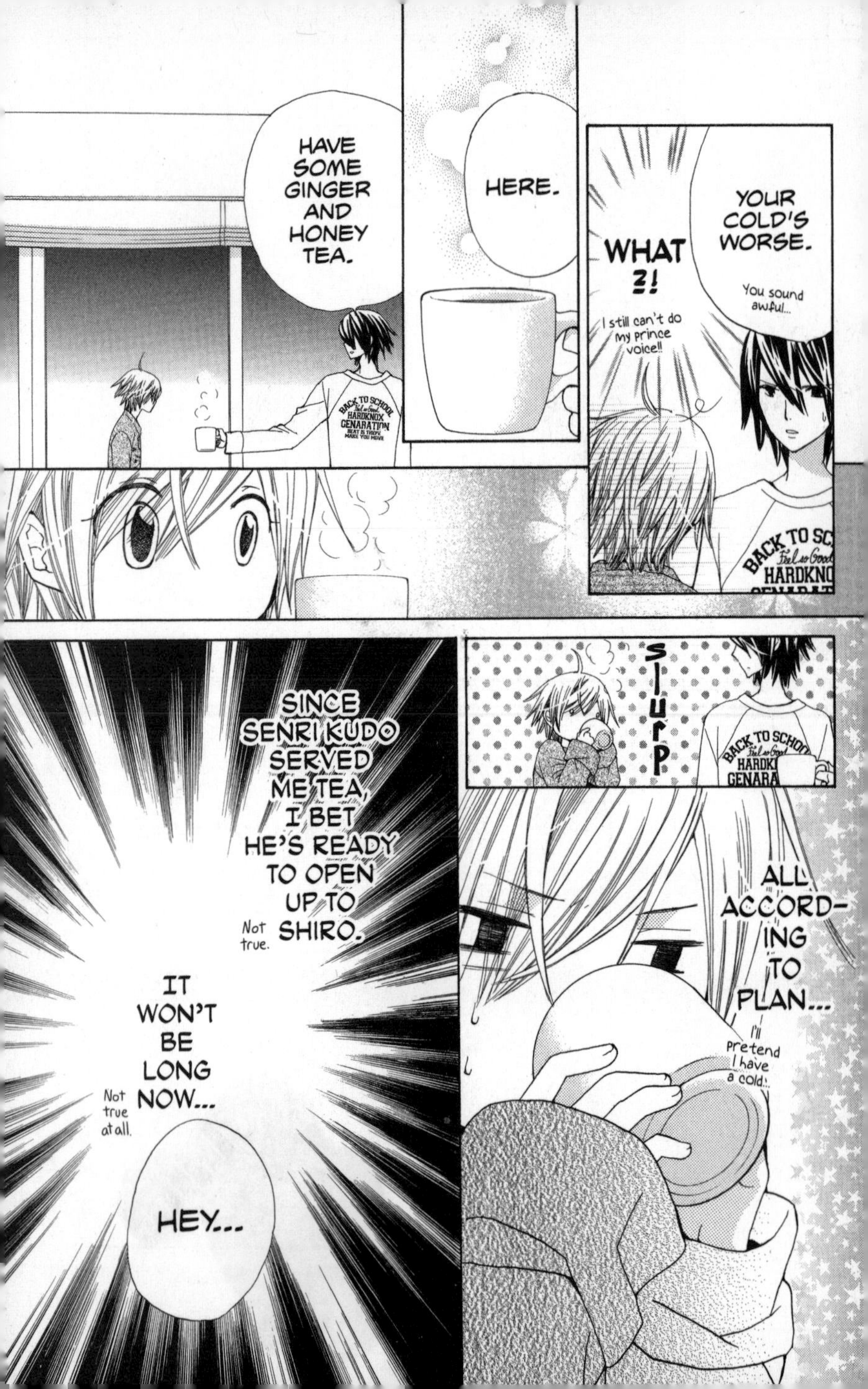
YOUR COLD'S WORSE.
You sound awful...
WHAT ?!
I still can't do my prince voice!!
HERE.
HAVE SOME GINGER AND HONEY TEA.
BACK TO SCHOOL Feel so Good HARDKNOX GENARATION BEAT IS THERE MAKE YOU MOVE
SLURP
ALL ACCORDING TO PLAN...
I'll pretend I have a cold...
SINCE SENRI KUDO SERVED ME TEA, I BET HE'S READY TO OPEN UP TO SHIRO.
Not true.
IT WON'T BE LONG NOW...
Not true at all.
HEY...

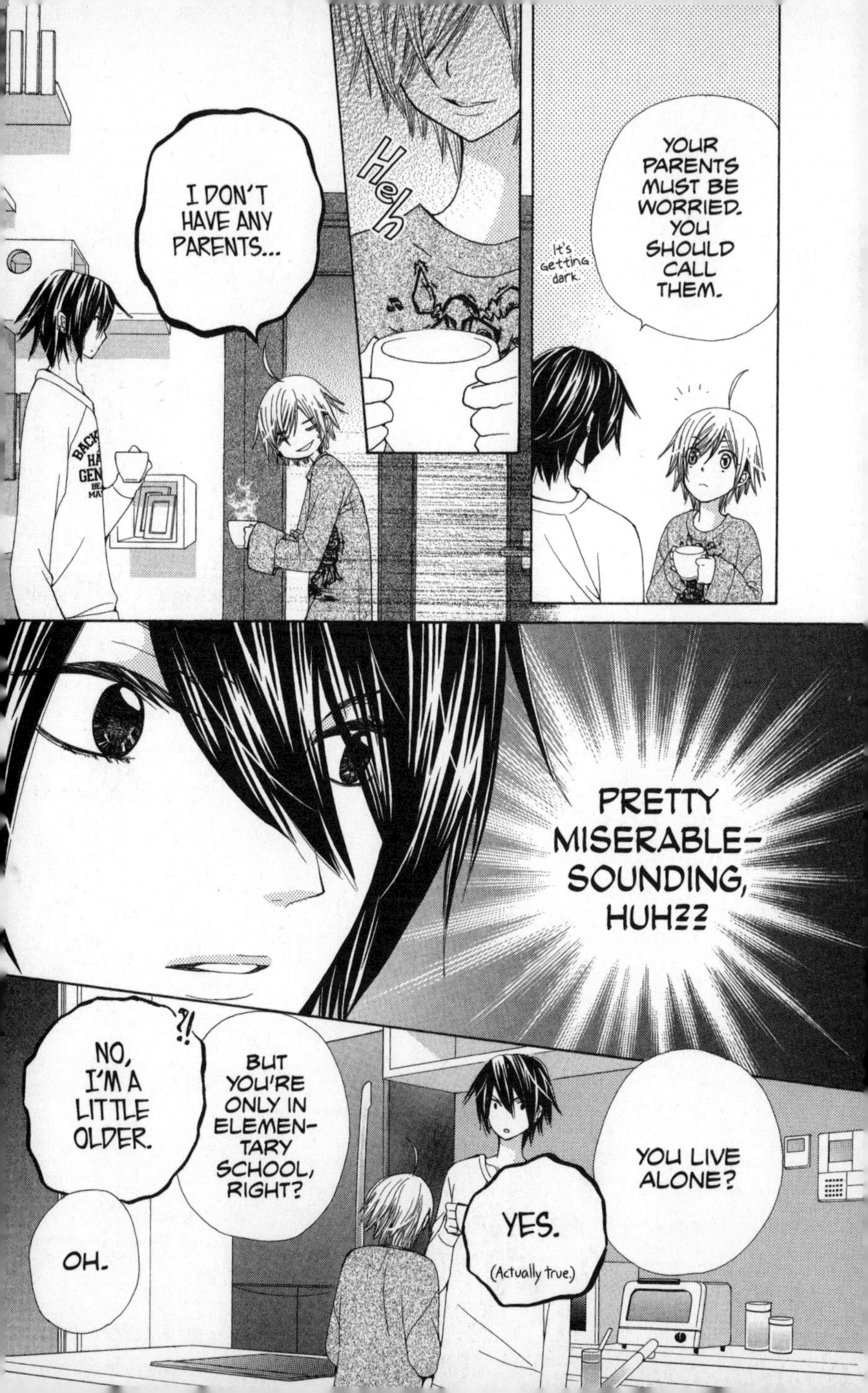
It's getting dark.
YOUR PARENTS MUST BE WORRIED. YOU SHOULD CALL THEM.
Heh
I DON'T HAVE ANY PARENTS...
PRETTY MISERABLE-SOUNDING, HUH??
YOU LIVE ALONE?
YES.
(Actually true.)
BUT YOU'RE ONLY IN ELEMENTARY SCHOOL, RIGHT?
?!
NO, I'M A LITTLE OLDER.
OH.

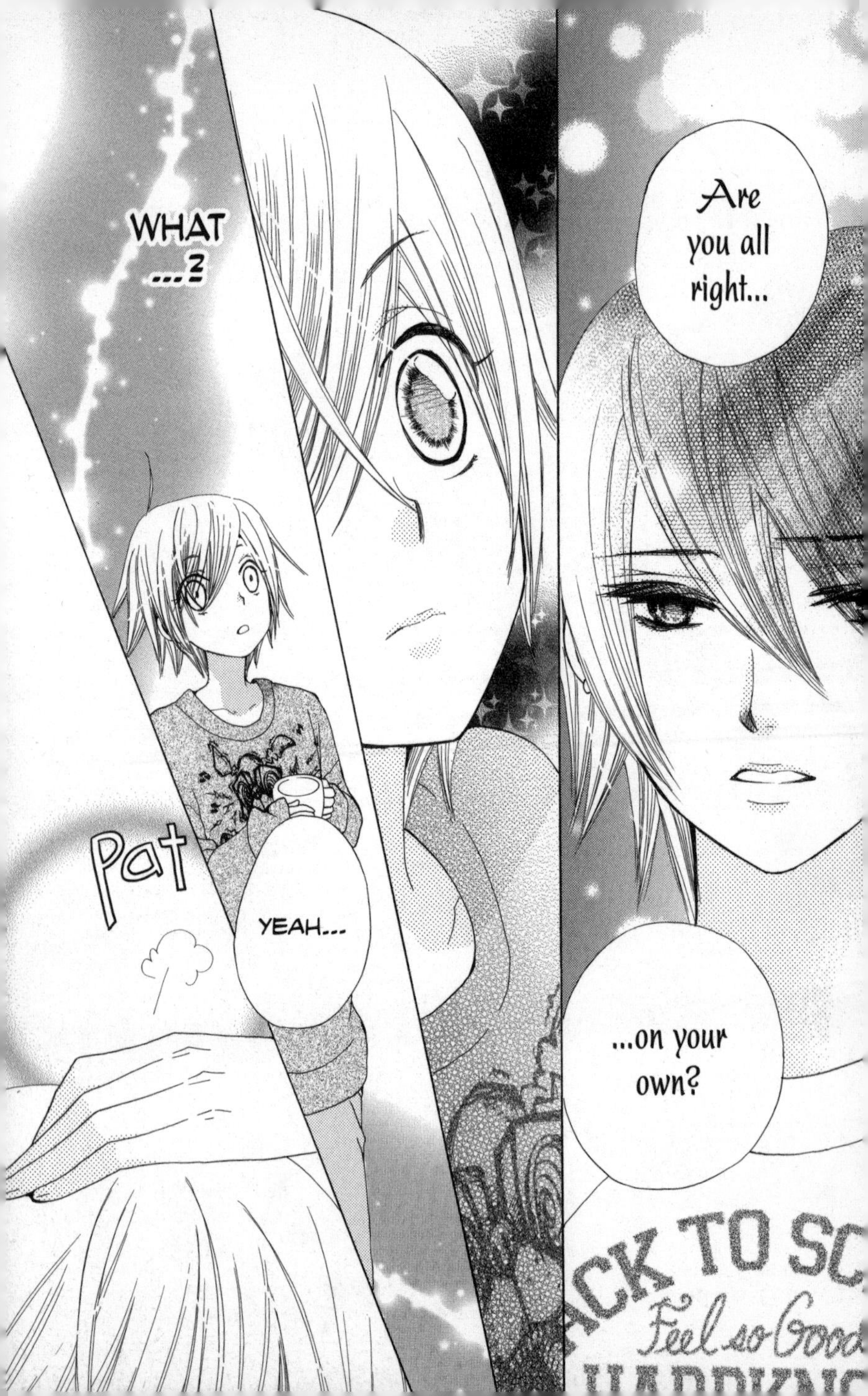
Are you all right...
...on your own?
WHAT ...?
Pat
YEAH...

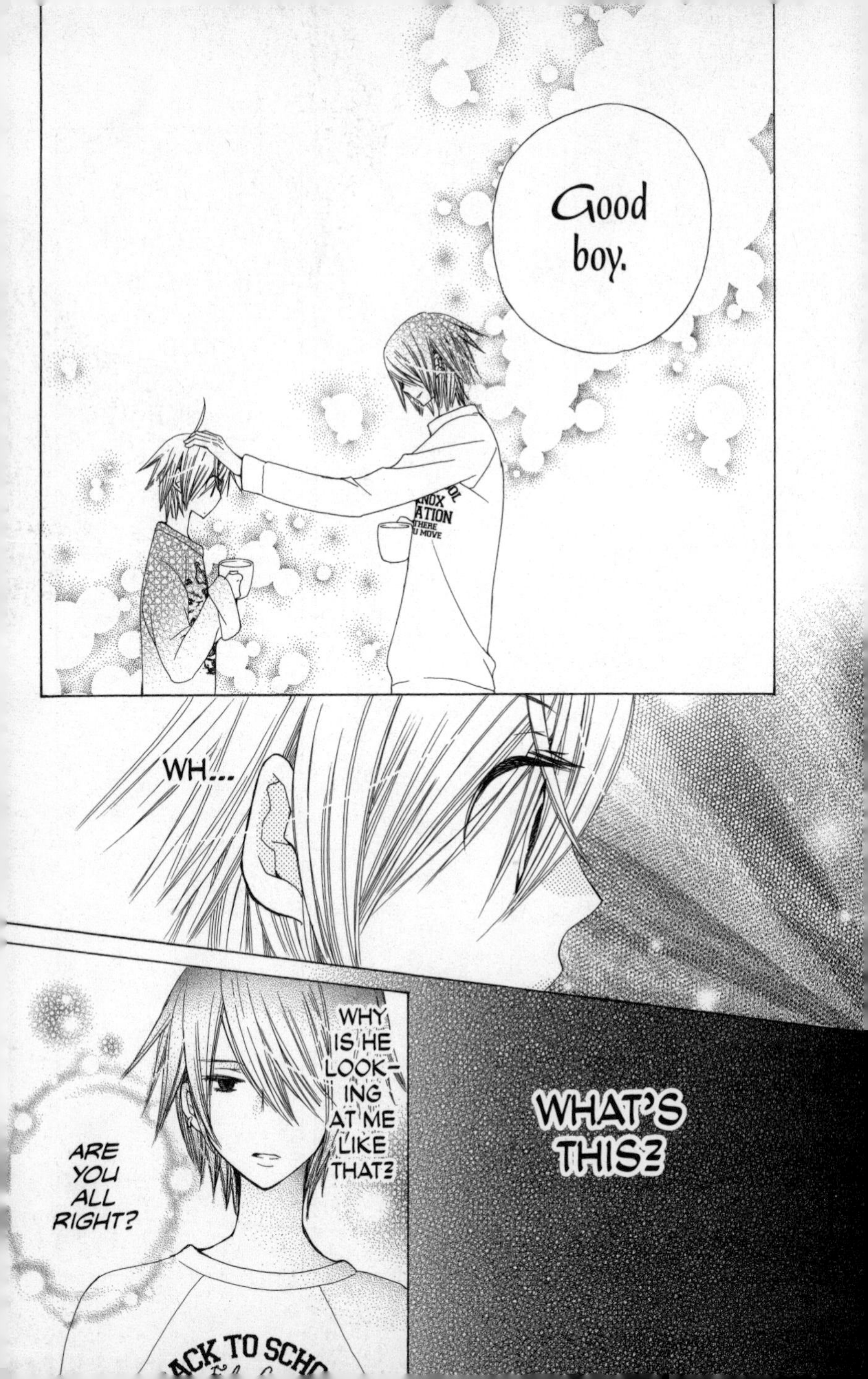
Good boy.
WH...
WHAT'S THIS?
WHY IS HE LOOKING AT ME LIKE THAT?
ARE YOU ALL RIGHT?

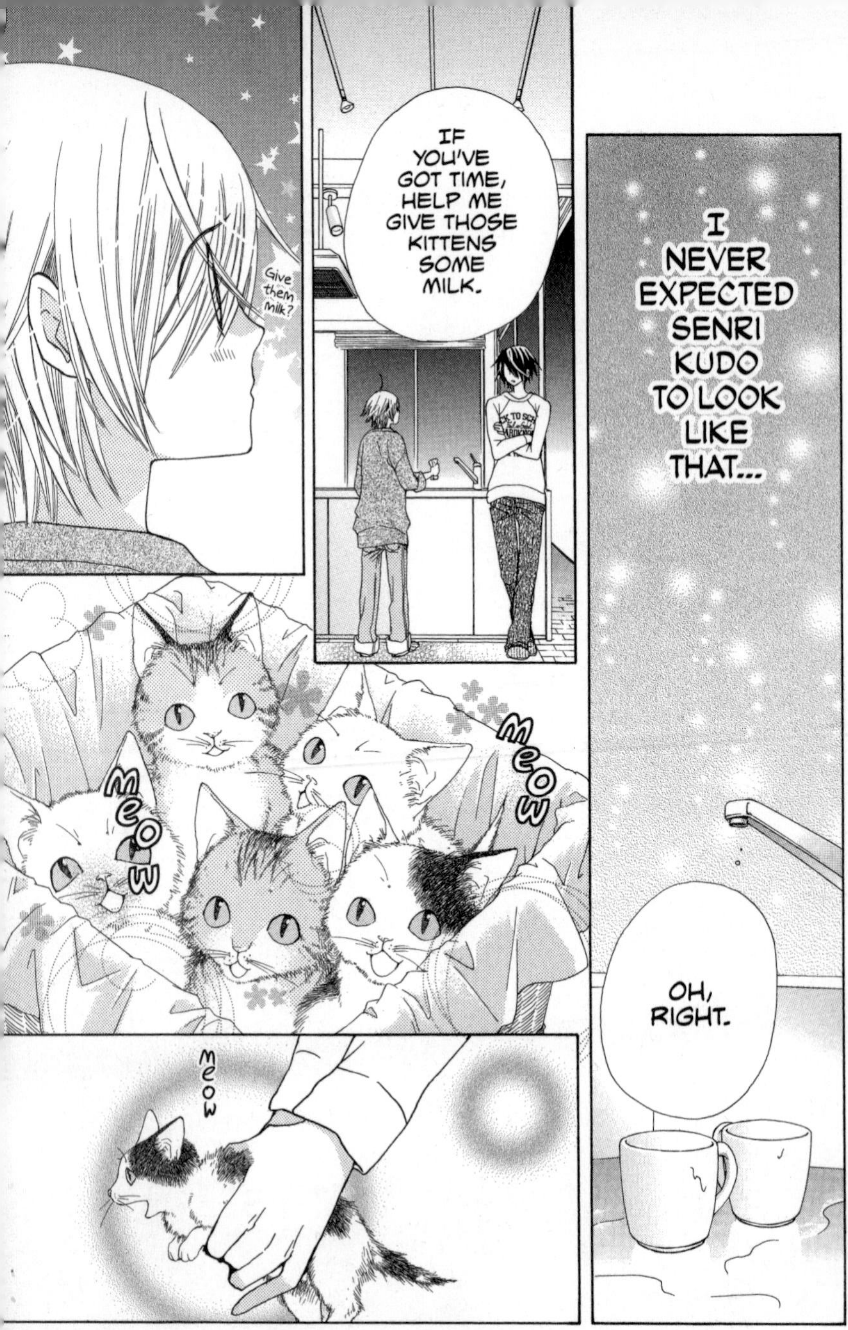
I NEVER EXPECTED SENRI KUDO TO LOOK LIKE THAT...
OH, RIGHT.
IF YOU'VE GOT TIME, HELP ME GIVE THOSE KITTENS SOME MILK.
Give them milk?
MEOW
MEOW
MEOW

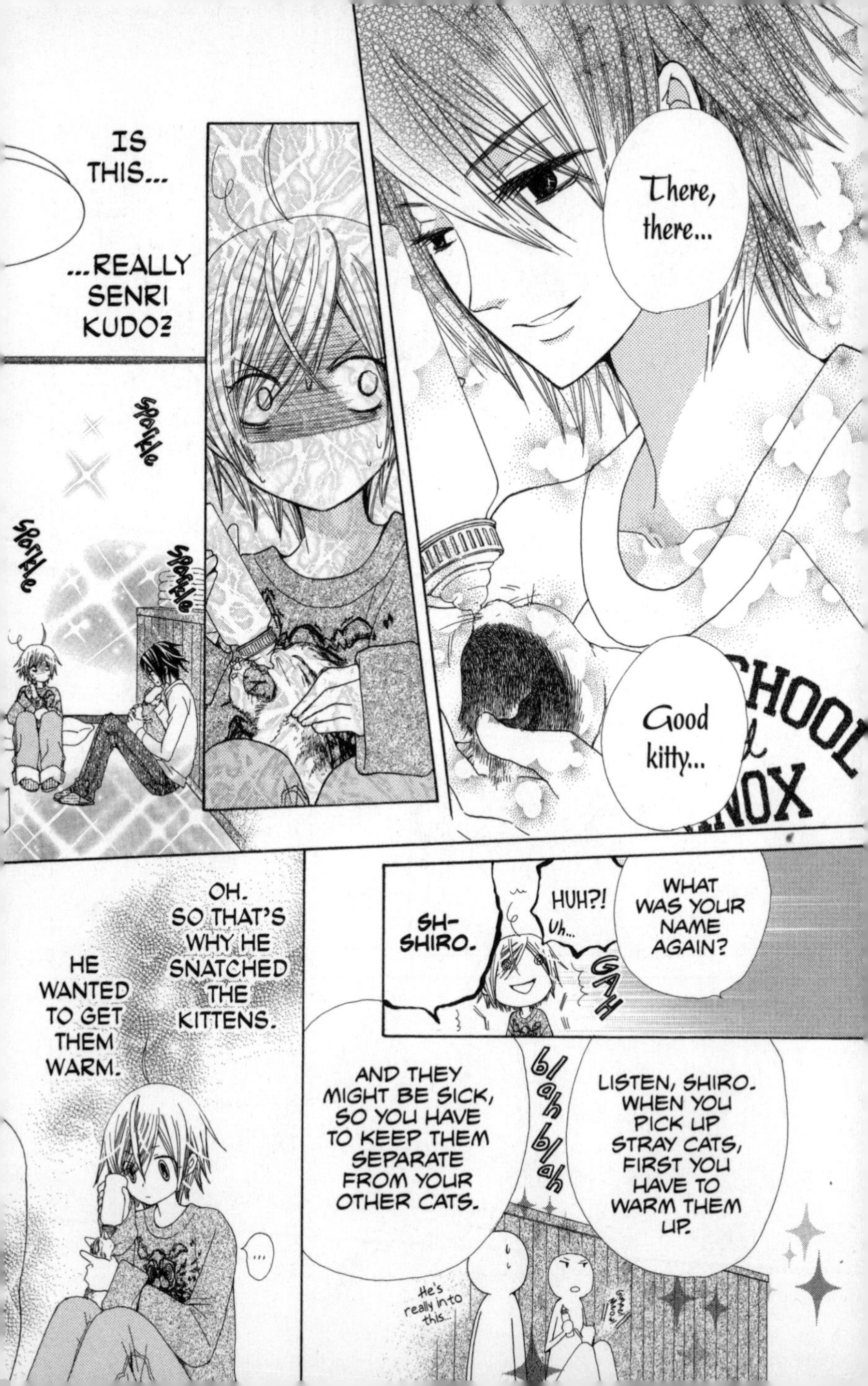

There, there...
Good kitty...
IS THIS...
...REALLY SENRI KUDO?
sparkle
sparkle
sparkle
WHAT WAS YOUR NAME AGAIN?
HUH?! Uh...
GAH
SH-SHIRO.
LISTEN, SHIRO. WHEN YOU PICK UP STRAY CATS, FIRST YOU HAVE TO WARM THEM UP.
blah blah
AND THEY MIGHT BE SICK, SO YOU HAVE TO KEEP THEM SEPARATE FROM YOUR OTHER CATS.
He's really into this...
OH. SO THAT'S WHY HE SNATCHED THE KITTENS.
HE WANTED TO GET THEM WARM.
...

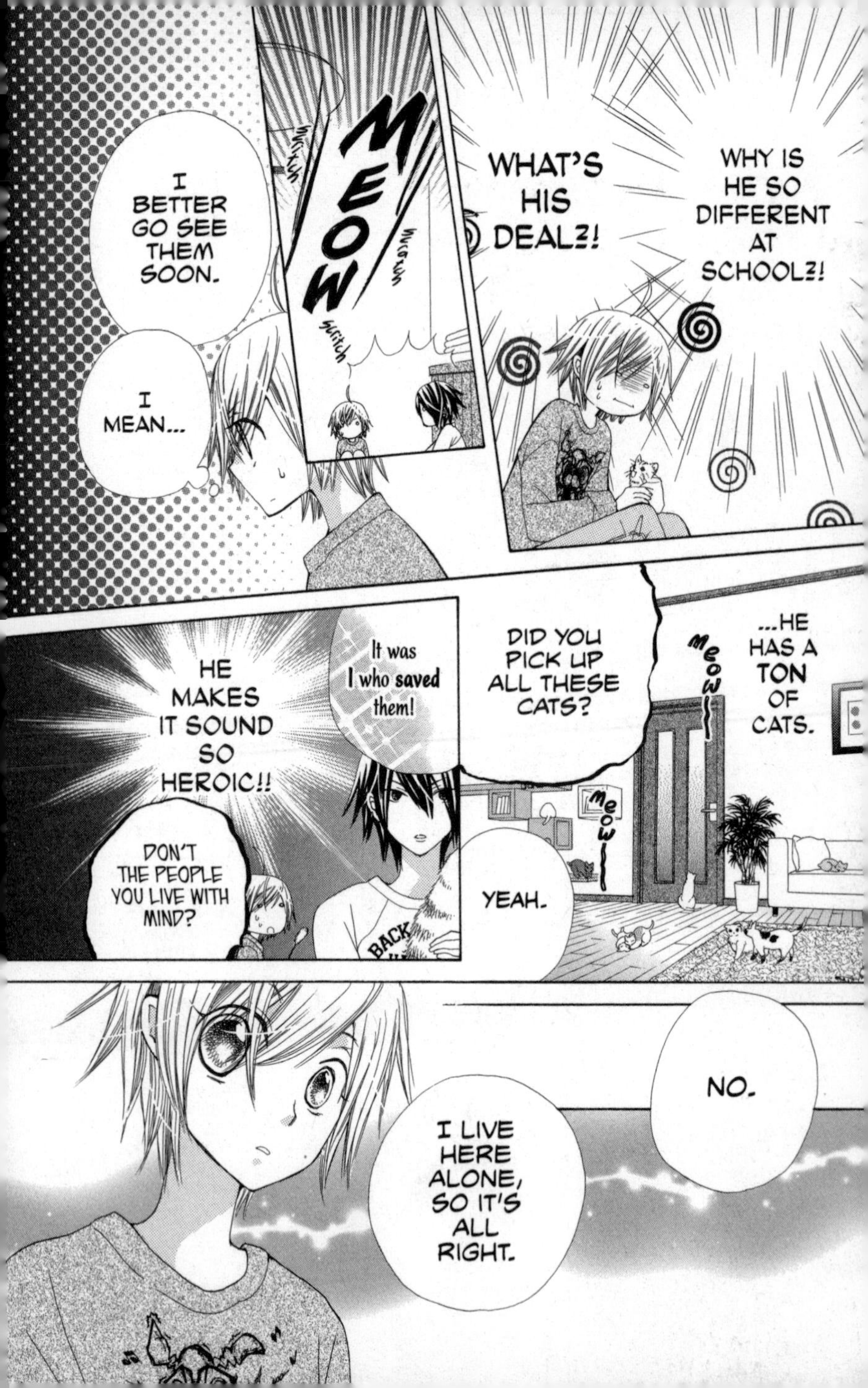
WHY IS HE SO DIFFERENT AT SCHOOL?!
WHAT'S HIS DEAL?!
MEOW
scritch
scritch
scritch
I BETTER GO SEE THEM SOON.
I MEAN...
...HE HAS A TON OF CATS.
MEOW~
DID YOU PICK UP ALL THESE CATS?
MEOW~
YEAH.
It was I who saved them!
HE MAKES IT SOUND SO HEROIC!!
DON'T THE PEOPLE YOU LIVE WITH MIND?
NO.
I LIVE HERE ALONE, SO IT'S ALL RIGHT.

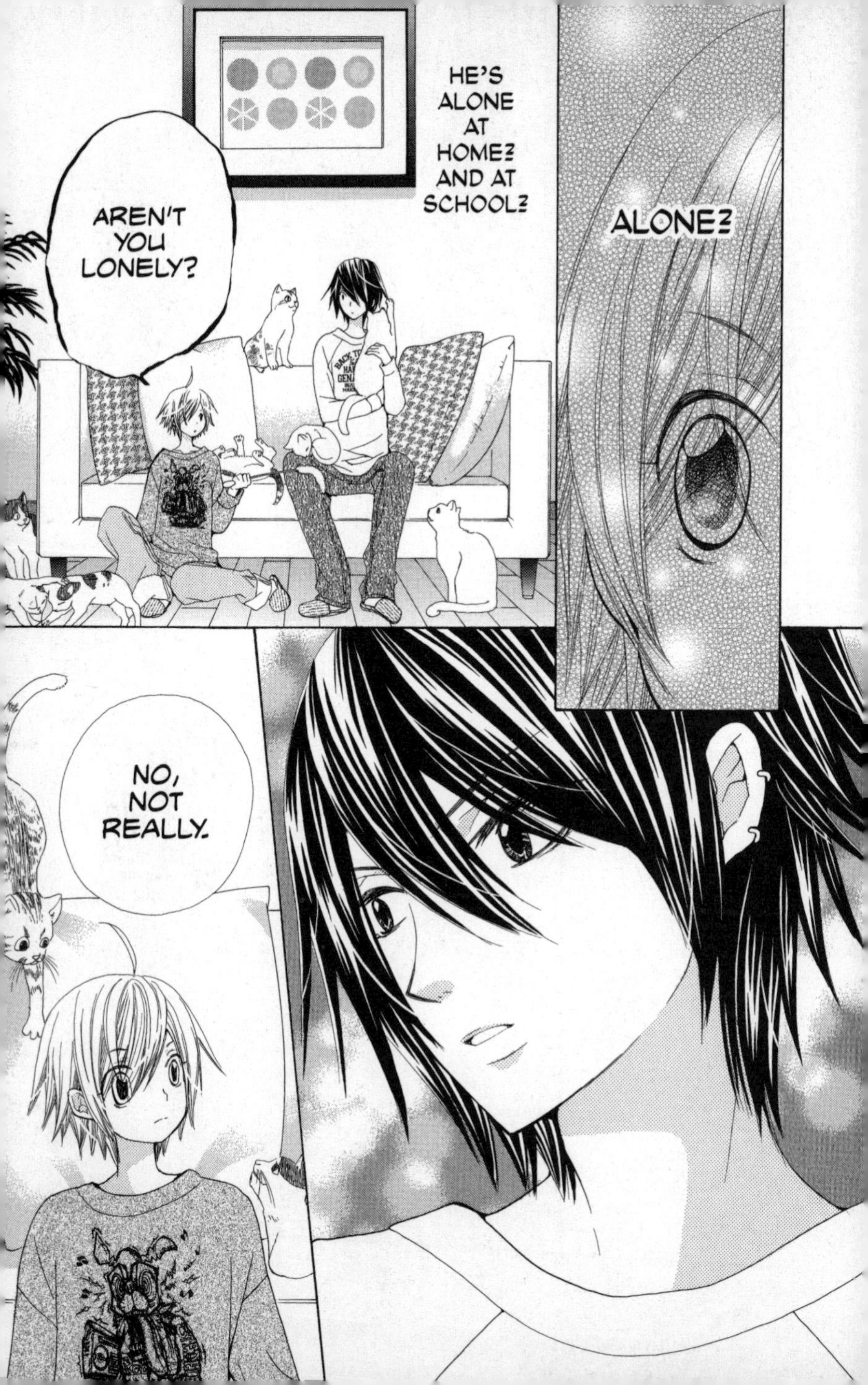
ALONE?
HE'S ALONE AT HOME? AND AT SCHOOL?
AREN'T YOU LONELY?
NO, NOT REALLY.

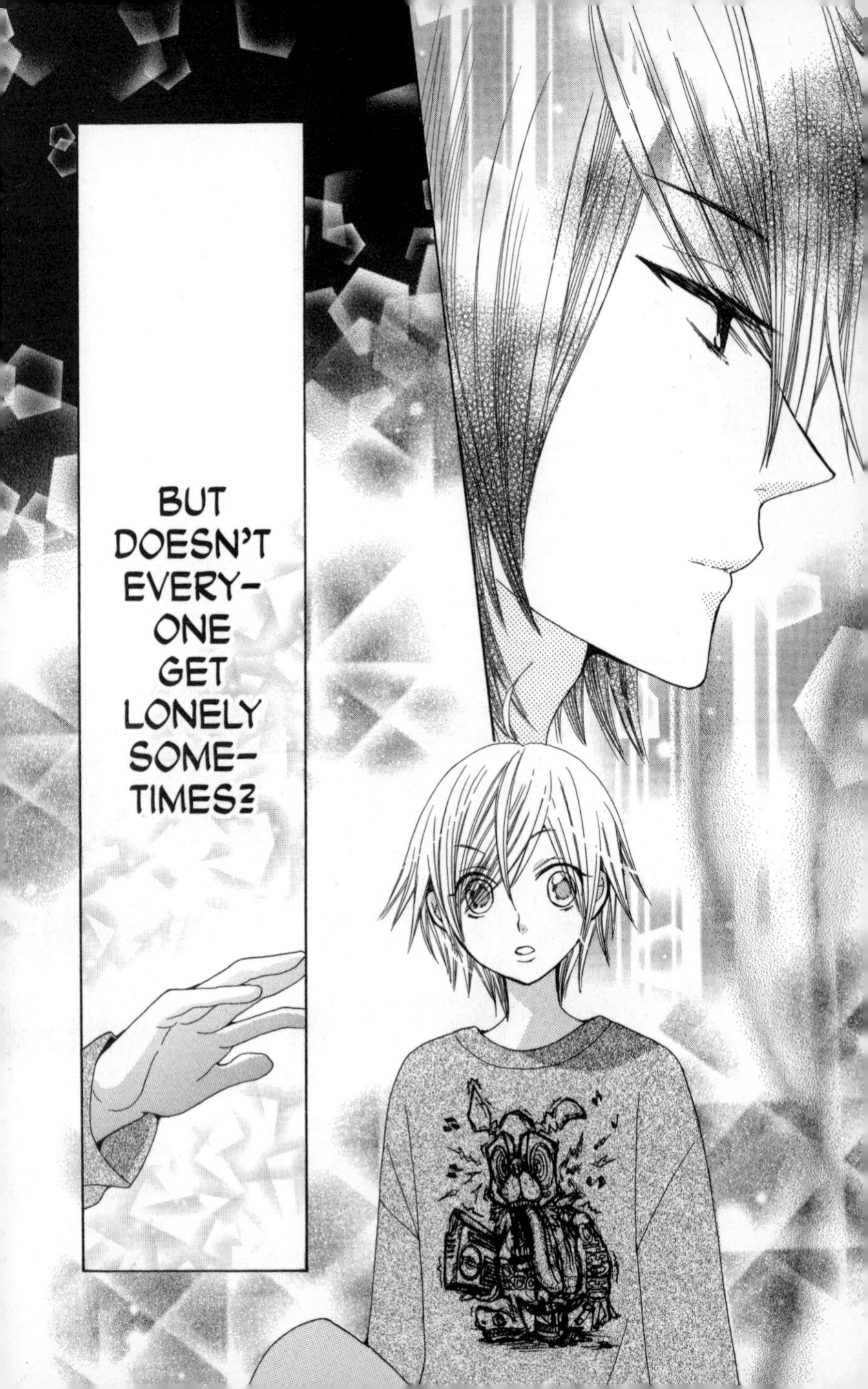
BUT DOESN'T EVERY-ONE GET LONELY SOME-TIMES?

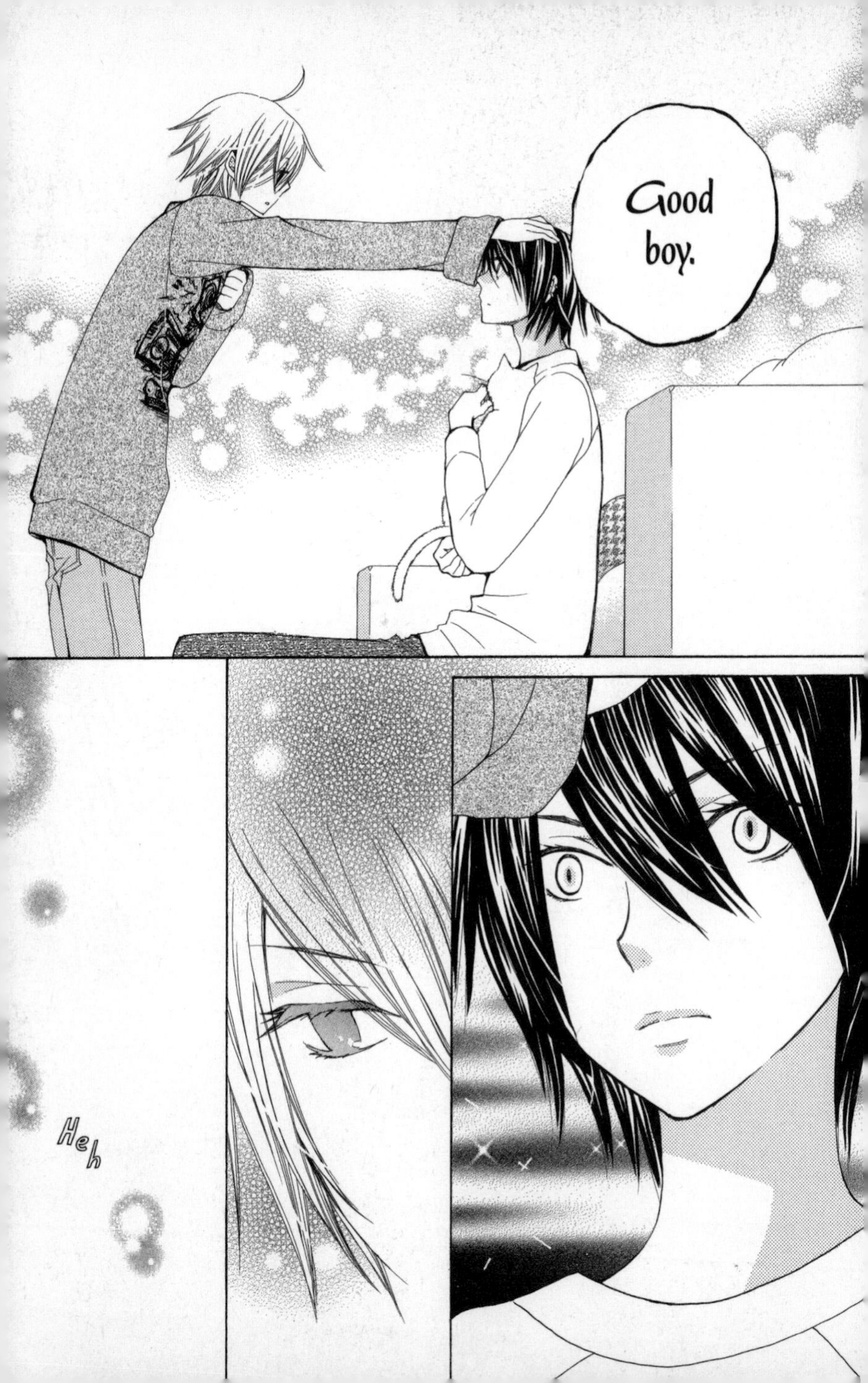
Good boy.
Heh

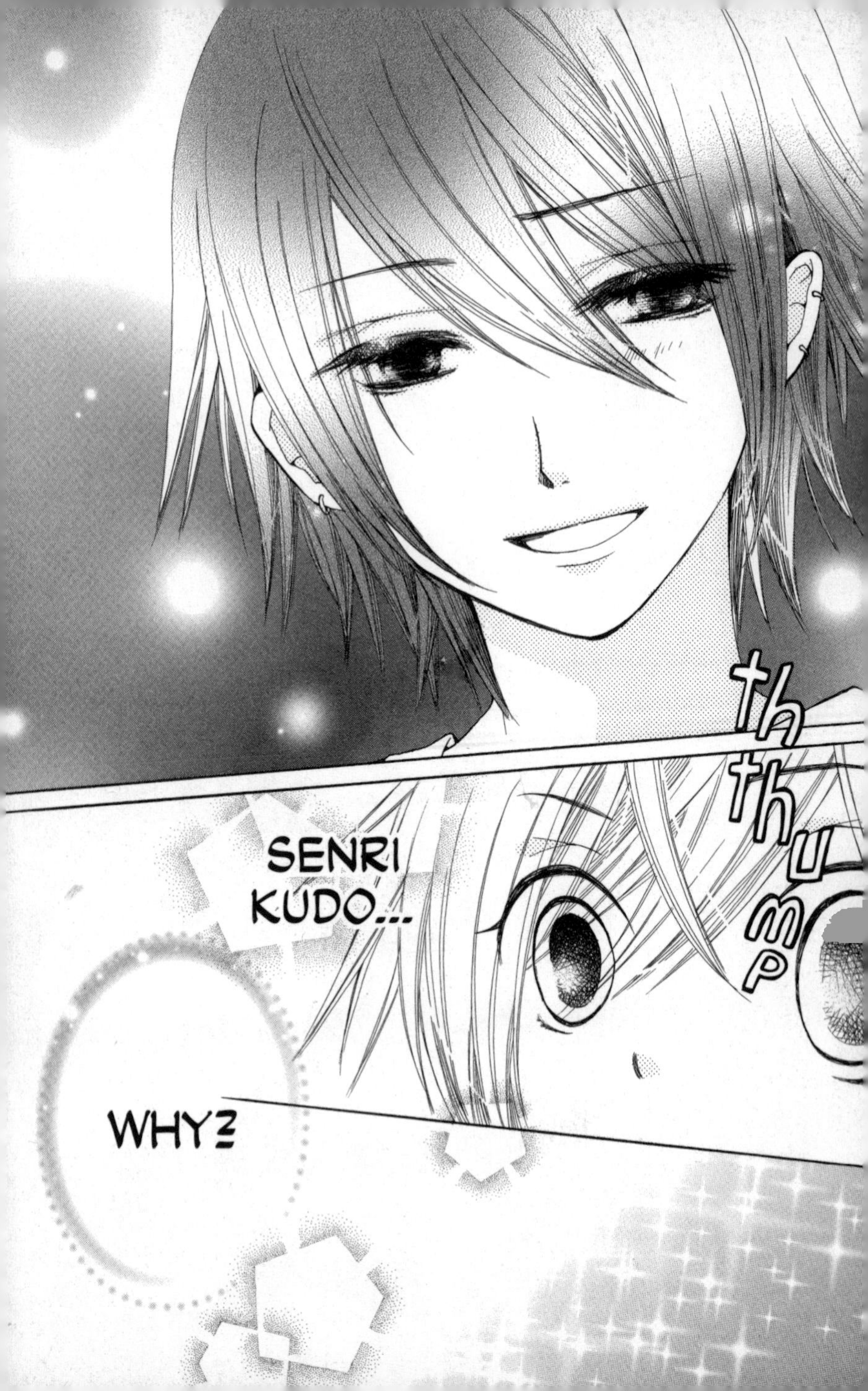
thump
SENRI KUDO...
WHY?

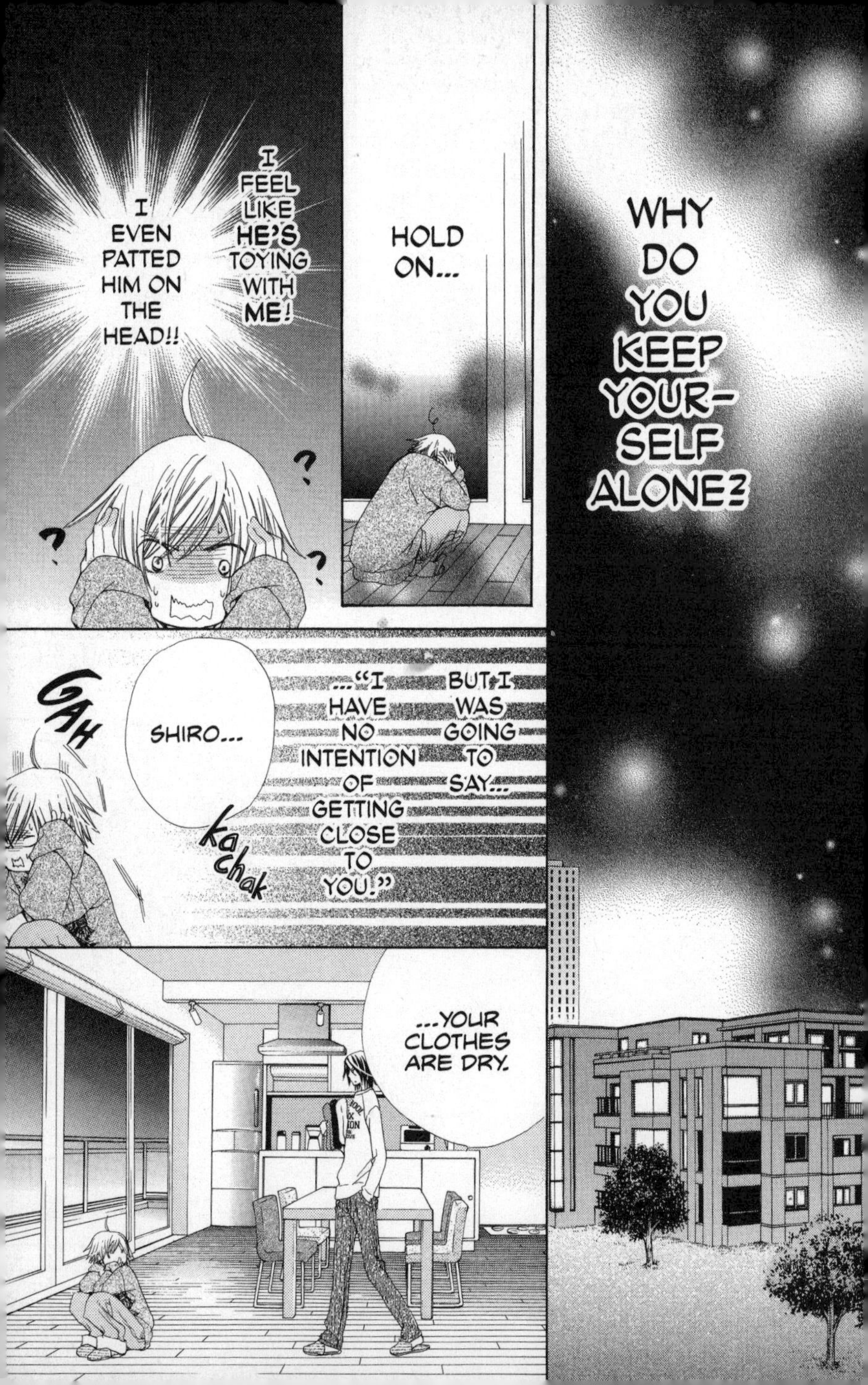
WHY DO YOU KEEP YOURSELF ALONE?
HOLD ON...
I FEEL LIKE HE'S TOYING WITH ME!
I EVEN PATTED HIM ON THE HEAD!!
BUT I WAS GOING TO SAY...
..."I HAVE NO INTENTION OF GETTING CLOSE TO YOU."
SHIRO...
GAH
kachak
...YOUR CLOTHES ARE DRY.

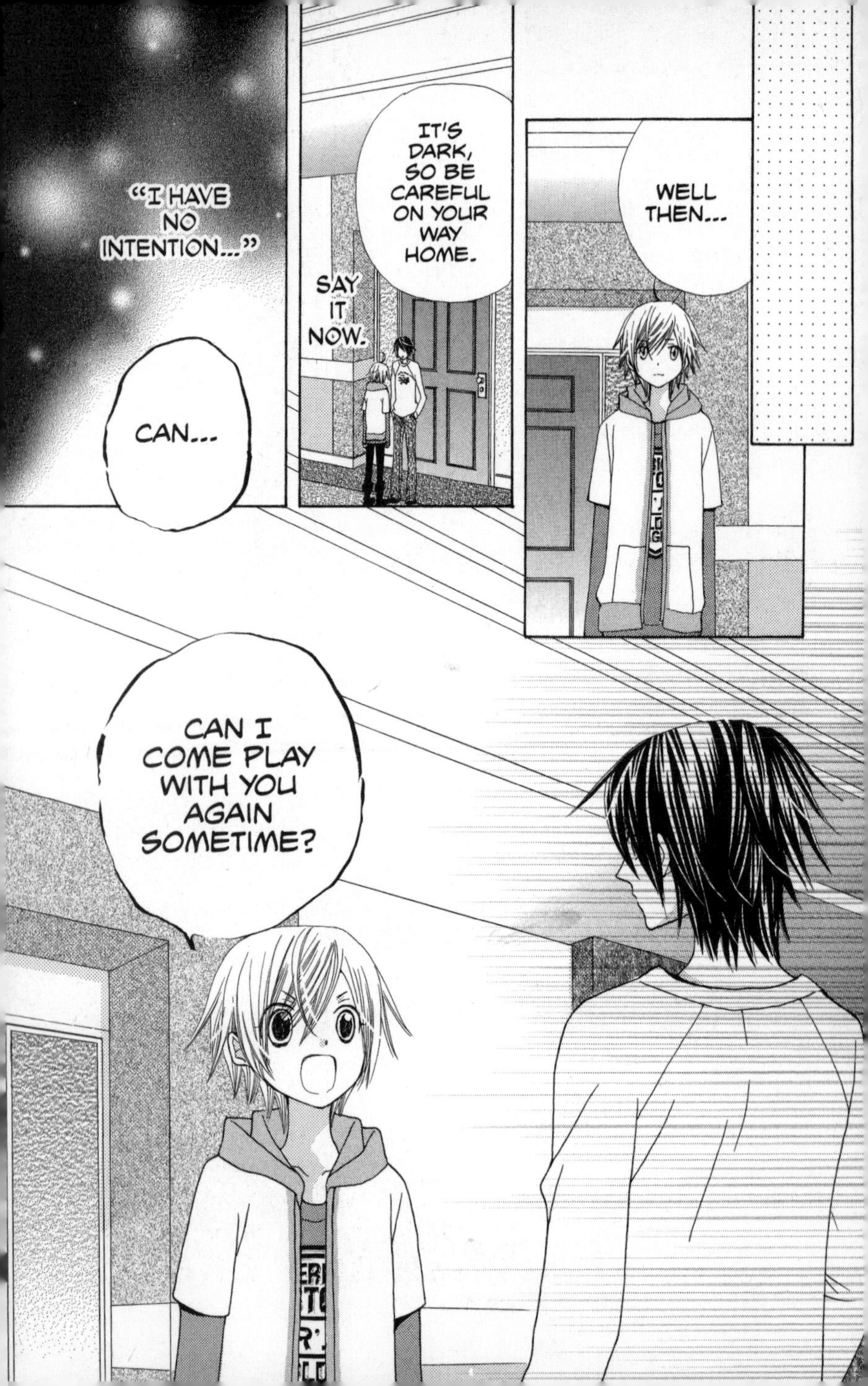
WELL THEN...
IT'S DARK, SO BE CAREFUL ON YOUR WAY HOME.
SAY IT NOW.
"I HAVE NO INTENTION..."
CAN...
CAN I COME PLAY WITH YOU AGAIN SOMETIME?

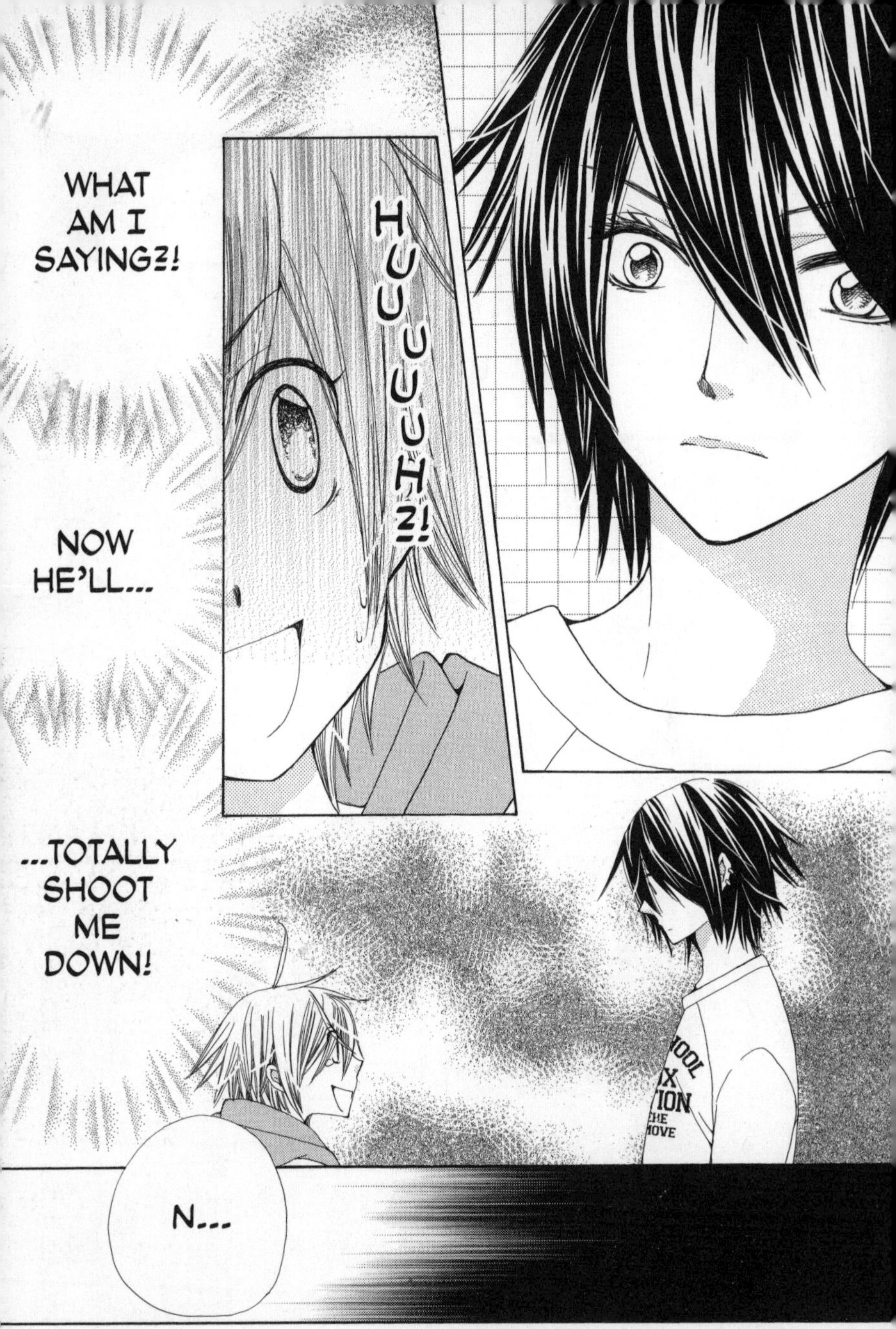
HUUUUUH?!
WHAT AM I SAYING?!
NOW HE'LL...
...TOTALLY SHOOT ME DOWN!
N...

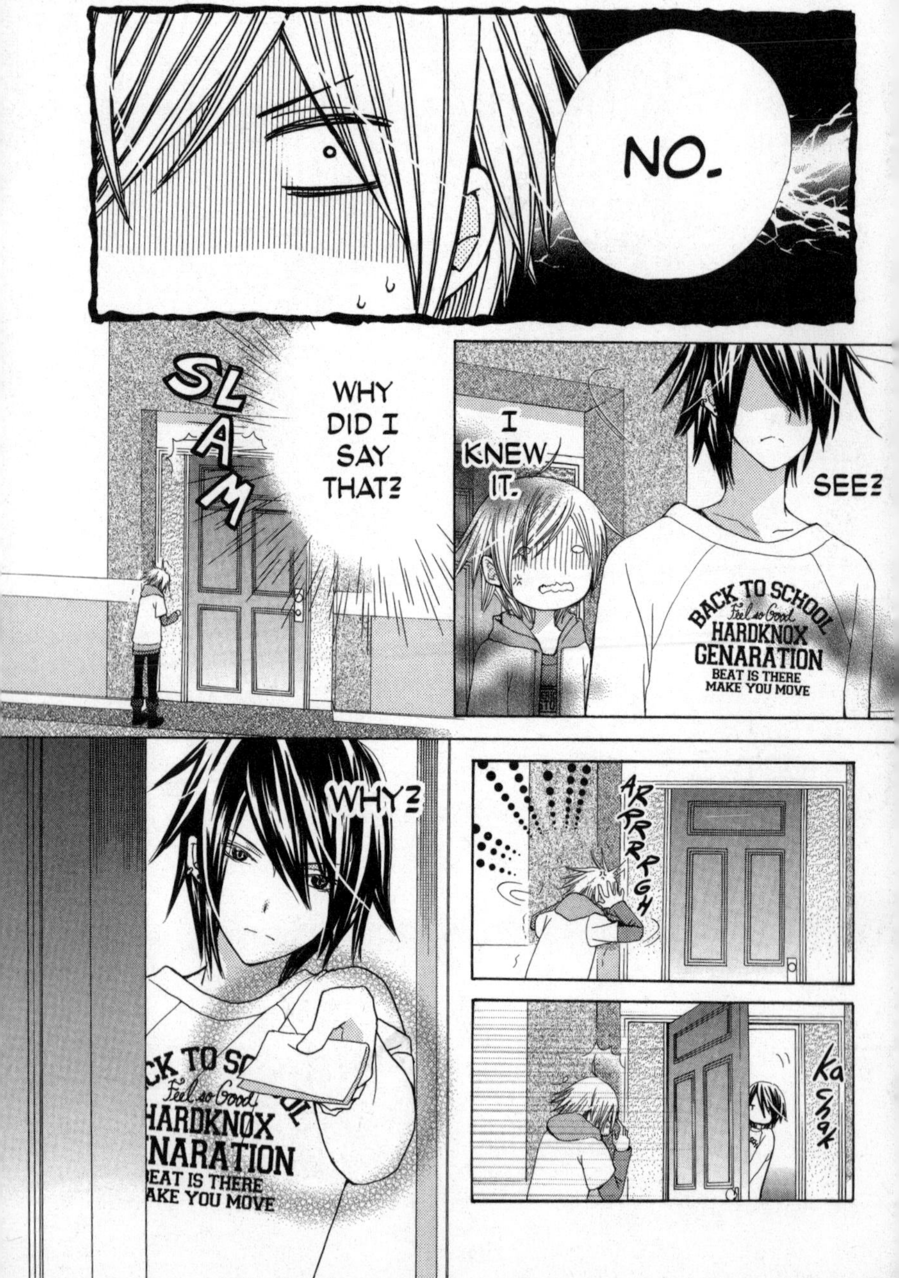
NO.
SEE?
I KNEW IT.
BACK TO SCHOOL
Feel so Good
HARDKNOX
GENARATION
BEAT IS THERE
MAKE YOU MOVE
WHY DID I SAY THAT?
SLAM
ARRRRGH
KA CHAK
WHY?

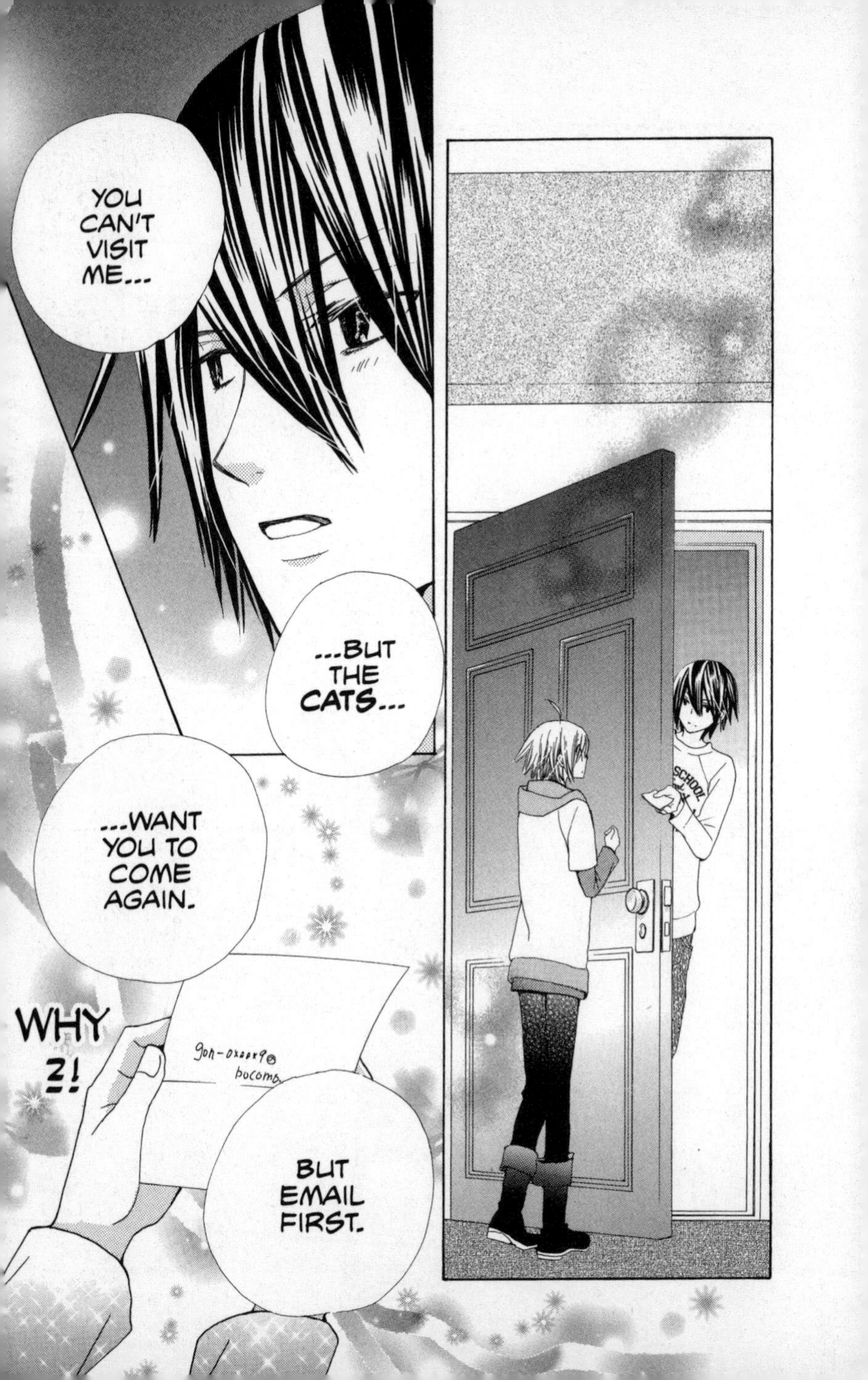
YOU CAN'T VISIT ME...
...BUT THE CATS...
...WANT YOU TO COME AGAIN.
WHY?!
BUT EMAIL FIRST.

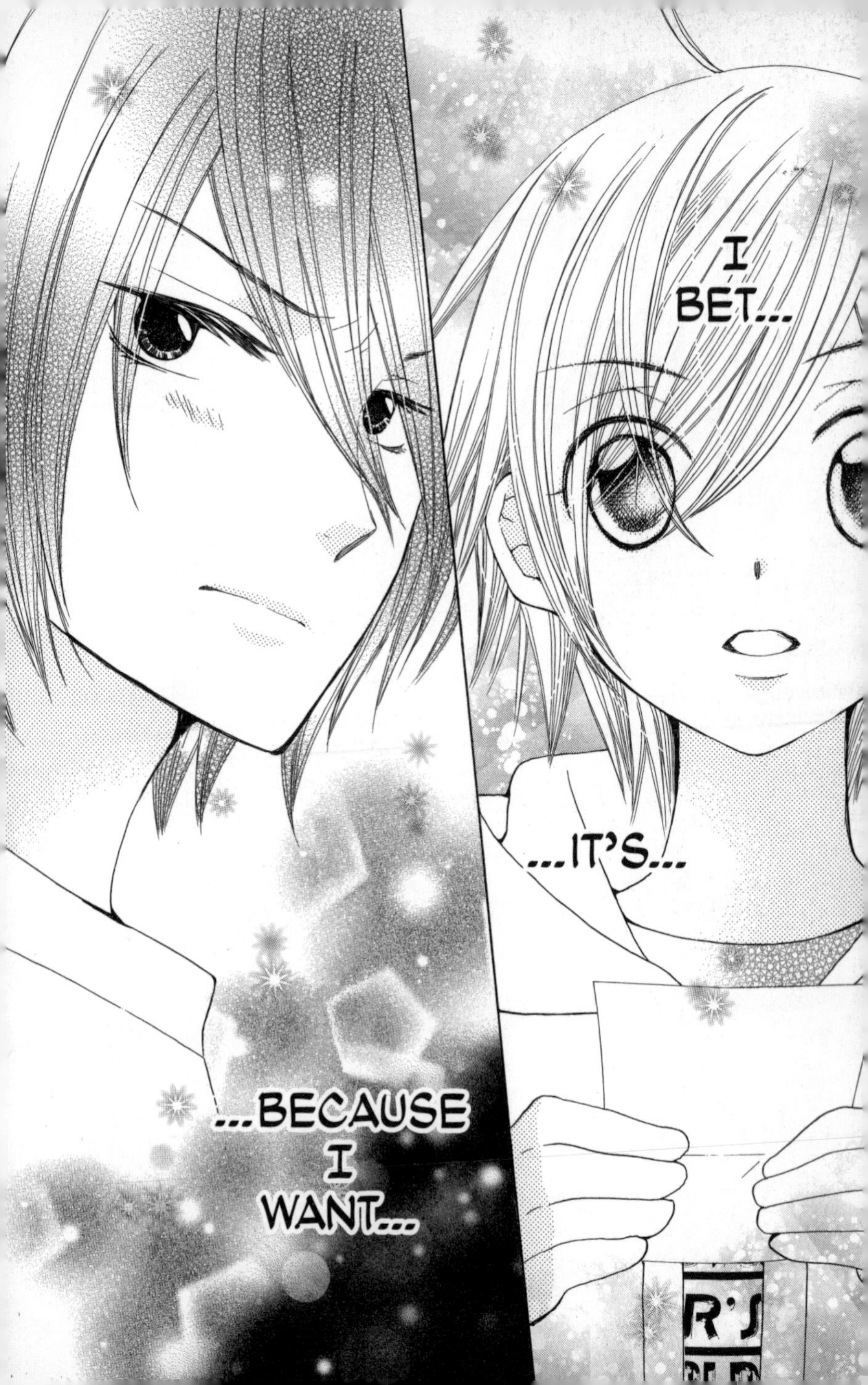
I BET...
...IT'S...
...BECAUSE I WANT...

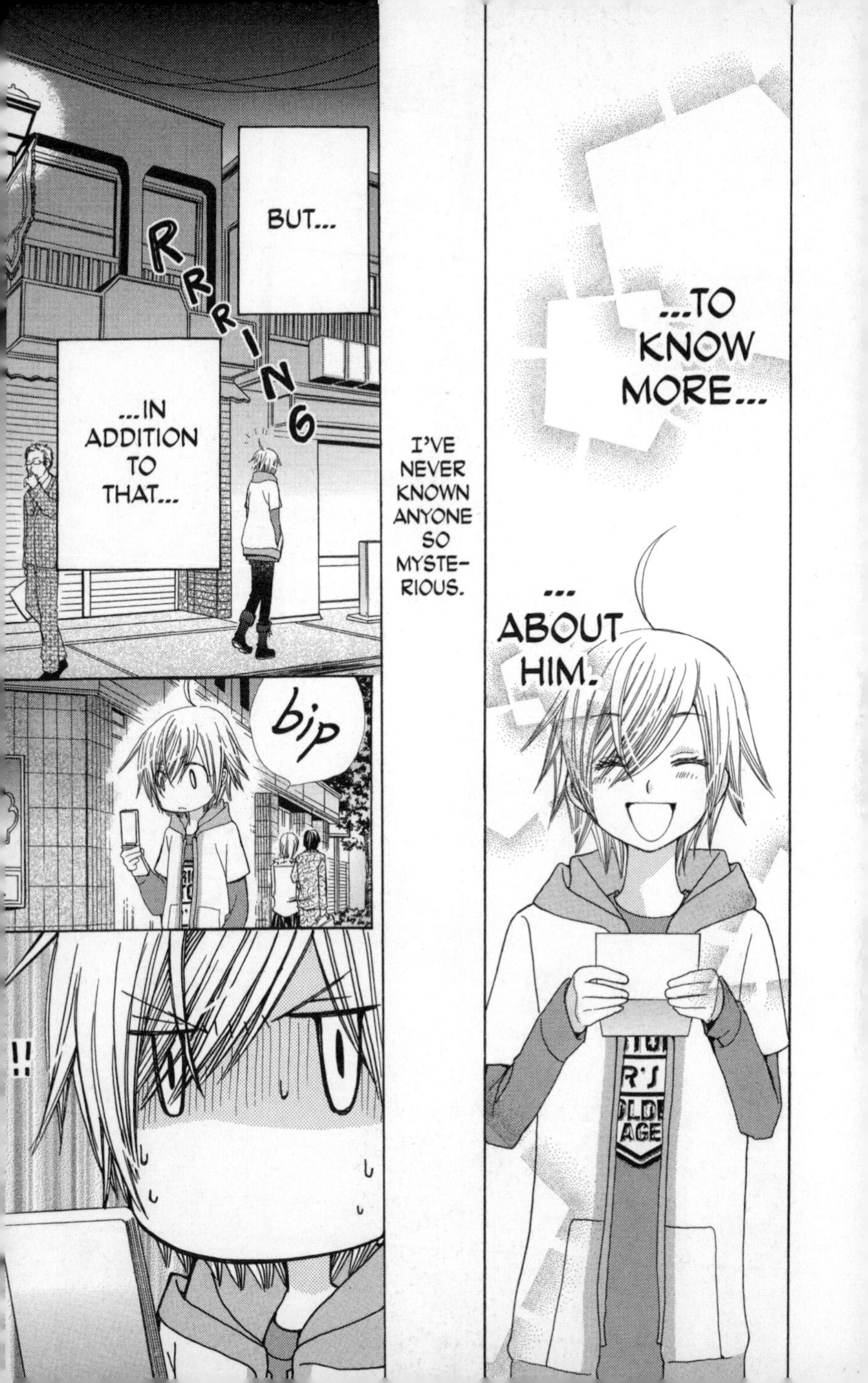
...TO KNOW MORE...
... ABOUT HIM.
I'VE NEVER KNOWN ANYONE SO MYSTERIOUS.
BUT...
RRRING
...IN ADDITION TO THAT...
bip
!!

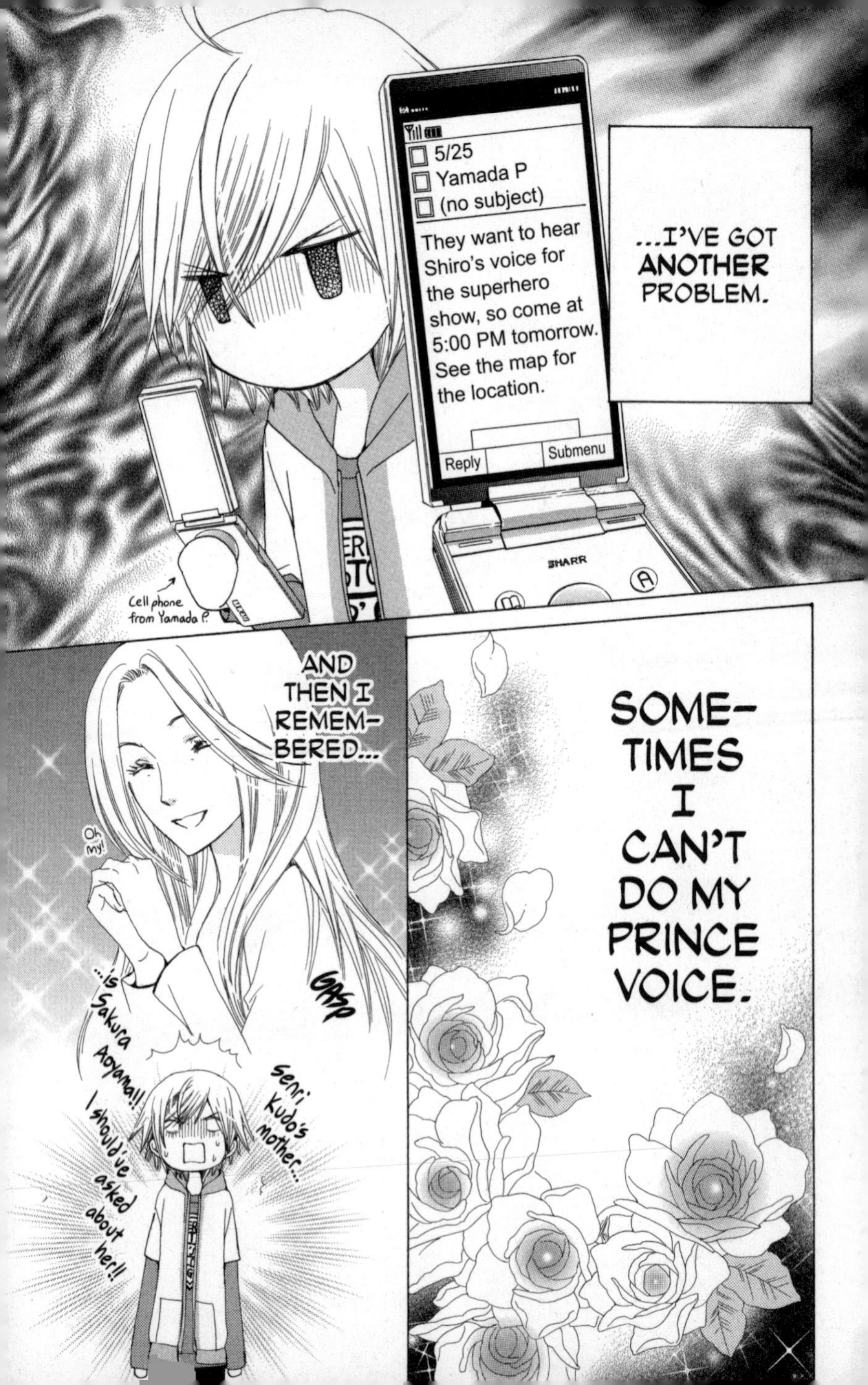
...I'VE GOT ANOTHER PROBLEM.
5/25
Yamada P
(no subject)
They want to hear Shiro's voice for the superhero show, so come at 5:00 PM tomorrow. See the map for the location.
Reply
Submenu
SHARR
Cell phone from Yamada P.
SOME-TIMES I CAN'T DO MY PRINCE VOICE.
AND THEN I REMEMBERED...
Oh my!
GASP
Senri Kudo's mother...
...is Sakura Aoyama!!
I should've asked about her!!

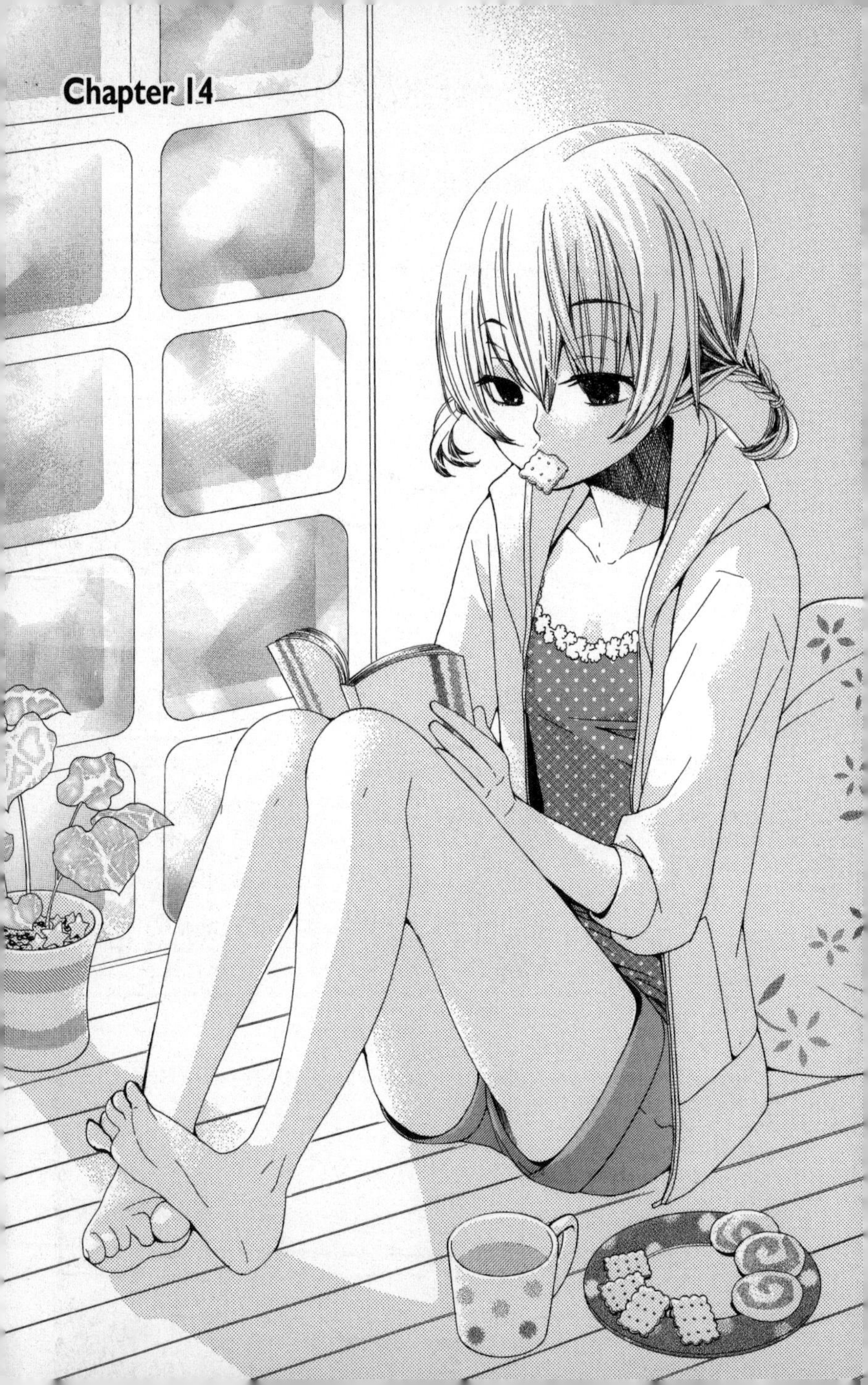
Chapter 14

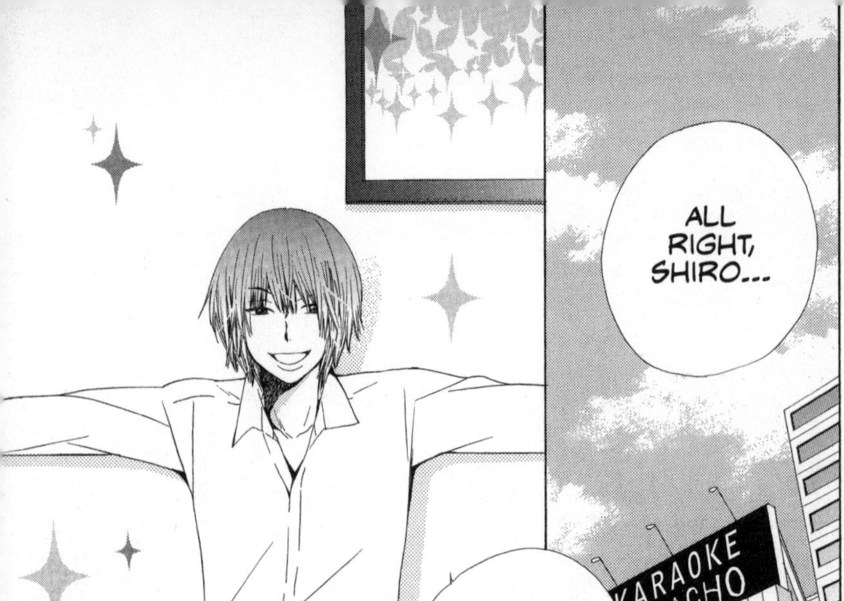
ALL RIGHT, SHIRO...
KARAOKE
PIG ACHO
PIG ACHO
PIG ACHO
PIG ACHO
PIG ACHO
I'M GOING TO TEST YOU.
USE YOUR PRINCE VOICE TO SAY THE LINES I GAVE YOU.

• Tones •

I get excited when screentones are on sale. I buy a lot, but then a bunch of the same tone shows up... *huff*

I'll be careful about that. *huff*

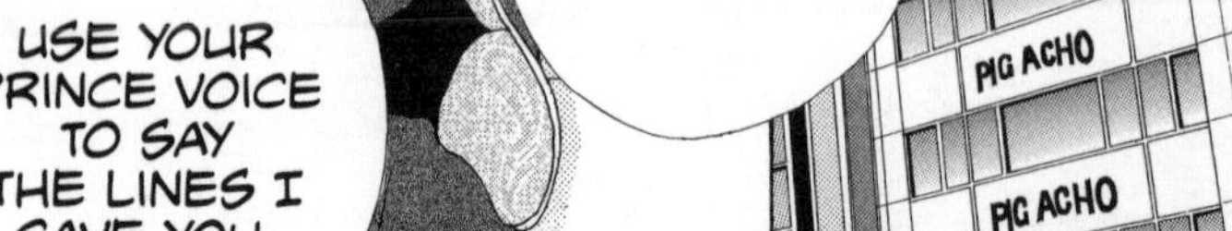

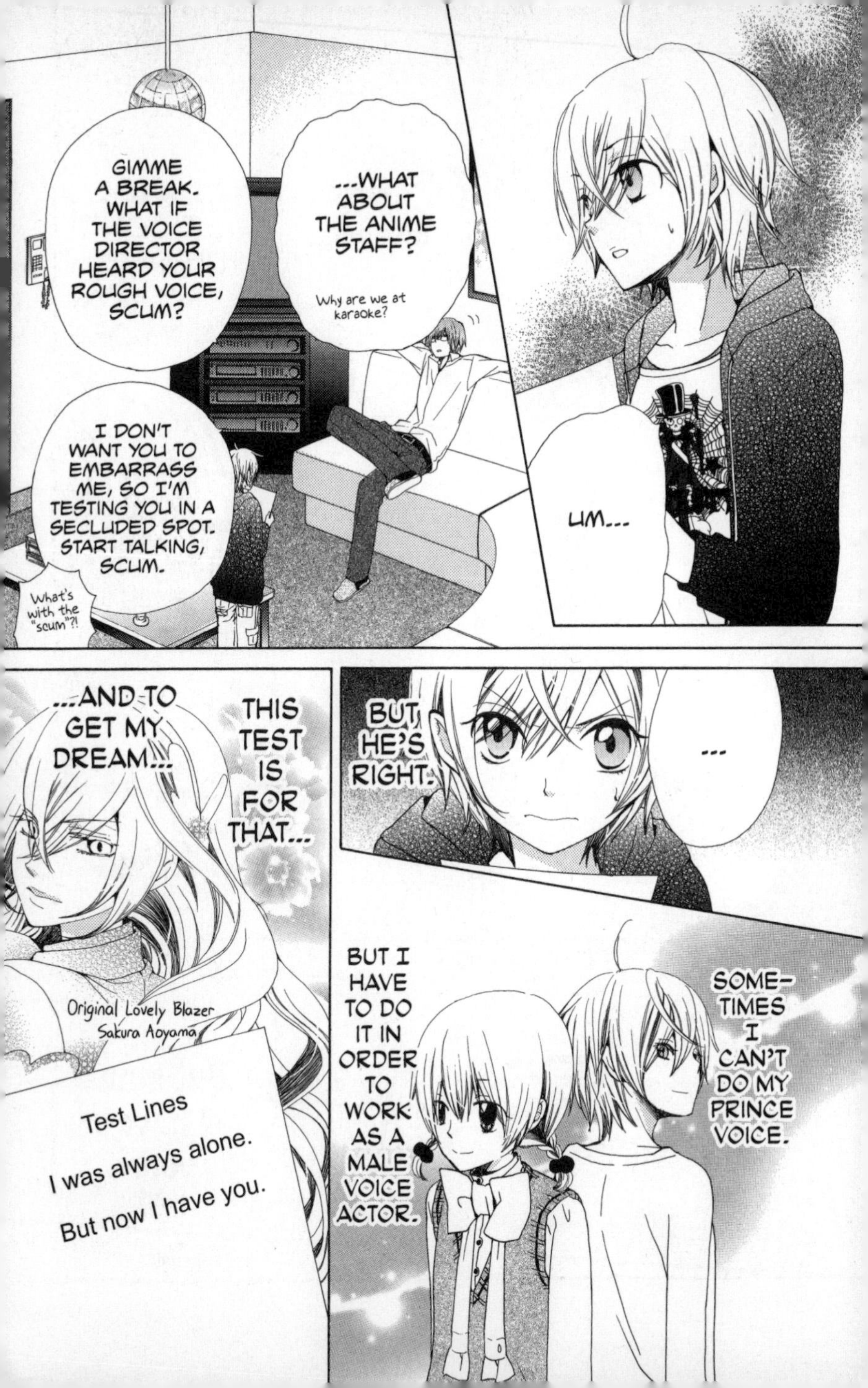
UM...
...WHAT ABOUT THE ANIME STAFF?
Why are we at karaoke?
GIMME A BREAK. WHAT IF THE VOICE DIRECTOR HEARD YOUR ROUGH VOICE, SCUM?
I DON'T WANT YOU TO EMBARRASS ME, SO I'M TESTING YOU IN A SECLUDED SPOT. START TALKING, SCUM.
What's with the "scum"?!
...
BUT HE'S RIGHT.
SOMETIMES I CAN'T DO MY PRINCE VOICE.
BUT I HAVE TO DO IT IN ORDER TO WORK AS A MALE VOICE ACTOR.
THIS TEST IS FOR THAT...
...AND TO GET MY DREAM...
Original Lovely Blazer Sakura Aoyama
Test Lines
I was always alone.
But now I have you.

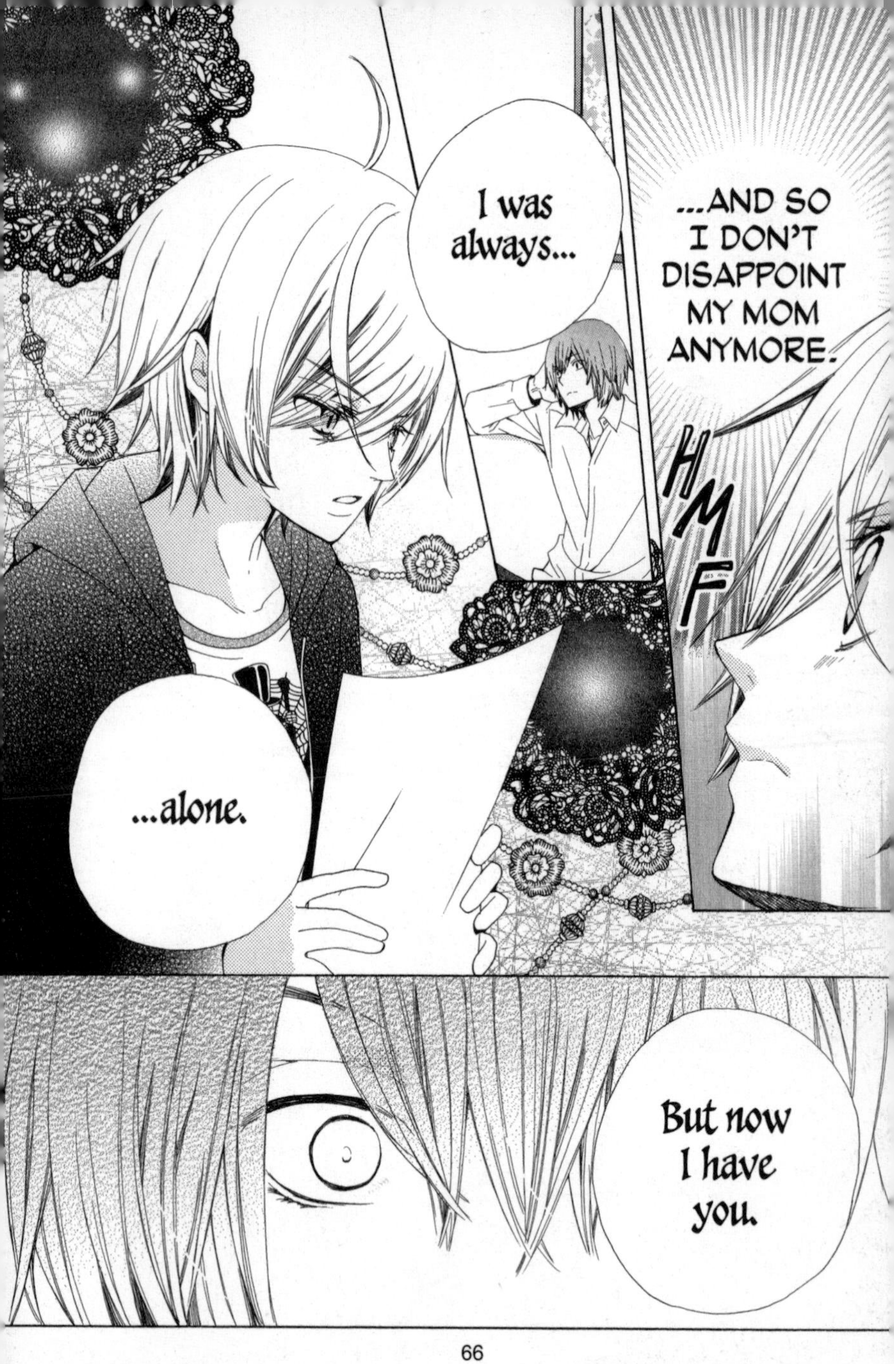
...AND SO I DON'T DISAPPOINT MY MOM ANYMORE.
HMF
I was always...
...alone.
But now I have you.

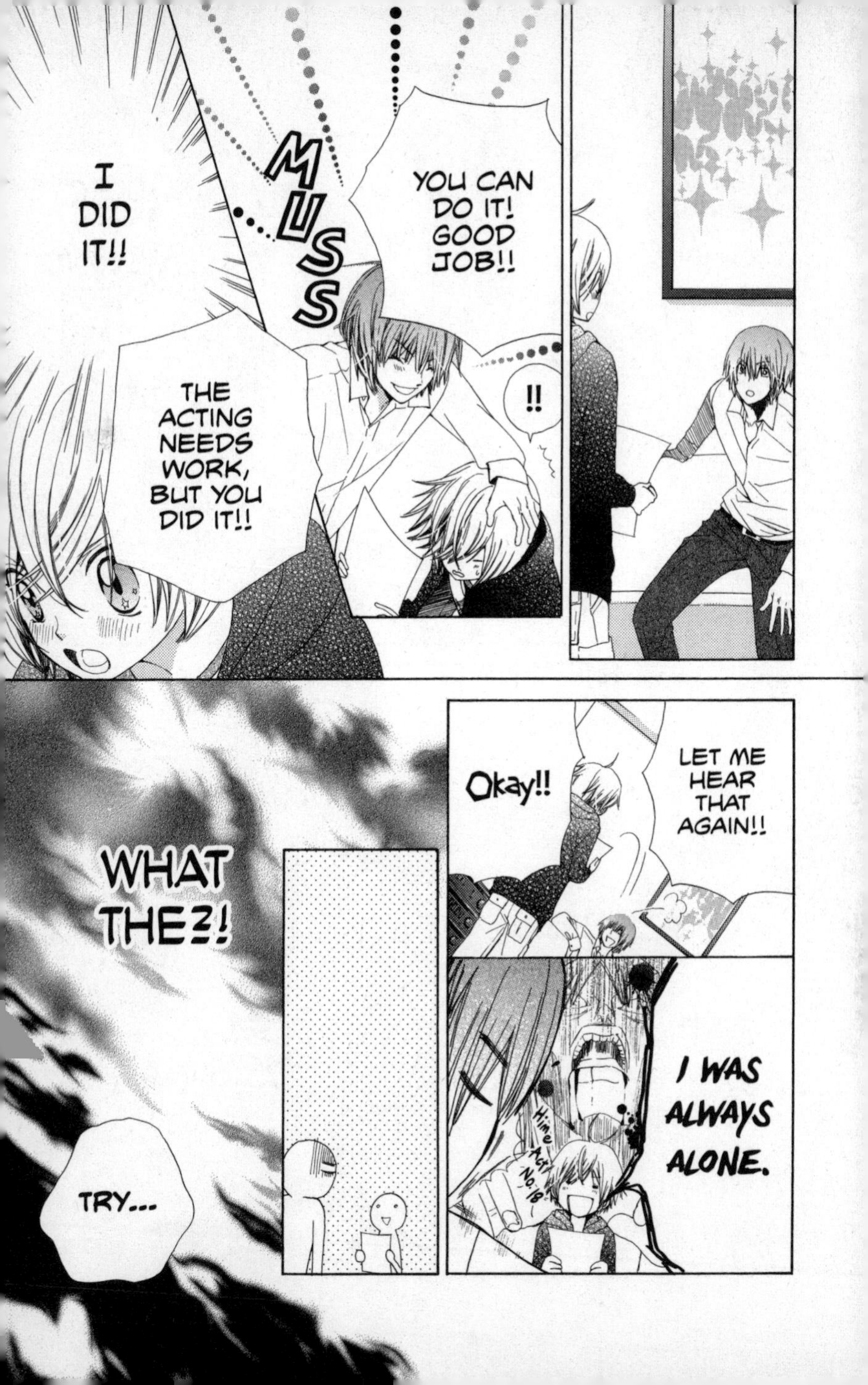
YOU CAN DO IT! GOOD JOB!!
MUSS
I DID IT!!
!!
THE ACTING NEEDS WORK, BUT YOU DID IT!!
LET ME HEAR THAT AGAIN!!
Okay!!
I WAS ALWAYS ALONE.
Hime Act No. 18
WHAT THE?!
TRY...

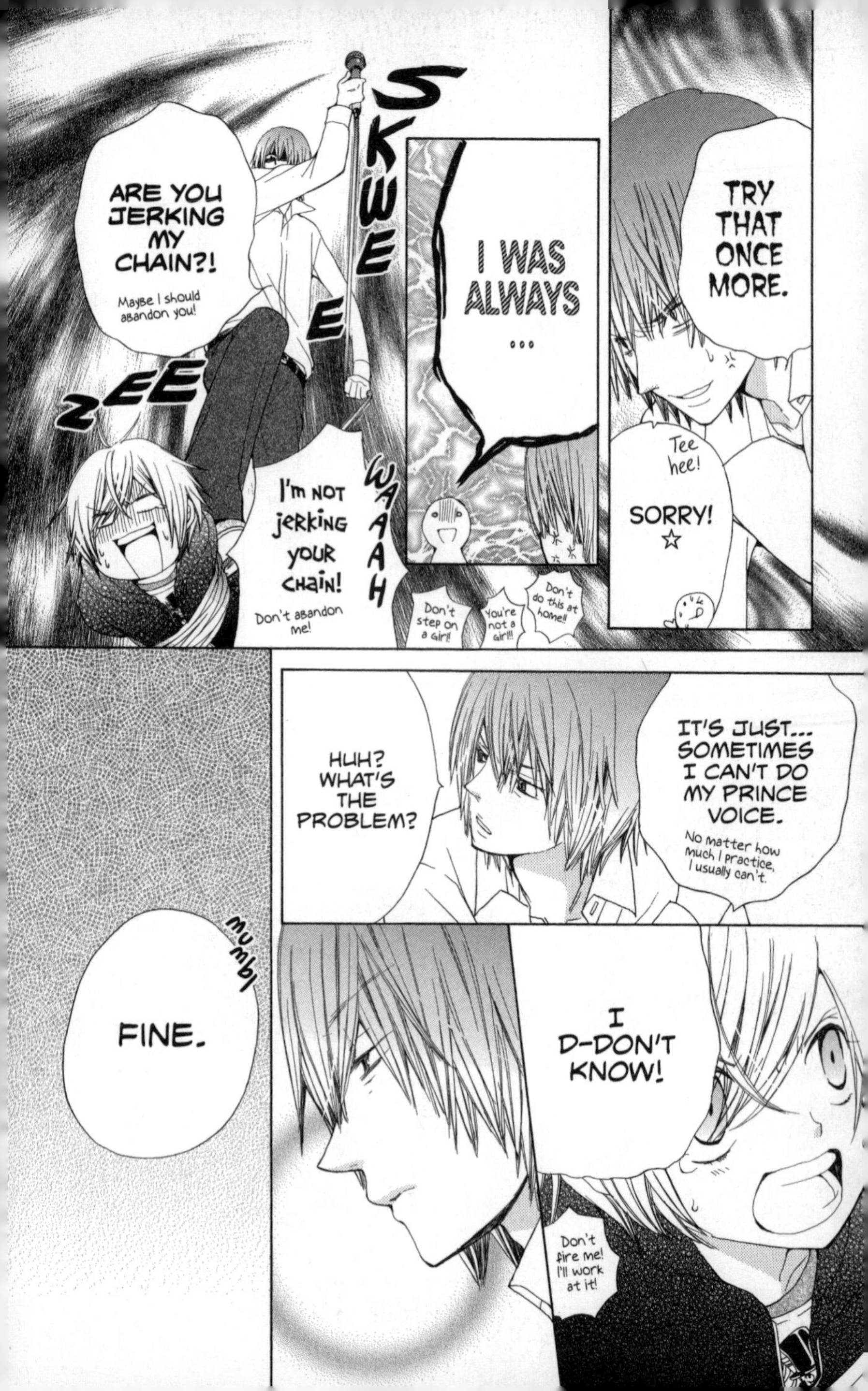
TRY THAT ONCE MORE.
Tee hee!
SORRY! ☆
I WAS ALWAYS...
SKWEEE
ARE YOU JERKING MY CHAIN?!
Maybe I should abandon you!
ZEE
WAAAAH
I'm NOT jerking your chain!
Don't abandon me!
Don't do this at home!!
You're not a Girl!!
Don't step on a Girl!
IT'S JUST... SOMETIMES I CAN'T DO MY PRINCE VOICE.
No matter how much I practice, I usually can't.
HUH? WHAT'S THE PROBLEM?
I D-DON'T KNOW!
Don't fire me! I'll work at it!
mumble
FINE.

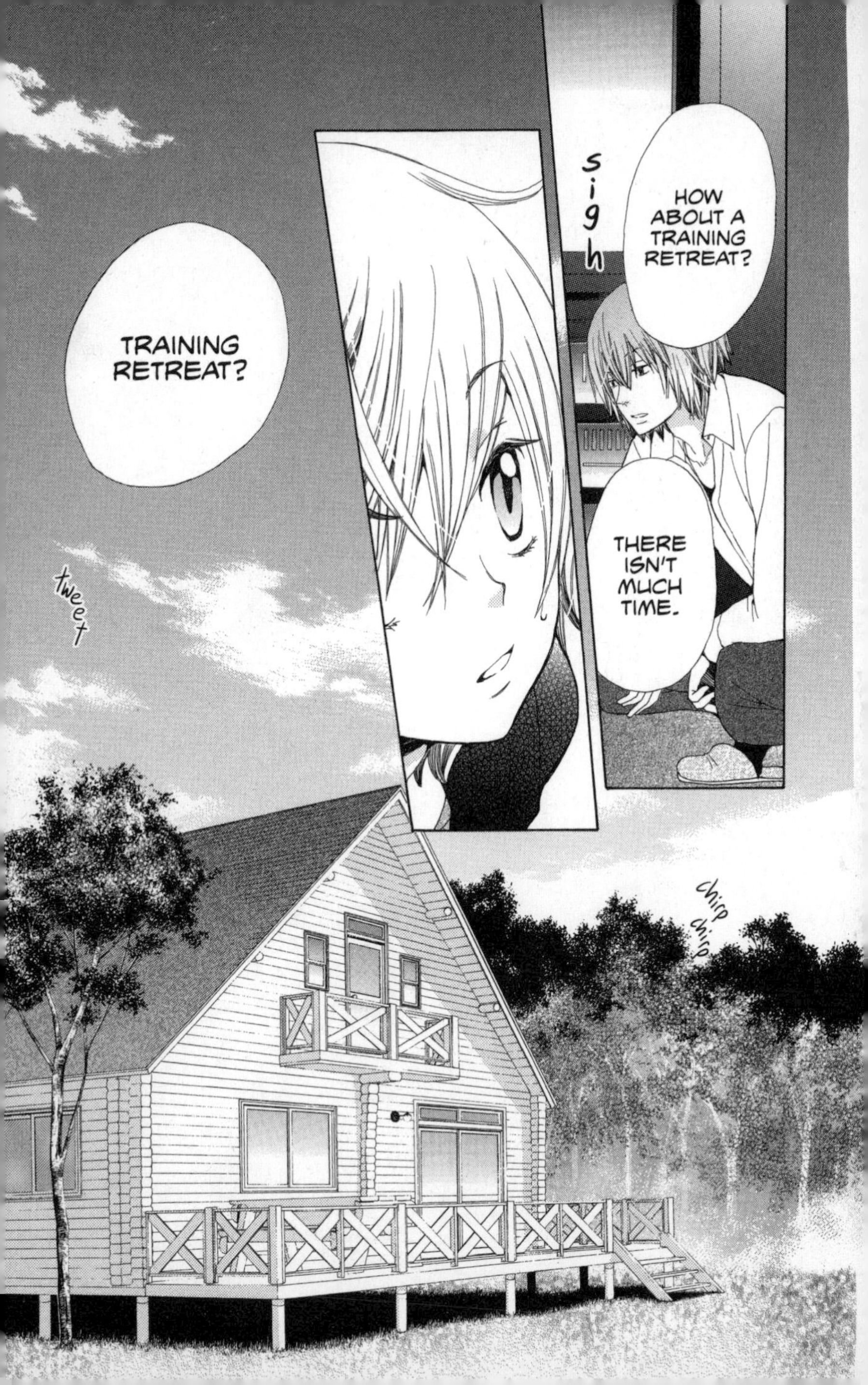
HOW ABOUT A TRAINING RETREAT?
sigh
THERE ISN'T MUCH TIME.
TRAINING RETREAT?
tweet
chirp chirp

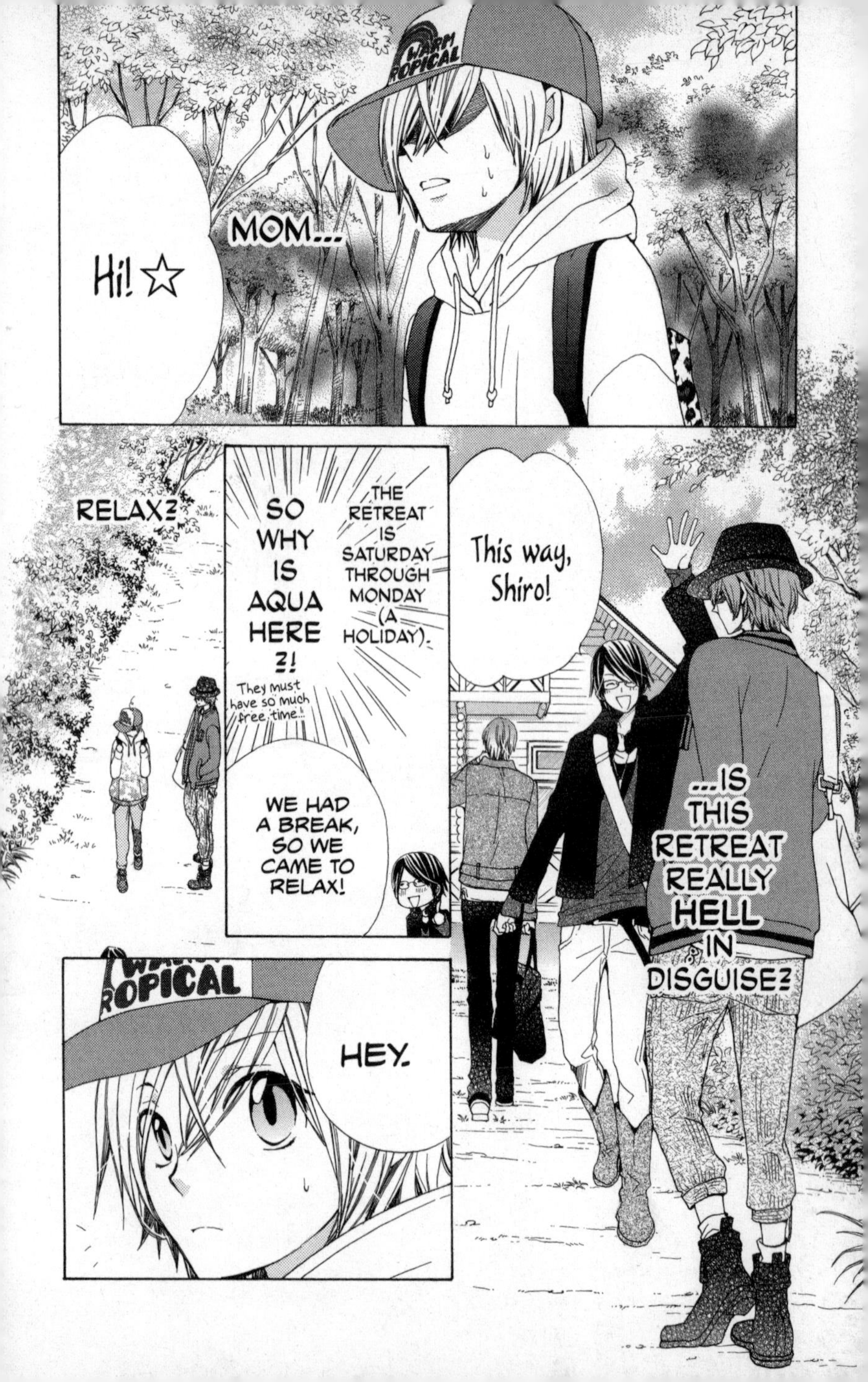
MOM...
Hi! ☆
This way, Shiro!
...IS THIS RETREAT REALLY HELL IN DISGUISE?
THE RETREAT IS SATURDAY THROUGH MONDAY (A HOLIDAY).
SO WHY IS AQUA HERE?!
They must have so much free time...
WE HAD A BREAK, SO WE CAME TO RELAX!
RELAX?
HEY.

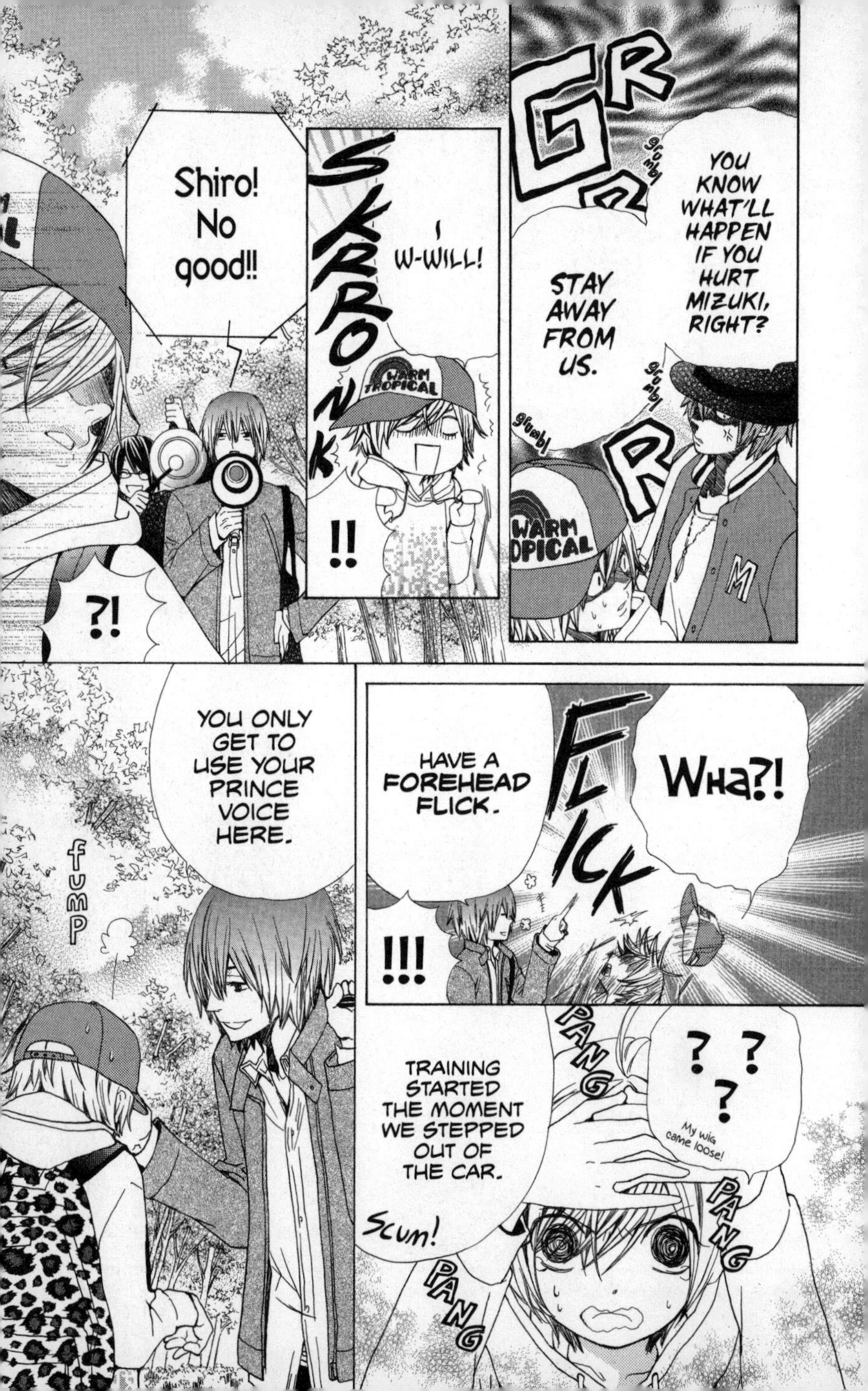
GRR
grumbl
YOU KNOW WHAT'LL HAPPEN IF YOU HURT MIZUKI, RIGHT?
STAY AWAY FROM US.
grumbl
grumbl
SKRRONK!!
I W-WILL!
Shiro! No good!!
?!
Wha?!
HAVE A FOREHEAD FLICK.
FLICK
!!!
???
My wig came loose!
PANG
PANG
TRAINING STARTED THE MOMENT WE STEPPED OUT OF THE CAR.
Scum!
PANG
YOU ONLY GET TO USE YOUR PRINCE VOICE HERE.
fump

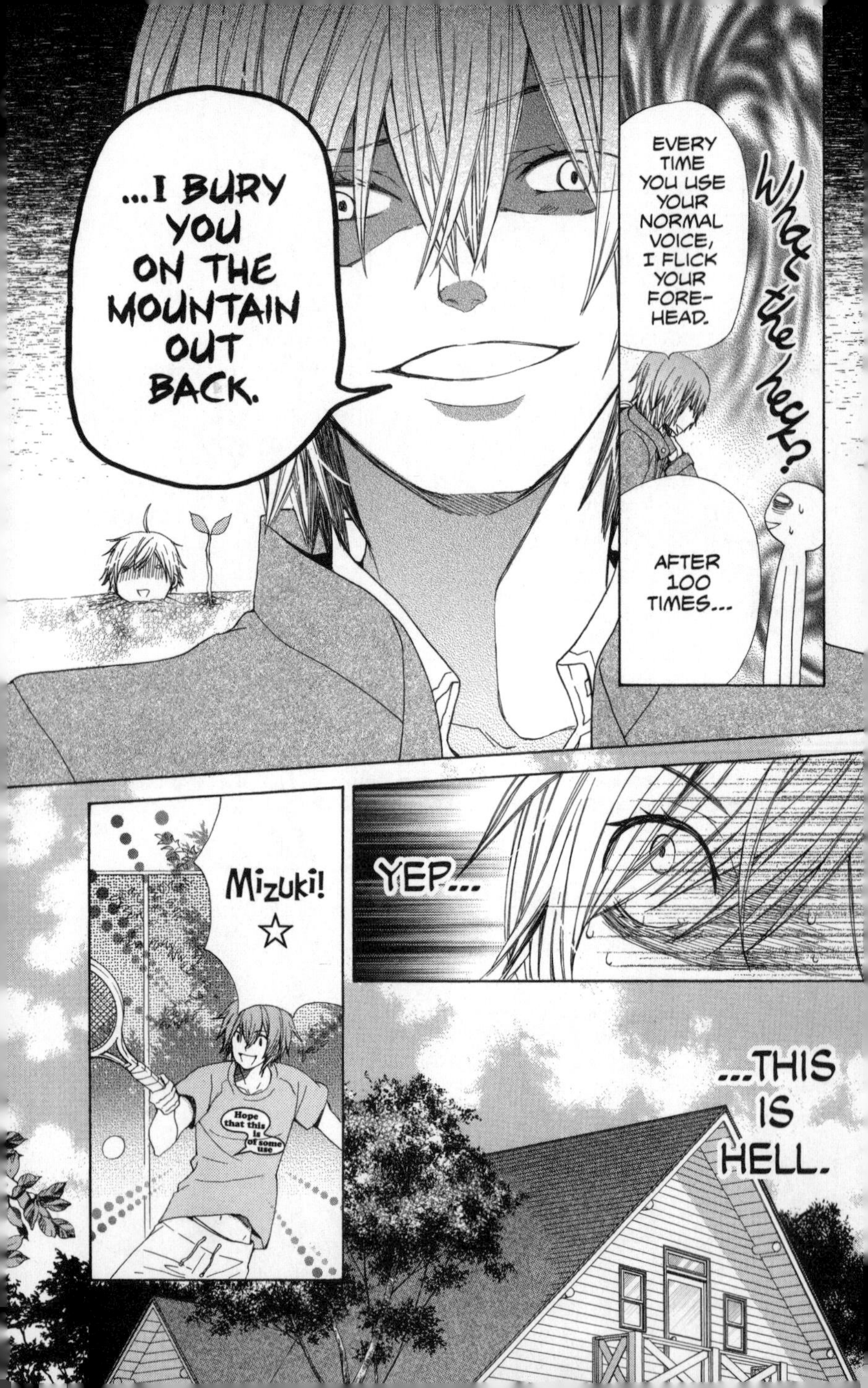
EVERY TIME YOU USE YOUR NORMAL VOICE, I FLICK YOUR FORE-HEAD.
What the heck?
AFTER 100 TIMES...
...I BURY YOU ON THE MOUNTAIN OUT BACK.
YEP...
...THIS IS HELL.
Mizuki! ☆
Hope that this is of some use

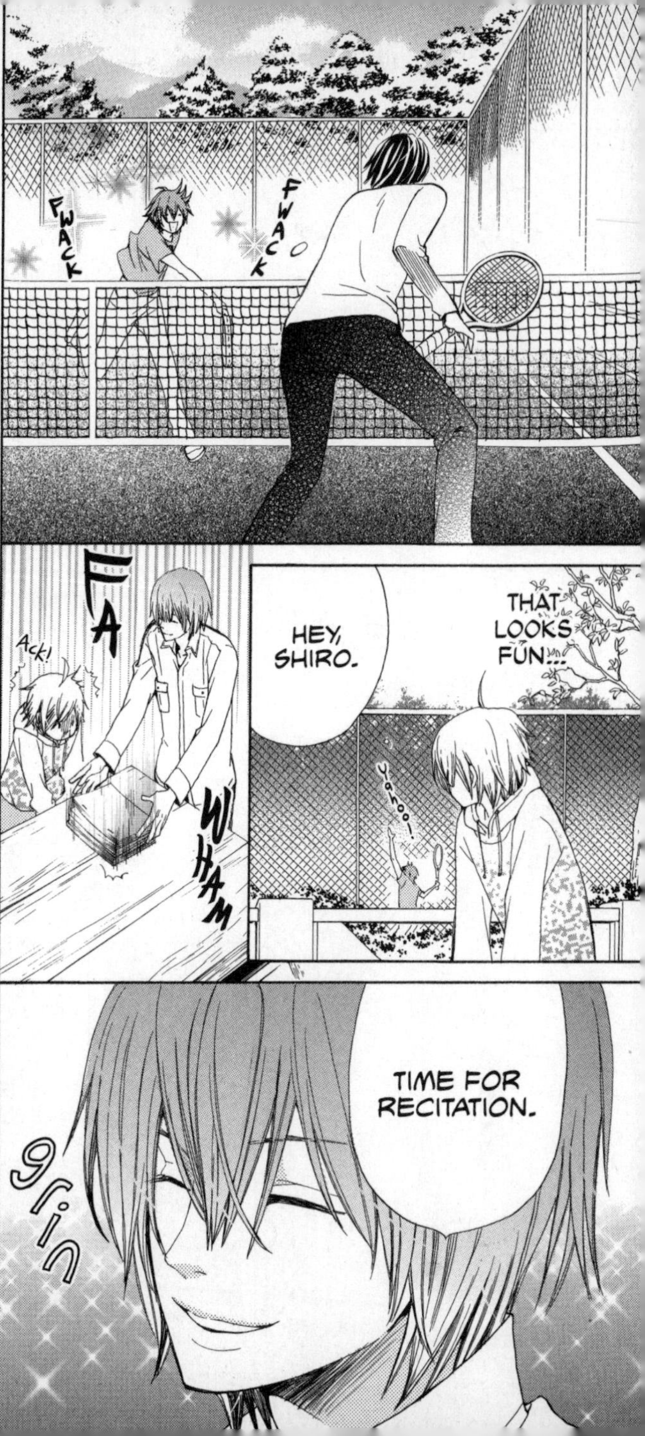
FWACK
FWACK
THAT LOOKS FUN...
HEY, SHIRO.
Yahoo!
FA
Ack!
WHAM
TIME FOR RECITATION.
grin

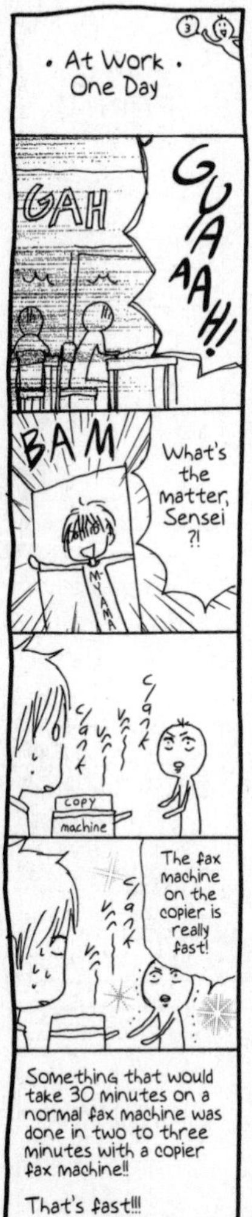
• At Work •
One Day
GUAAAAH!
GAH
BAM
What's the matter, Sensei?!
MIYAMA
clank
vrrr
clank
vrrr
clank
copy
machine
The fax machine on the copier is really fast!
clank
vrrr
vrrr
Something that would take 30 minutes on a normal fax machine was done in two to three minutes with a copier fax machine!!
That's fast!!!
Oh.
Senri (age 6)

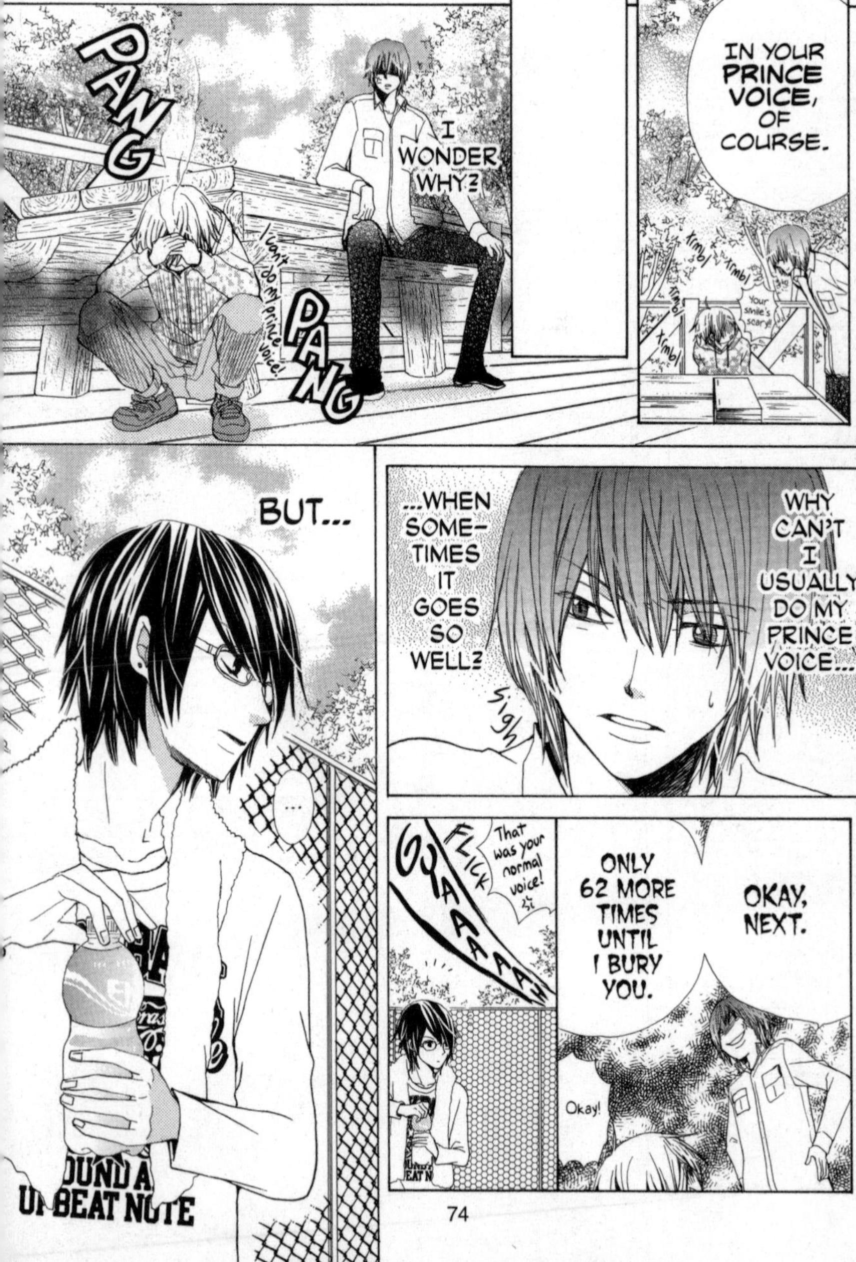
IN YOUR PRINCE VOICE, OF COURSE.
trmbl trmbl trmbl trmbl
Your smile's scary!
PANG PANG
I WONDER WHY?
I can't do my prince voice!
WHY CAN'T I USUALLY DO MY PRINCE VOICE...
...WHEN SOMETIMES IT GOES SO WELL?
sigh
OKAY, NEXT.
ONLY 62 MORE TIMES UNTIL I BURY YOU.
Okay!
That was your normal voice!
FLICK
GYAAAAA
BUT...
...

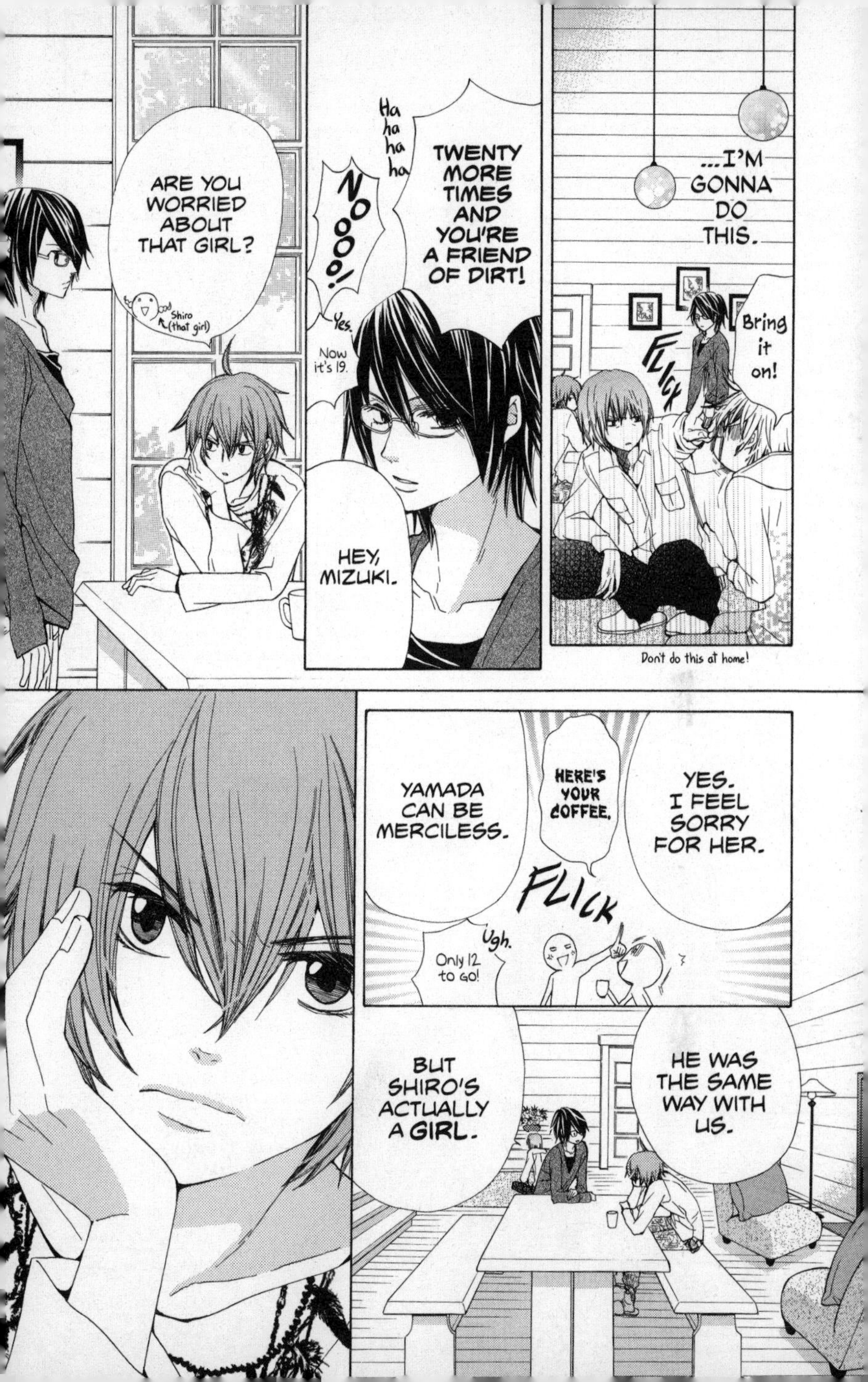
...I'M GONNA DO THIS.
Bring it on!
FLICK
Don't do this at home!
TWENTY MORE TIMES AND YOU'RE A FRIEND OF DIRT!
Ha ha ha ha
NOOOO!
Yes.
Now it's 19.
HEY, MIZUKI.
ARE YOU WORRIED ABOUT THAT GIRL?
Shiro (that girl)
YES. I FEEL SORRY FOR HER.
HERE'S YOUR COFFEE.
YAMADA CAN BE MERCILESS.
FLICK
Ugh.
Only 12 to go!
HE WAS THE SAME WAY WITH US.
BUT SHIRO'S ACTUALLY A GIRL.

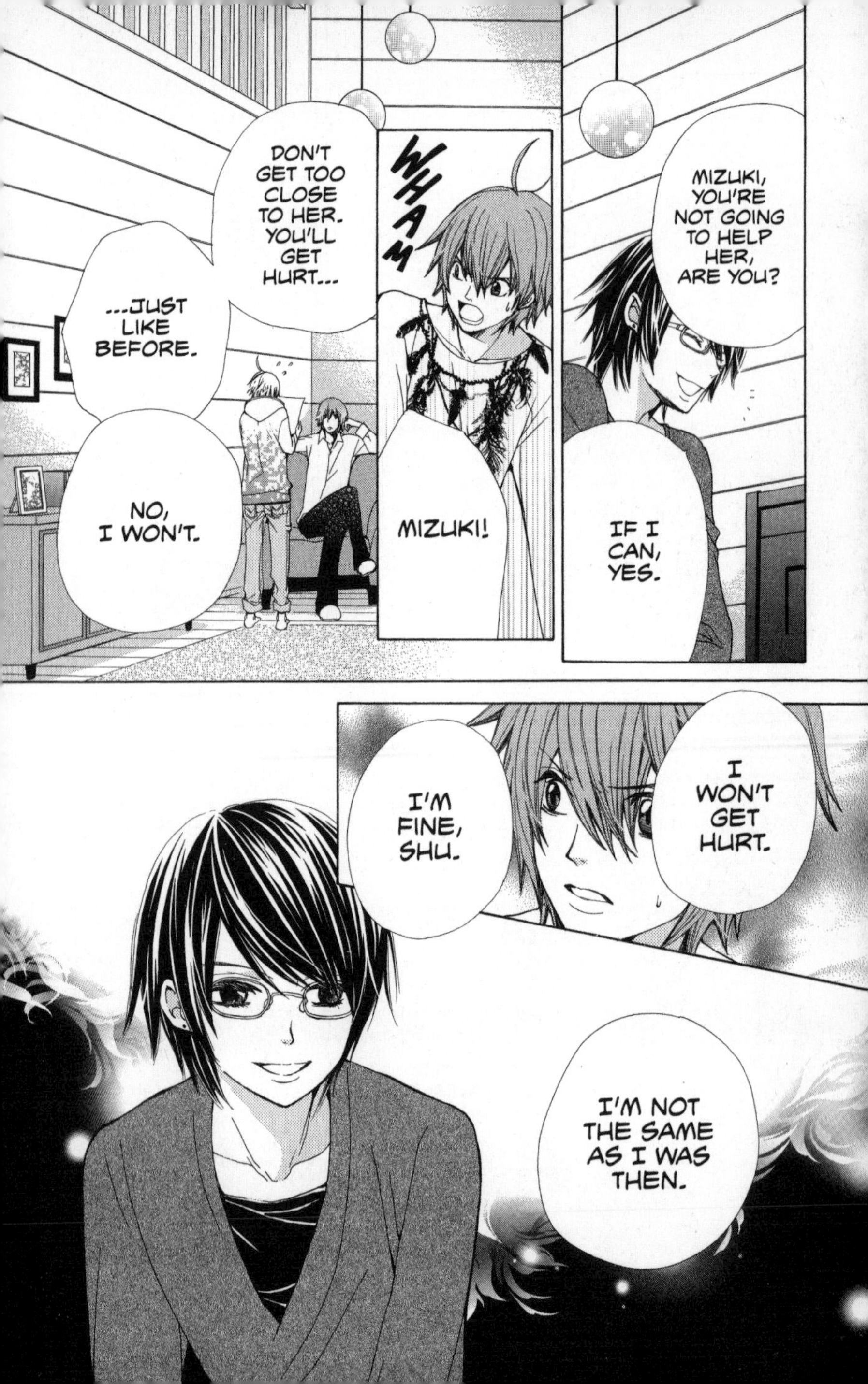
MIZUKI, YOU'RE NOT GOING TO HELP HER, ARE YOU?
IF I CAN, YES.
WHAM
MIZUKI!
DON'T GET TOO CLOSE TO HER. YOU'LL GET HURT...
...JUST LIKE BEFORE.
NO, I WON'T.
I WON'T GET HURT.
I'M FINE, SHU.
I'M NOT THE SAME AS I WAS THEN.

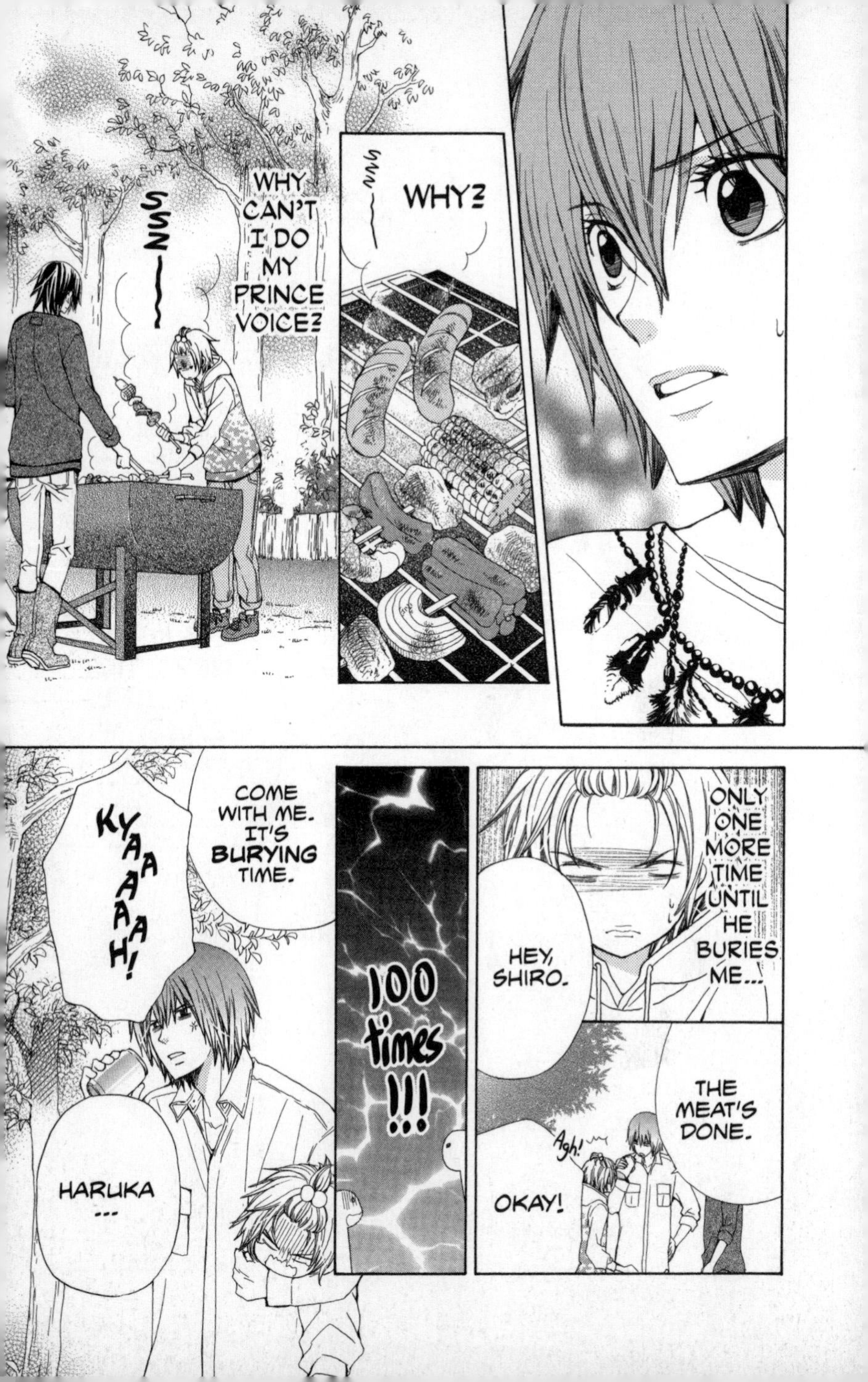
SSS~
WHY?
WHY CAN'T I DO MY PRINCE VOICE?
SSZ~
ONLY ONE MORE TIME UNTIL HE BURIES ME...
HEY, SHIRO.
THE MEAT'S DONE.
Agh!
OKAY!
100 times!!!
COME WITH ME. IT'S BURYING TIME.
KYAAAAAH!
HARUKA...

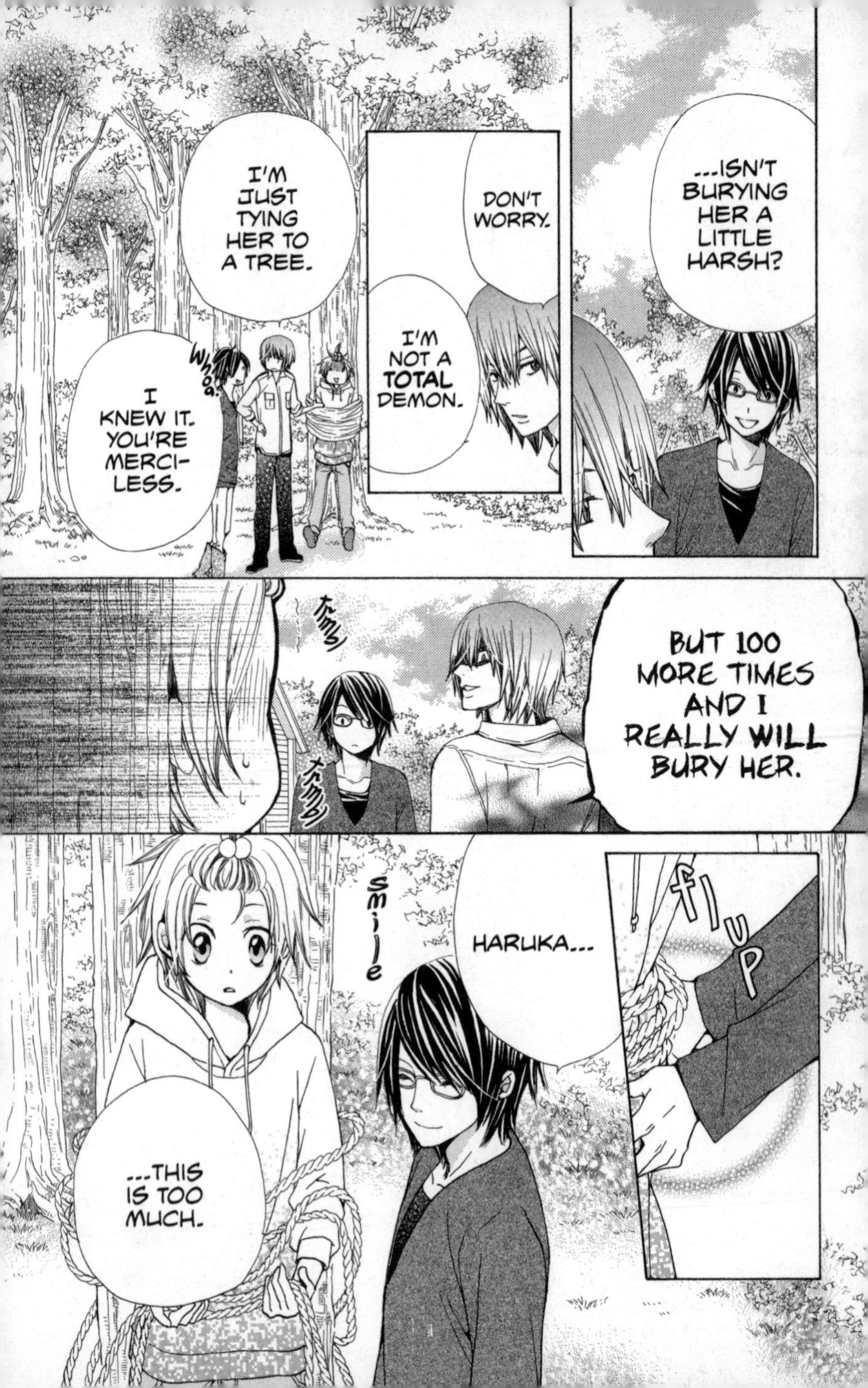
...ISN'T BURYING HER A LITTLE HARSH?
DON'T WORRY.
I'M NOT A TOTAL DEMON.
I'M JUST TYING HER TO A TREE.
Whoa.
I KNEW IT. YOU'RE MERCILESS.
BUT 100 MORE TIMES AND I REALLY WILL BURY HER.
flup
HARUKA...
smile
...THIS IS TOO MUCH.

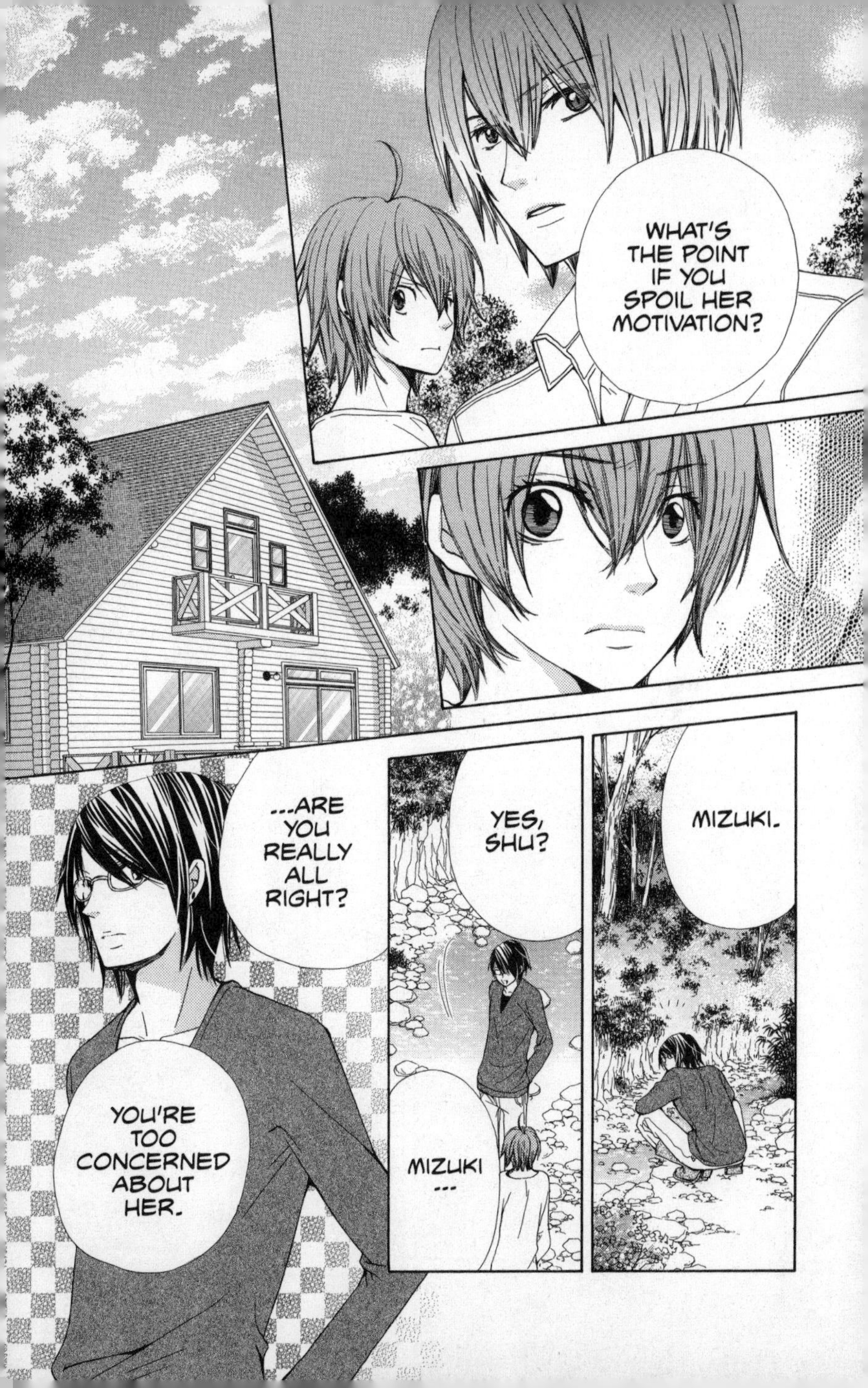
WHAT'S THE POINT IF YOU SPOIL HER MOTIVATION?
MIZUKI.
YES, SHU?
MIZUKI...
...ARE YOU REALLY ALL RIGHT?
YOU'RE TOO CONCERNED ABOUT HER.

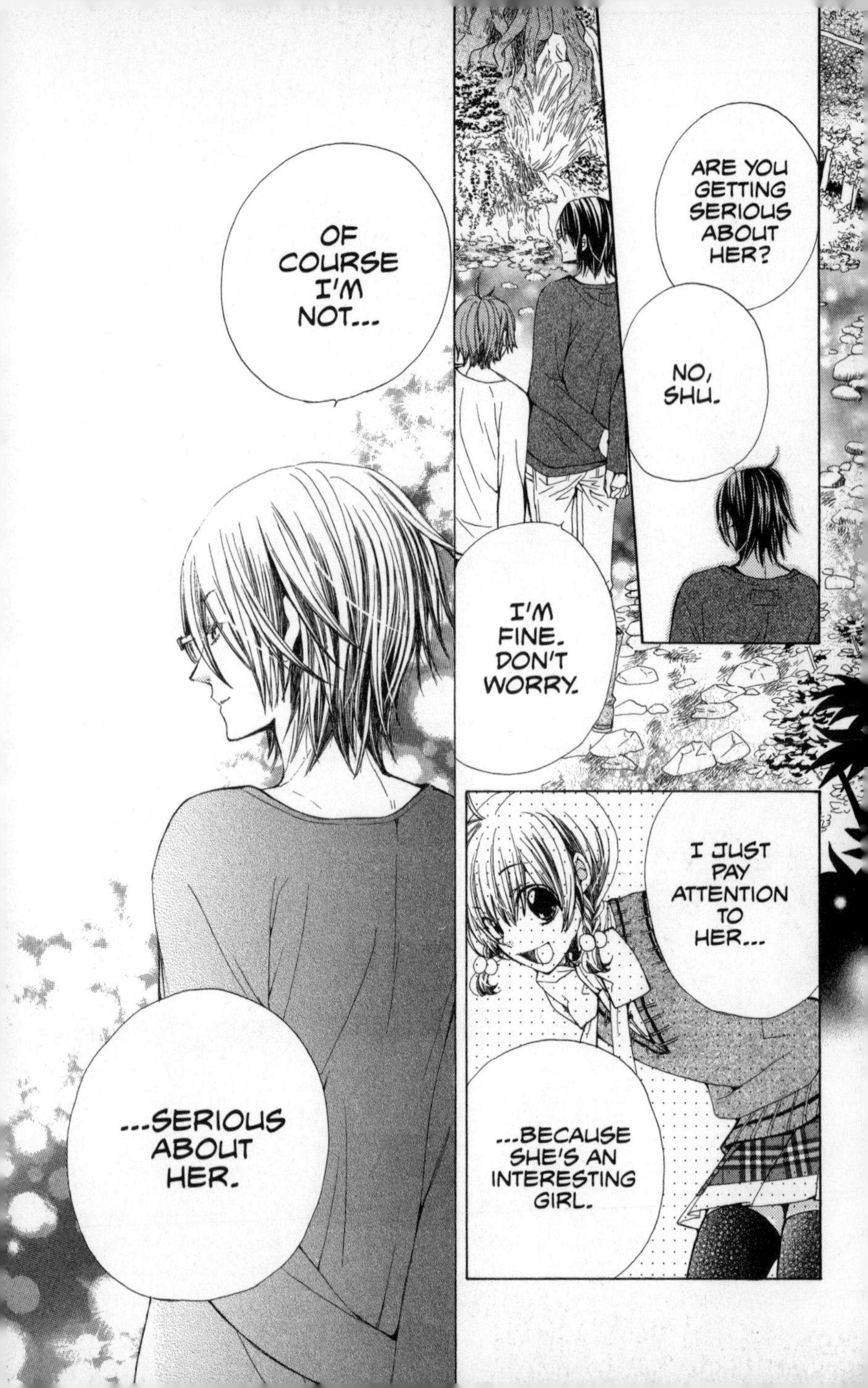
ARE YOU GETTING SERIOUS ABOUT HER?
NO, SHU.
I'M FINE. DON'T WORRY.
I JUST PAY ATTENTION TO HER...
...BECAUSE SHE'S AN INTERESTING GIRL.
OF COURSE I'M NOT...
...SERIOUS ABOUT HER.

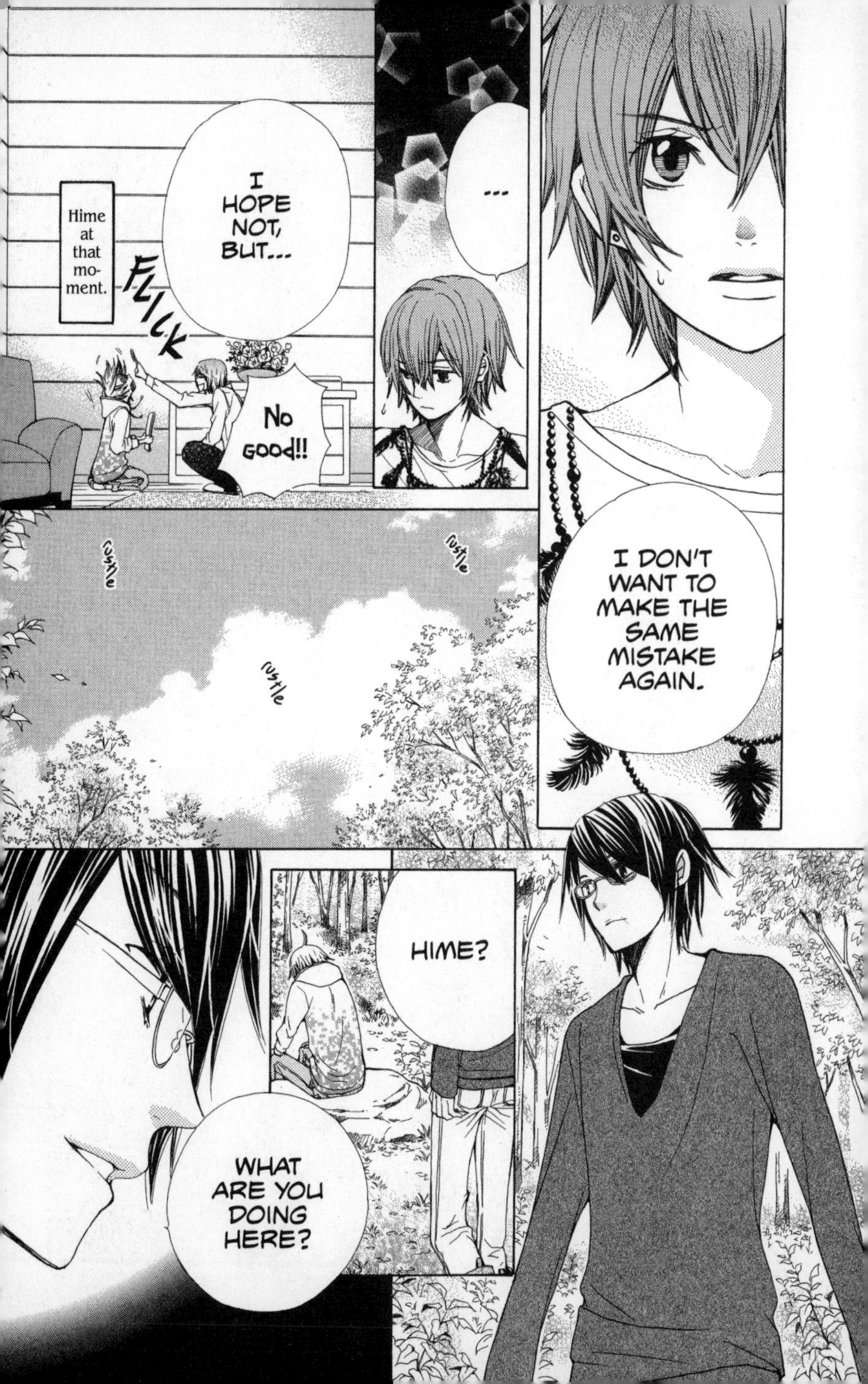
I DON'T WANT TO MAKE THE SAME MISTAKE AGAIN.
...
I HOPE NOT, BUT...
Hime at that mo-ment.
FLICK
No good!!
rustle
rustle
rustle
HIME?
WHAT ARE YOU DOING HERE?

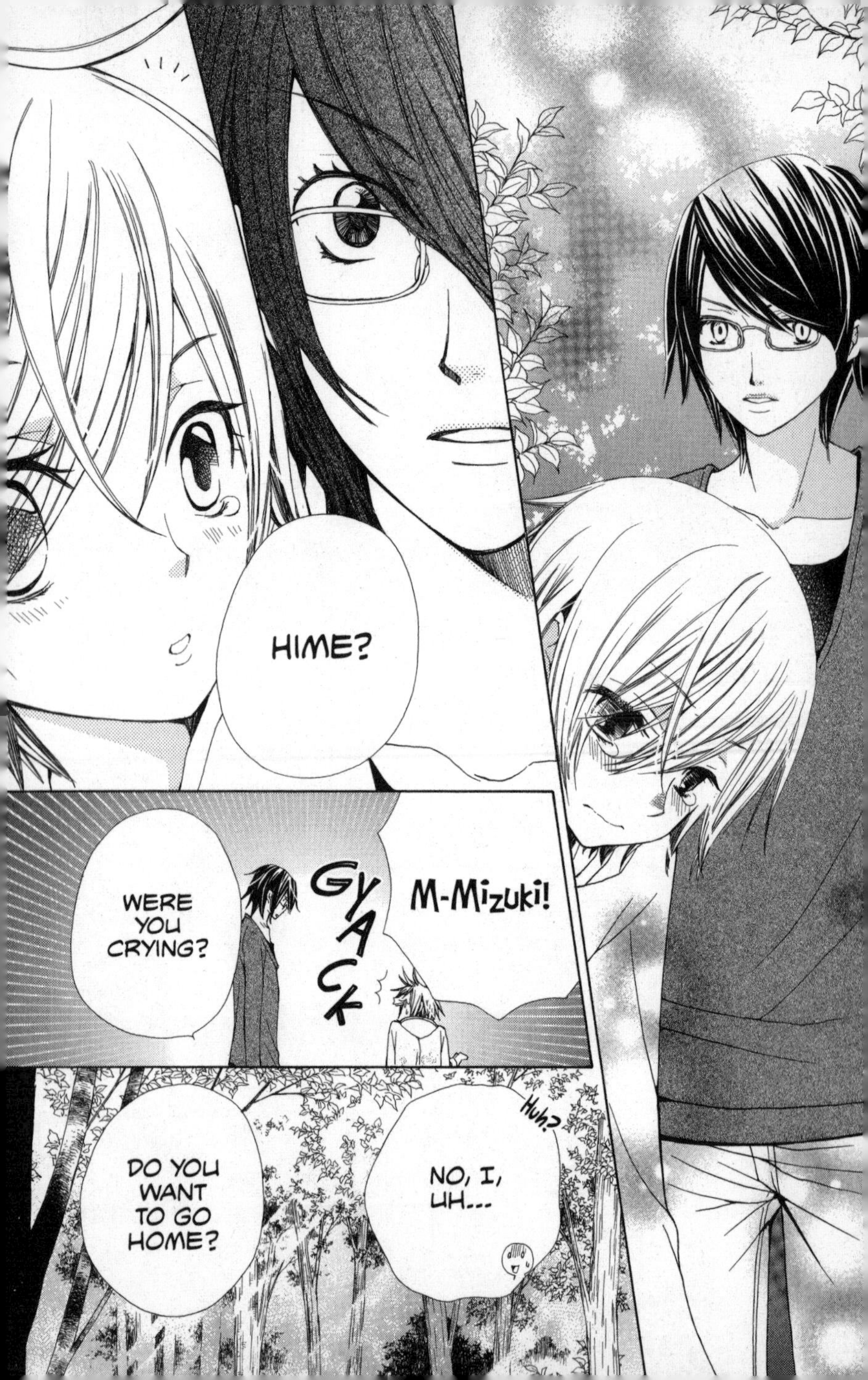
HIME?
M-Mizuki!
GYACK
WERE YOU CRYING?
Huh?
NO, I, UH...
DO YOU WANT TO GO HOME?

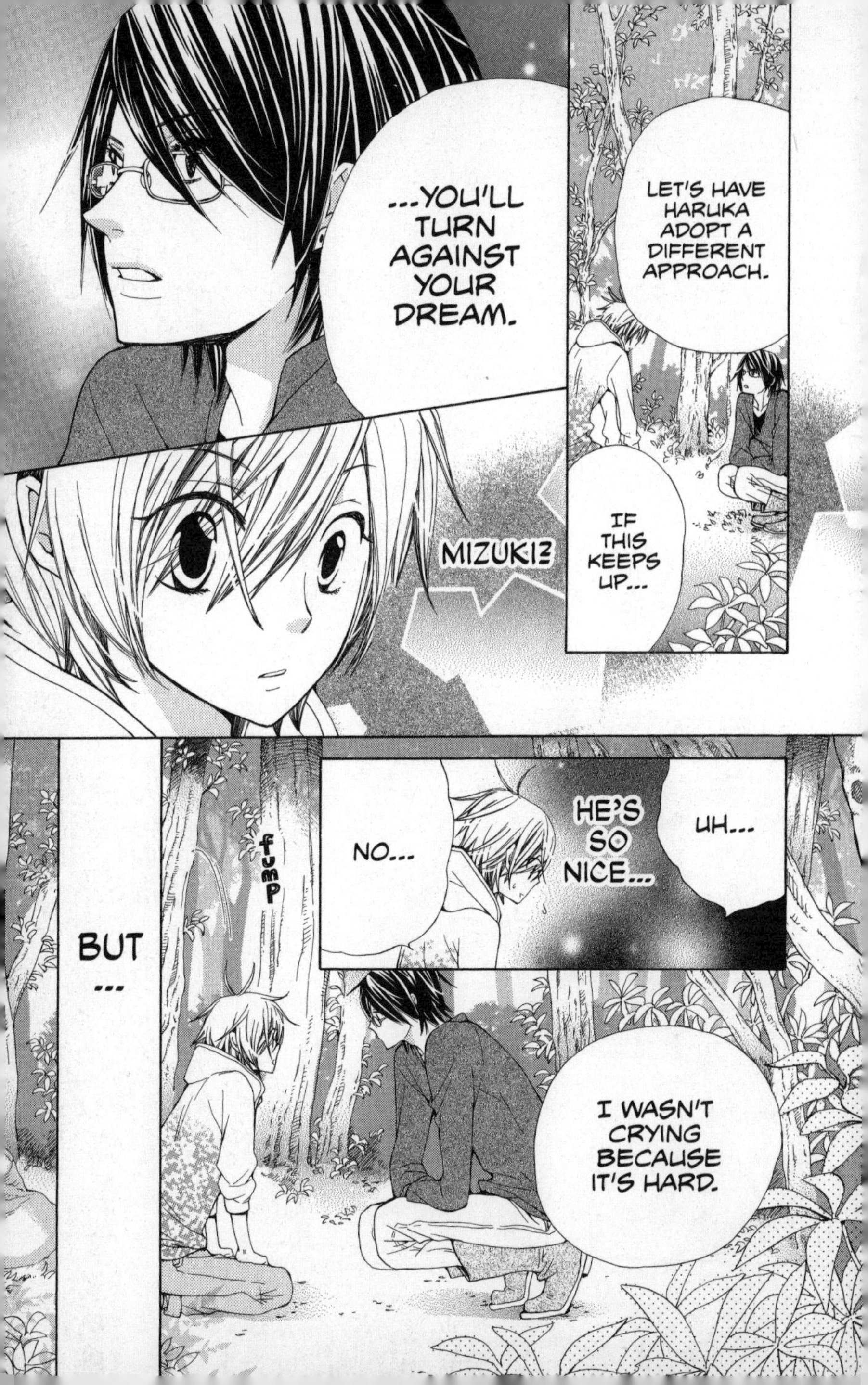
LET'S HAVE HARUKA ADOPT A DIFFERENT APPROACH.
IF THIS KEEPS UP...
...YOU'LL TURN AGAINST YOUR DREAM.
MIZUKI?
UH...
HE'S SO NICE...
NO...
I WASN'T CRYING BECAUSE IT'S HARD.
fump
BUT ...

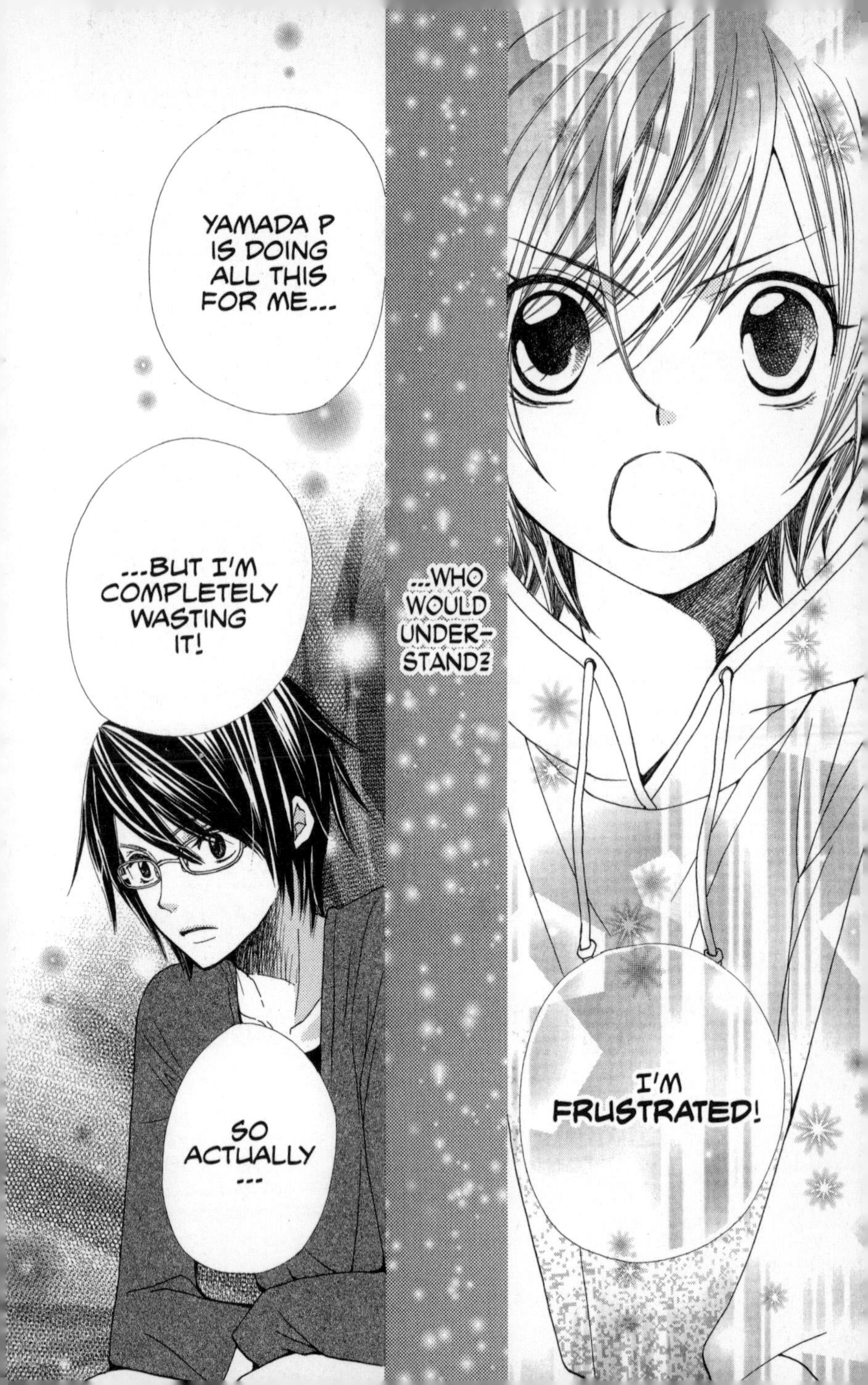
YAMADA P IS DOING ALL THIS FOR ME...
...BUT I'M COMPLETELY WASTING IT!
SO ACTUALLY ...
...WHO WOULD UNDERSTAND?
I'M FRUSTRATED!

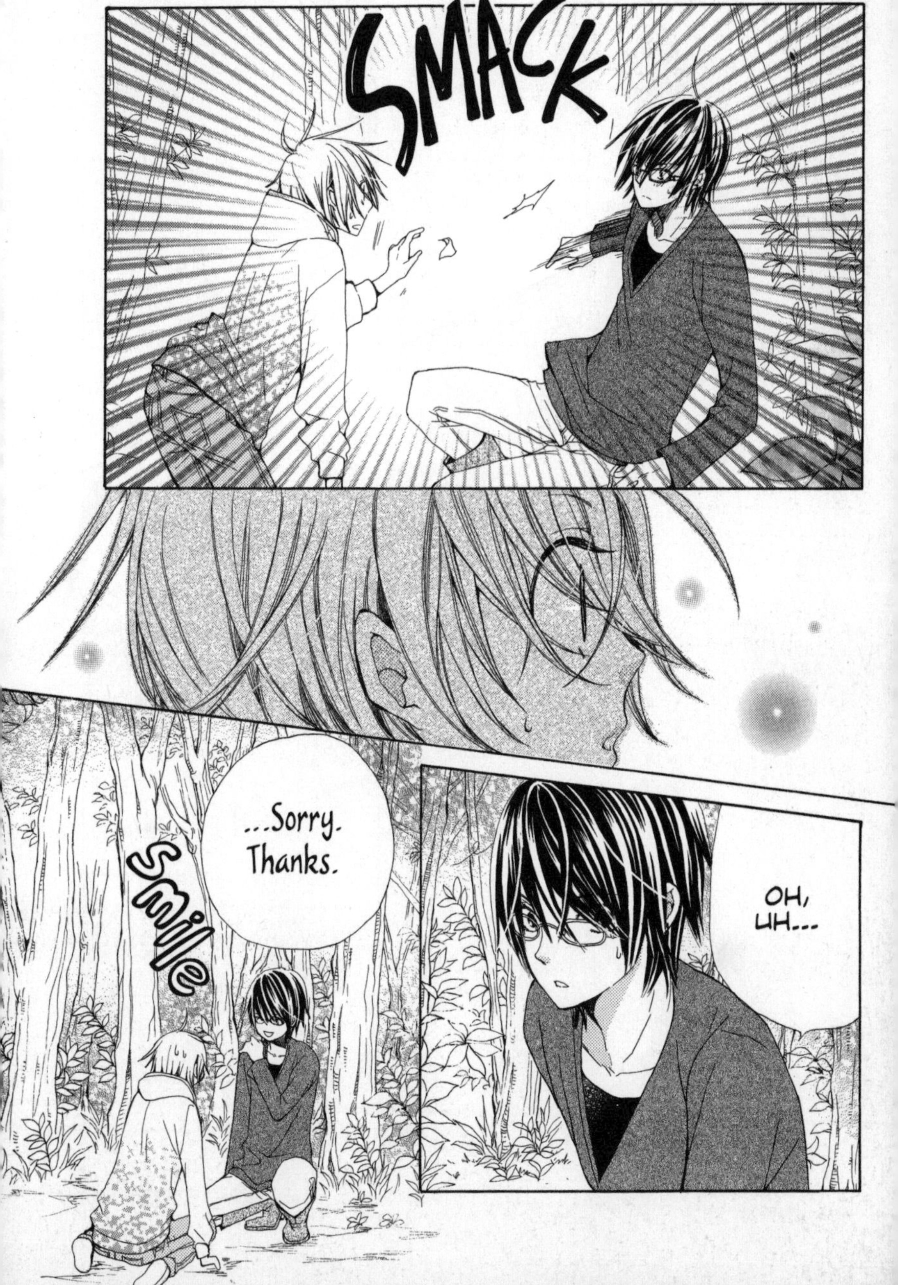
SMACK
OH, UH...
...Sorry. Thanks.
Smile

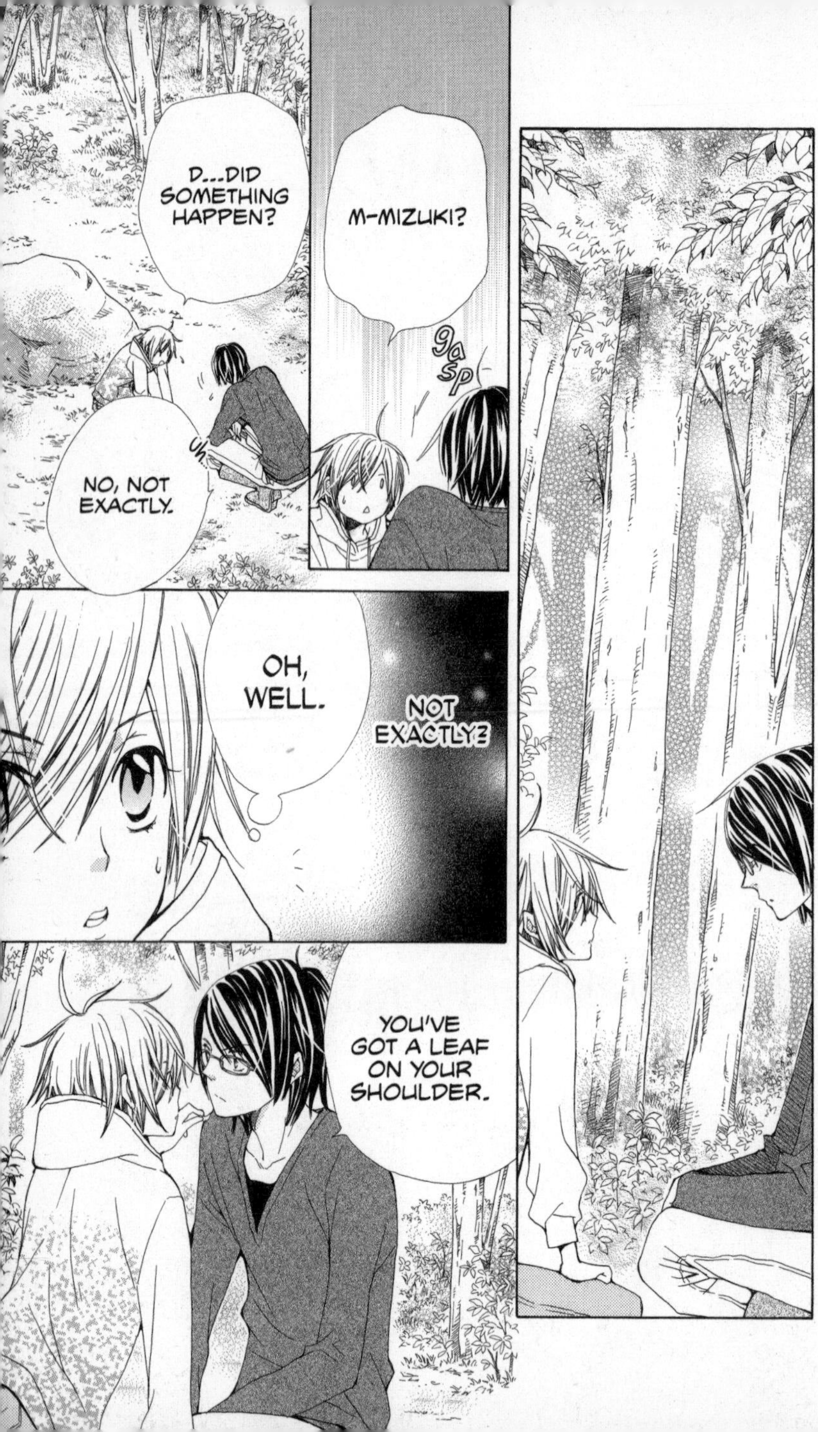
M-MIZUKI?
gasp
D...DID SOMETHING HAPPEN?
NO, NOT EXACTLY.
OH, WELL.
NOT EXACTLY?
YOU'VE GOT A LEAF ON YOUR SHOULDER.

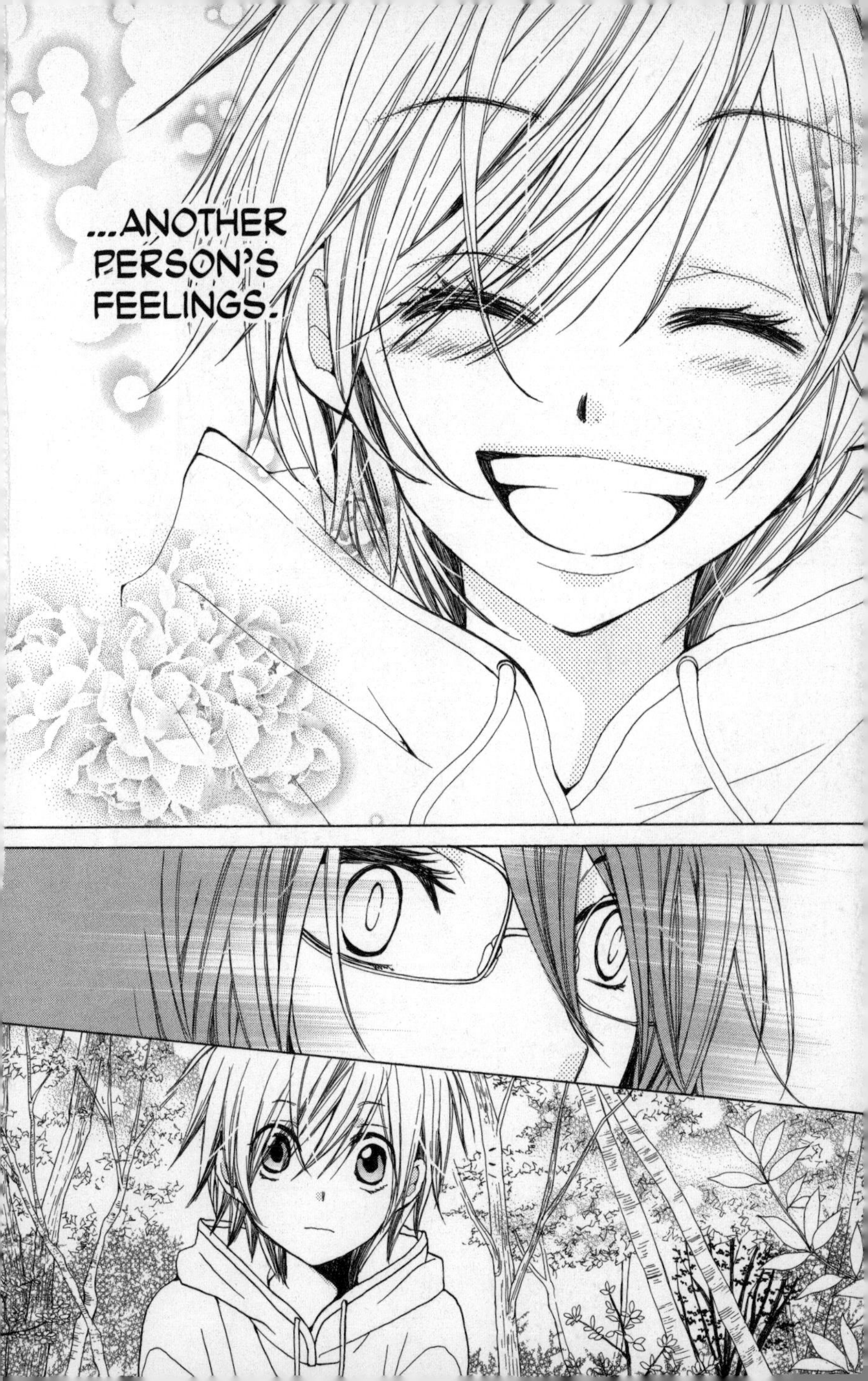
...ANOTHER PERSON'S FEELINGS.

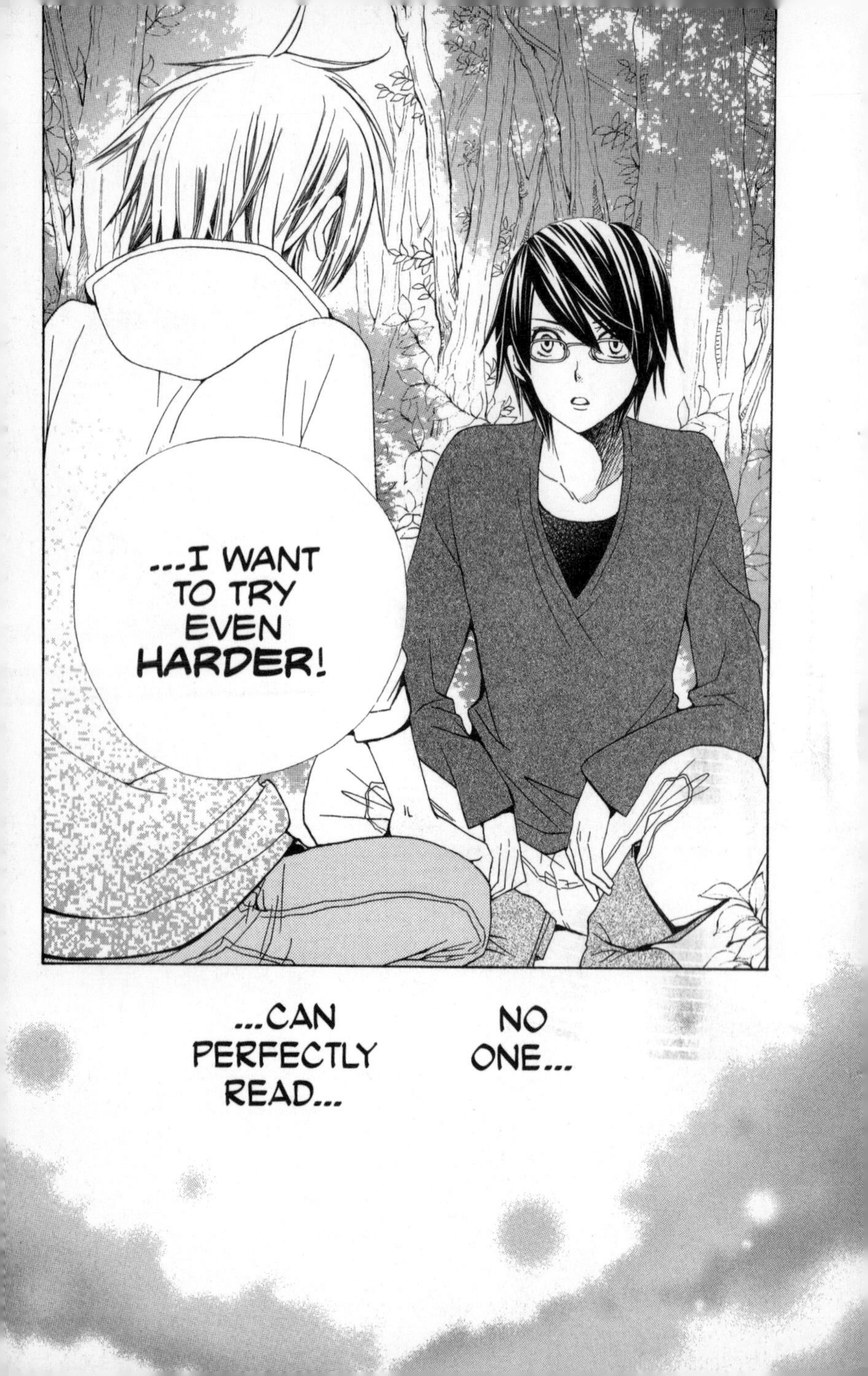
...I WANT TO TRY EVEN HARDER!
NO ONE...
...CAN PERFECTLY READ...

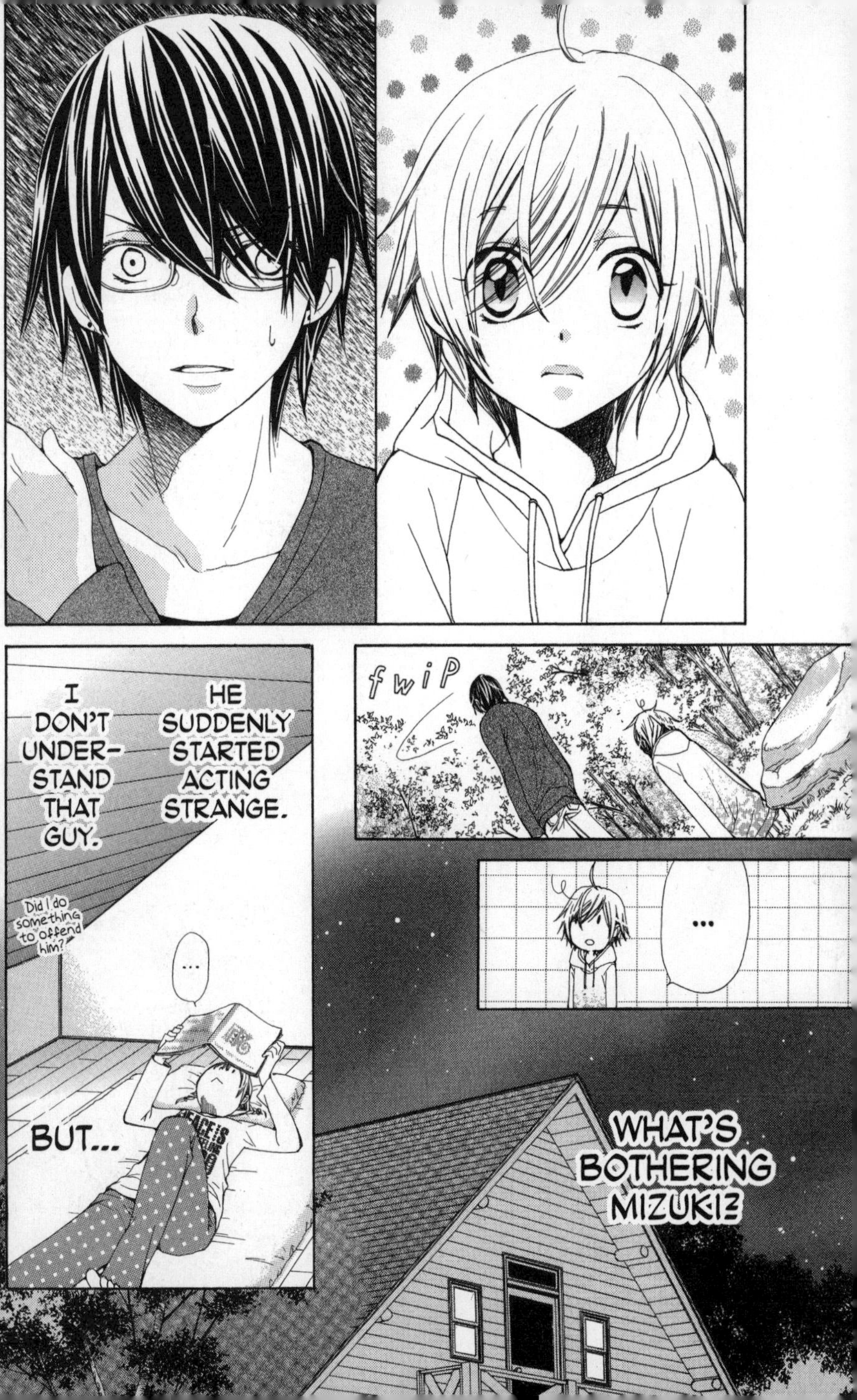
fwiP
...
HE SUDDENLY STARTED ACTING STRANGE.
I DON'T UNDER-STAND THAT GUY.
Did I do something to offend him?
...
BUT...
WHAT'S BOTHERING MIZUKI?

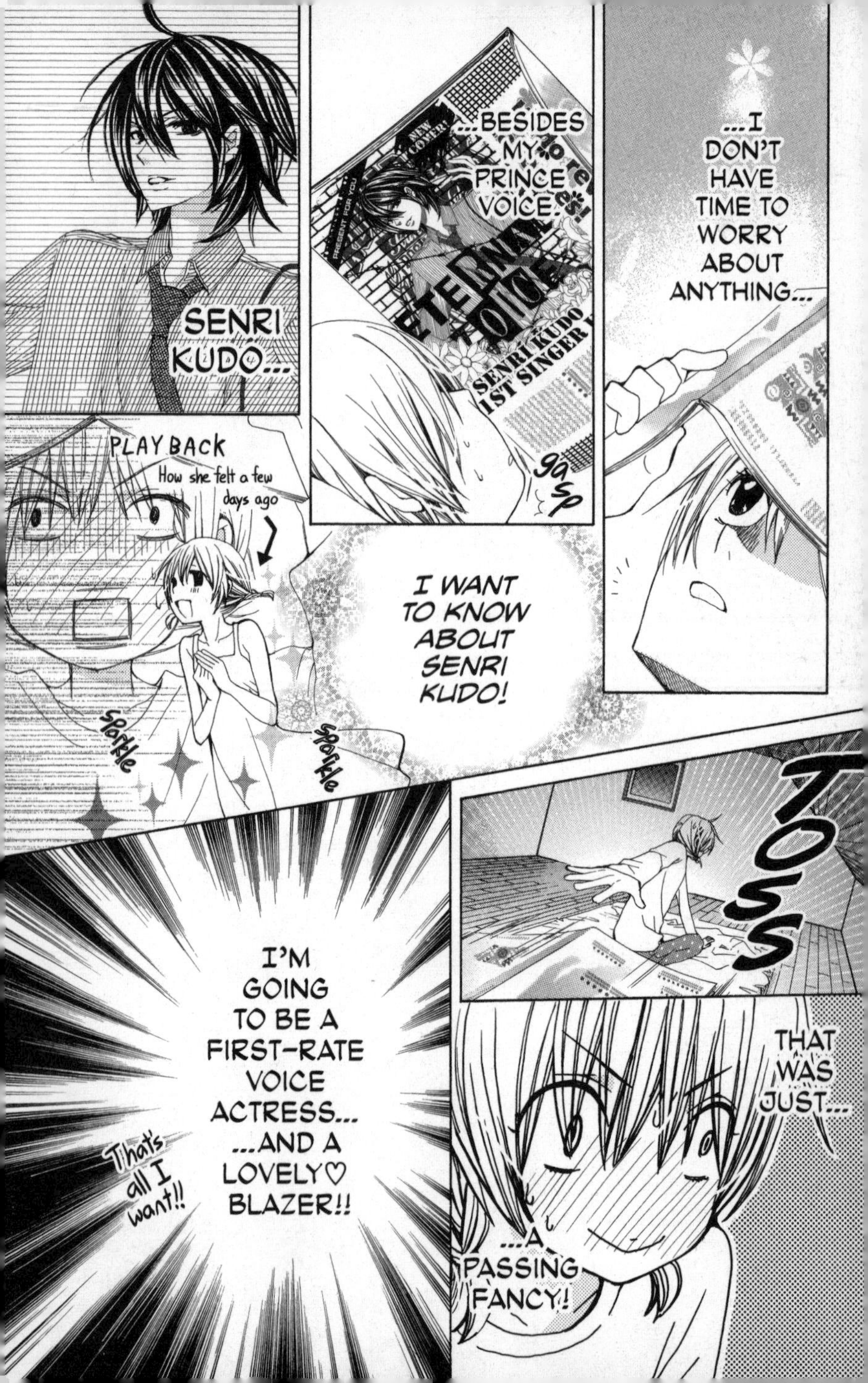

...I DON'T HAVE TIME TO WORRY ABOUT ANYTHING...
...BESIDES MY PRINCE VOICE.
SENRI KUDO
1ST SINGER
gasp
SENRI KUDO...
PLAY BACK
How she felt a few days ago
I WANT TO KNOW ABOUT SENRI KUDO!
sparkle
sparkle
TOSS
THAT WAS JUST...
...A PASSING FANCY!
I'M GOING TO BE A FIRST-RATE VOICE ACTRESS...
...AND A LOVELY♡ BLAZER!!
That's all I want!!

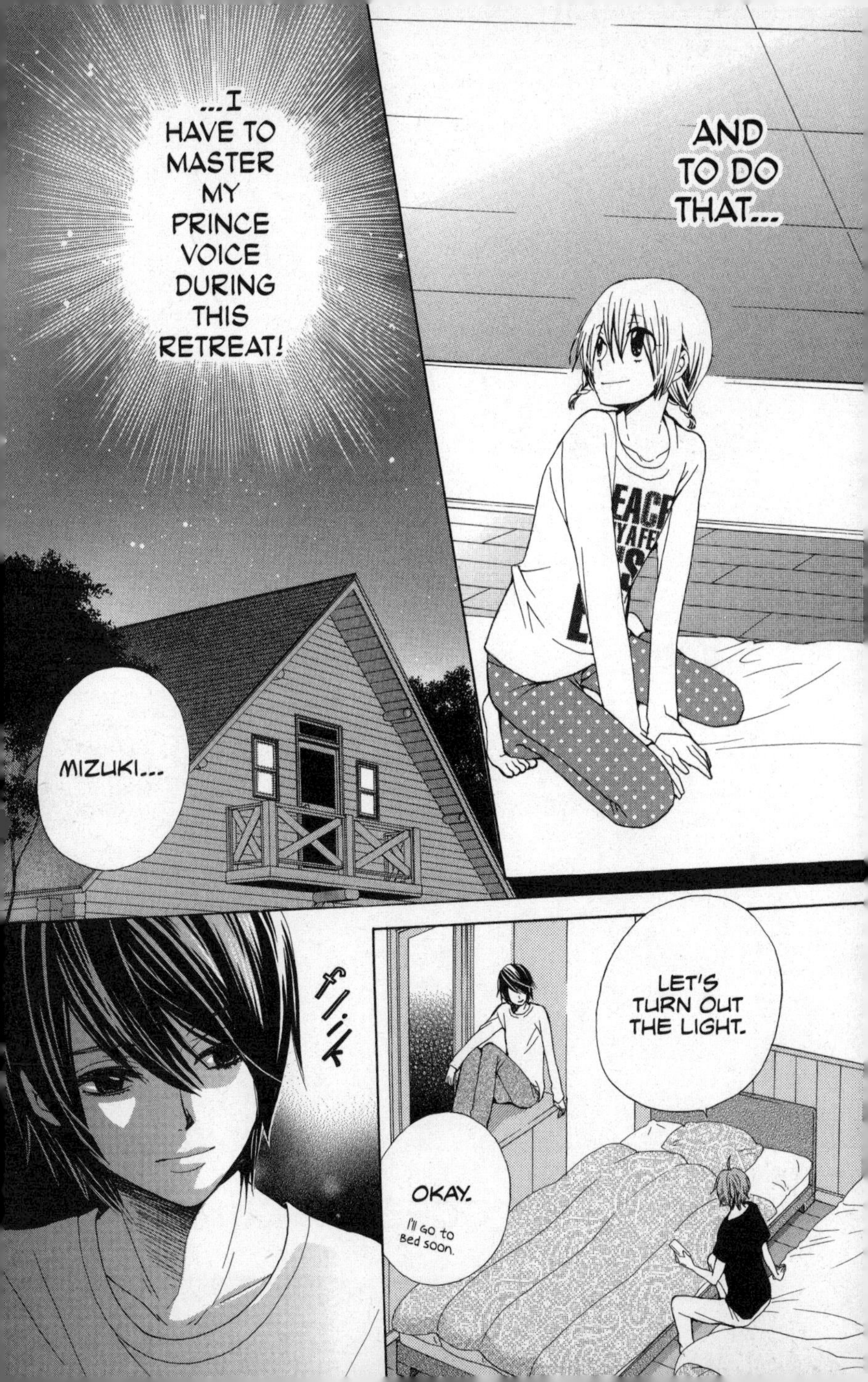
AND TO DO THAT...
...I HAVE TO MASTER MY PRINCE VOICE DURING THIS RETREAT!
MIZUKI...
LET'S TURN OUT THE LIGHT.
OKAY.
I'll go to bed soon.
flik

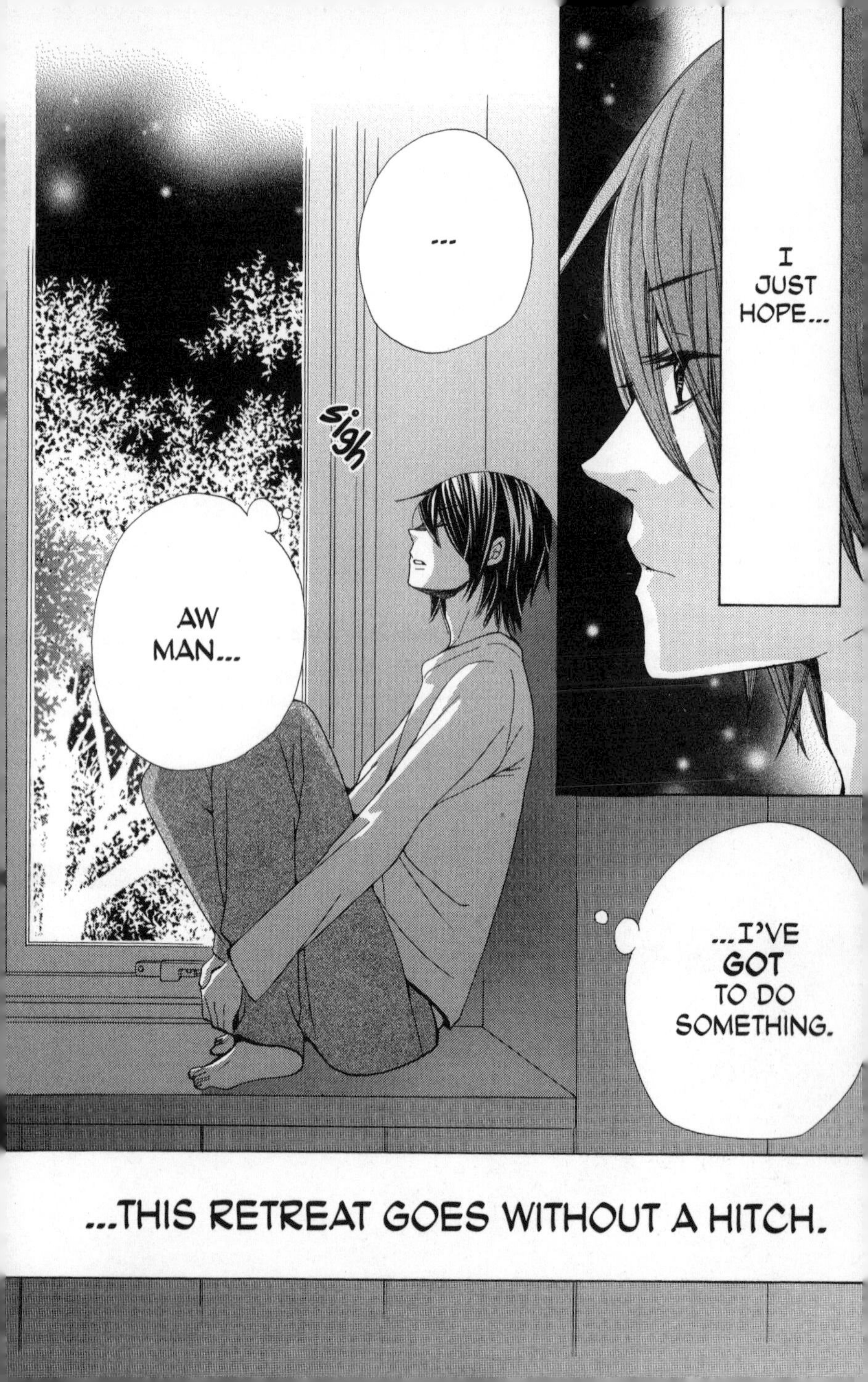
I JUST HOPE...
...
sigh
AW MAN...
...I'VE GOT TO DO SOMETHING.
...THIS RETREAT GOES WITHOUT A HITCH.

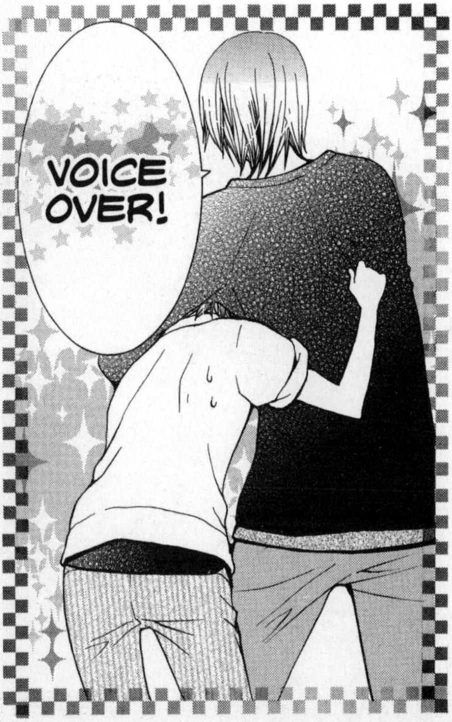
VOICE OVER!

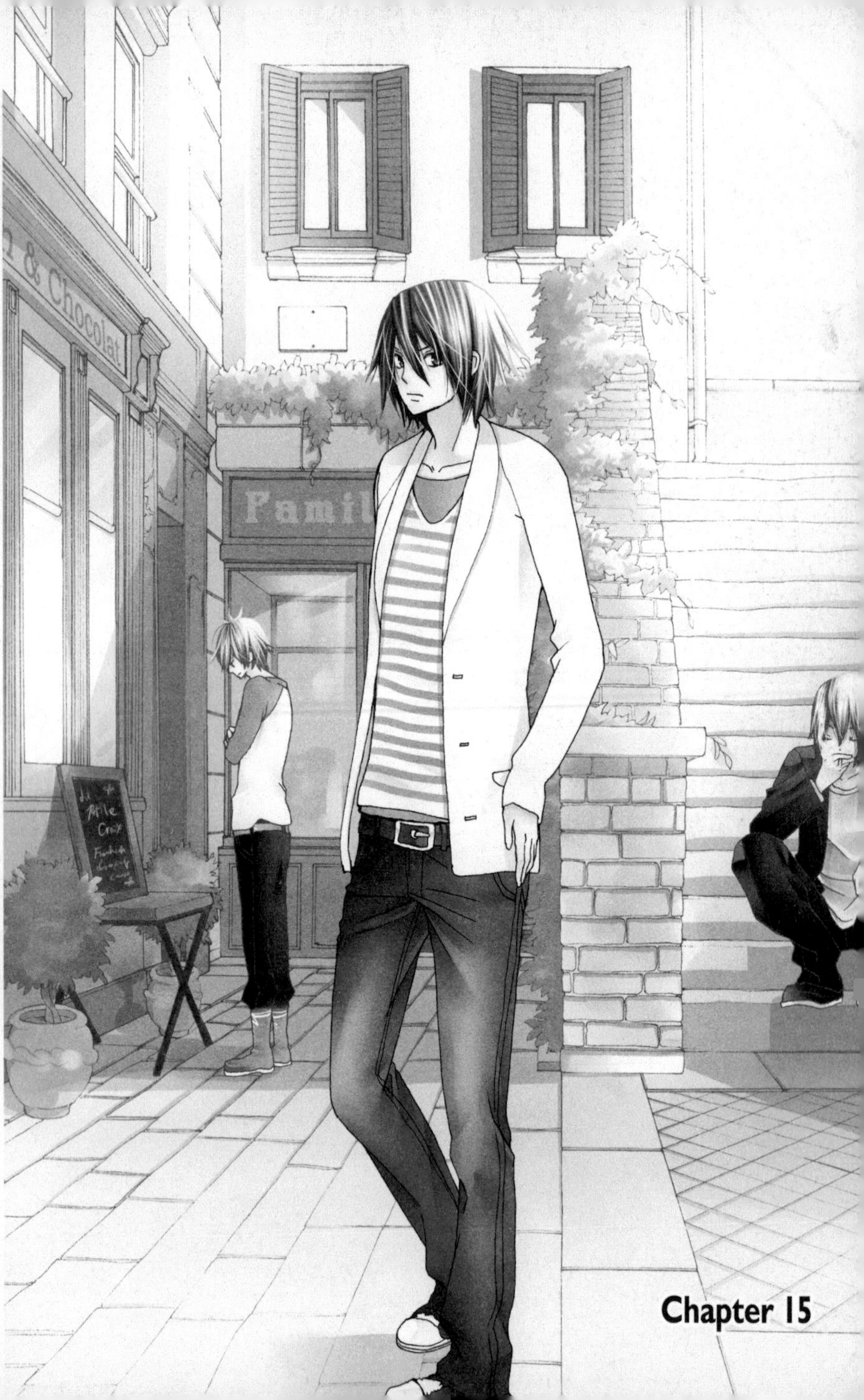
& Chocolat
Famil

Chapter 15

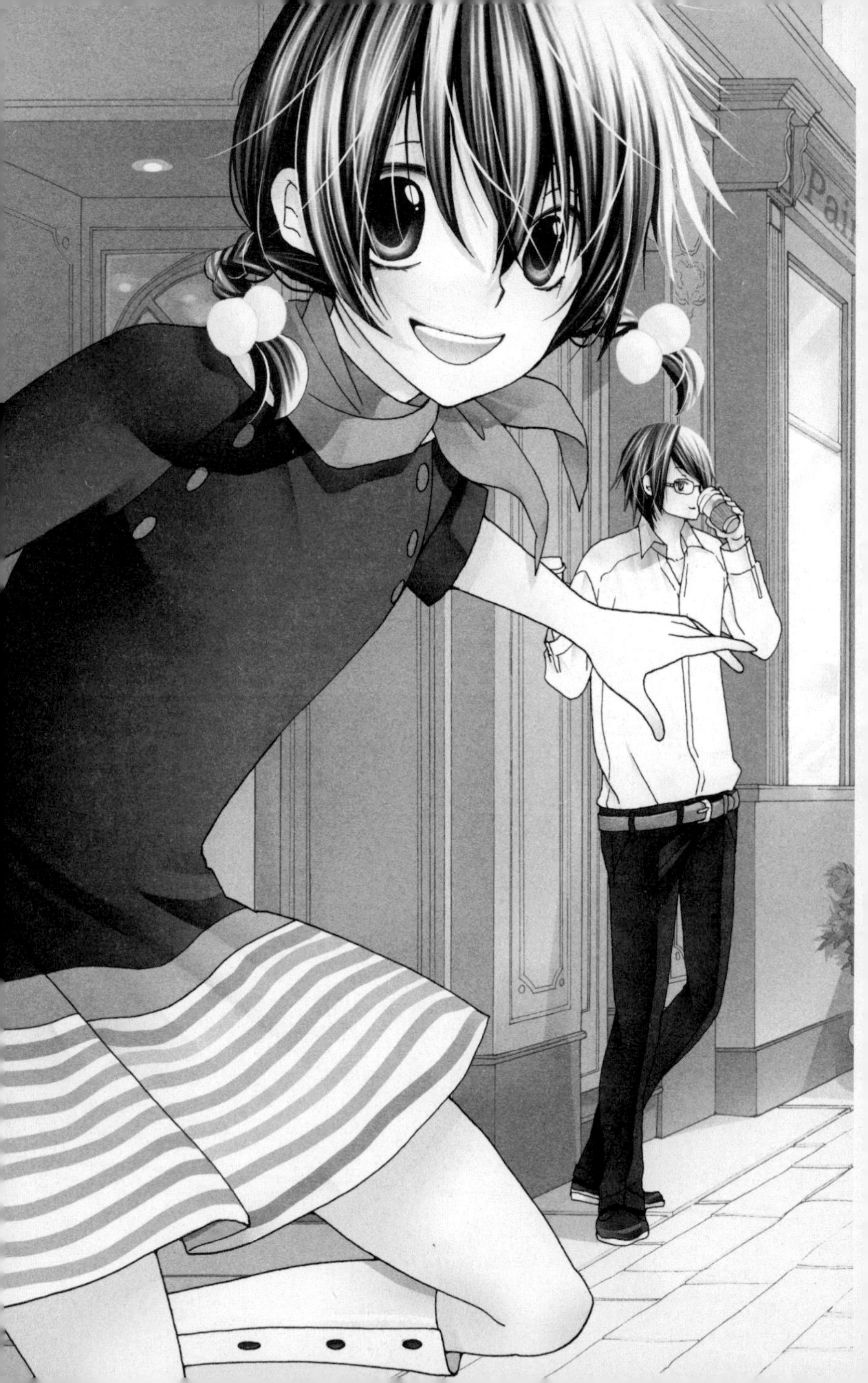

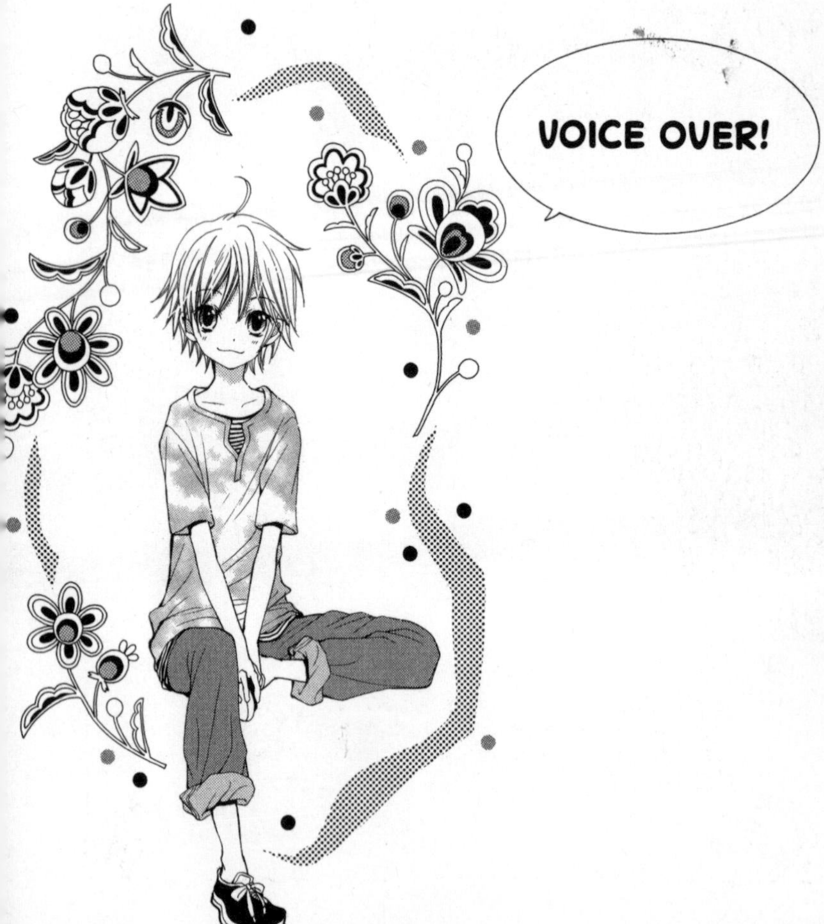
VOICE OVER!

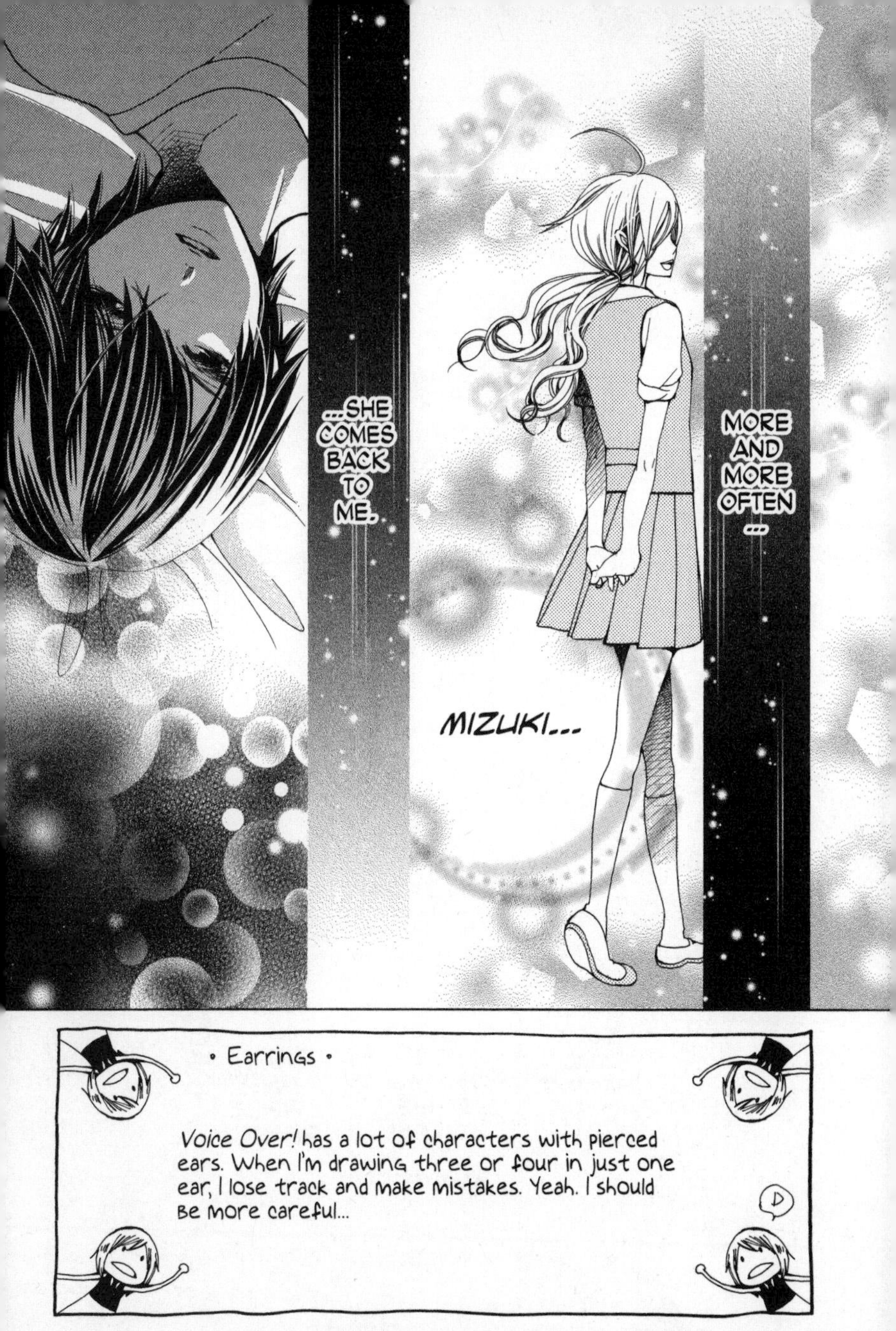
MORE AND MORE OFTEN...
MIZUKI...
...SHE COMES BACK TO ME.

• Earrings •

Voice Over! has a lot of characters with pierced ears. When I'm drawing three or four in just one ear, I lose track and make mistakes. Yeah. I should be more careful...

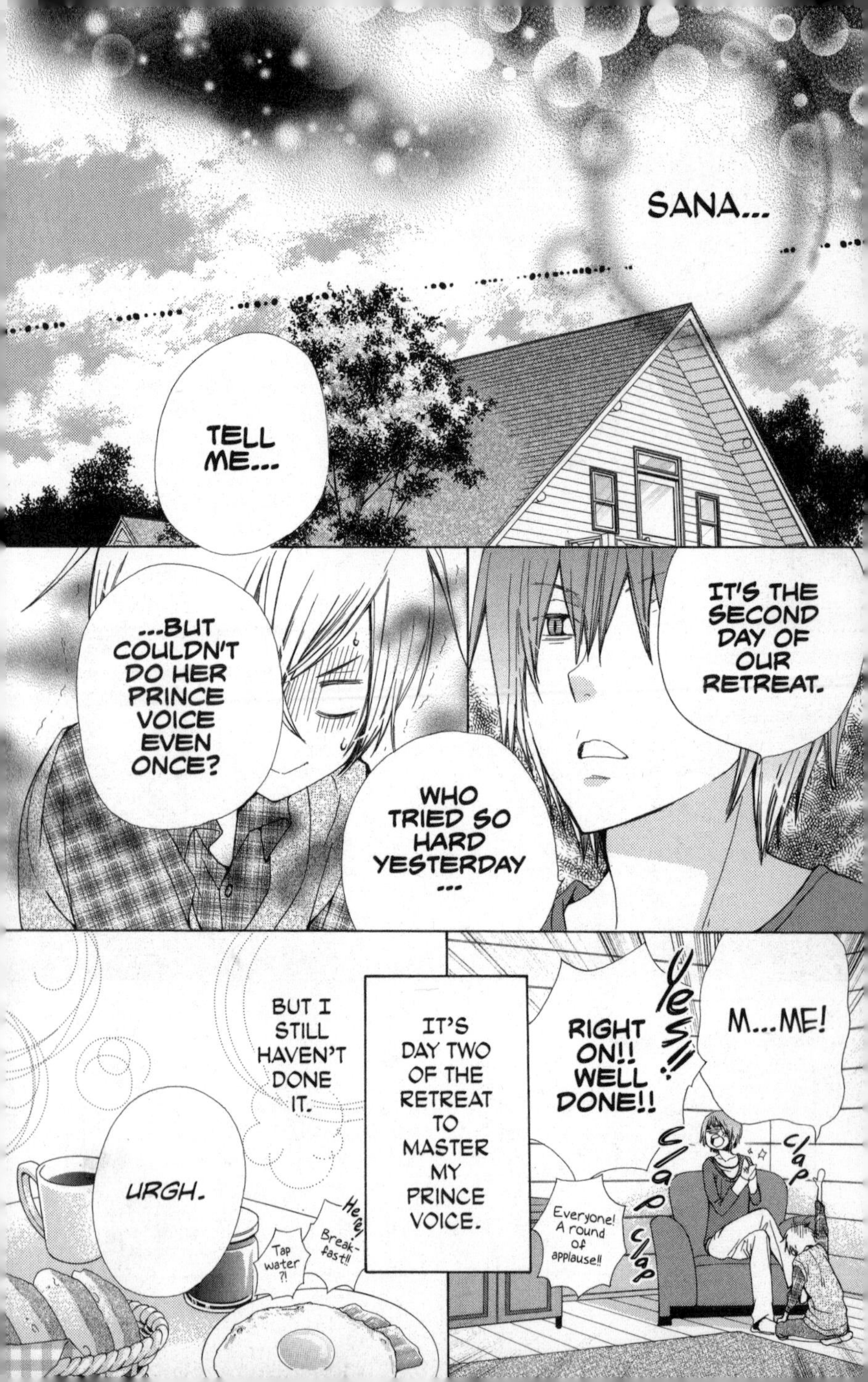
SANA...
TELL ME...
IT'S THE SECOND DAY OF OUR RETREAT.
WHO TRIED SO HARD YESTERDAY...
...BUT COULDN'T DO HER PRINCE VOICE EVEN ONCE?
M...ME!
YES!!
RIGHT ON!! WELL DONE!!
Clap
Clap
Clap clap
Everyone! A round of applause!!
IT'S DAY TWO OF THE RETREAT TO MASTER MY PRINCE VOICE.
BUT I STILL HAVEN'T DONE IT.
URGH.
Here! Breakfast!!
Tap water?!

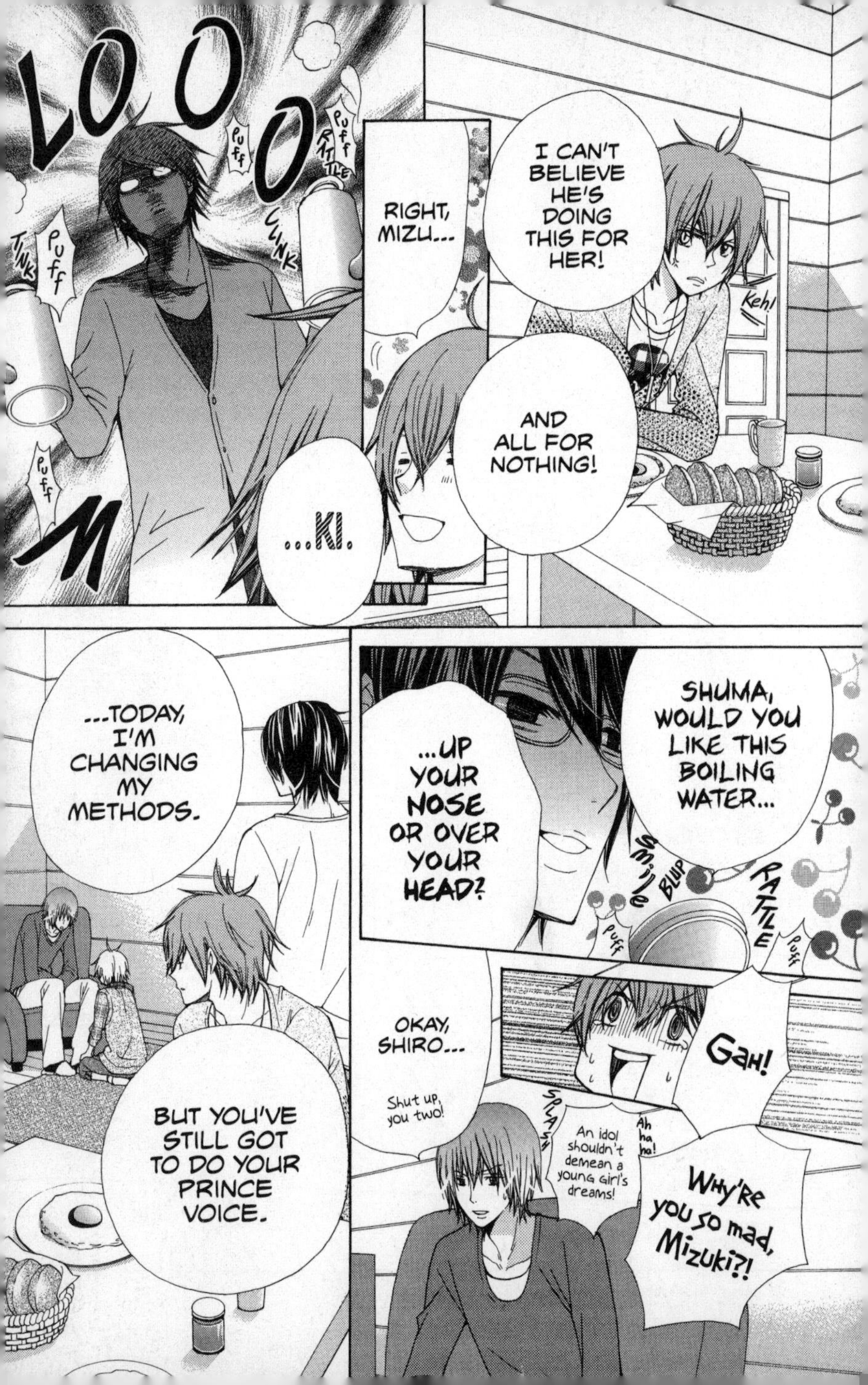
I CAN'T BELIEVE HE'S DOING THIS FOR HER!
Keh!
AND ALL FOR NOTHING!
RIGHT, MIZU...
...KI.
LOOOOM
Puff
RATTLE
Puff
CLINK
TINK
Puff
Puff
SHUMA, WOULD YOU LIKE THIS BOILING WATER...
...UP YOUR NOSE OR OVER YOUR HEAD?
Smile
BLUP
RATTLE
Puff
Puff
Gah!
Why're you so mad, Mizuki?!
Ah ha ha!
An idol shouldn't demean a young girl's dreams!
SPLASH
OKAY, SHIRO...
Shut up, you two!
...TODAY, I'M CHANGING MY METHODS.
BUT YOU'VE STILL GOT TO DO YOUR PRINCE VOICE.

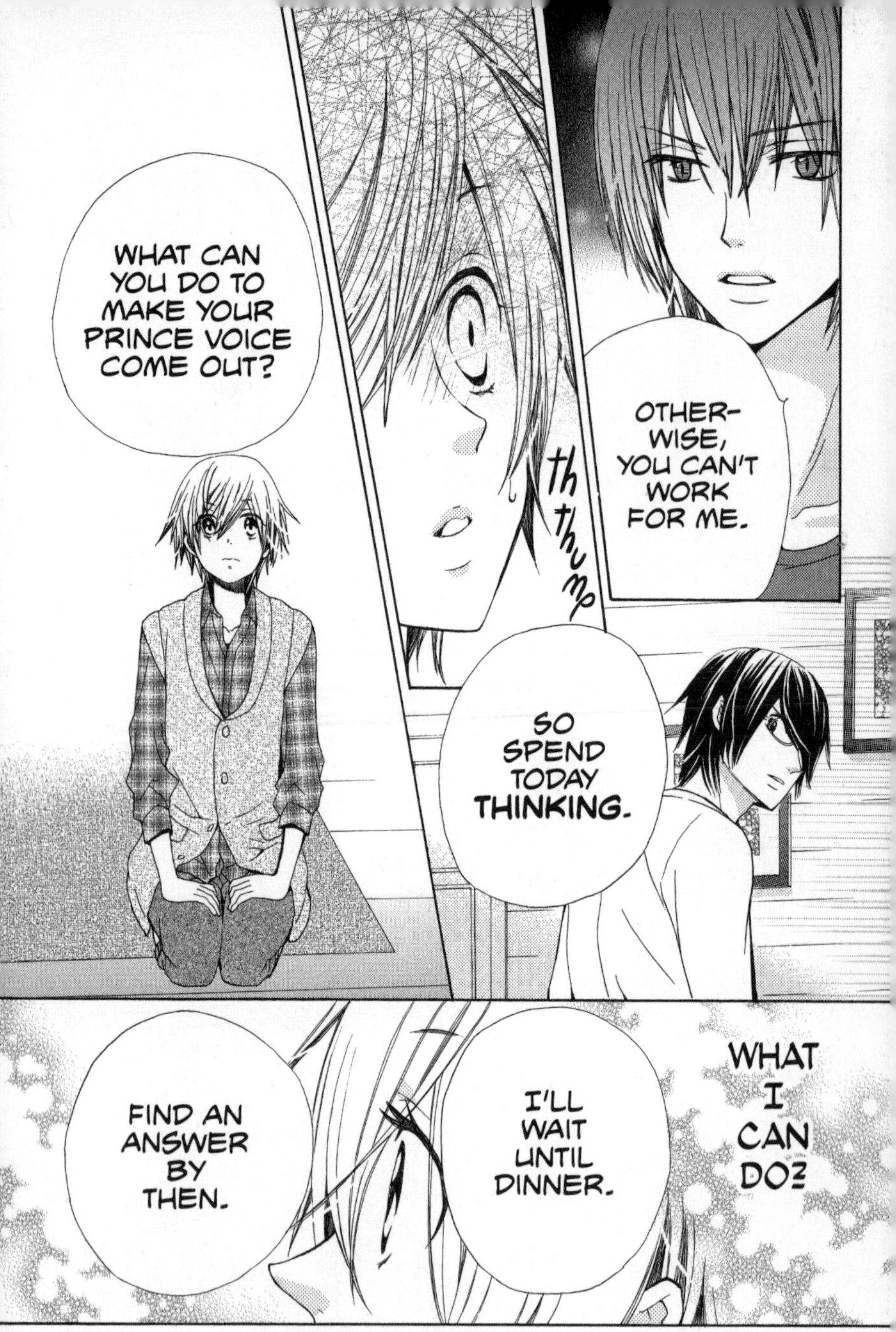
OTHER-WISE, YOU CAN'T WORK FOR ME.
th thump
SO SPEND TODAY **THINKING.**
WHAT CAN YOU DO TO MAKE YOUR PRINCE VOICE COME OUT?
WHAT I CAN DO?
I'LL WAIT UNTIL DINNER.
FIND AN ANSWER BY THEN.

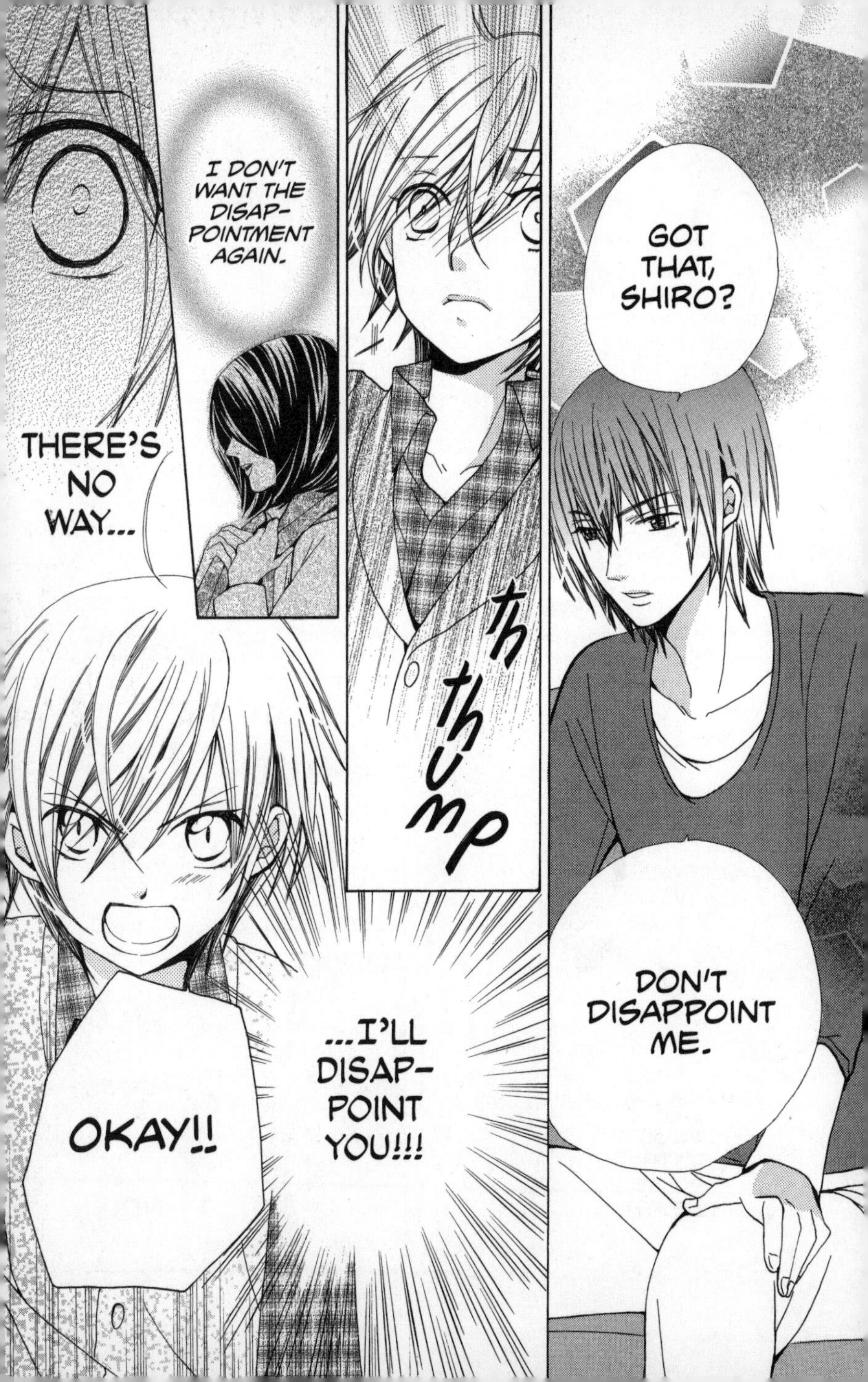
GOT THAT, SHIRO?
DON'T DISAPPOINT ME.
THUMP THUMP
I DON'T WANT THE DISAP-POINTMENT AGAIN.
THERE'S NO WAY...
...I'LL DISAP-POINT YOU!!!
OKAY!!

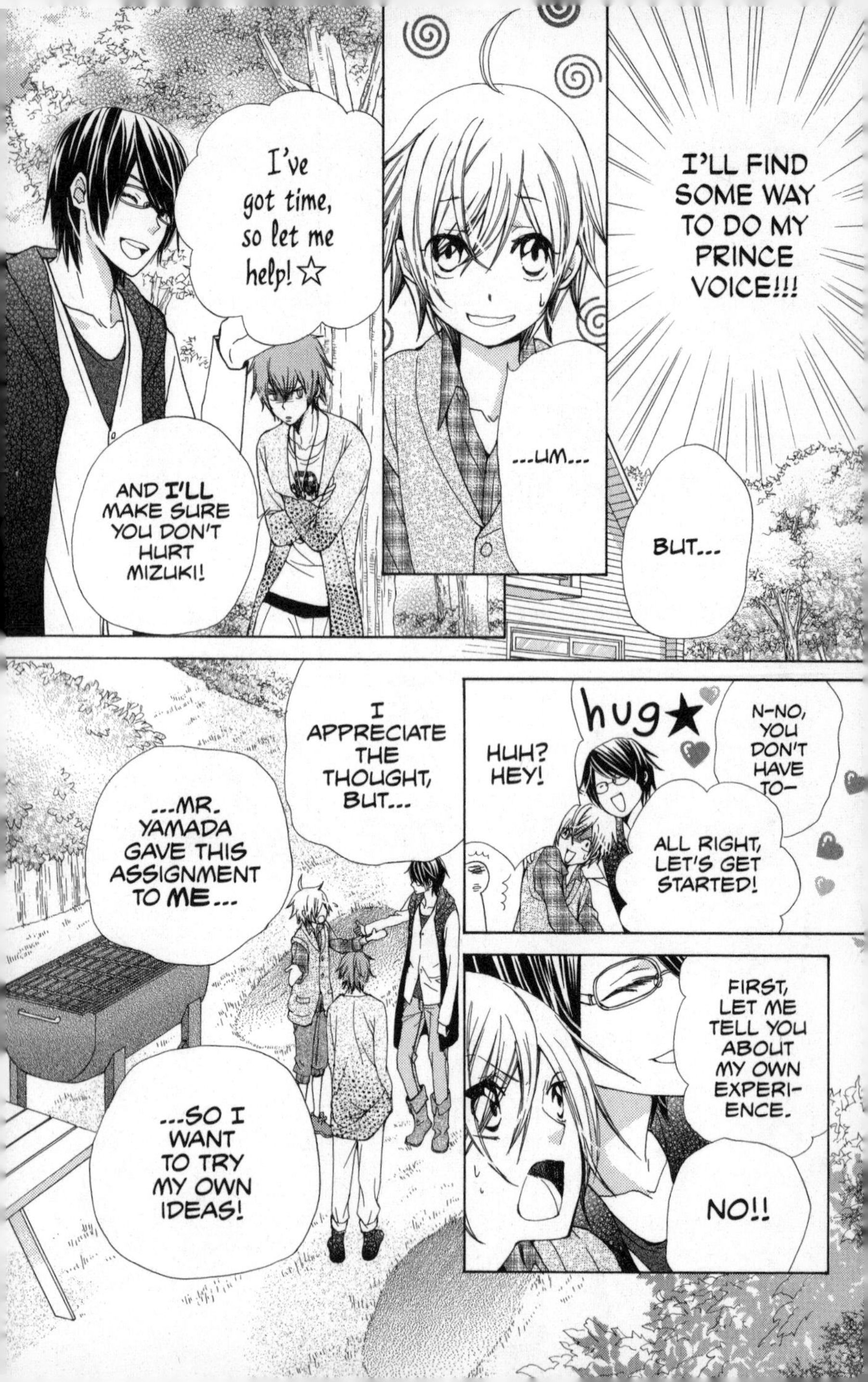
I'LL FIND SOME WAY TO DO MY PRINCE VOICE!!!
BUT...
...UM...
I've got time, so let me help! ☆
AND I'LL MAKE SURE YOU DON'T HURT MIZUKI!
N-NO, YOU DON'T HAVE TO—
hug★
HUH? HEY!
ALL RIGHT, LET'S GET STARTED!
FIRST, LET ME TELL YOU ABOUT MY OWN EXPERIENCE.
NO!!
I APPRECIATE THE THOUGHT, BUT...
...MR. YAMADA GAVE THIS ASSIGNMENT TO ME...
...SO I WANT TO TRY MY OWN IDEAS!

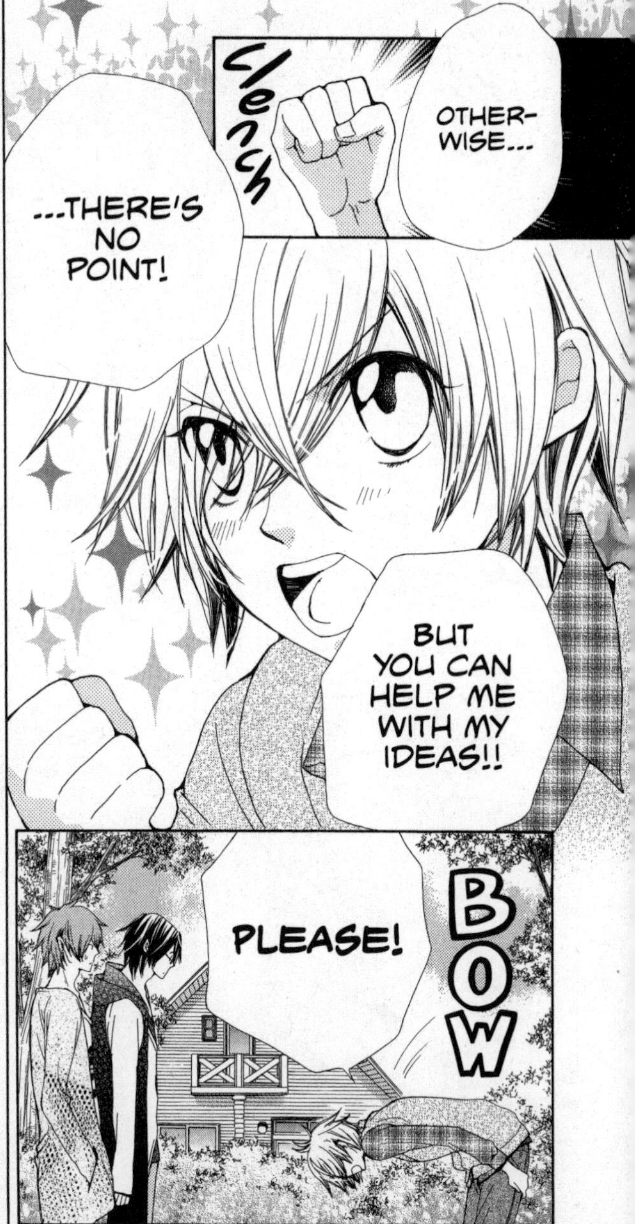
OTHER-WISE...
CLENCH
...THERE'S NO POINT!
BUT YOU CAN HELP ME WITH MY IDEAS!!
BOW
PLEASE!

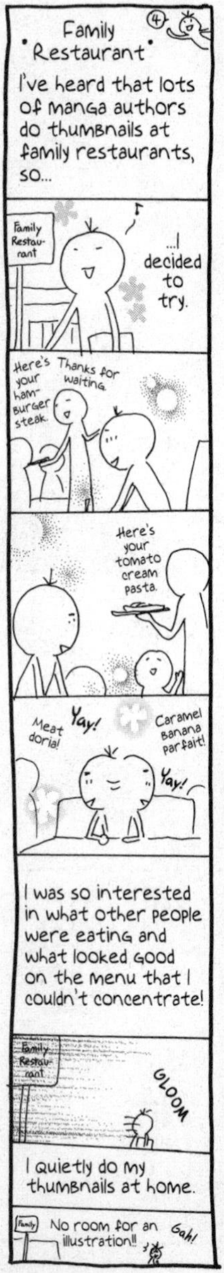
Family Restaurant ④
I've heard that lots of manga authors do thumbnails at family restaurants, so...
Family Restaurant
...I decided to try.
Here's your hamburger steak.
Thanks for waiting.
Here's your tomato cream pasta.
Meat doria!
Yay!
Caramel Banana parfait!
Yay!
I was so interested in what other people were eating and what looked good on the menu that I couldn't concentrate!
Family Restaurant
GLOOM
I quietly do my thumbnails at home.
Family
No room for an illustration!!
Gah!

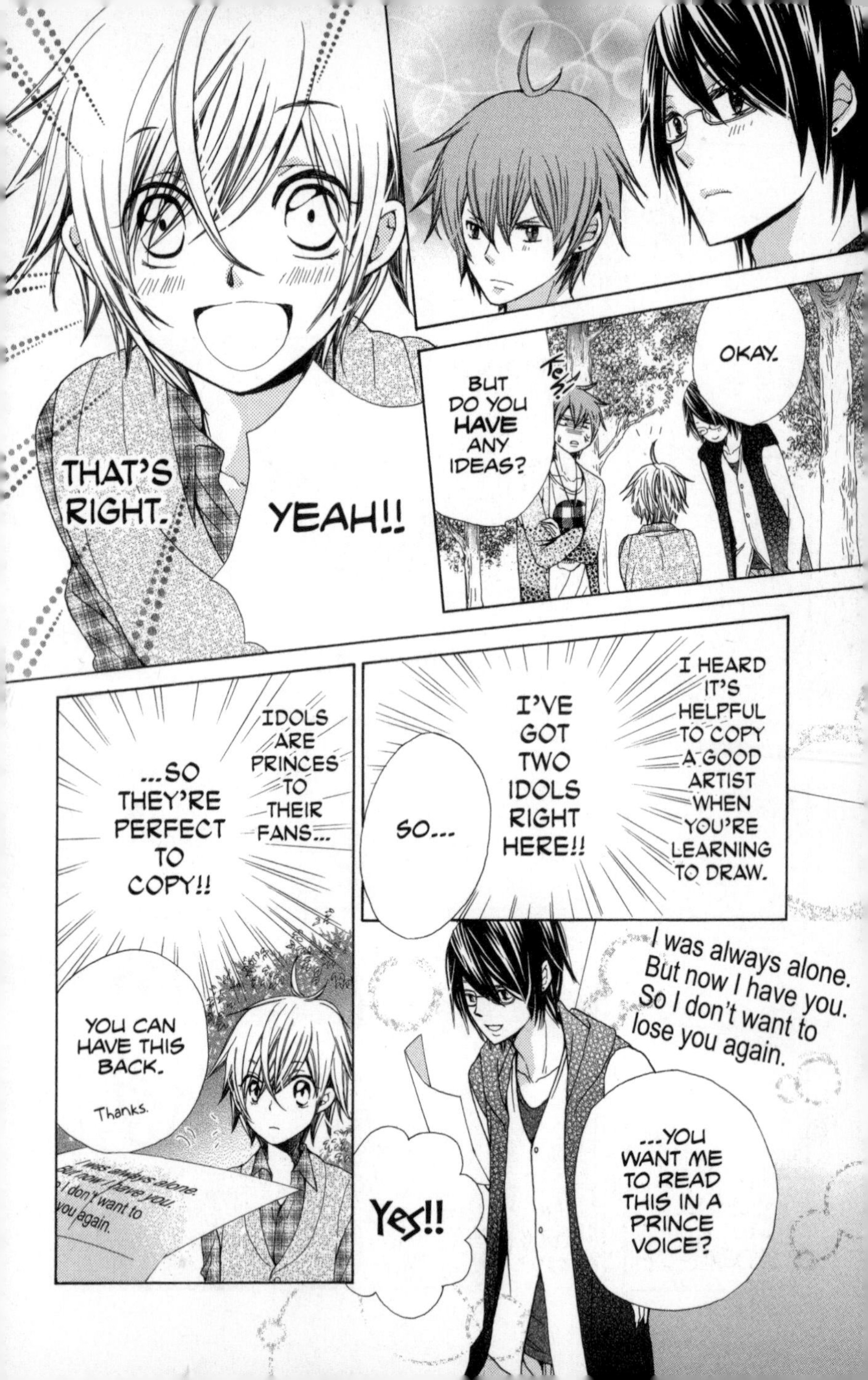
OKAY.
KCH!
BUT DO YOU HAVE ANY IDEAS?
THAT'S RIGHT.
YEAH!!
I HEARD IT'S HELPFUL TO COPY A GOOD ARTIST WHEN YOU'RE LEARNING TO DRAW.
I'VE GOT TWO IDOLS RIGHT HERE!!
SO...
IDOLS ARE PRINCES TO THEIR FANS...
...SO THEY'RE PERFECT TO COPY!!
YOU CAN HAVE THIS BACK.
Thanks.
I was always alone. But now I have you. So I don't want to lose you again.
...YOU WANT ME TO READ THIS IN A PRINCE VOICE?
Yes!!

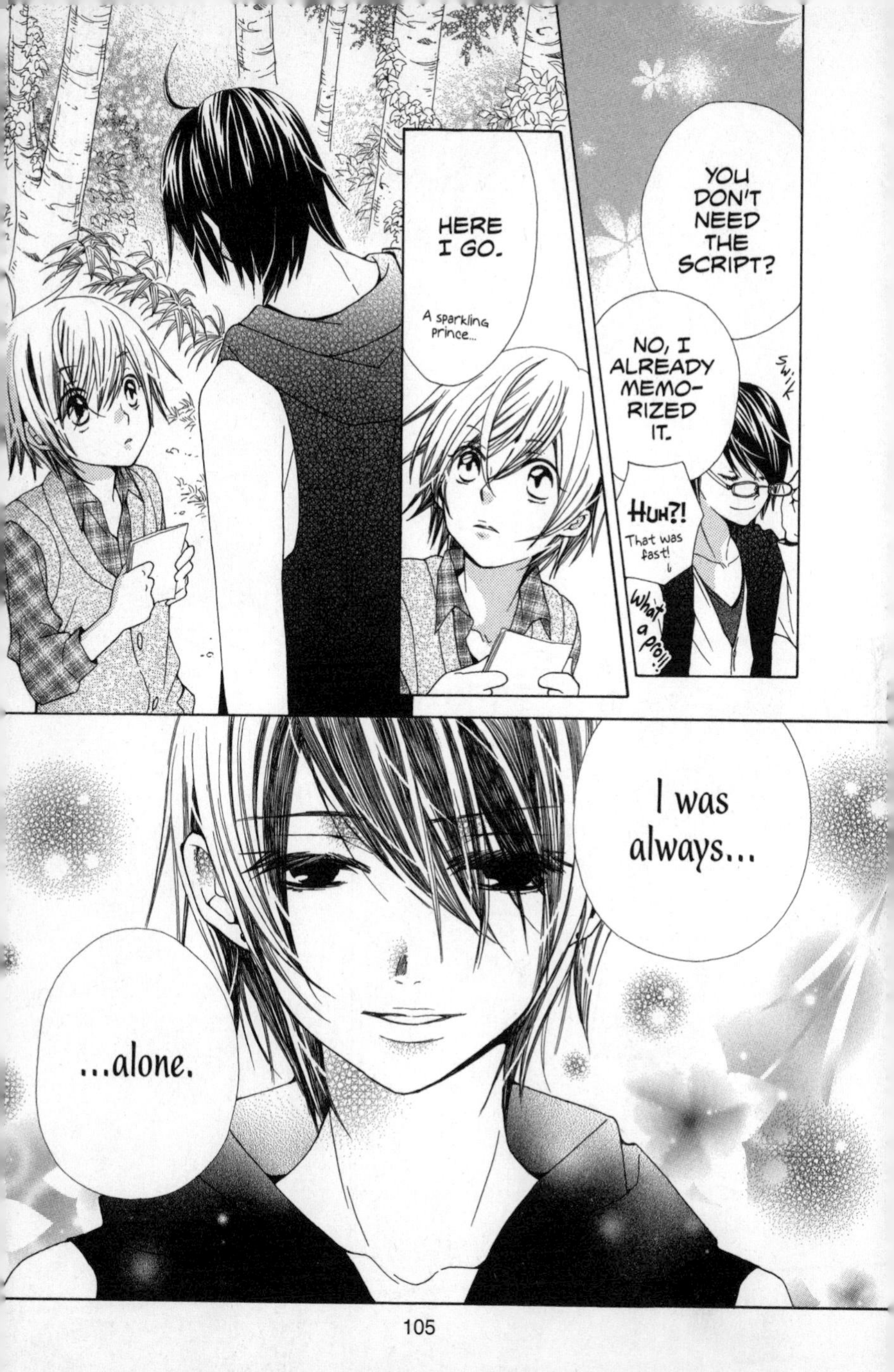
YOU DON'T NEED THE SCRIPT?
NO, I ALREADY MEMO-RIZED IT.
SWIK
HUH?!
That was fast!
What a pro!!
HERE I GO.
A sparkling prince...
I was always...
...alone.

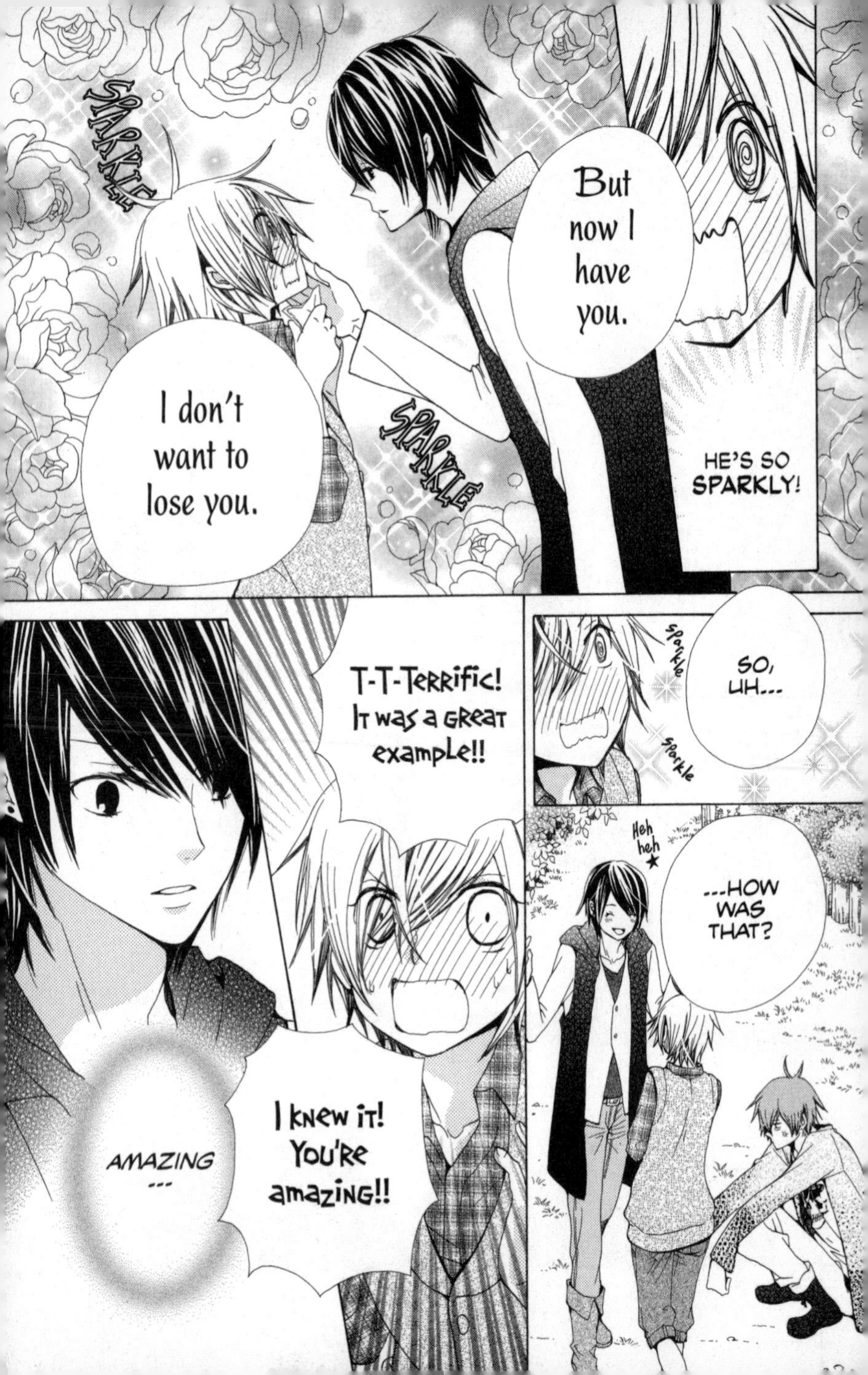
But now I have you.
HE'S SO SPARKLY!
SPARKLE
SPARKLE
I don't want to lose you.
SO, UH...
Sparkle
Sparkle
Heh heh ★
...HOW WAS THAT?
T-T-Terrific! It was a great example!!
I knew it! You're amazing!!
AMAZING ---

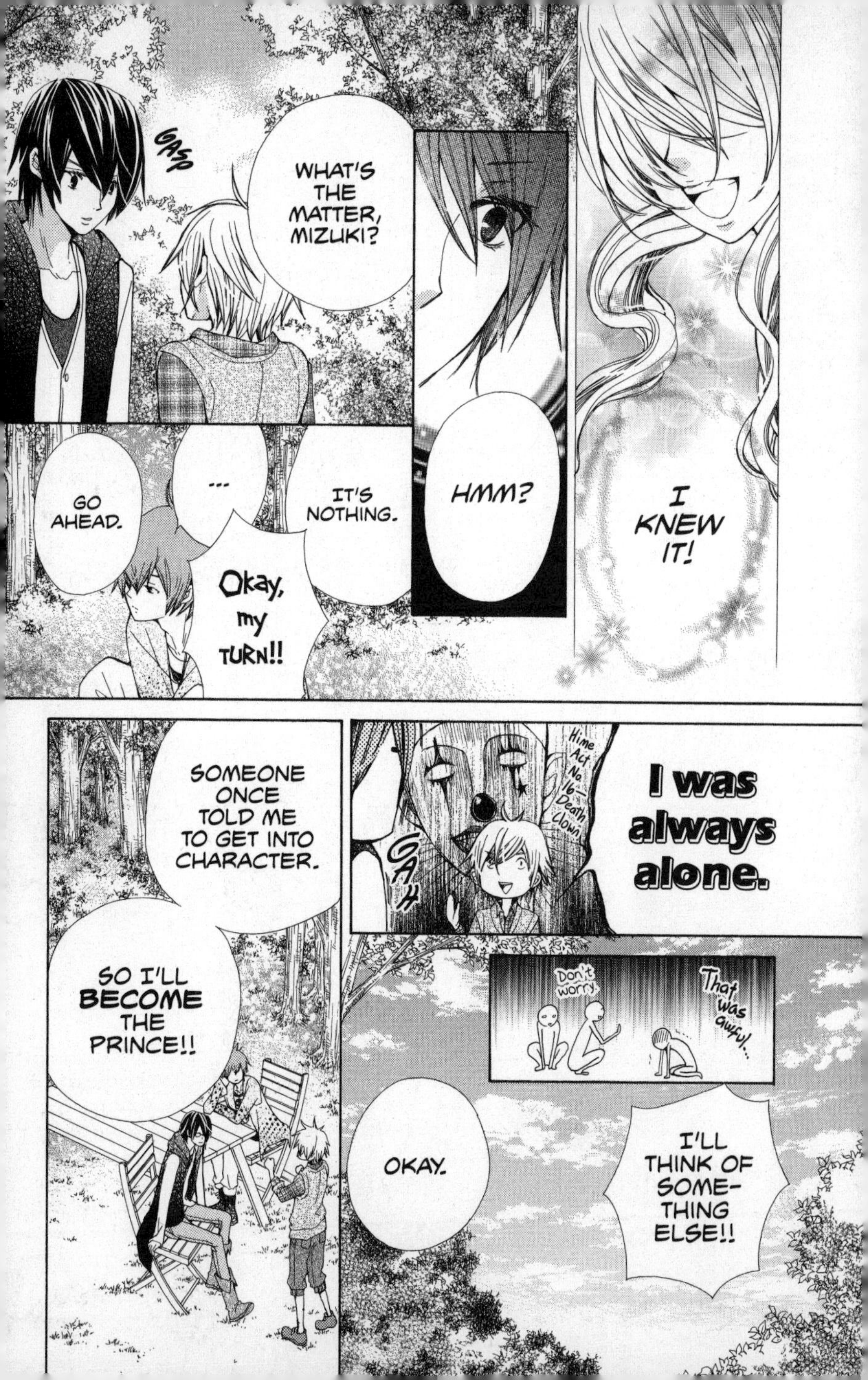
I KNEW IT!
HMM?
WHAT'S THE MATTER, MIZUKI?
GASP
IT'S NOTHING.
...
GO AHEAD.
Okay, my TURN!!
I was always alone.
Hime Act No. 16—Death Clown
GAH
That was awful...
Don't worry
I'LL THINK OF SOMETHING ELSE!!
OKAY.
SOMEONE ONCE TOLD ME TO GET INTO CHARACTER.
SO I'LL BECOME THE PRINCE!!

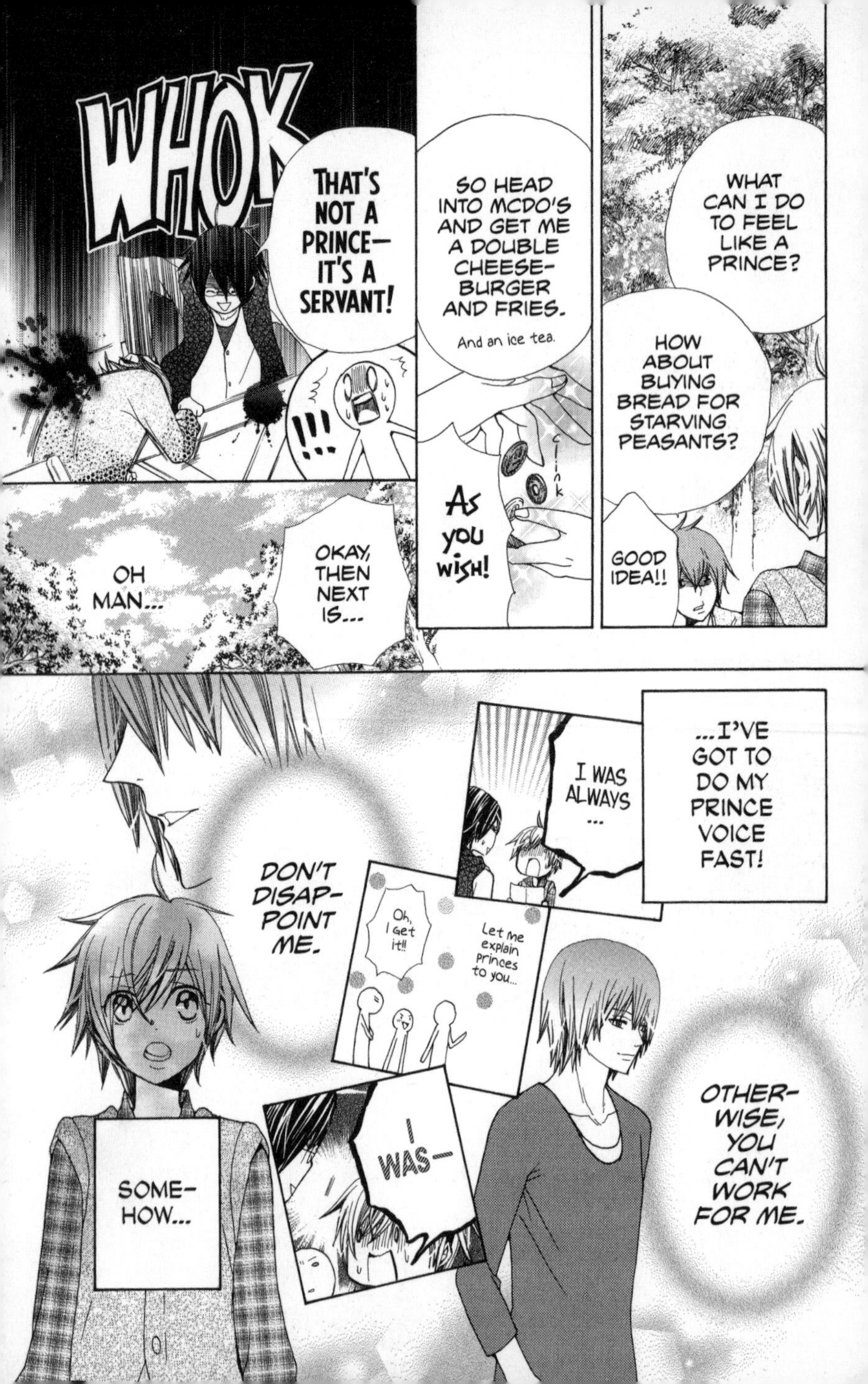
WHAT CAN I DO TO FEEL LIKE A PRINCE?
HOW ABOUT BUYING BREAD FOR STARVING PEASANTS?
GOOD IDEA!!
SO HEAD INTO MCDO'S AND GET ME A DOUBLE CHEESE-BURGER AND FRIES.
And an ice tea.
clink
As you wish!
WHOK
THAT'S NOT A PRINCE—IT'S A SERVANT!
!!!
OKAY, THEN NEXT IS...
OH MAN...
...I'VE GOT TO DO MY PRINCE VOICE FAST!
I WAS ALWAYS ...
Let me explain princes to you...
Oh, I get it!!
DON'T DISAP-POINT ME.
OTHER-WISE, YOU CAN'T WORK FOR ME.
I WAS—
SOME-HOW...

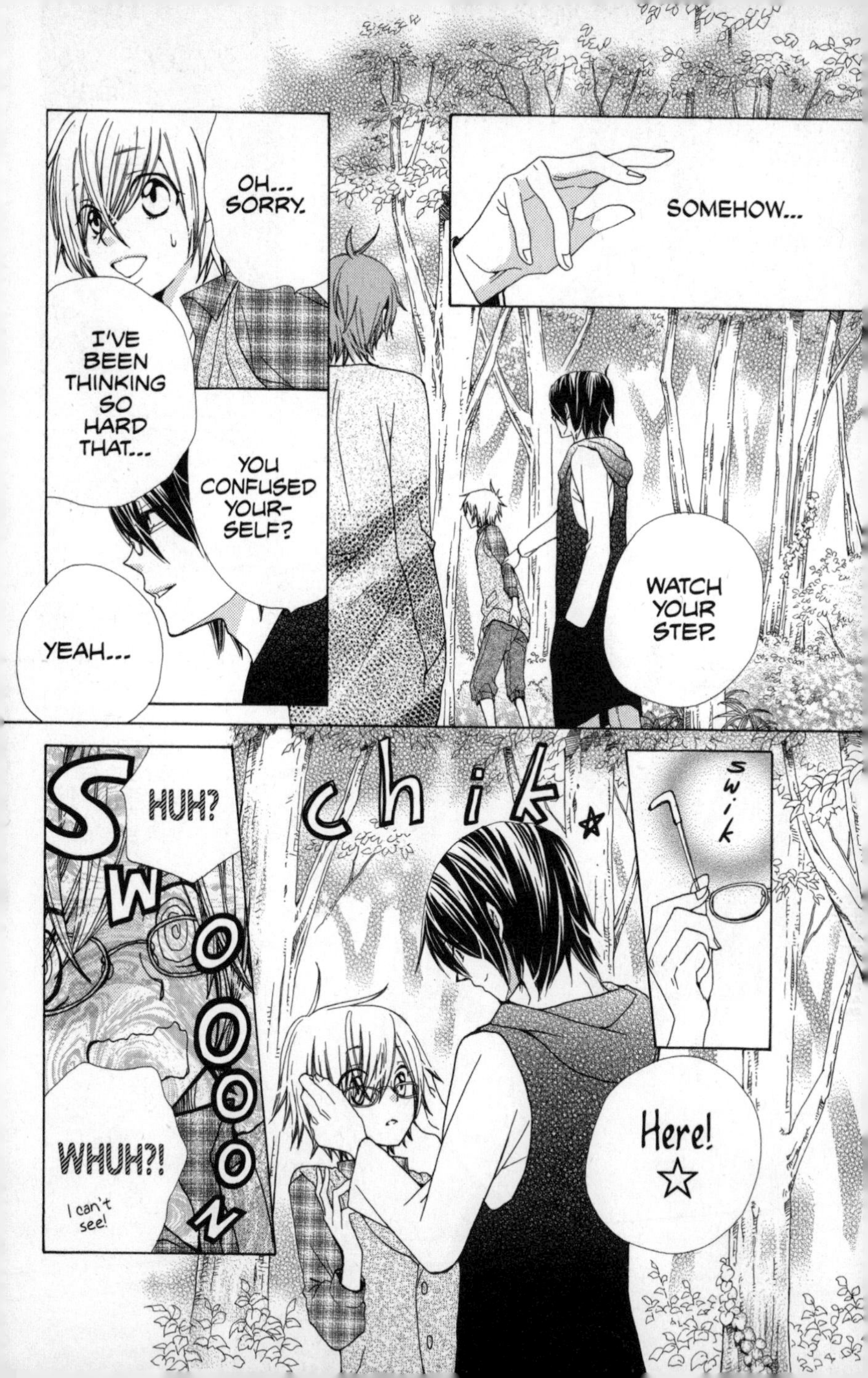
SOMEHOW...
WATCH YOUR STEP.
OH... SORRY.
I'VE BEEN THINKING SO HARD THAT...
YOU CONFUSED YOURSELF?
YEAH...
swik
Schik☆
Here! ☆
HUH?
SWOOOOON
WHUH?!
I can't see!

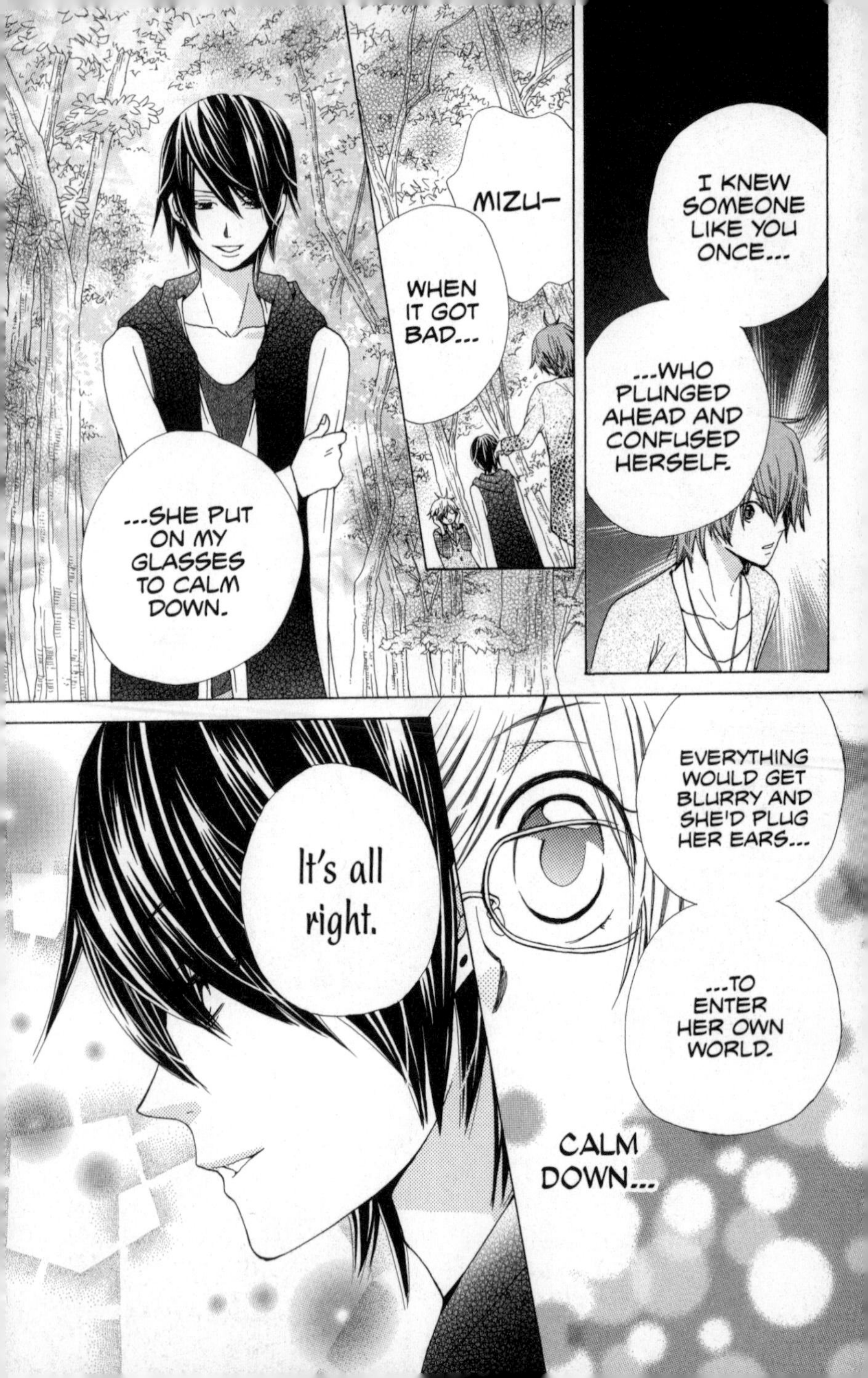
I KNEW SOMEONE LIKE YOU ONCE...
...WHO PLUNGED AHEAD AND CONFUSED HERSELF.
MIZU-
WHEN IT GOT BAD...
...SHE PUT ON MY GLASSES TO CALM DOWN.
EVERYTHING WOULD GET BLURRY AND SHE'D PLUG HER EARS...
...TO ENTER HER OWN WORLD.
It's all right.
CALM DOWN...

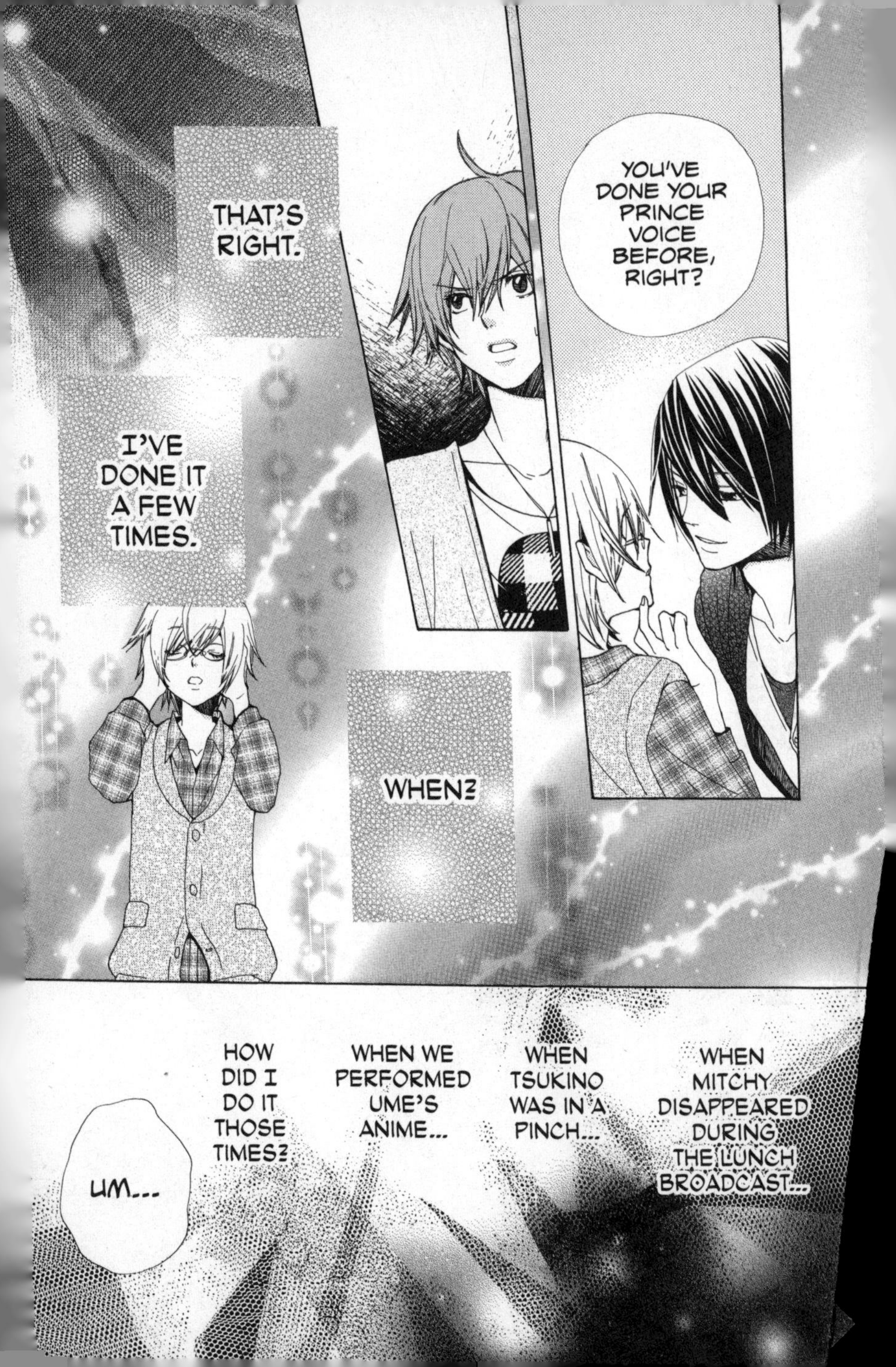
YOU'VE DONE YOUR PRINCE VOICE BEFORE, RIGHT?
THAT'S RIGHT.
I'VE DONE IT A FEW TIMES.
WHEN?
WHEN MITCHY DISAPPEARED DURING THE LUNCH BROADCAST...
WHEN TSUKINO WAS IN A PINCH...
WHEN WE PERFORMED UME'S ANIME...
HOW DID I DO IT THOSE TIMES?
UM...

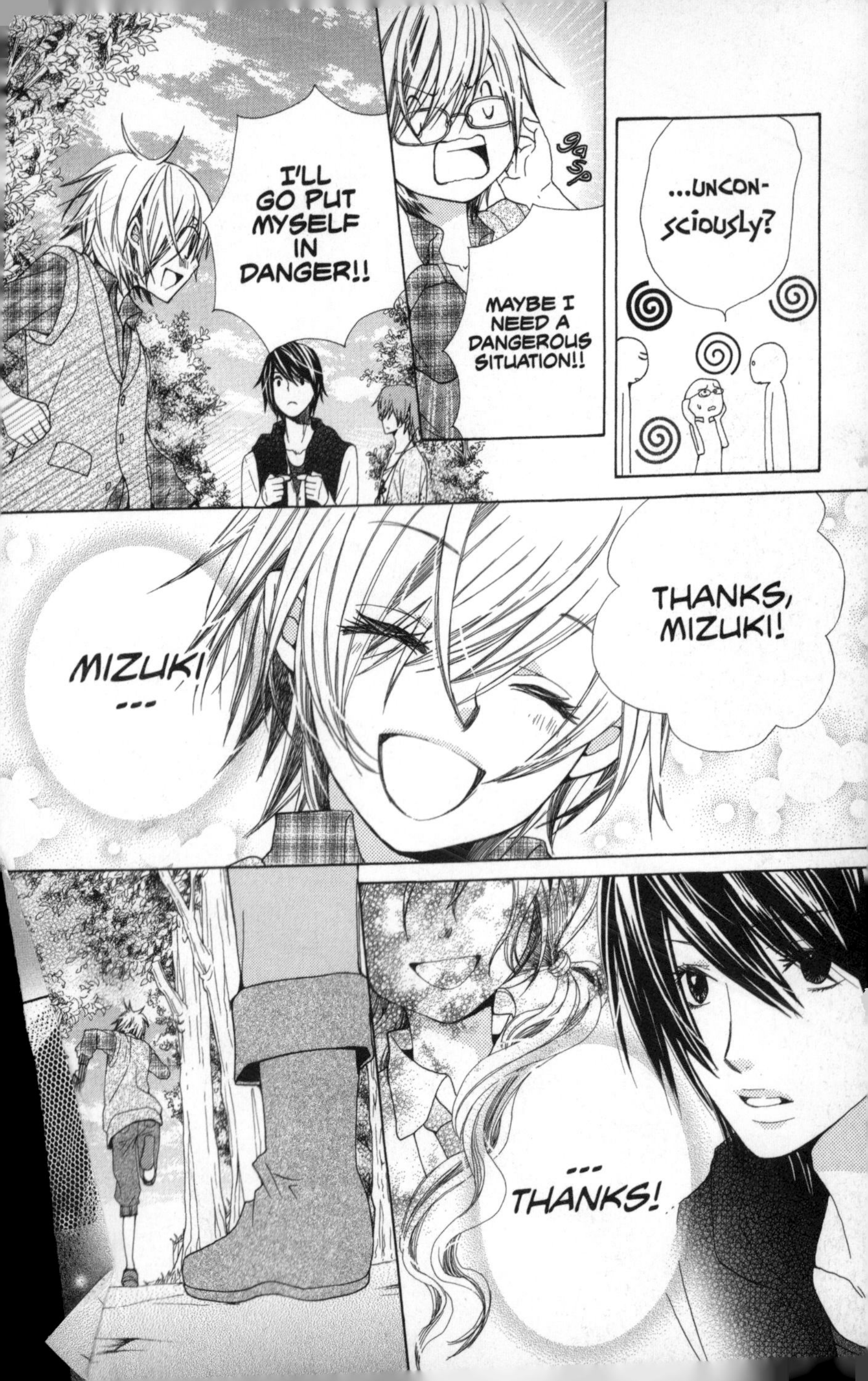
...UNCON-SCIOUSLY?
gasp
MAYBE I NEED A DANGEROUS SITUATION!!
I'LL GO PUT MYSELF IN DANGER!!
THANKS, MIZUKI!
MIZUKI...
...THANKS!

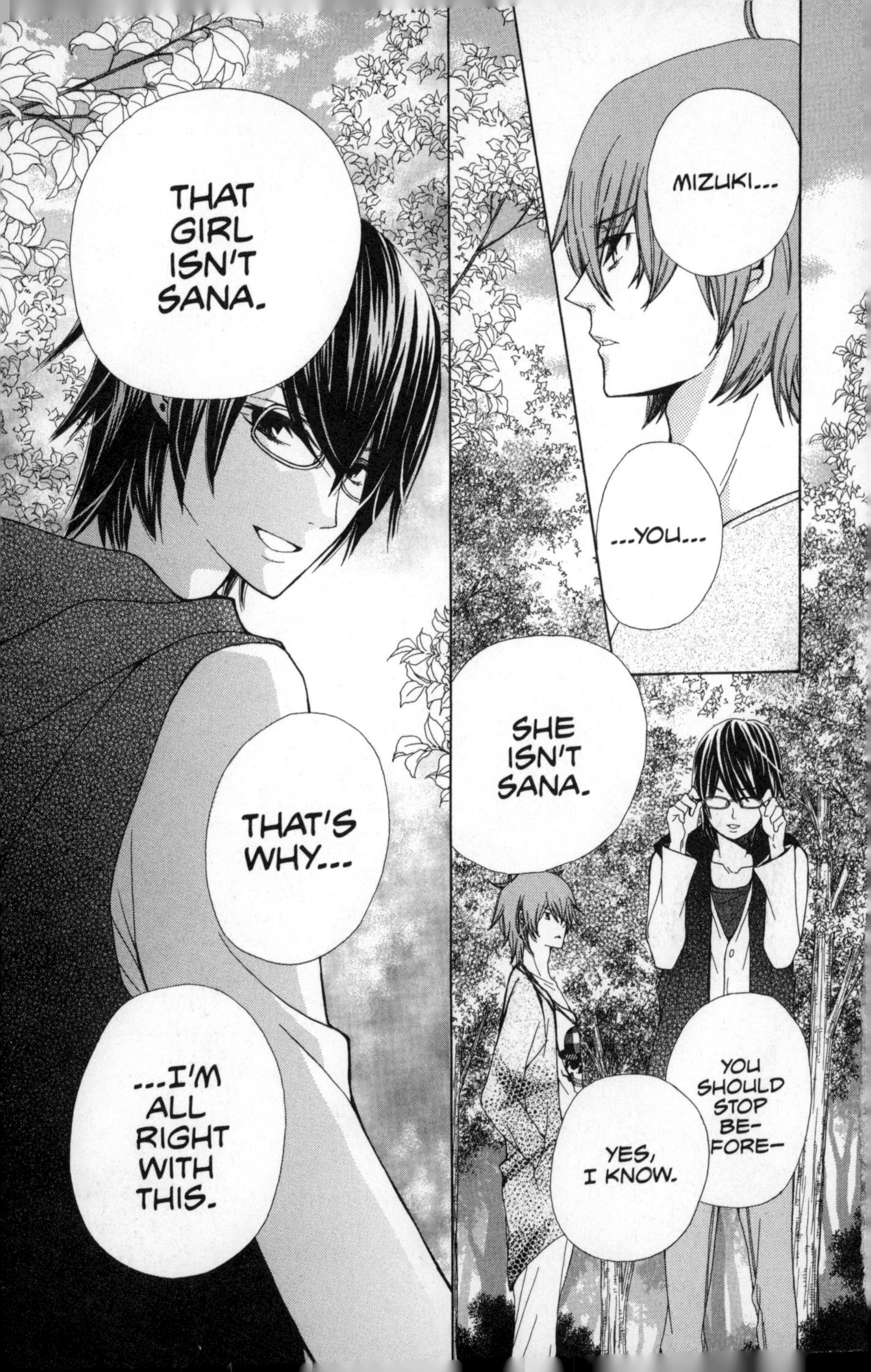
MIZUKI...
...YOU...
SHE ISN'T SANA.
YOU SHOULD STOP BE-FORE—
YES, I KNOW.
THAT GIRL ISN'T SANA.
THAT'S WHY...
...I'M ALL RIGHT WITH THIS.

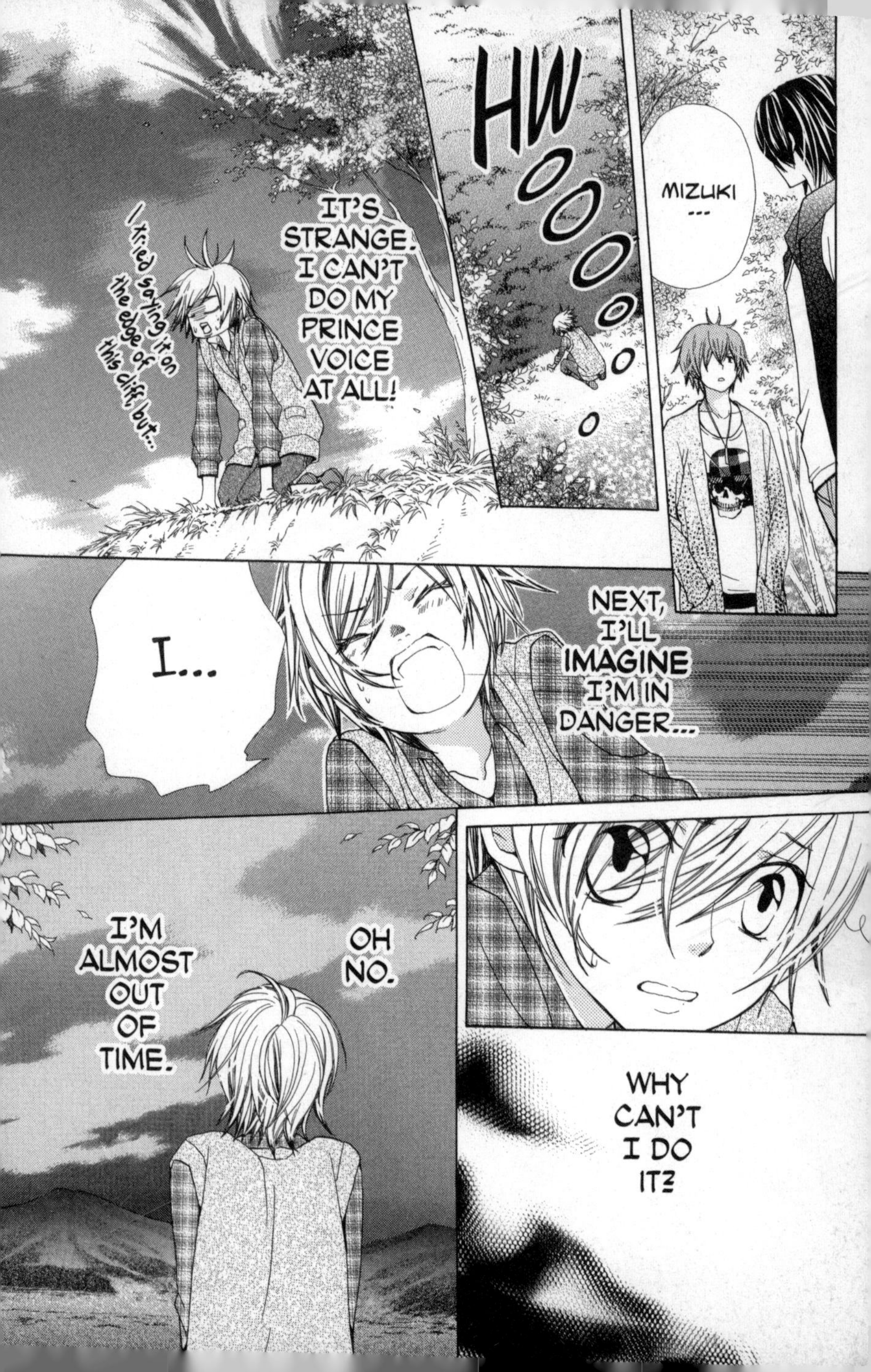
MIZUKI ...
HWOOOOOOO
IT'S STRANGE. I CAN'T DO MY PRINCE VOICE AT ALL!
I tried saying it on the edge of this cliff, but...
NEXT, I'LL IMAGINE I'M IN DANGER...
I...
WHY CAN'T I DO IT?
OH NO.
I'M ALMOST OUT OF TIME.

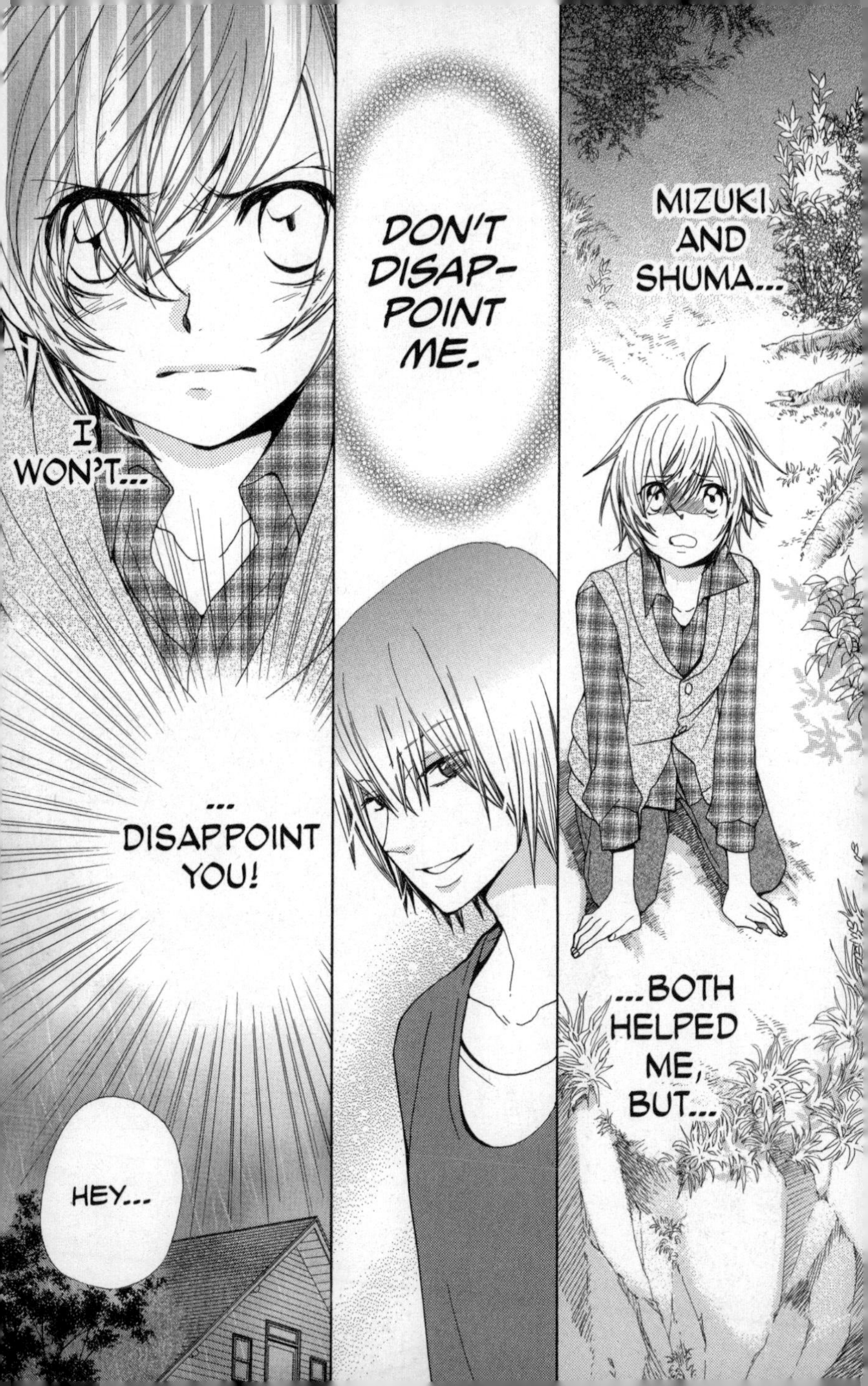
MIZUKI AND SHUMA...
...BOTH HELPED ME, BUT...
DON'T DISAP-POINT ME.
I WON'T...
...DISAPPOINT YOU!
HEY...

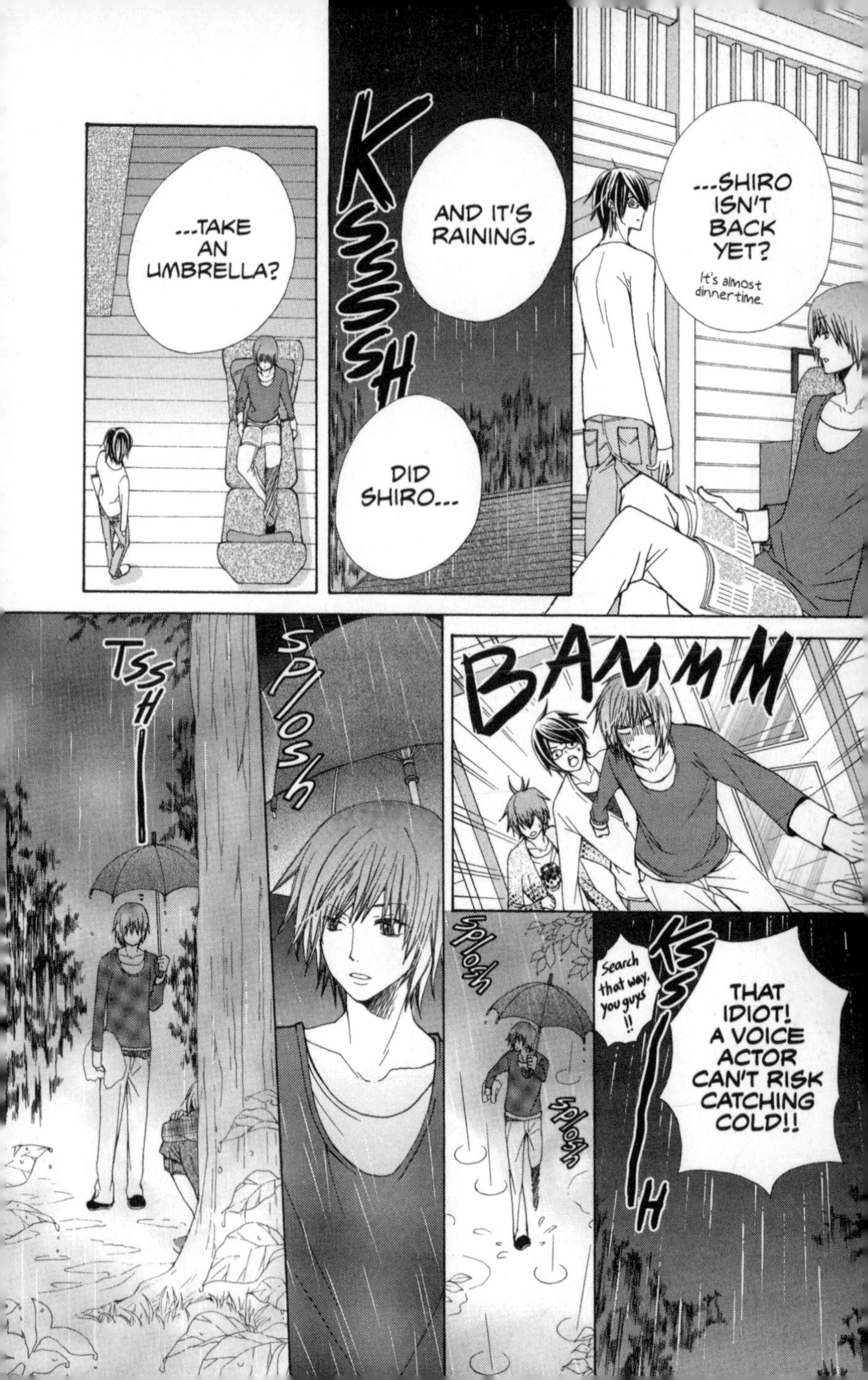

...SHIRO ISN'T BACK YET?
It's almost dinnertime.
KSSSSH
AND IT'S RAINING.
DID SHIRO...
...TAKE AN UMBRELLA?
BAMMM
KSSH
THAT IDIOT! A VOICE ACTOR CAN'T RISK CATCHING COLD!!
Search that way, you guys!!
splosh
splosh
splosh
TSSH

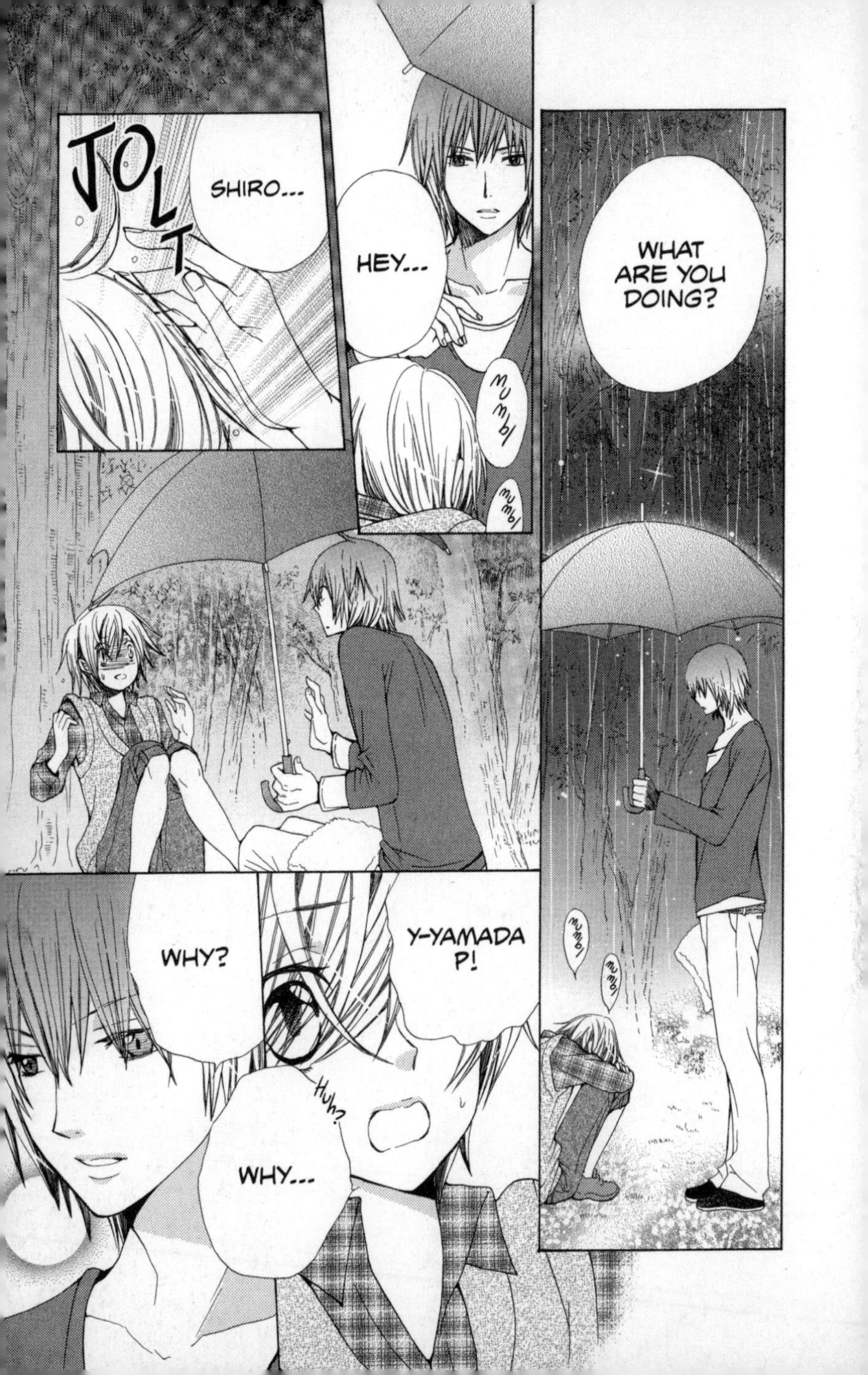
WHAT ARE YOU DOING?
mumbl
mumbl
HEY...
mumbl
mumbl
SHIRO...
JOLT
Y-YAMADA P!
Huh?
WHY?
WHY...

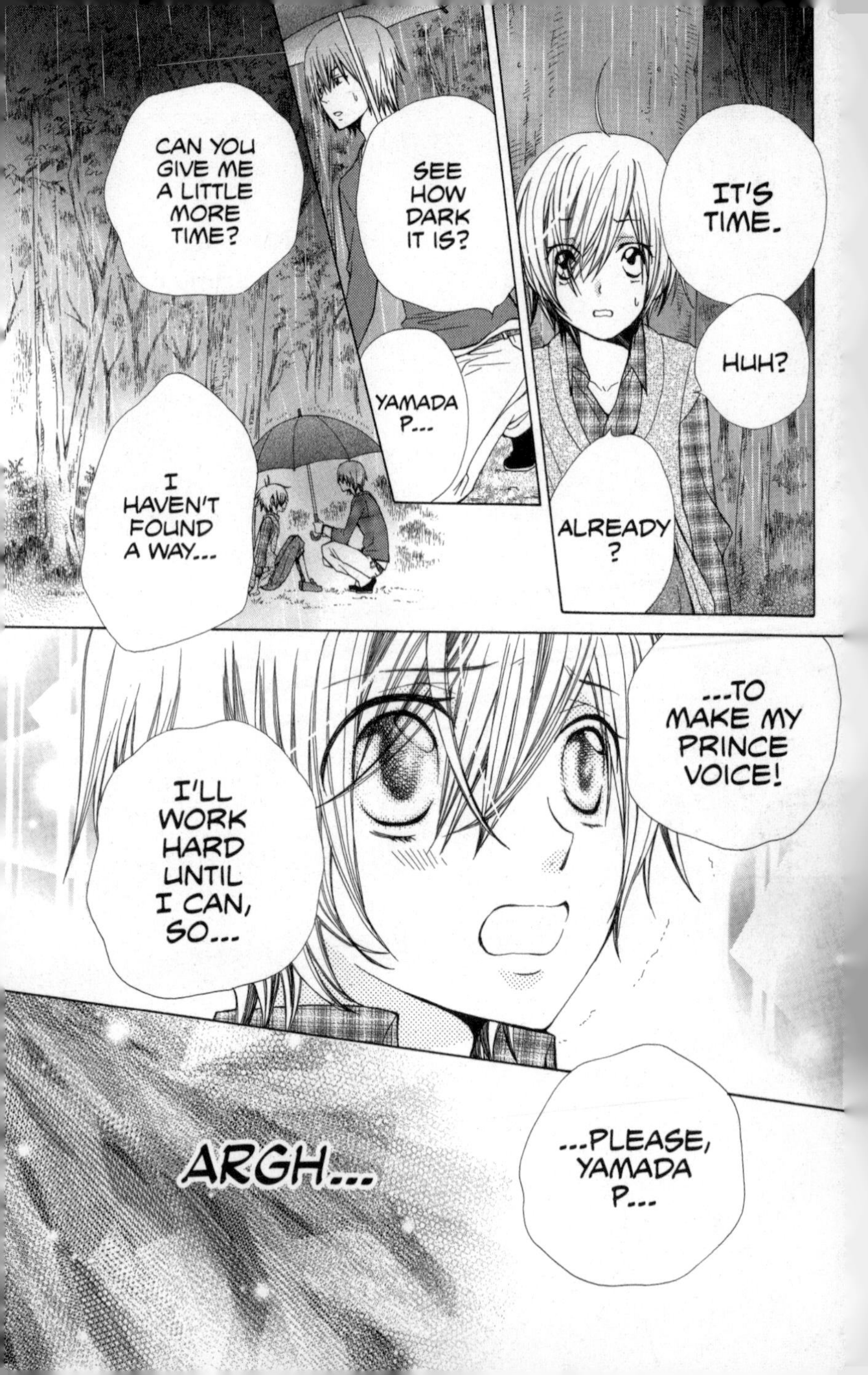
IT'S TIME.
HUH?
ALREADY?
SEE HOW DARK IT IS?
YAMADA P...
CAN YOU GIVE ME A LITTLE MORE TIME?
I HAVEN'T FOUND A WAY...
...TO MAKE MY PRINCE VOICE!
I'LL WORK HARD UNTIL I CAN, SO...
...PLEASE, YAMADA P...
ARGH...

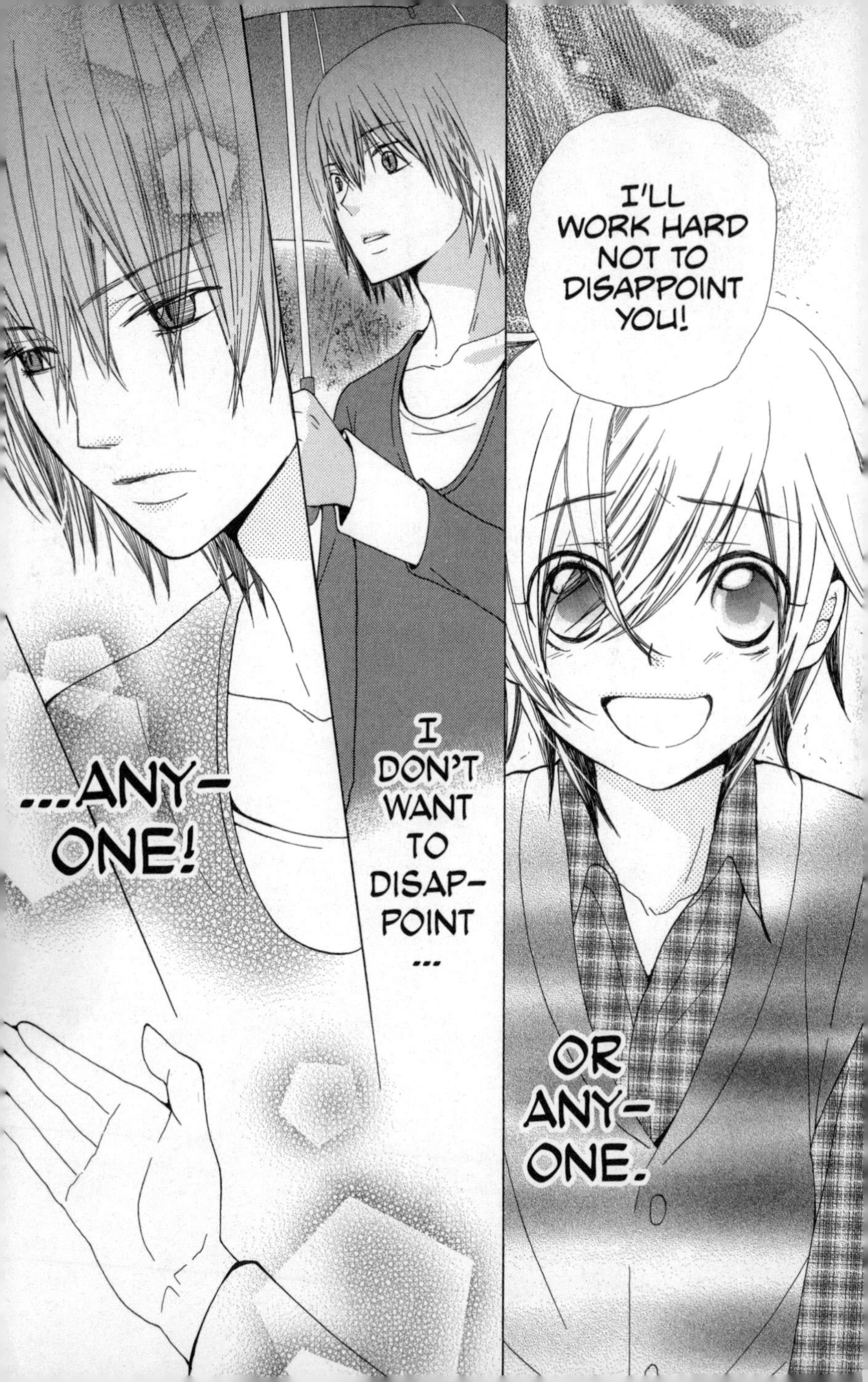
I'LL WORK HARD NOT TO DISAPPOINT YOU!
OR ANY-ONE.
I DON'T WANT TO DISAP-POINT ...
...ANY-ONE!

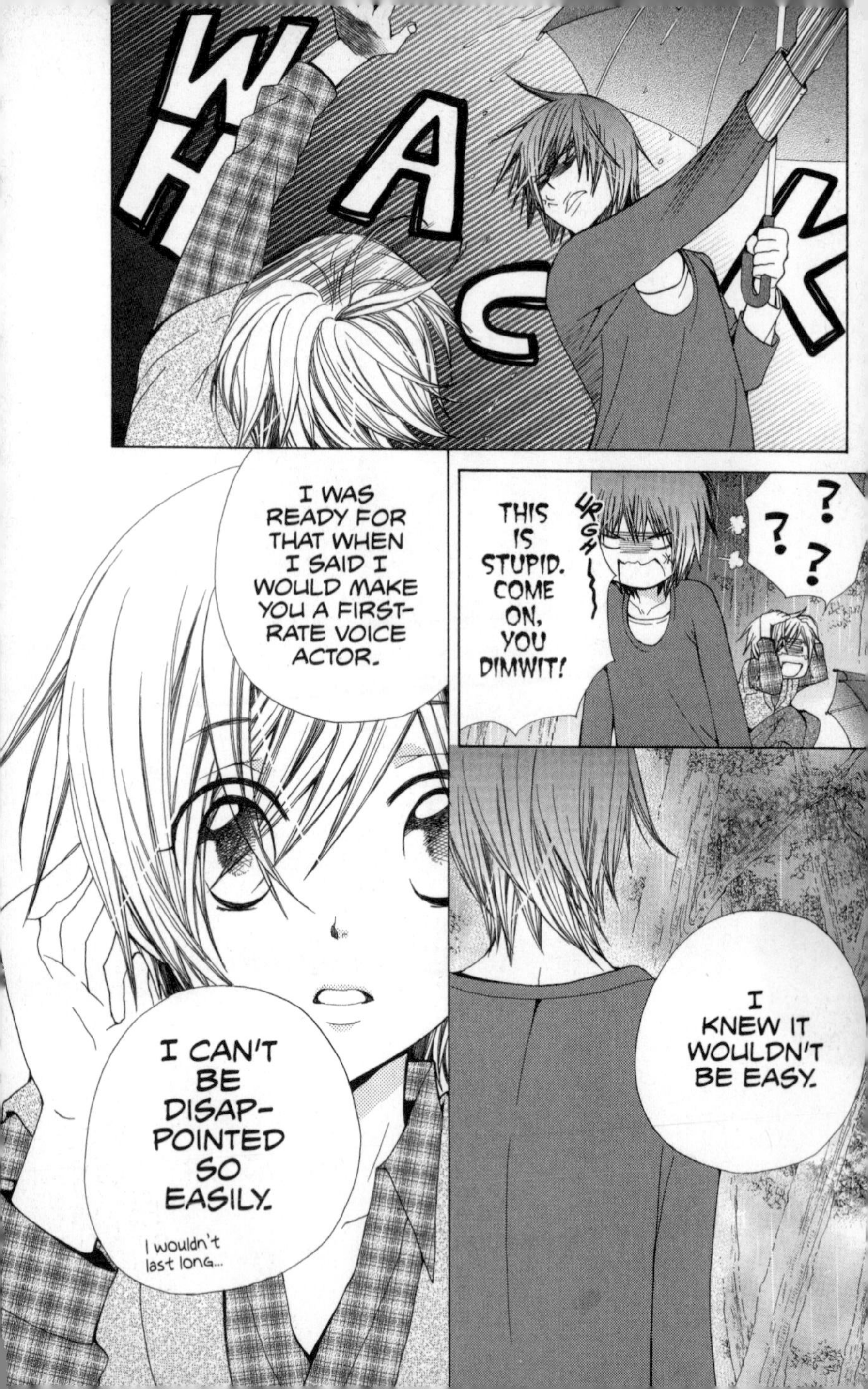
WHACK
???
URGH
THIS IS STUPID. COME ON, YOU DIMWIT!
I KNEW IT WOULDN'T BE EASY.
I WAS READY FOR THAT WHEN I SAID I WOULD MAKE YOU A FIRST-RATE VOICE ACTOR.
I CAN'T BE DISAPPOINTED SO EASILY.
I wouldn't last long...

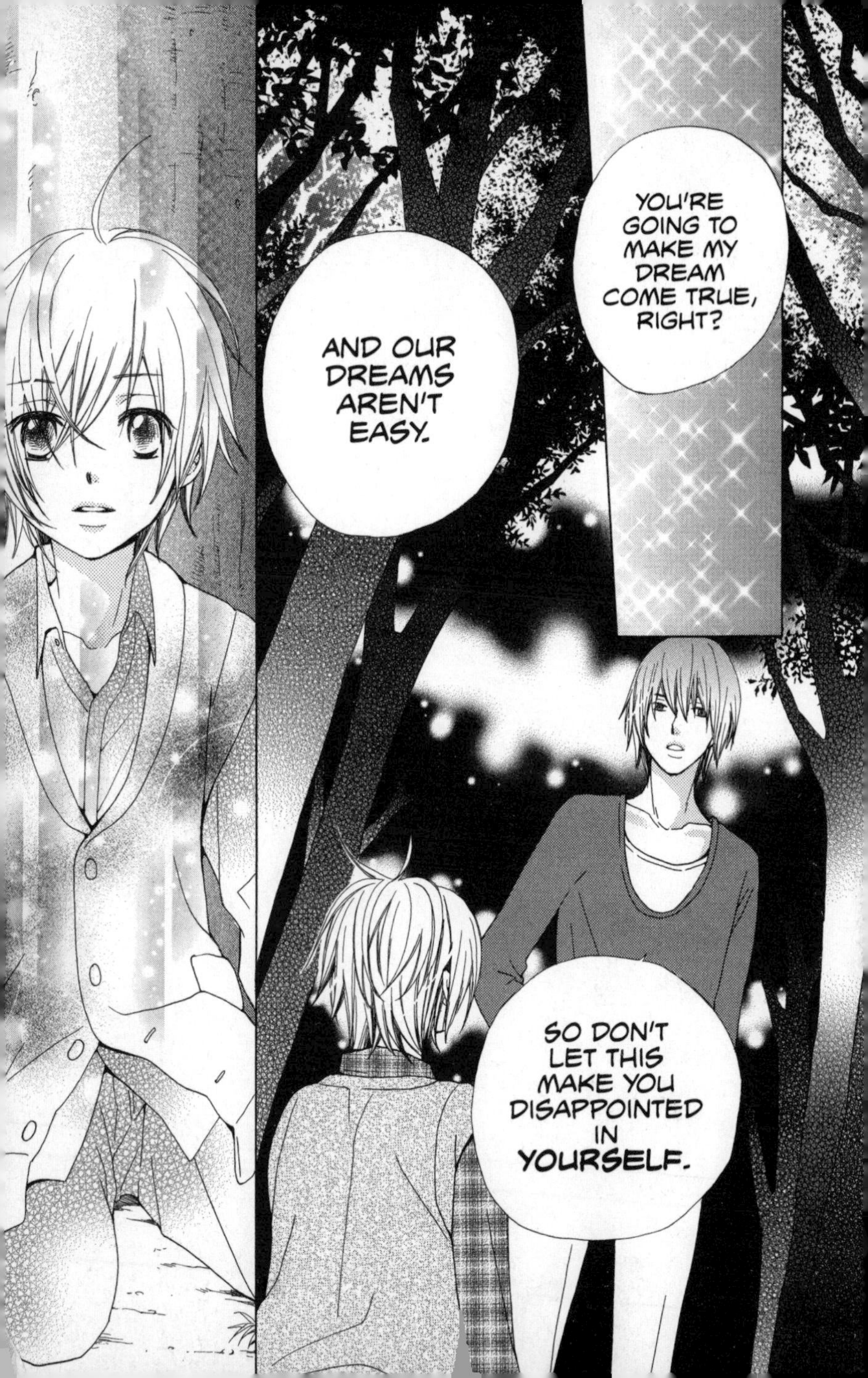
YOU'RE GOING TO MAKE MY DREAM COME TRUE, RIGHT?
AND OUR DREAMS AREN'T EASY.
SO DON'T LET THIS MAKE YOU DISAPPOINTED IN YOURSELF.

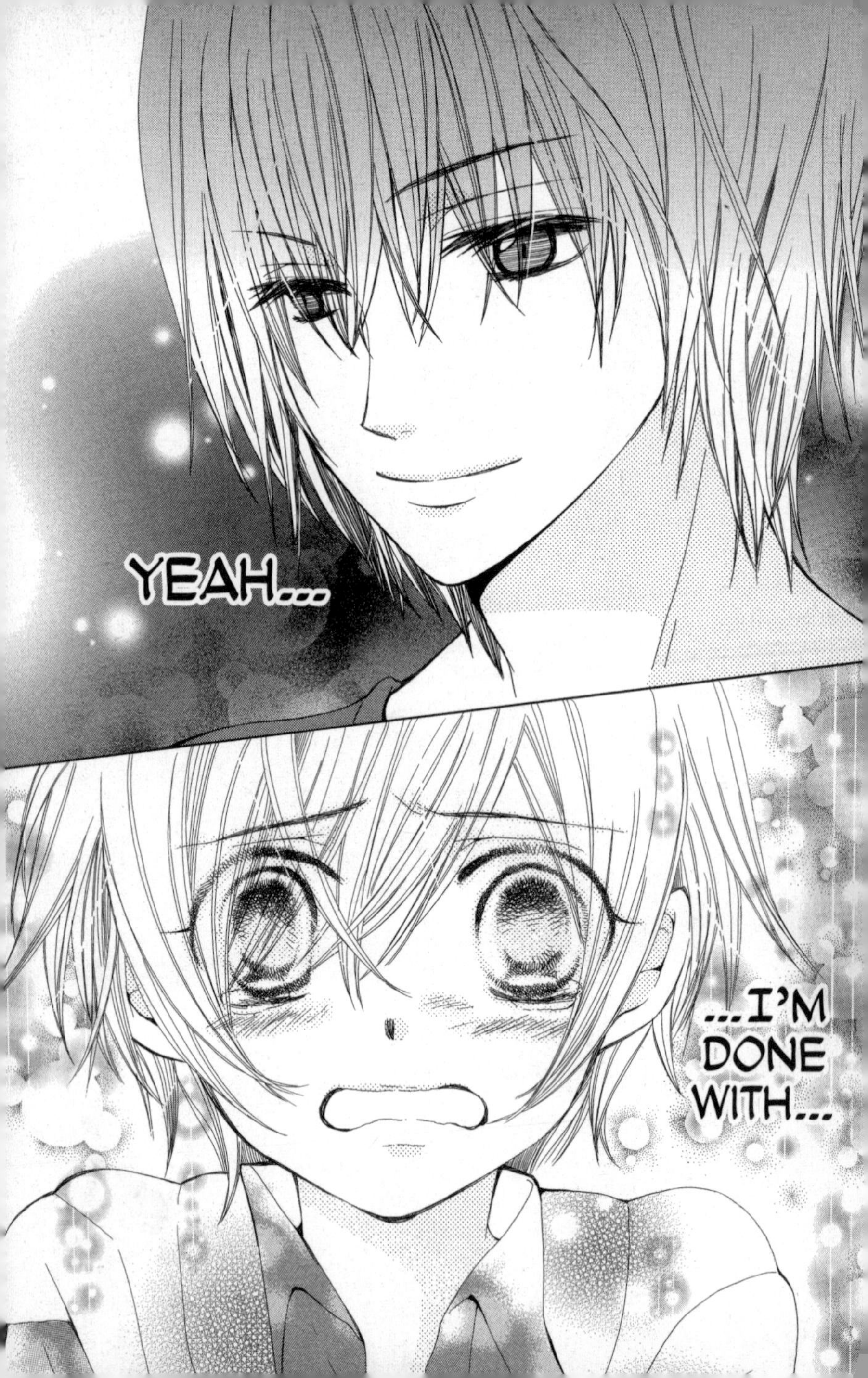
YEAH...
...I'M DONE WITH...

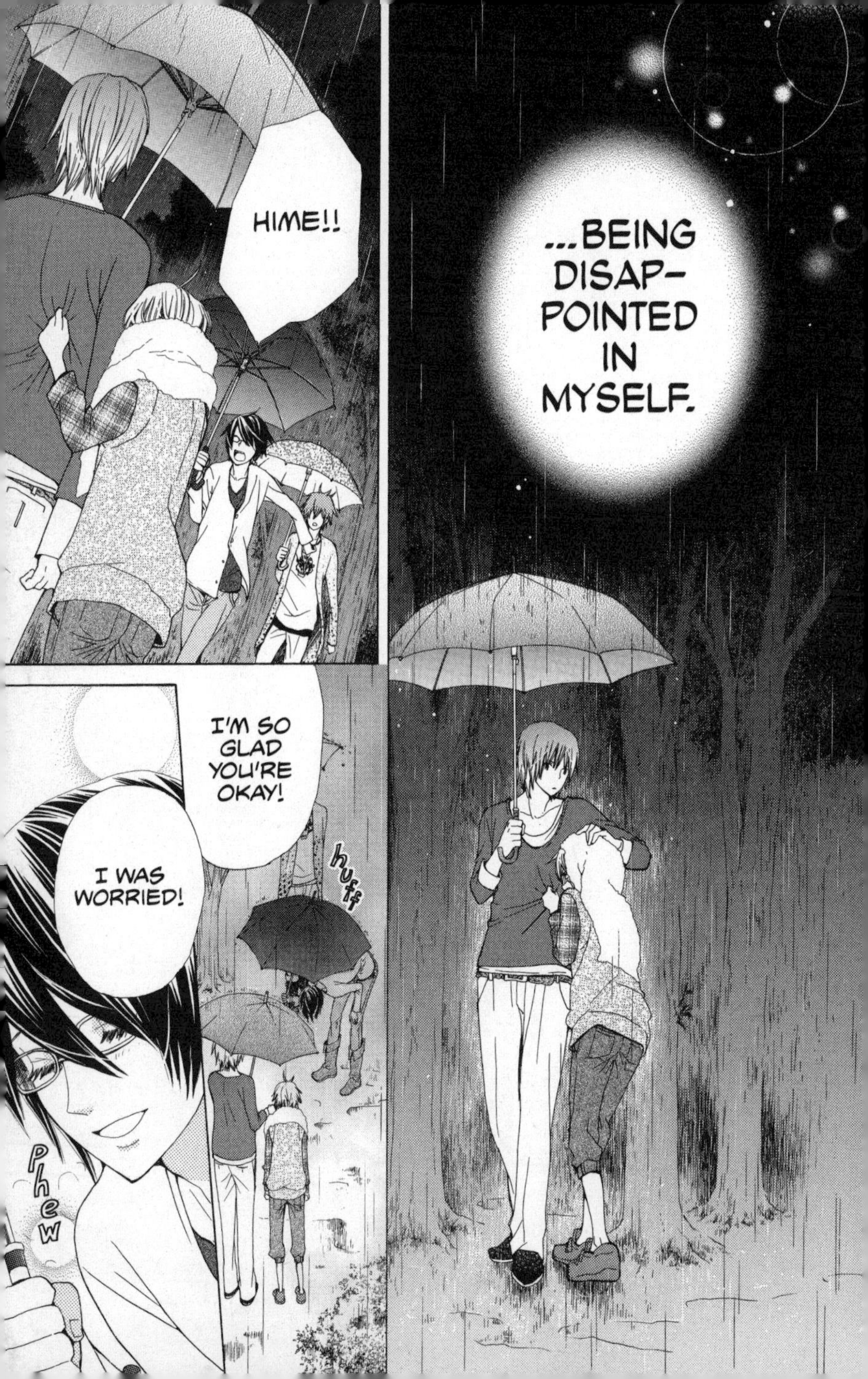
...BEING DISAPPOINTED IN MYSELF.
HIME!!
I'M SO GLAD YOU'RE OKAY!
huff
I WAS WORRIED!
Phew

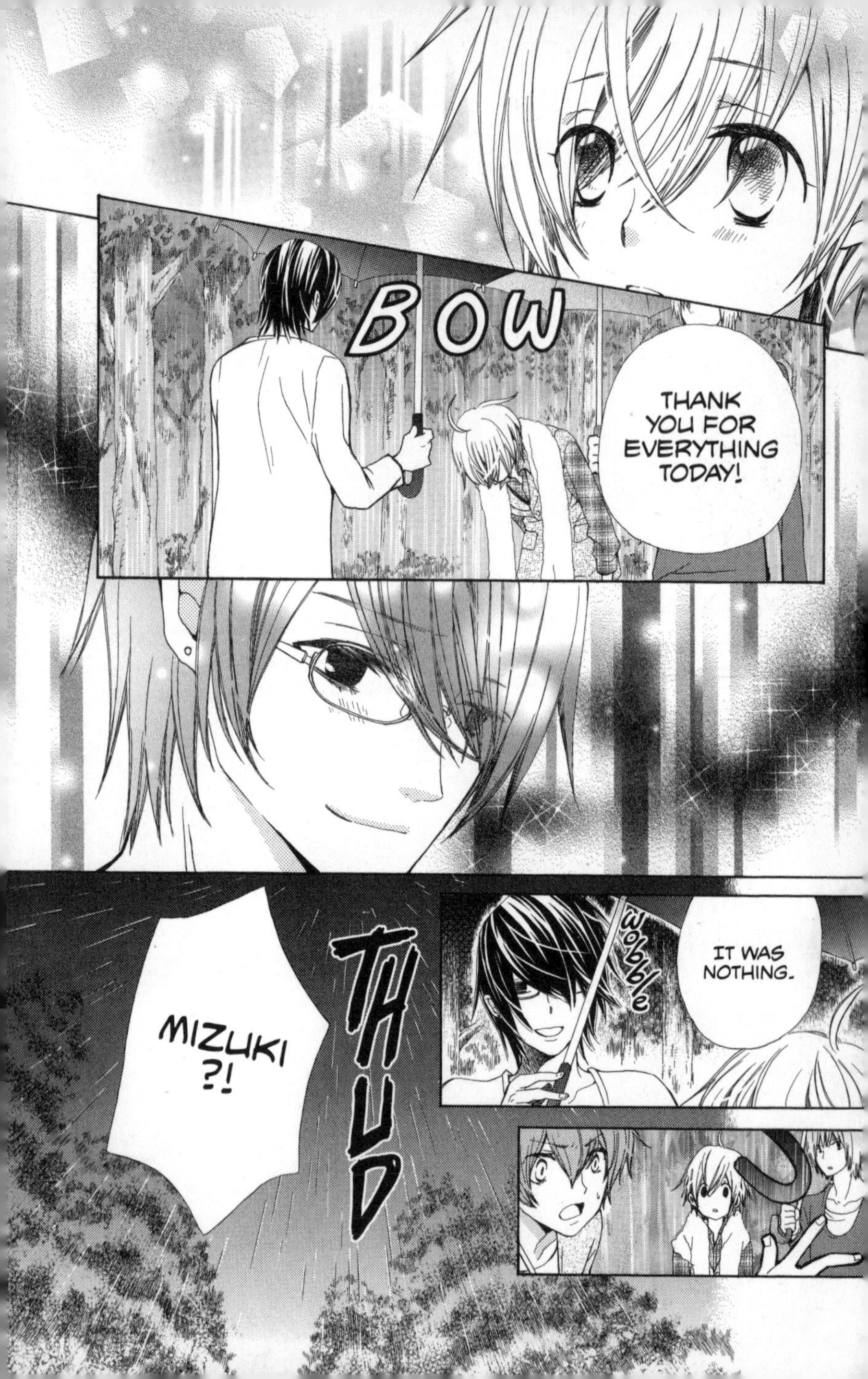
THANK YOU FOR EVERYTHING TODAY!
BOW
IT WAS NOTHING.
wobble
THUD
MIZUKI ?!

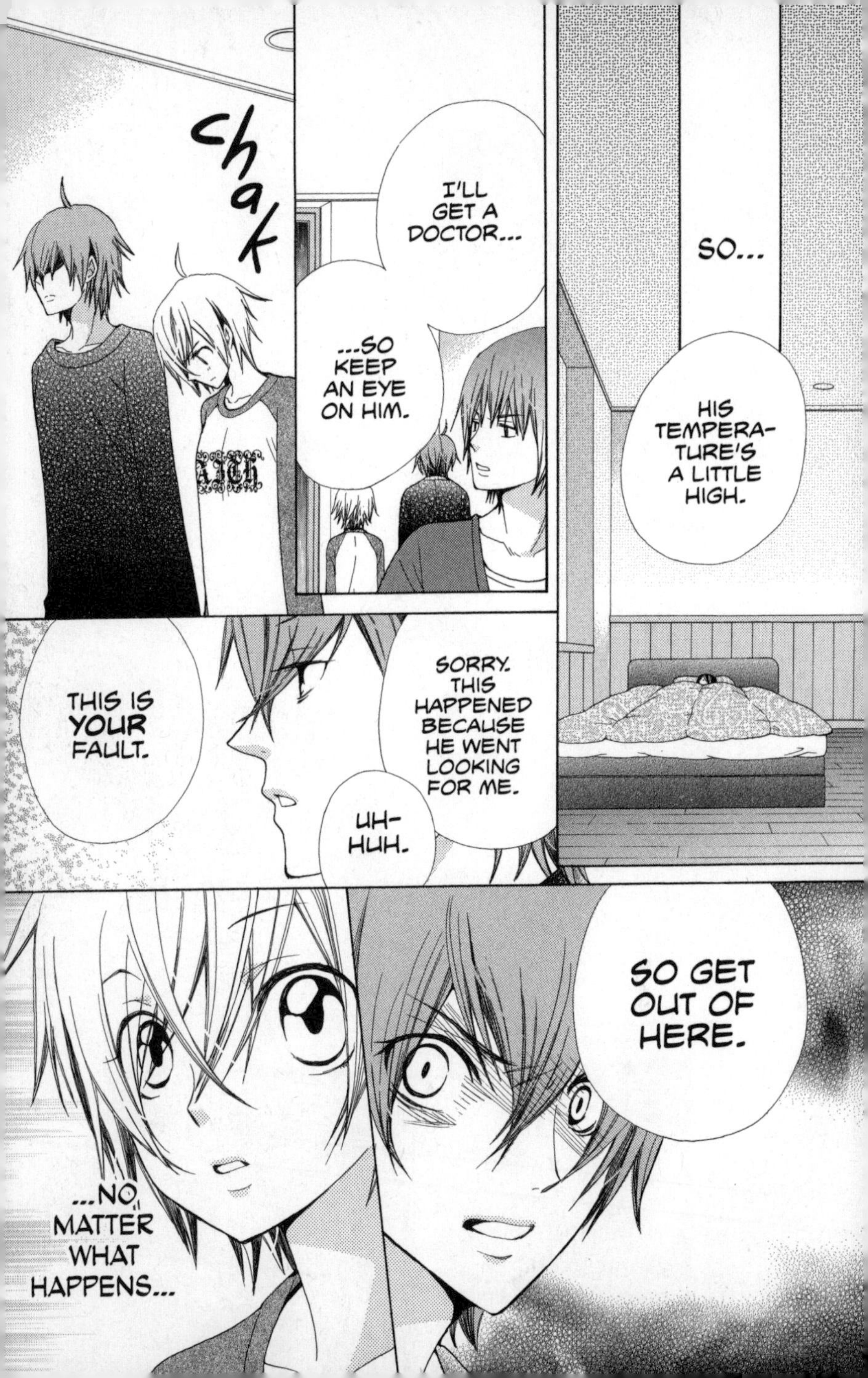
SO...
HIS TEMPERA-TURE'S A LITTLE HIGH.
I'LL GET A DOCTOR...
...SO KEEP AN EYE ON HIM.
chak
SORRY. THIS HAPPENED BECAUSE HE WENT LOOKING FOR ME.
UH-HUH.
THIS IS YOUR FAULT.
SO GET OUT OF HERE.
...NO MATTER WHAT HAPPENS...

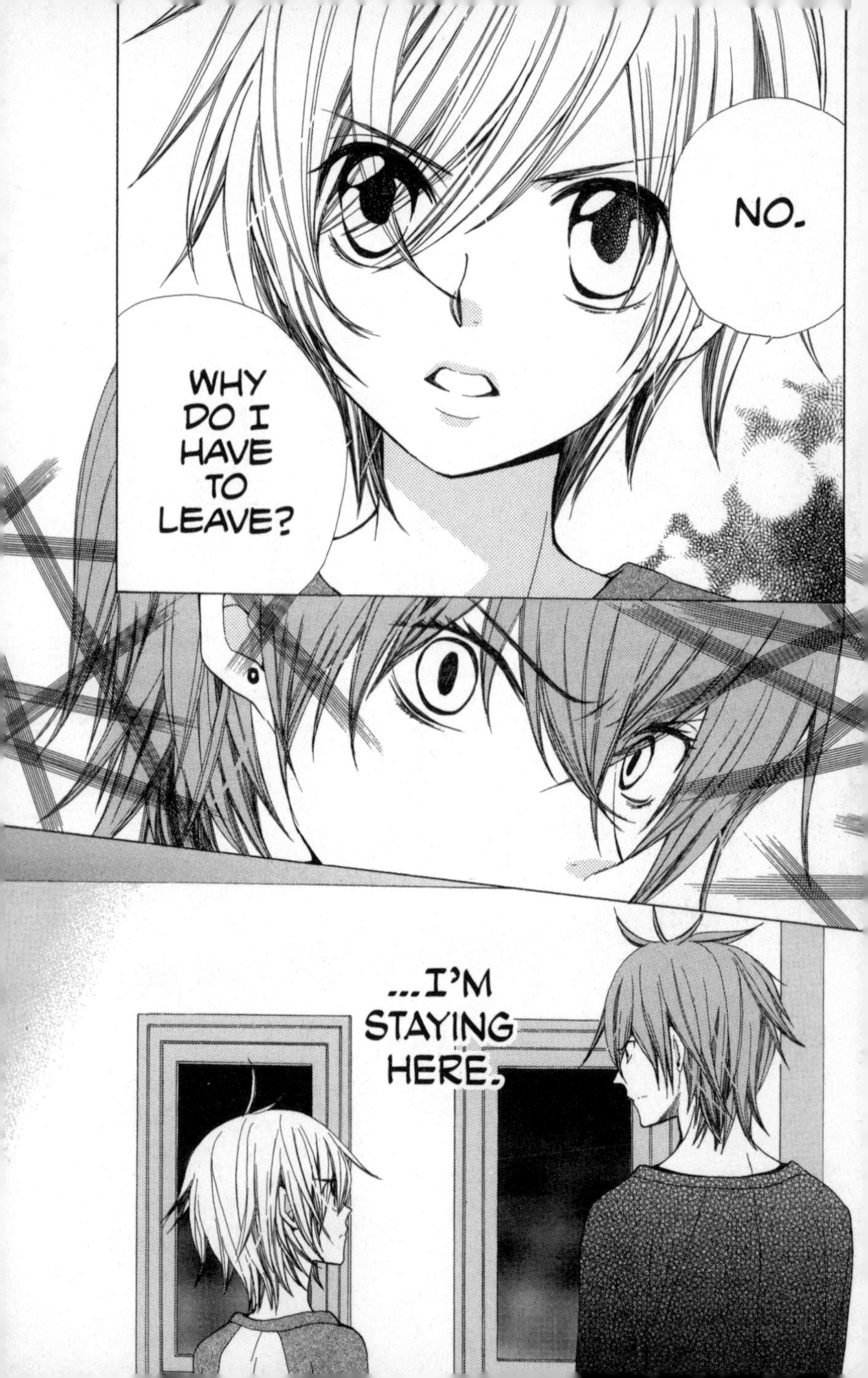
NO.
WHY DO I HAVE TO LEAVE?
...I'M STAYING HERE.

Chapter 16

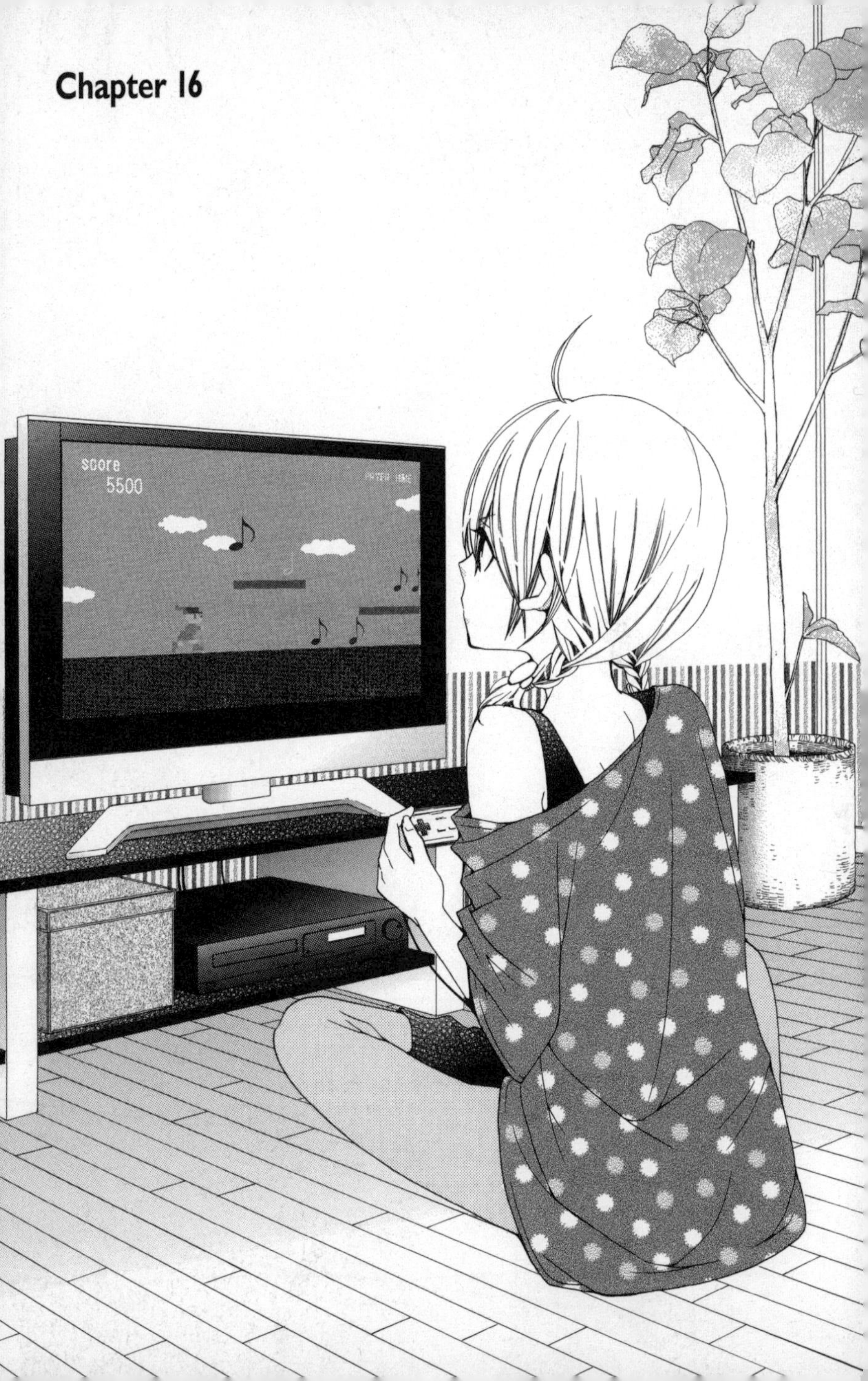
score
5500

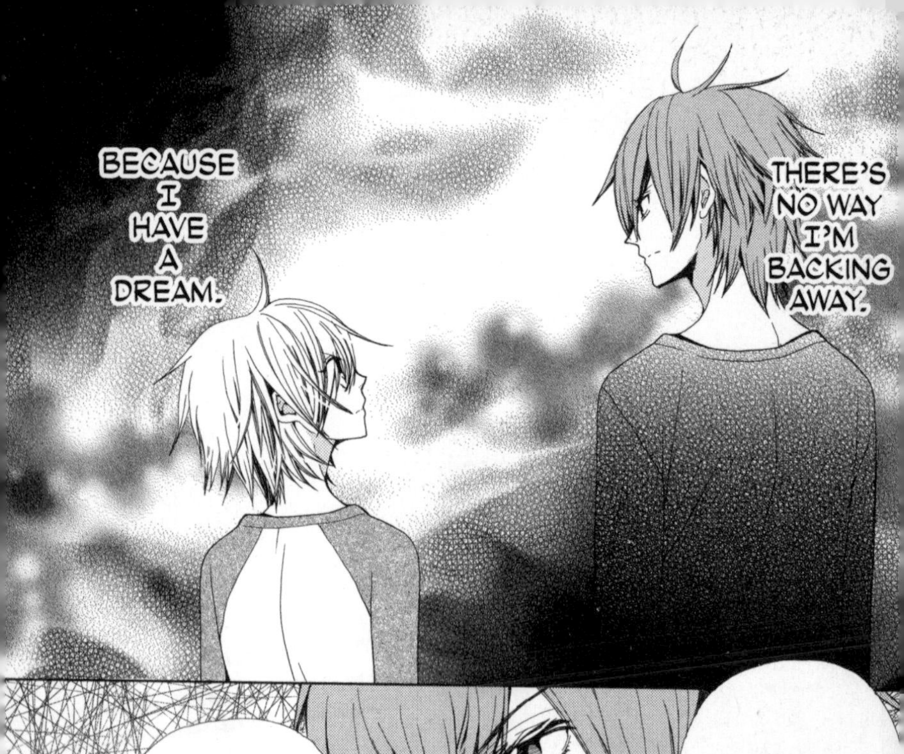
THERE'S NO WAY I'M BACKING AWAY.
BECAUSE I HAVE A DREAM.

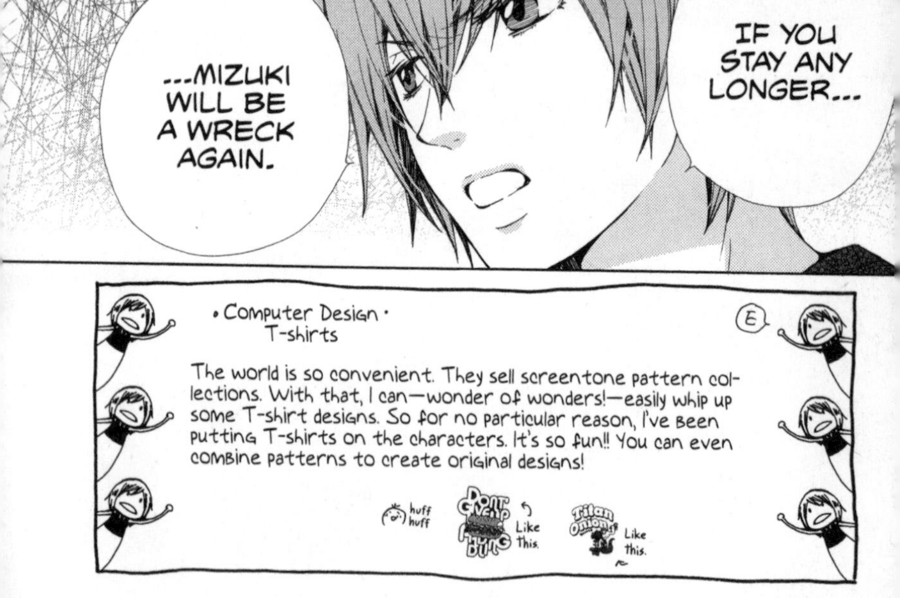
IF YOU STAY ANY LONGER...
...MIZUKI WILL BE A WRECK AGAIN.

• Computer Design •
T-shirts

The world is so convenient. They sell screentone pattern collections. With that, I can—wonder of wonders!—easily whip up some T-shirt designs. So for no particular reason, I've been putting T-shirts on the characters. It's so fun!! You can even combine patterns to create original designs!

huff huff

Like this.

Like this.

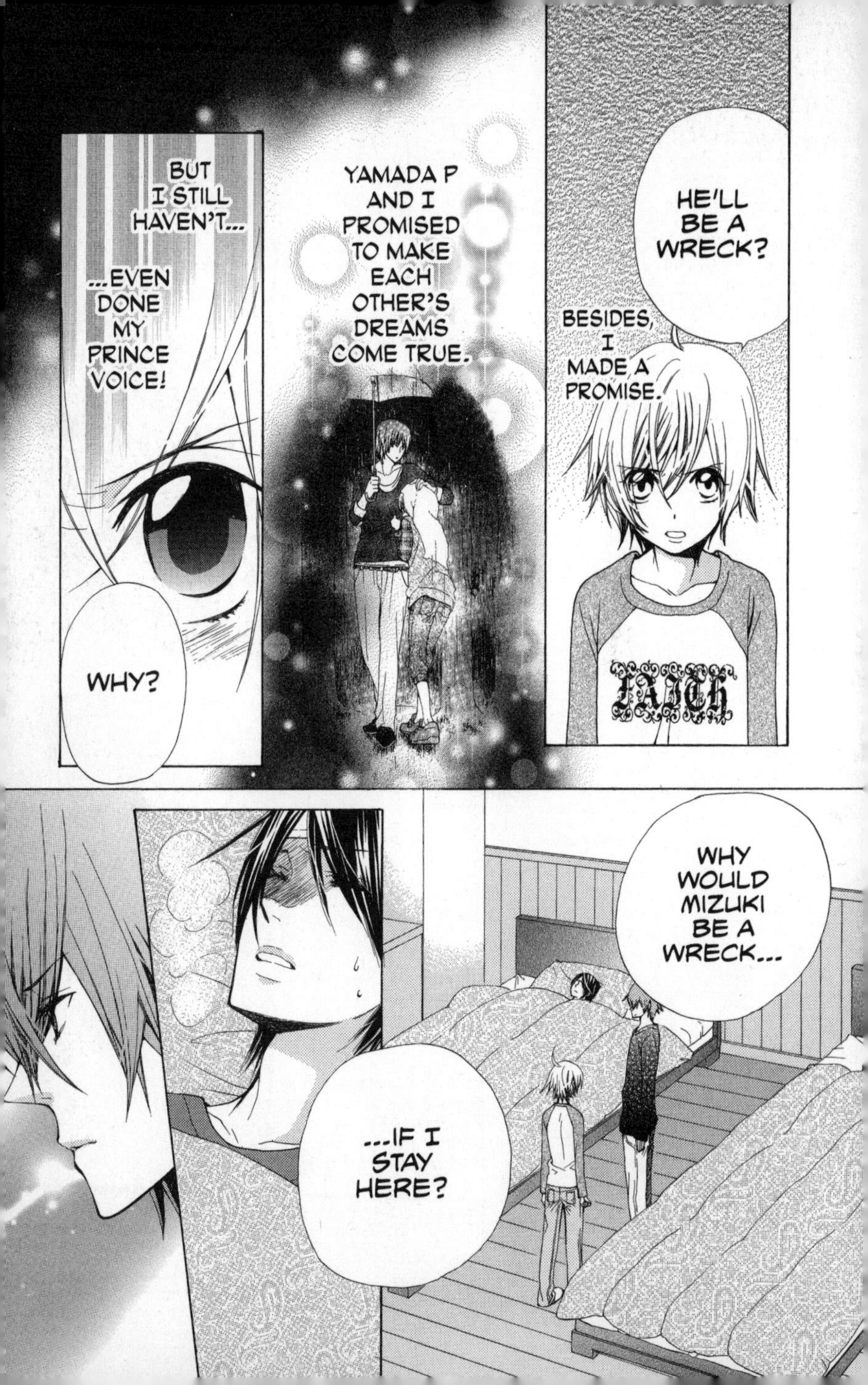
HE'LL BE A WRECK?
BESIDES, I MADE A PROMISE.
FAITH
YAMADA P AND I PROMISED TO MAKE EACH OTHER'S DREAMS COME TRUE.
BUT I STILL HAVEN'T...
...EVEN DONE MY PRINCE VOICE!
WHY?
WHY WOULD MIZUKI BE A WRECK...
...IF I STAY HERE?

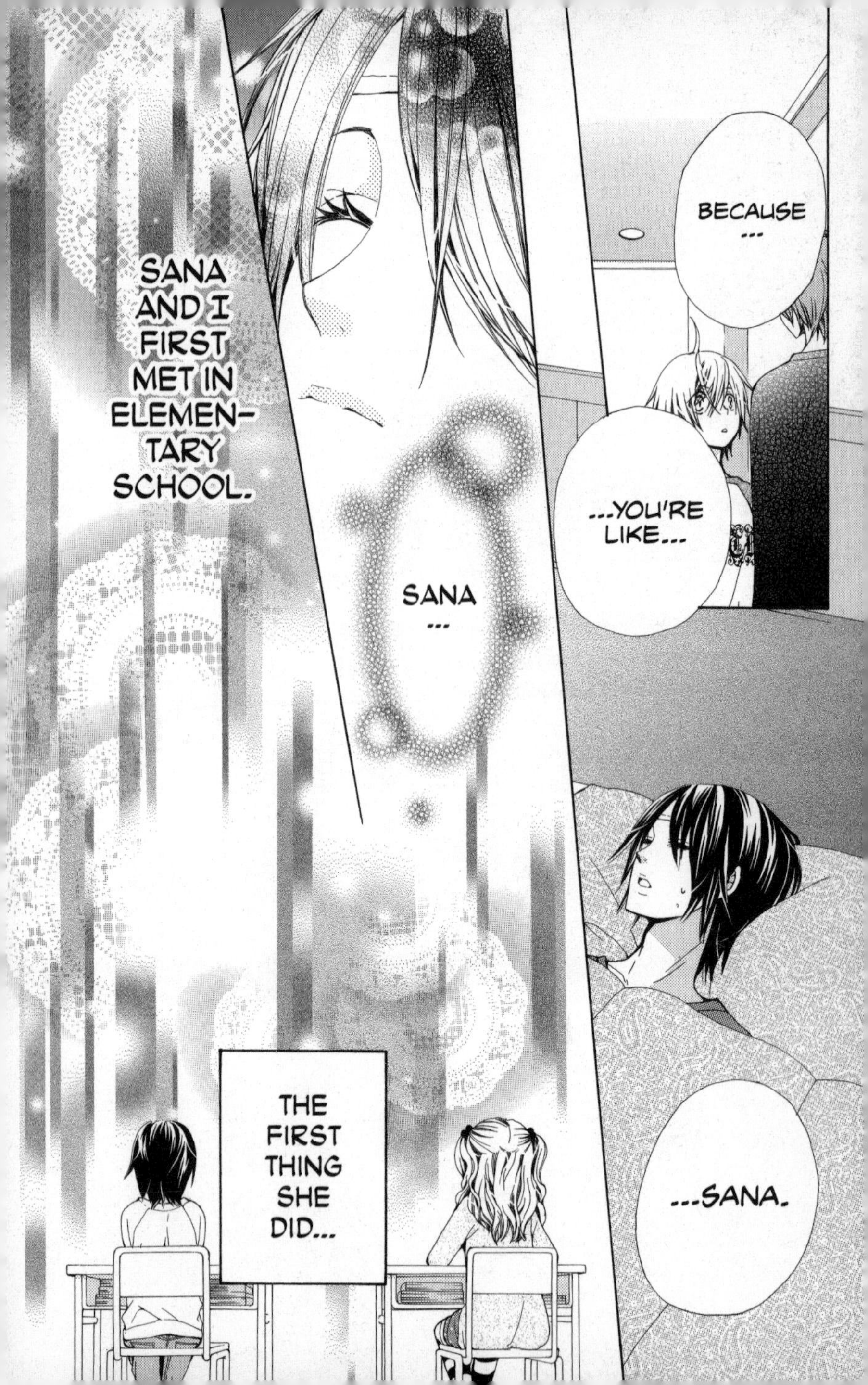
BECAUSE ...
...YOU'RE LIKE...
...SANA.
SANA ...
SANA AND I FIRST MET IN ELEMEN-TARY SCHOOL.
THE FIRST THING SHE DID...

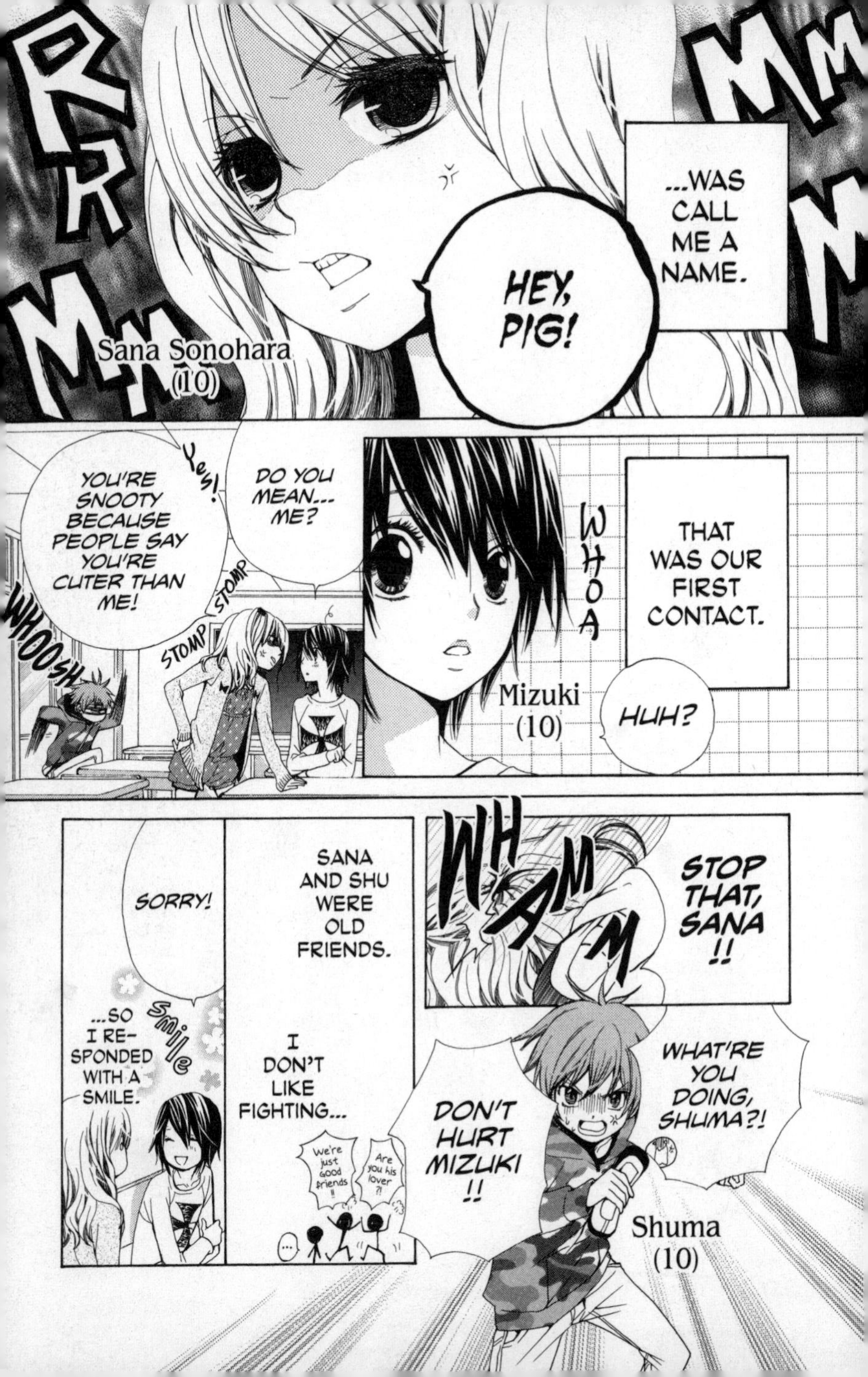
MMMM
...WAS CALL ME A NAME.
HEY, PIG!
RRMM
Sana Sonohara (10)
THAT WAS OUR FIRST CONTACT.
WHOA
HUH?
Mizuki (10)
DO YOU MEAN... ME?
Yes!
YOU'RE SNOOTY BECAUSE PEOPLE SAY YOU'RE CUTER THAN ME!
STOMP STOMP
WHOOSH
STOP THAT, SANA!!
WHAM
WHAT'RE YOU DOING, SHUMA?!
DON'T HURT MIZUKI!!
Shuma (10)
SANA AND SHU WERE OLD FRIENDS.
I DON'T LIKE FIGHTING...
Are you his lover?!
We're just Good friends!!
...
SORRY!
...SO I RE- SPONDED WITH A SMILE.
Smile

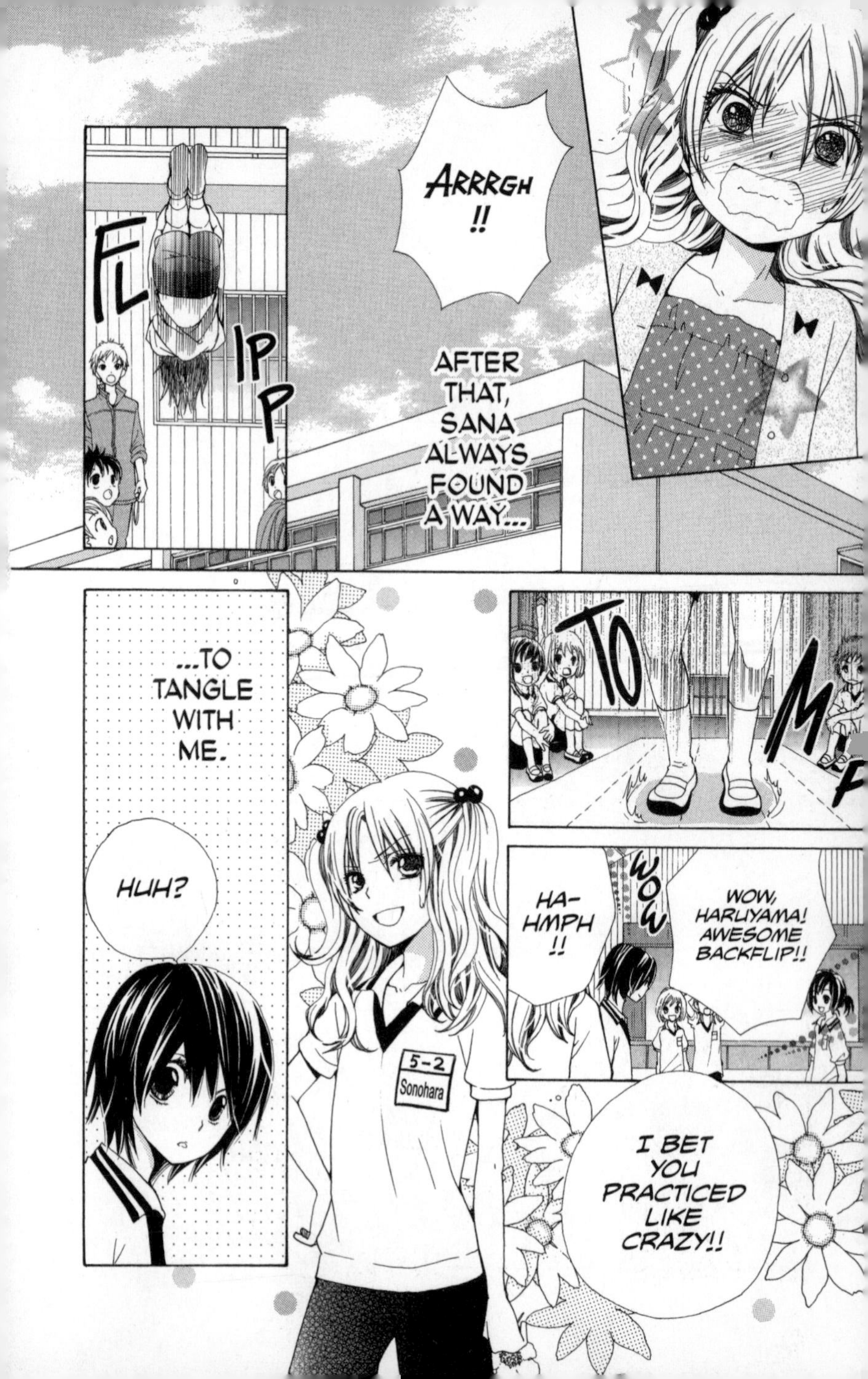
ARRRGH !!
AFTER THAT, SANA ALWAYS FOUND A WAY...
FLIPP
TOMP
WOW, HARUYAMA! AWESOME BACKFLIP!!
WOW
HA-HMPH !!
I BET YOU PRACTICED LIKE CRAZY!!
5-2
Sonohara
...TO TANGLE WITH ME.
HUH?

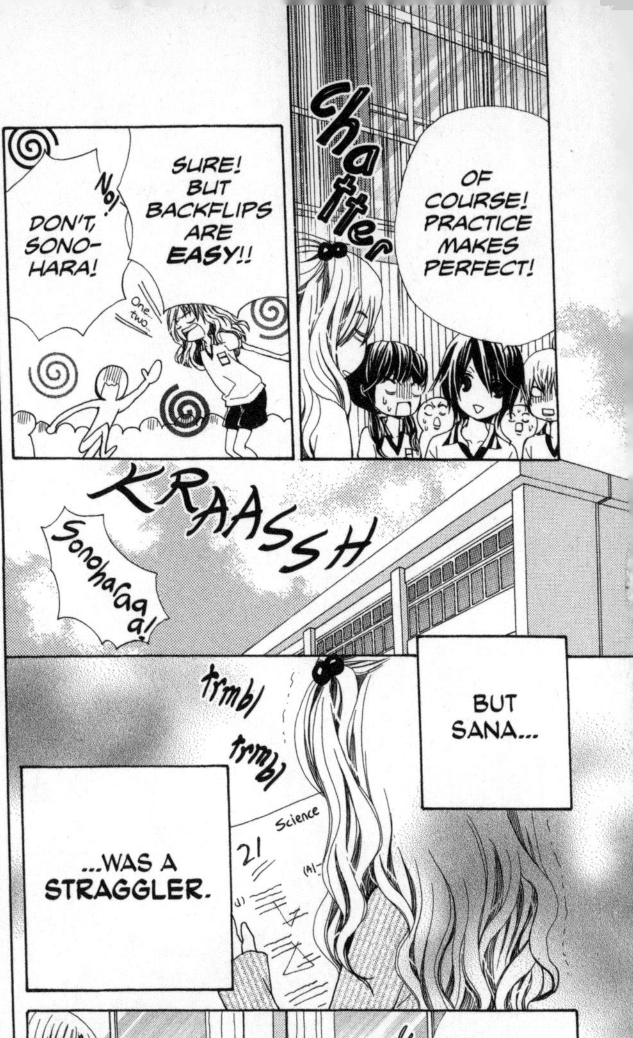
Chatter
OF COURSE! PRACTICE MAKES PERFECT!
SURE! BUT BACKFLIPS ARE EASY!!
No!
DON'T, SONO-HARA!
One... two...
KRAASSH
Sonoharaaa!
BUT SANA...
trmbl
trmbl
Science
21
...WAS A STRAGGLER.
Yay
WOW, HARUYAMA!
YOU PLAY PIANO SO WELL FOR SOMEONE WHO DOESN'T TAKE LESSONS!
Yay

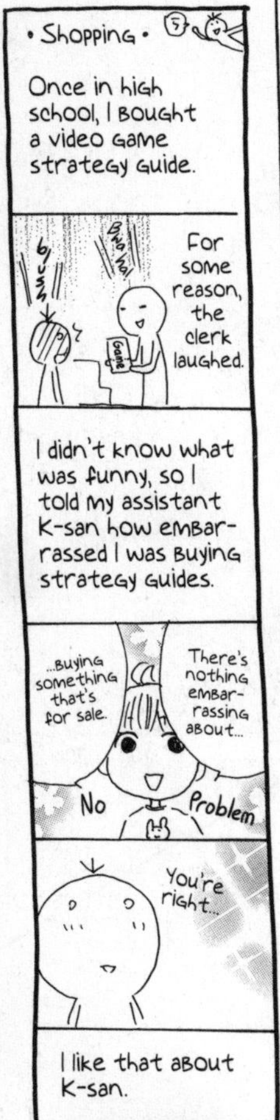
• Shopping •
Once in high school, I bought a video game strategy guide.
For some reason, the clerk laughed.
Game
I didn't know what was funny, so I told my assistant K-san how embarrassed I was buying strategy guides.
There's nothing embarrassing about...
...buying something that's for sale.
No
Problem
You're right...
I like that about K-san.
Mizuki (age 6)

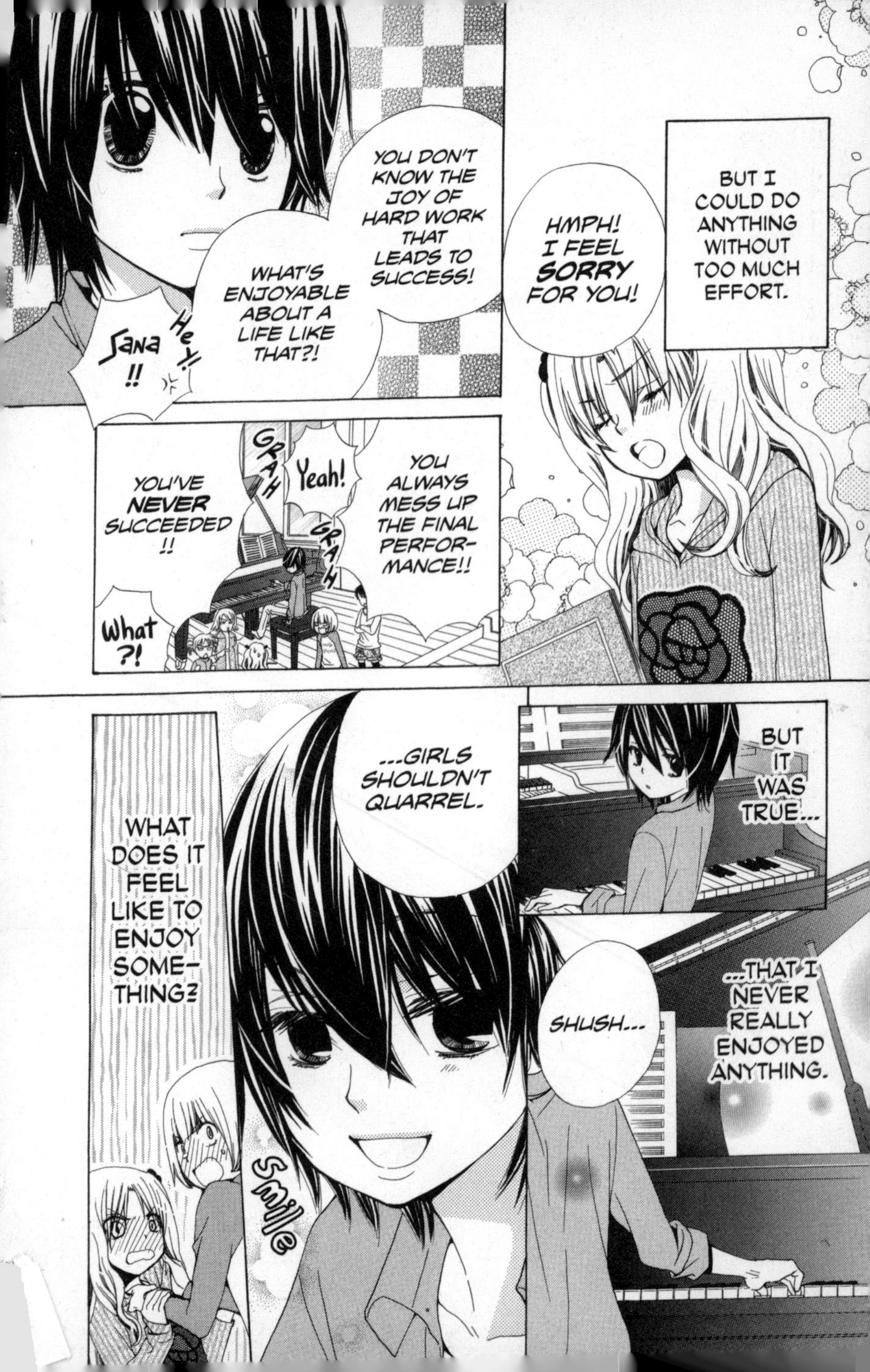
BUT I COULD DO ANYTHING WITHOUT TOO MUCH EFFORT.
HMPH! I FEEL **SORRY** FOR YOU!
YOU DON'T KNOW THE JOY OF HARD WORK THAT LEADS TO SUCCESS!
WHAT'S ENJOYABLE ABOUT A LIFE LIKE THAT?!
Hey!! Sana!!
YOU ALWAYS MESS UP THE FINAL PERFORMANCE!!
Yeah!
GRAH GRAH
YOU'VE **NEVER** SUCCEEDED!!
What?!
BUT IT WAS TRUE...
...THAT I NEVER REALLY ENJOYED ANYTHING.
...GIRLS SHOULDN'T QUARREL.
SHUSH...
WHAT DOES IT FEEL LIKE TO ENJOY SOMETHING?
Smile

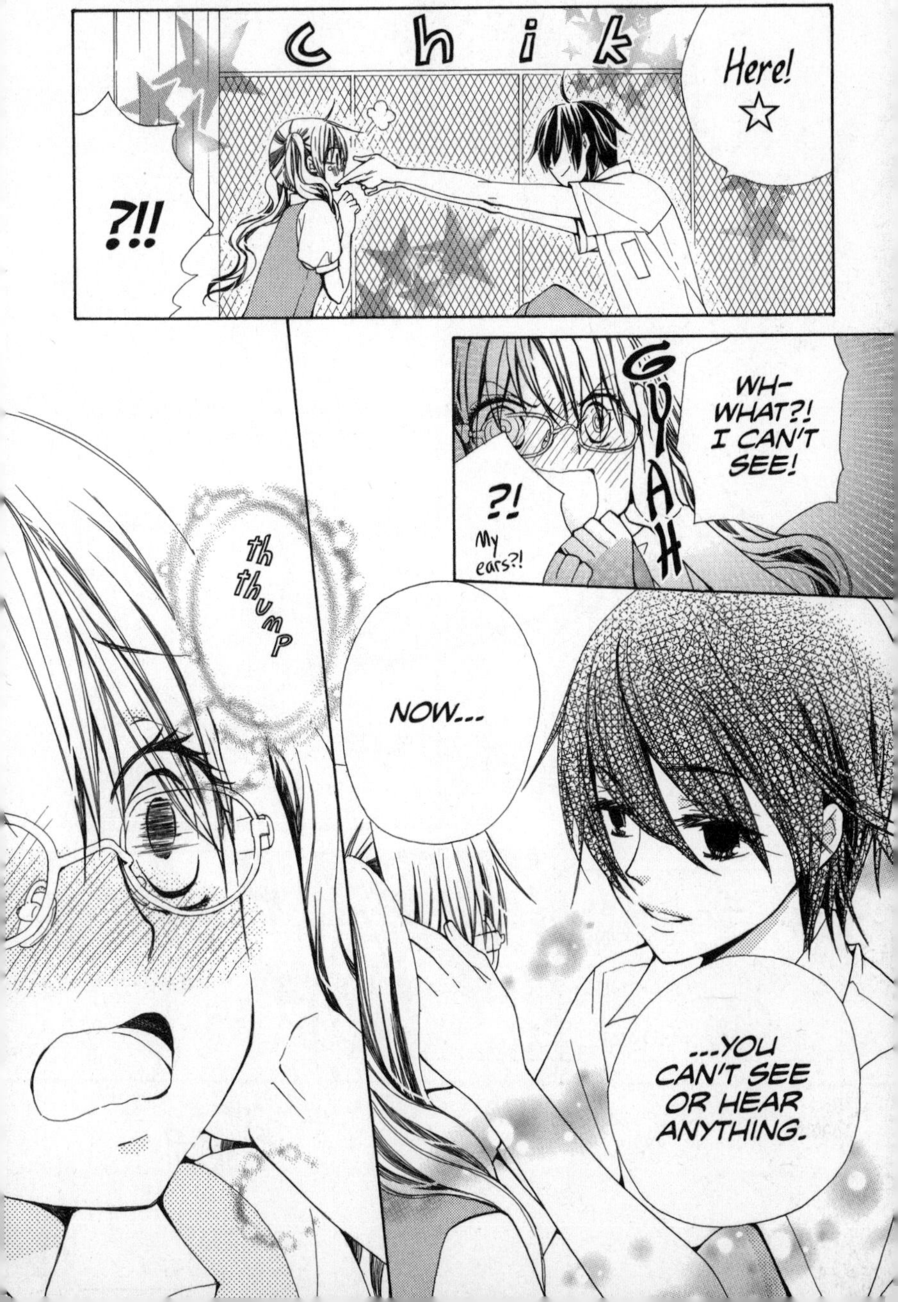
Here! ☆
chik
?!!
WH- WHAT?! I CAN'T SEE!
GYAH
?!
My ears?!
NOW...
...YOU CAN'T SEE OR HEAR ANYTHING.
th thump

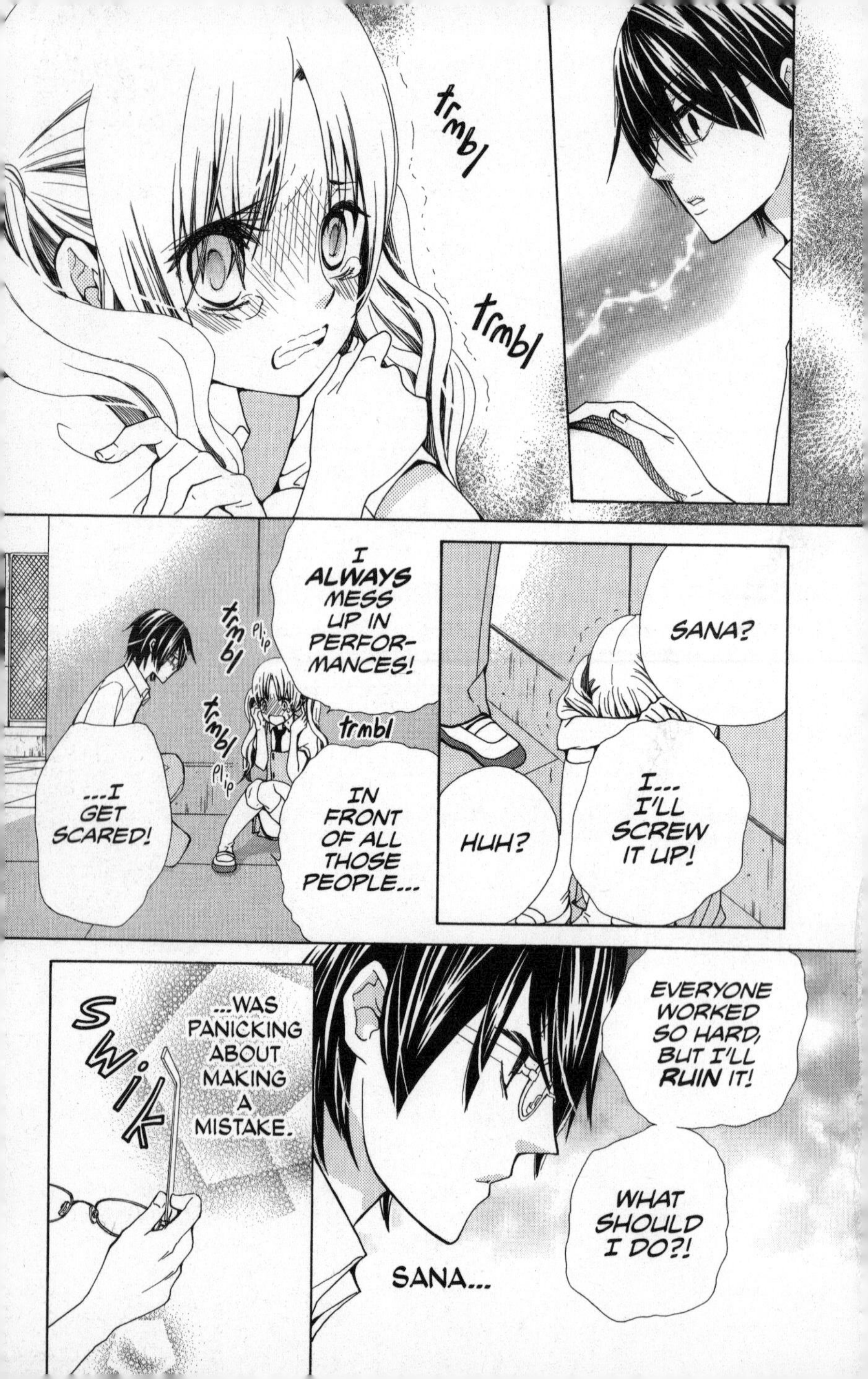

trmbl
trmbl
SANA?
I... I'LL SCREW IT UP!
HUH?
I ALWAYS MESS UP IN PERFORMANCES!
trmbl
IN FRONT OF ALL THOSE PEOPLE...
trmbl
plip
trmbl
plip
...I GET SCARED!
EVERYONE WORKED SO HARD, BUT I'LL RUIN IT!
WHAT SHOULD I DO?!
SANA...
...WAS PANICKING ABOUT MAKING A MISTAKE.
SWIK

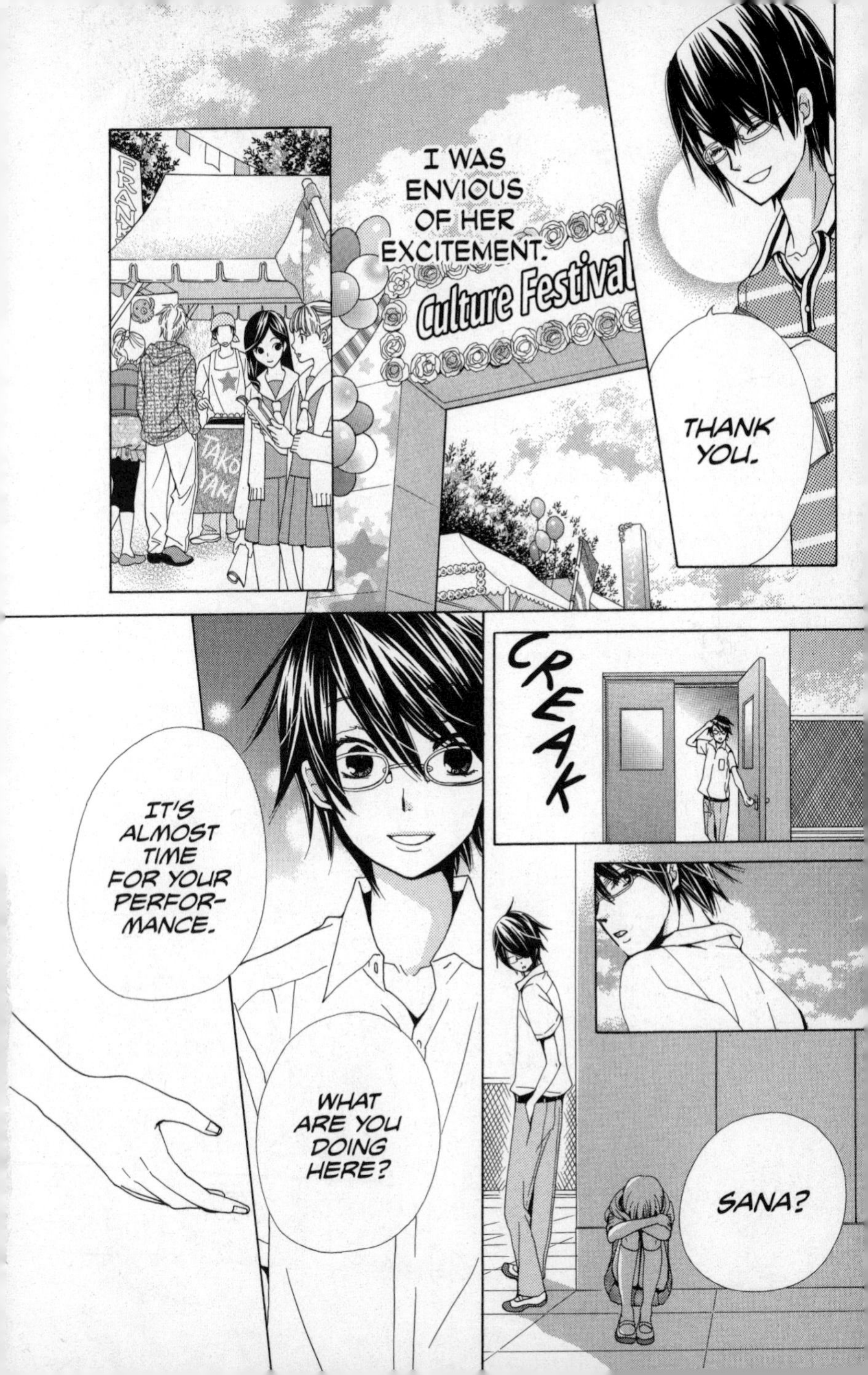
THANK YOU.
I WAS ENVIOUS OF HER EXCITEMENT.
Culture Festival
TAKO YAKI
CREAK
SANA?
IT'S ALMOST TIME FOR YOUR PERFORMANCE.
WHAT ARE YOU DOING HERE?

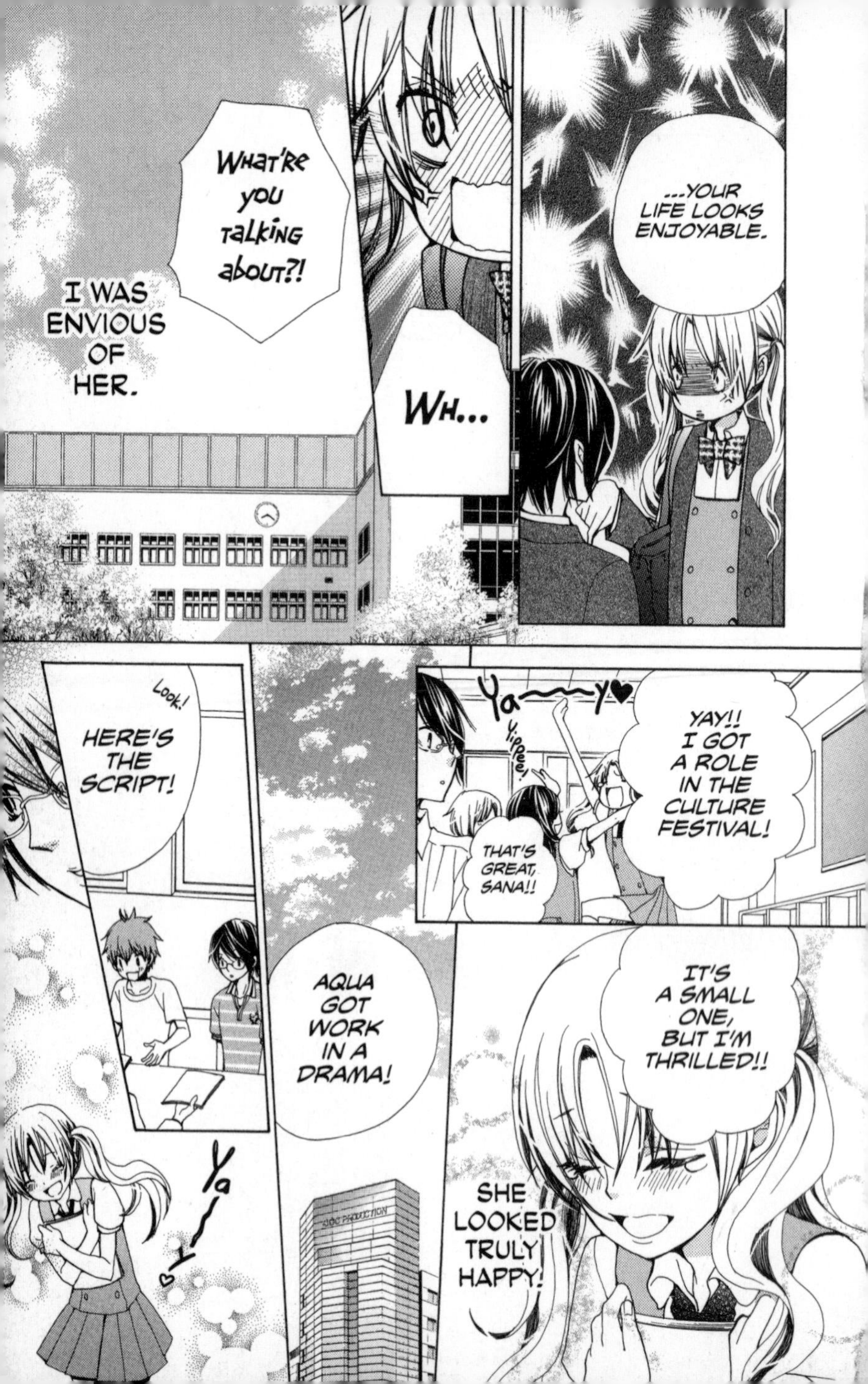
...YOUR LIFE LOOKS ENJOYABLE.
WH...
What're you talking about?!
I WAS ENVIOUS OF HER.
Ya~~y♥
YAY!! I GOT A ROLE IN THE CULTURE FESTIVAL!
Yippee!
THAT'S GREAT, SANA!!
IT'S A SMALL ONE, BUT I'M THRILLED!!
SHE LOOKED TRULY HAPPY.
AQUA GOT WORK IN A DRAMA!
Look!
HERE'S THE SCRIPT!
Ya~~y♥

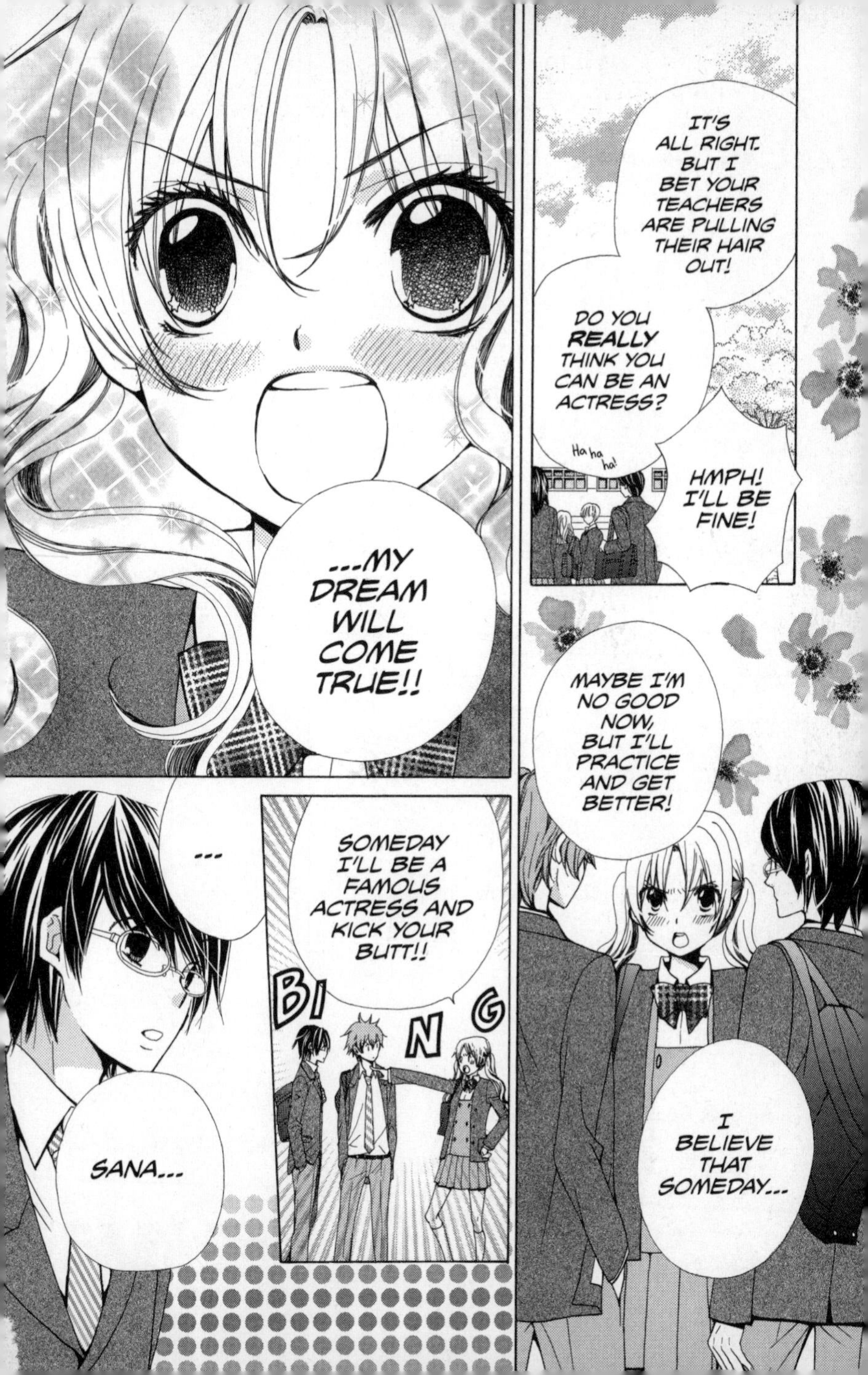

IT'S ALL RIGHT. BUT I BET YOUR TEACHERS ARE PULLING THEIR HAIR OUT!
DO YOU **REALLY** THINK YOU CAN BE AN ACTRESS?
Ha ha ha!
HMPH! I'LL BE FINE!
MAYBE I'M NO GOOD NOW, BUT I'LL PRACTICE AND GET BETTER!
I BELIEVE THAT SOMEDAY...
...MY DREAM WILL COME TRUE!!
SOMEDAY I'LL BE A FAMOUS ACTRESS AND KICK YOUR BUTT!!
BING
...
SANA...

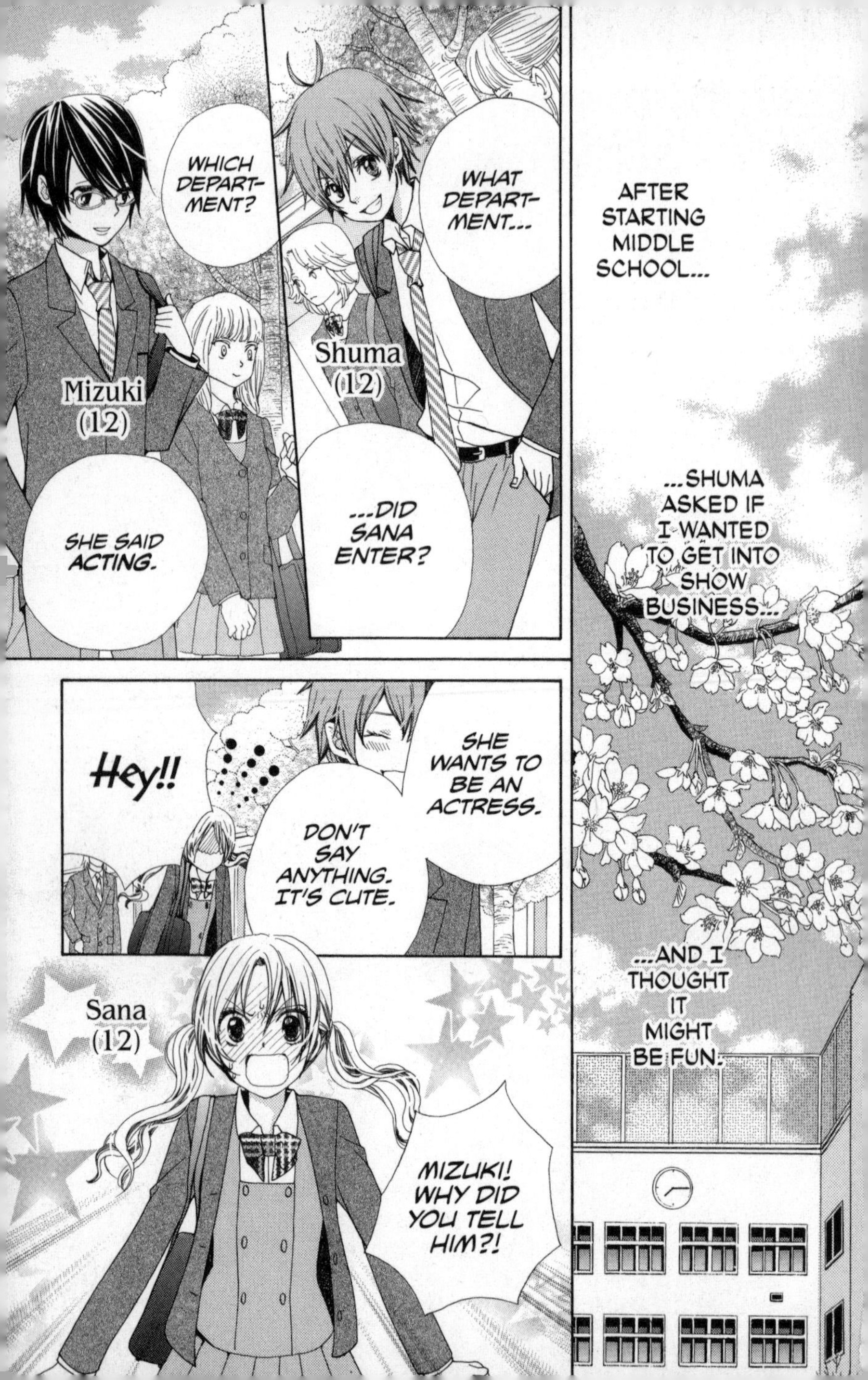
AFTER STARTING MIDDLE SCHOOL...
...SHUMA ASKED IF I WANTED TO GET INTO SHOW BUSINESS...
...AND I THOUGHT IT MIGHT BE FUN.
WHAT DEPARTMENT...
Shuma (12)
...DID SANA ENTER?
WHICH DEPARTMENT?
Mizuki (12)
SHE SAID ACTING.
SHE WANTS TO BE AN ACTRESS.
DON'T SAY ANYTHING. IT'S CUTE.
Hey!!
Sana (12)
MIZUKI! WHY DID YOU TELL HIM?!

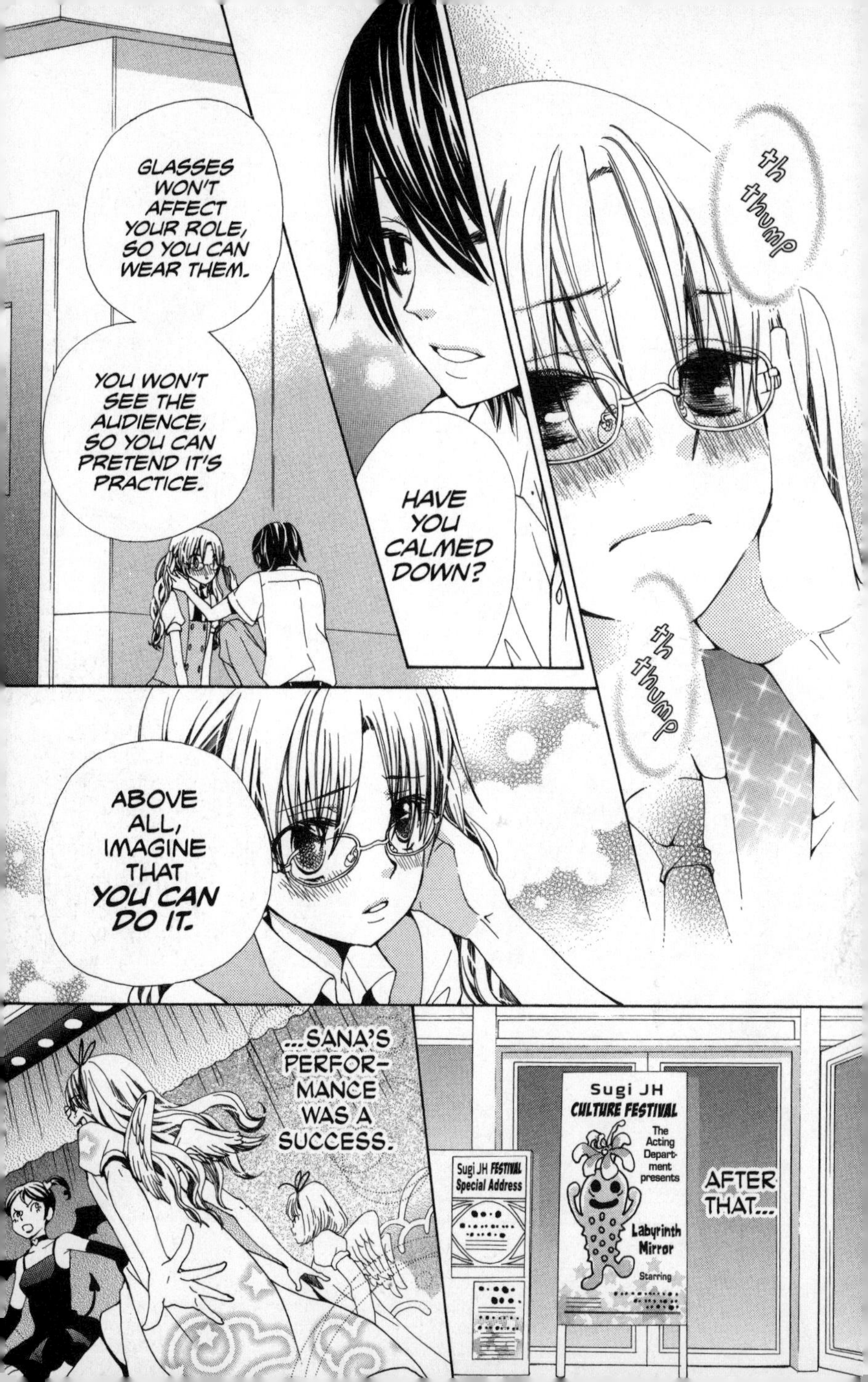
th thump
th thump
HAVE YOU CALMED DOWN?
GLASSES WON'T AFFECT YOUR ROLE, SO YOU CAN WEAR THEM.
YOU WON'T SEE THE AUDIENCE, SO YOU CAN PRETEND IT'S PRACTICE.
ABOVE ALL, IMAGINE THAT YOU CAN DO IT.
AFTER THAT...
Sugi JH CULTURE FESTIVAL
The Acting Department presents
Labyrinth Mirror
Starring
Sugi JH FESTIVAL Special Address
...SANA'S PERFOR-MANCE WAS A SUCCESS.

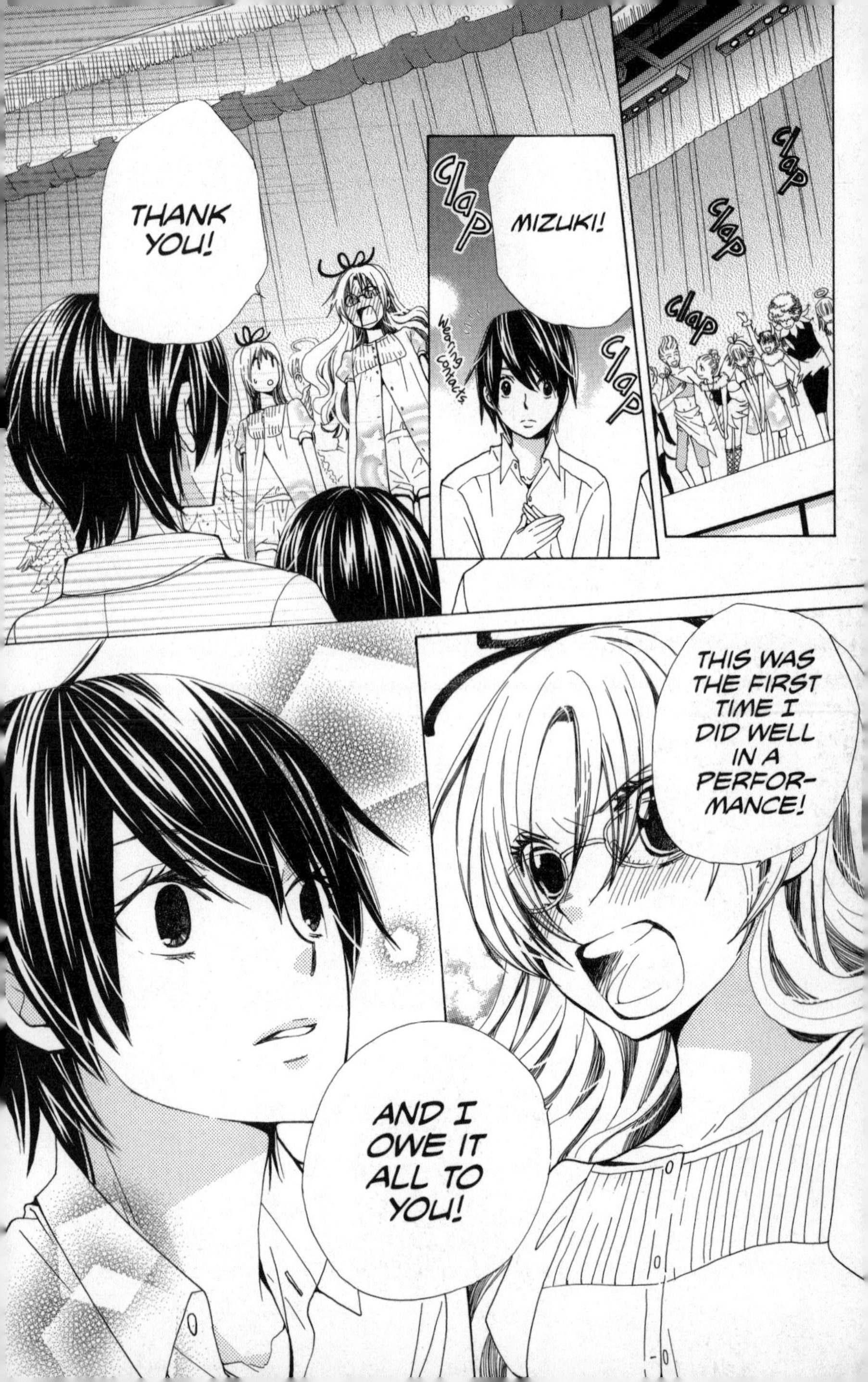
clap
clap
clap
clap
MIZUKI!
clap
Wearing contacts.
THANK YOU!
THIS WAS THE FIRST TIME I DID WELL IN A PERFORMANCE!
AND I OWE IT ALL TO YOU!

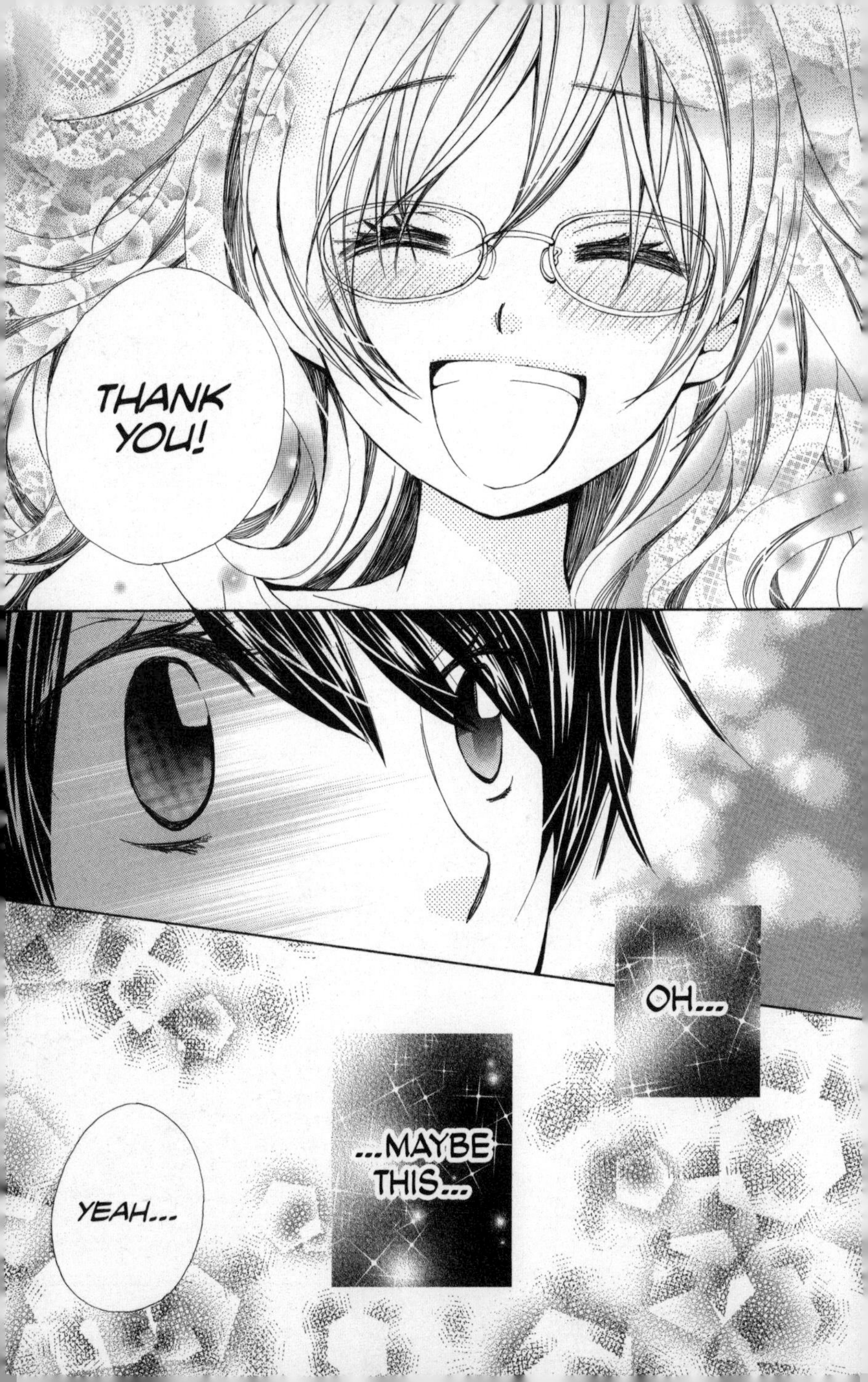
THANK YOU!
OH...
...MAYBE THIS...
YEAH...

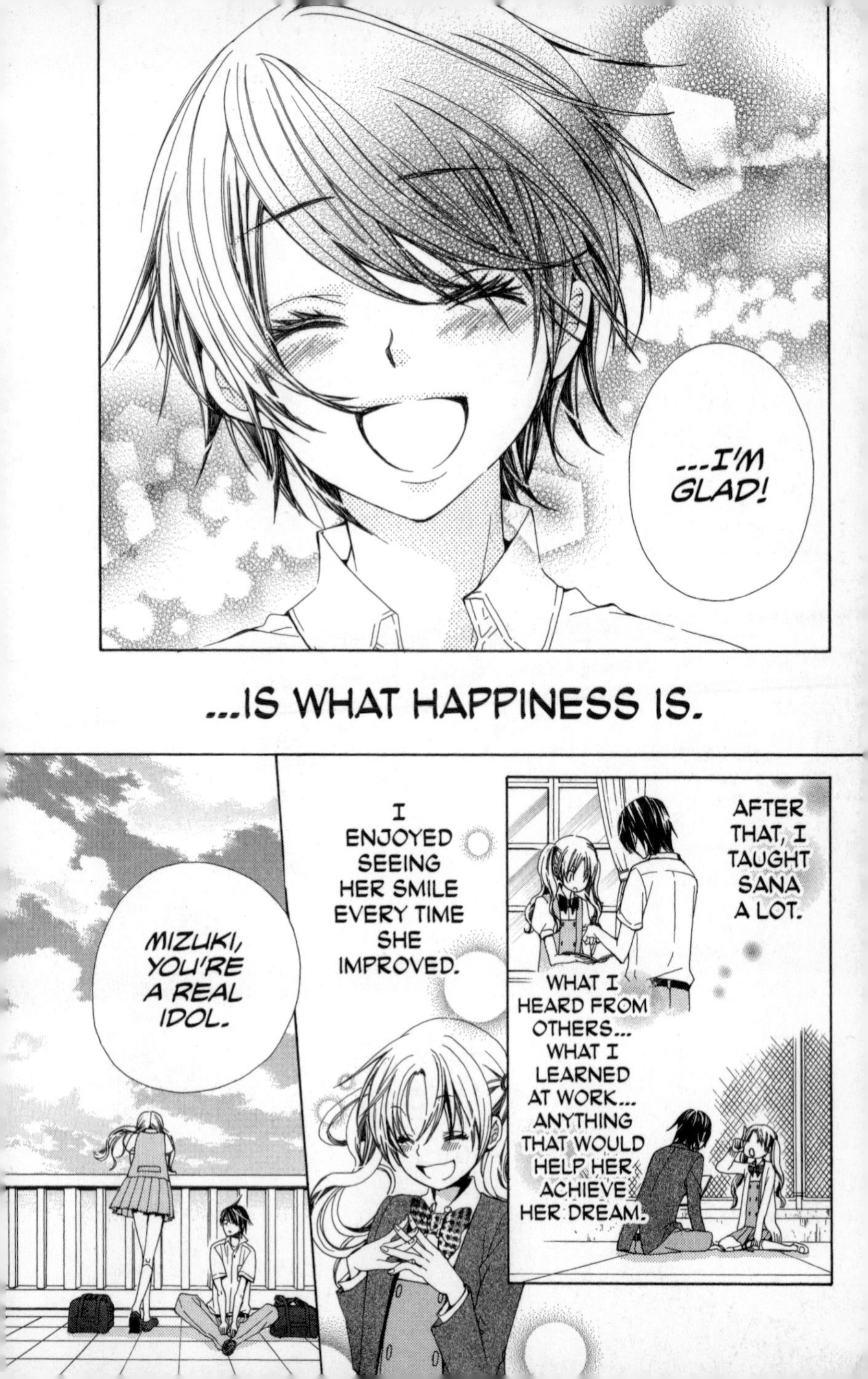
...I'M GLAD!
...IS WHAT HAPPINESS IS.
AFTER THAT, I TAUGHT SANA A LOT.
WHAT I HEARD FROM OTHERS... WHAT I LEARNED AT WORK... ANYTHING THAT WOULD HELP HER ACHIEVE HER DREAM.
I ENJOYED SEEING HER SMILE EVERY TIME SHE IMPROVED.
MIZUKI, YOU'RE A REAL IDOL.

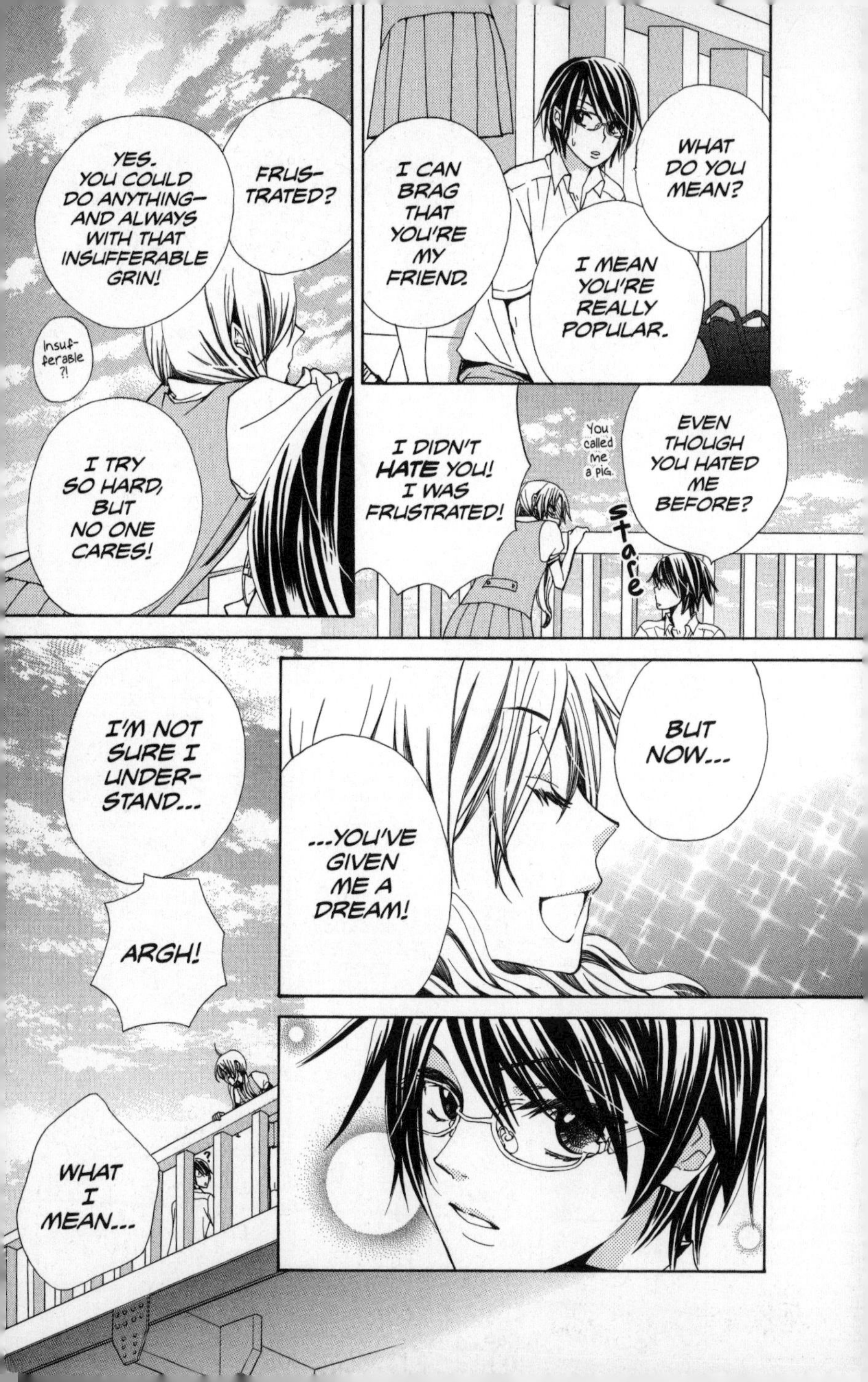
I CAN BRAG THAT YOU'RE MY FRIEND.
WHAT DO YOU MEAN?
I MEAN YOU'RE REALLY POPULAR.
EVEN THOUGH YOU HATED ME BEFORE?
You called me a pig.
stare
I DIDN'T HATE YOU! I WAS FRUSTRATED!
FRUS-TRATED?
YES. YOU COULD DO ANYTHING— AND ALWAYS WITH THAT INSUFFERABLE GRIN!
Insuf-ferable ?!
I TRY SO HARD, BUT NO ONE CARES!
BUT NOW...
...YOU'VE GIVEN ME A DREAM!
I'M NOT SURE I UNDER-STAND...
ARGH!
WHAT I MEAN...

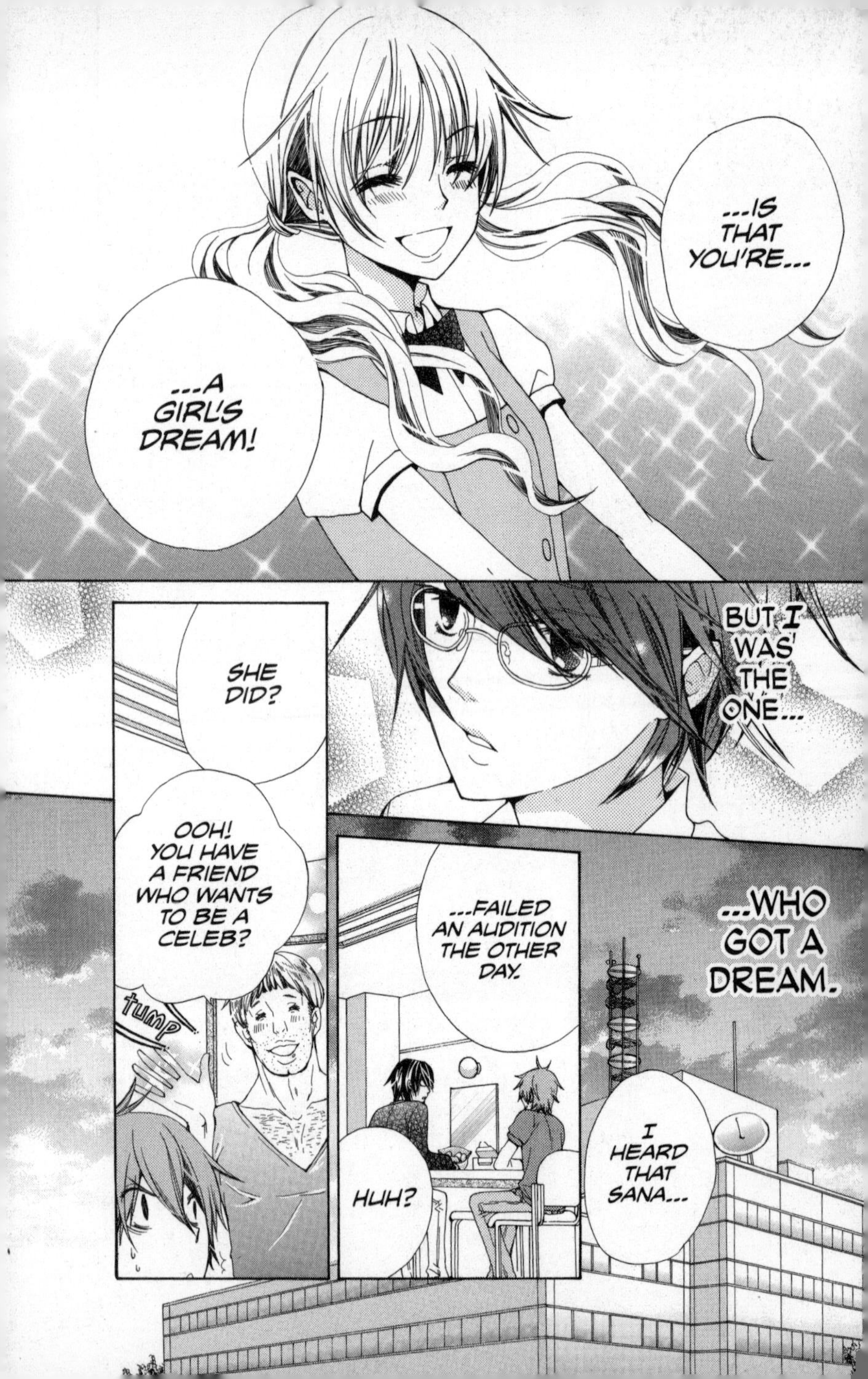
...IS THAT YOU'RE...
...A GIRL'S DREAM!
BUT I WAS THE ONE...
...WHO GOT A DREAM.
I HEARD THAT SANA...
...FAILED AN AUDITION THE OTHER DAY.
HUH?
SHE DID?
OOH! YOU HAVE A FRIEND WHO WANTS TO BE A CELEB?
tump

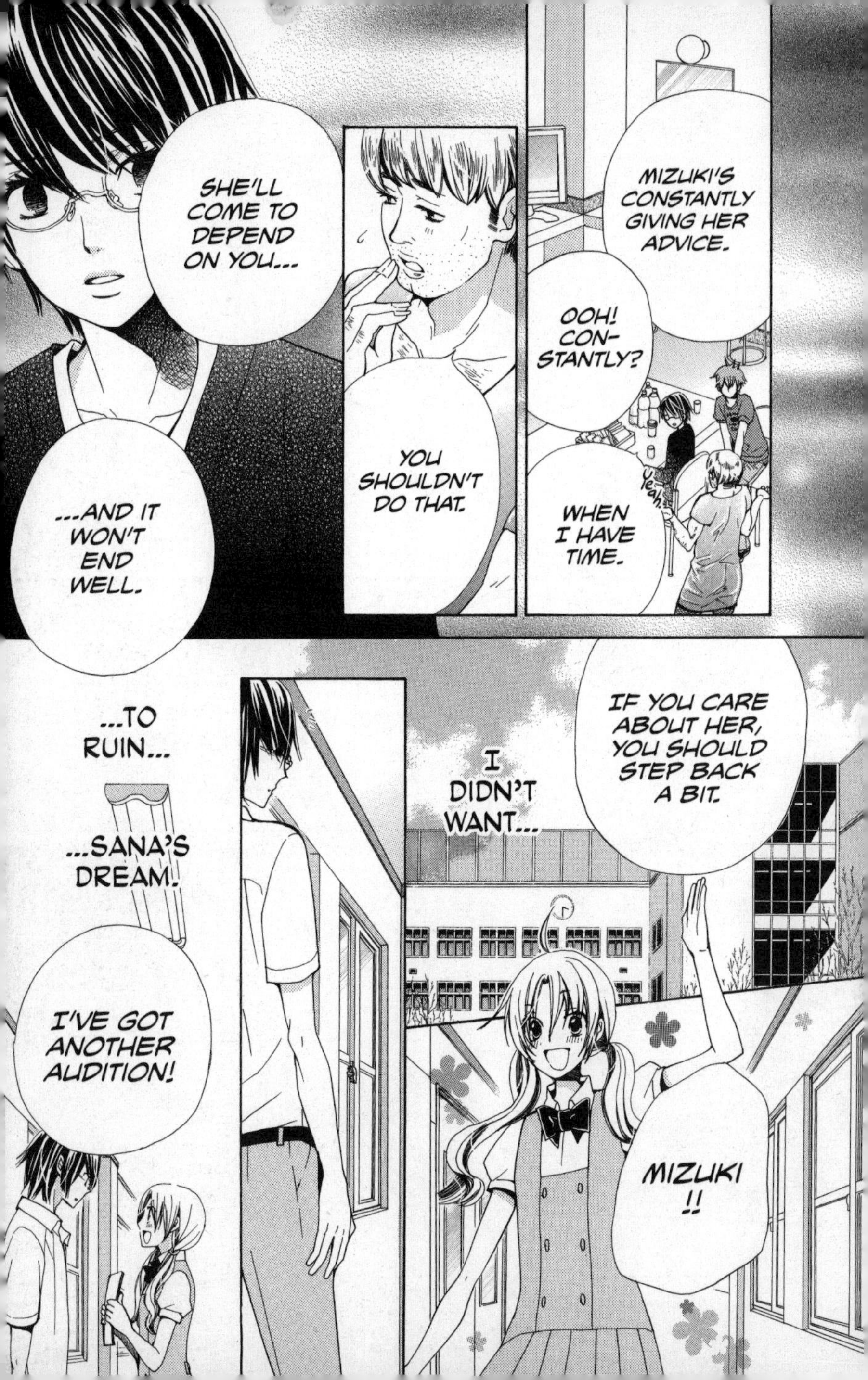
MIZUKI'S CONSTANTLY GIVING HER ADVICE.
OOH! CON-STANTLY?
WHEN I HAVE TIME.
Yeah
YOU SHOULDN'T DO THAT.
SHE'LL COME TO DEPEND ON YOU...
...AND IT WON'T END WELL.
IF YOU CARE ABOUT HER, YOU SHOULD STEP BACK A BIT.
I DIDN'T WANT...
MIZUKI !!
...TO RUIN...
...SANA'S DREAM.
I'VE GOT ANOTHER AUDITION!

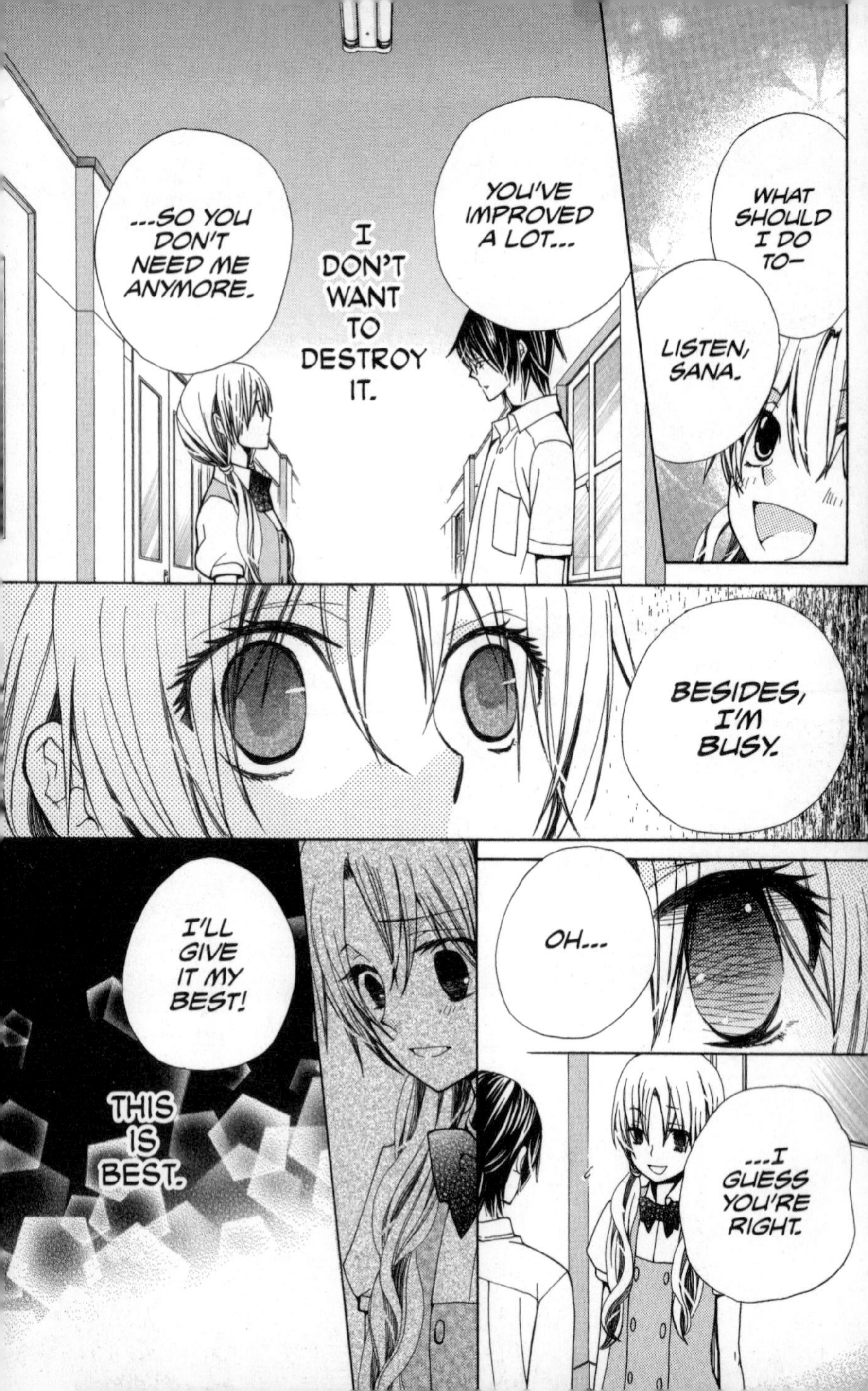
WHAT SHOULD I DO TO—
LISTEN, SANA.
YOU'VE IMPROVED A LOT...
I DON'T WANT TO DESTROY IT.
...SO YOU DON'T NEED ME ANYMORE.
BESIDES, I'M BUSY.
OH...
...I GUESS YOU'RE RIGHT.
I'LL GIVE IT MY BEST!
THIS IS BEST.

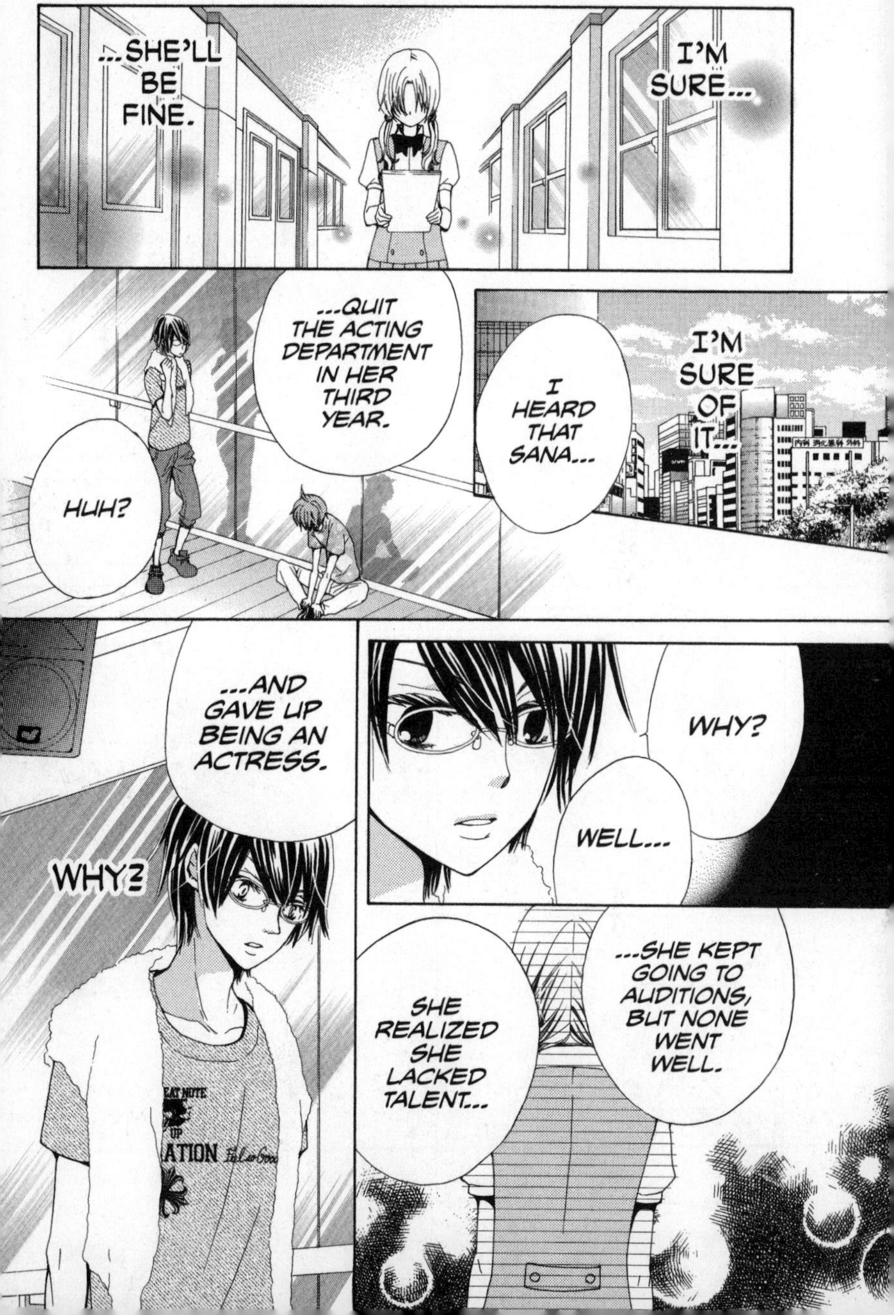
I'M SURE...
...SHE'LL BE FINE.
I'M SURE OF IT...
I HEARD THAT SANA...
...QUIT THE ACTING DEPARTMENT IN HER THIRD YEAR.
HUH?
WHY?
WELL...
...SHE KEPT GOING TO AUDITIONS, BUT NONE WENT WELL.
SHE REALIZED SHE LACKED TALENT...
...AND GAVE UP BEING AN ACTRESS.
WHY?

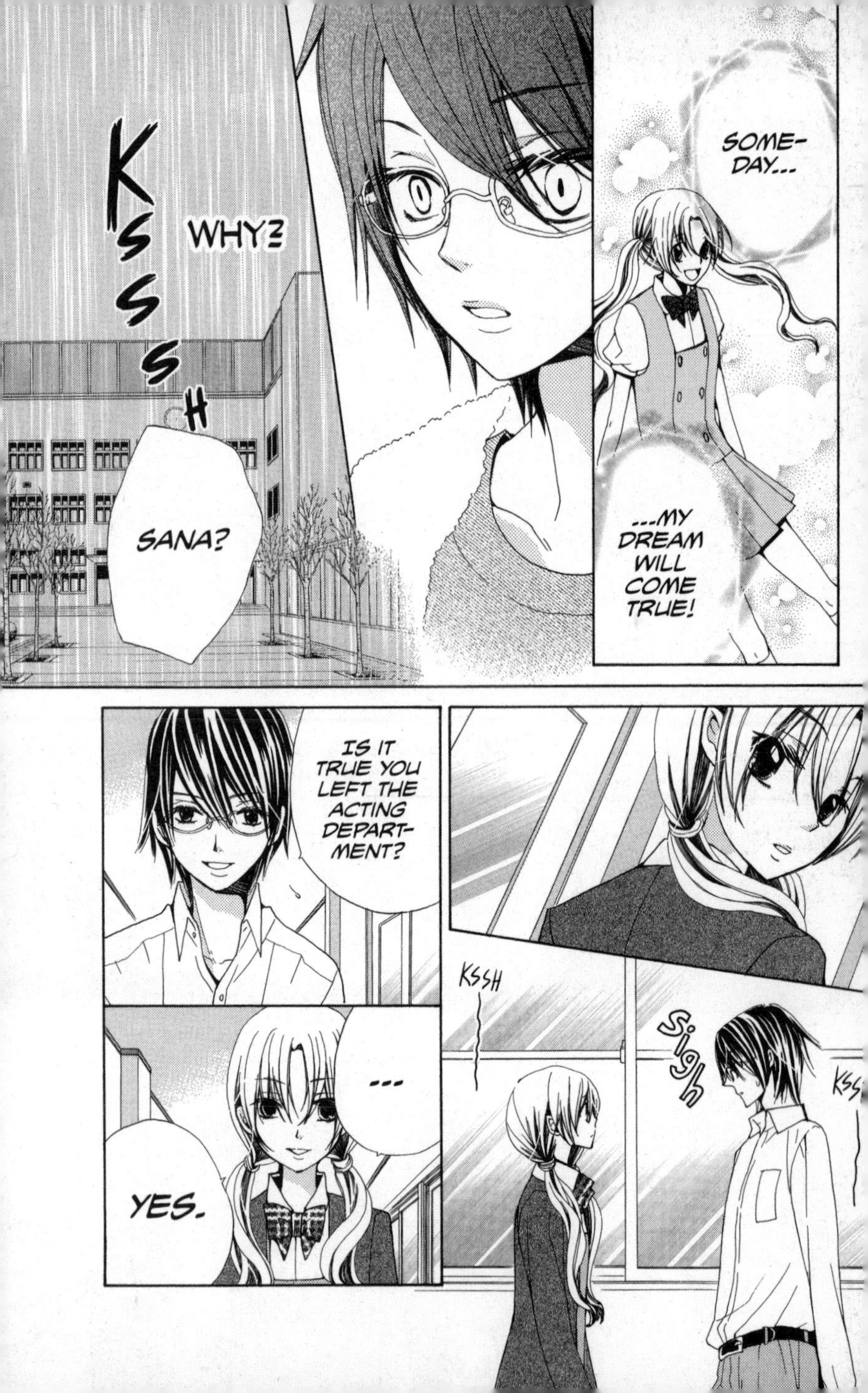
SOME-DAY...
...MY DREAM WILL COME TRUE!
KSSSH
WHY?
SANA?
IS IT TRUE YOU LEFT THE ACTING DEPART-MENT?
KSS
Sigh
KSSH
...
YES.

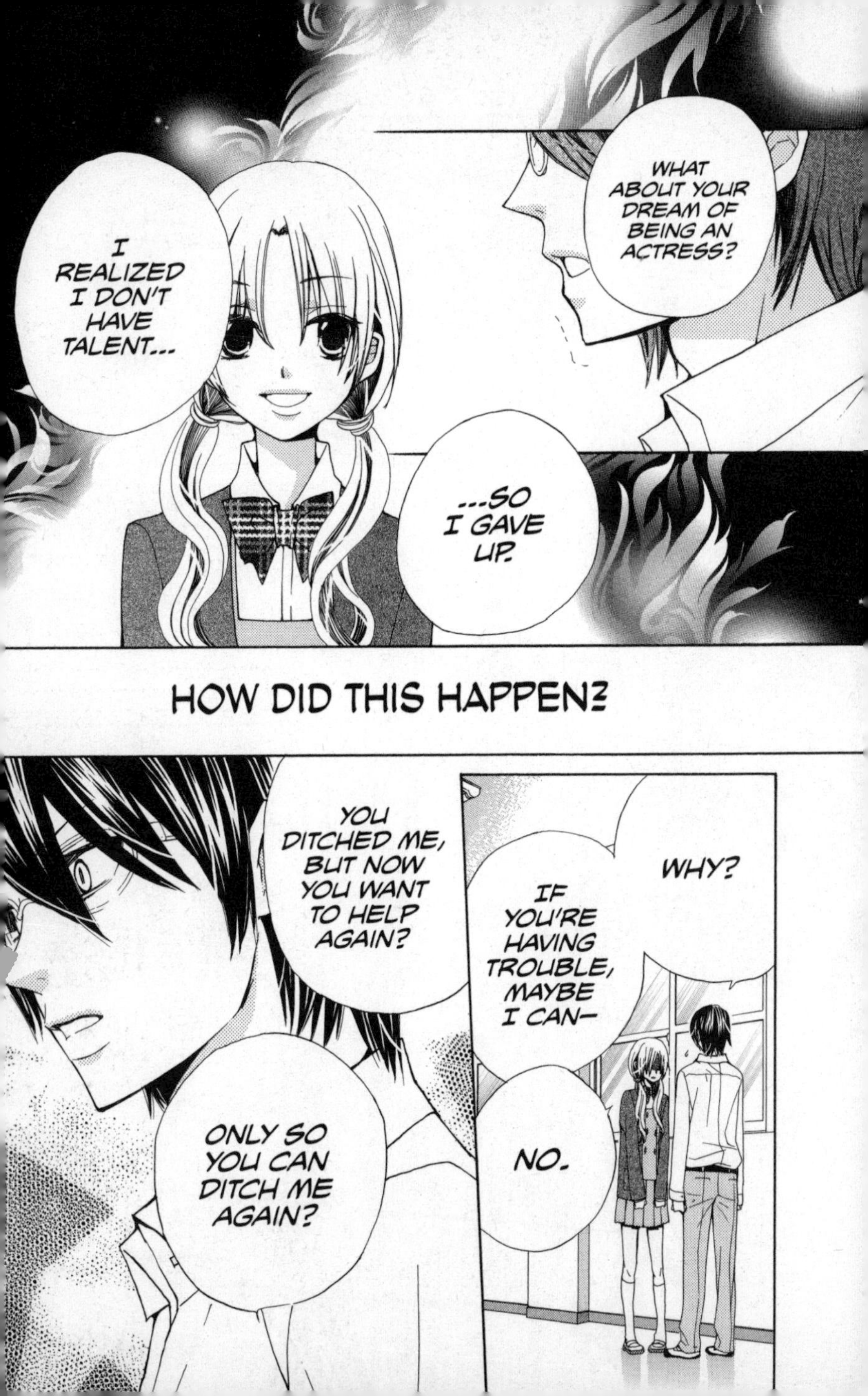
WHAT ABOUT YOUR DREAM OF BEING AN ACTRESS?
I REALIZED I DON'T HAVE TALENT...
...SO I GAVE UP.
HOW DID THIS HAPPEN?
WHY?
IF YOU'RE HAVING TROUBLE, MAYBE I CAN—
NO.
YOU DITCHED ME, BUT NOW YOU WANT TO HELP AGAIN?
ONLY SO YOU CAN DITCH ME AGAIN?

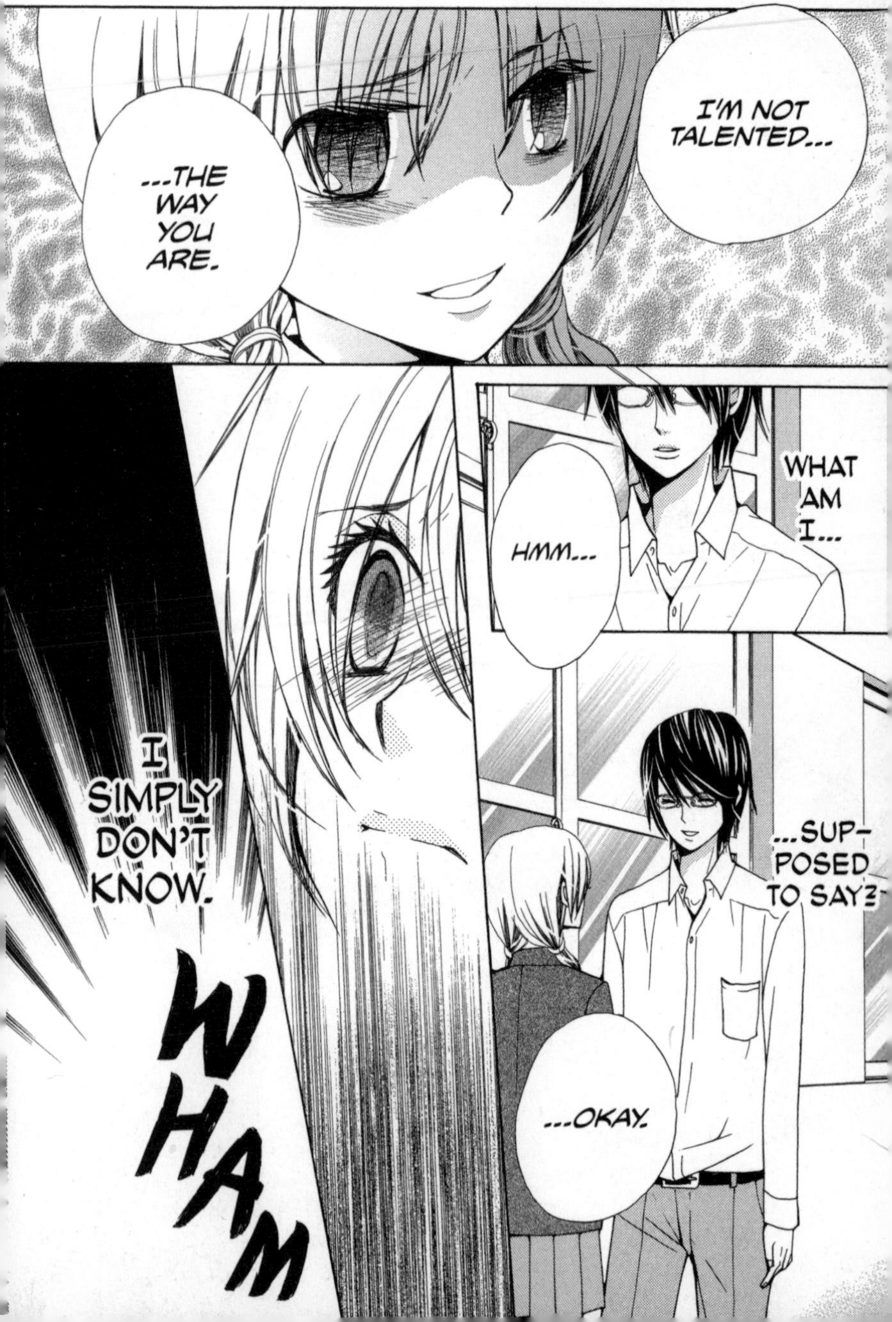
I'M NOT TALENTED...
...THE WAY YOU ARE.
WHAT AM I...
HMM...
...SUP-POSED TO SAY?
...OKAY.
I SIMPLY DON'T KNOW.
WHAM

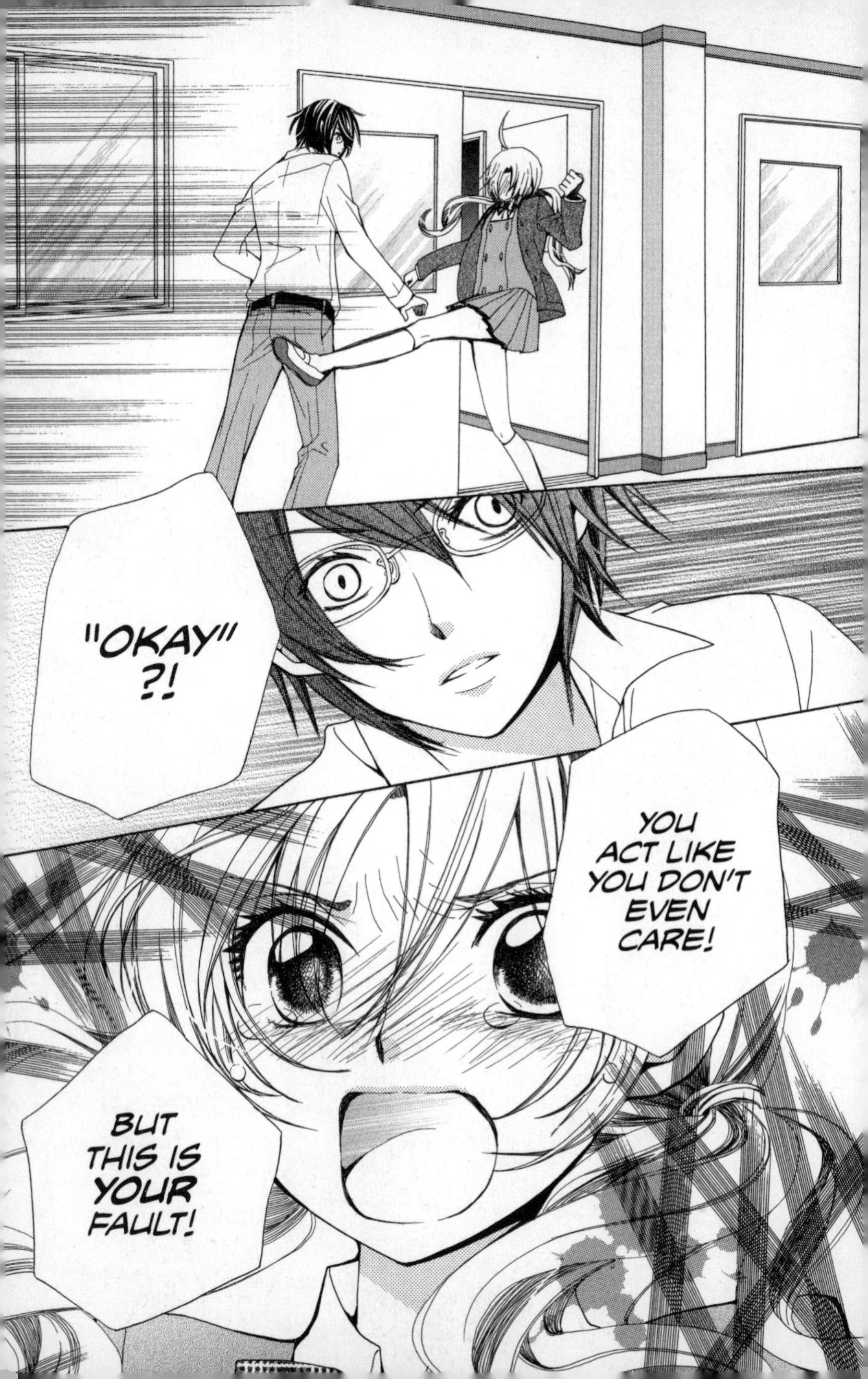
"OKAY" ?!
YOU ACT LIKE YOU DON'T EVEN CARE!
BUT THIS IS YOUR FAULT!

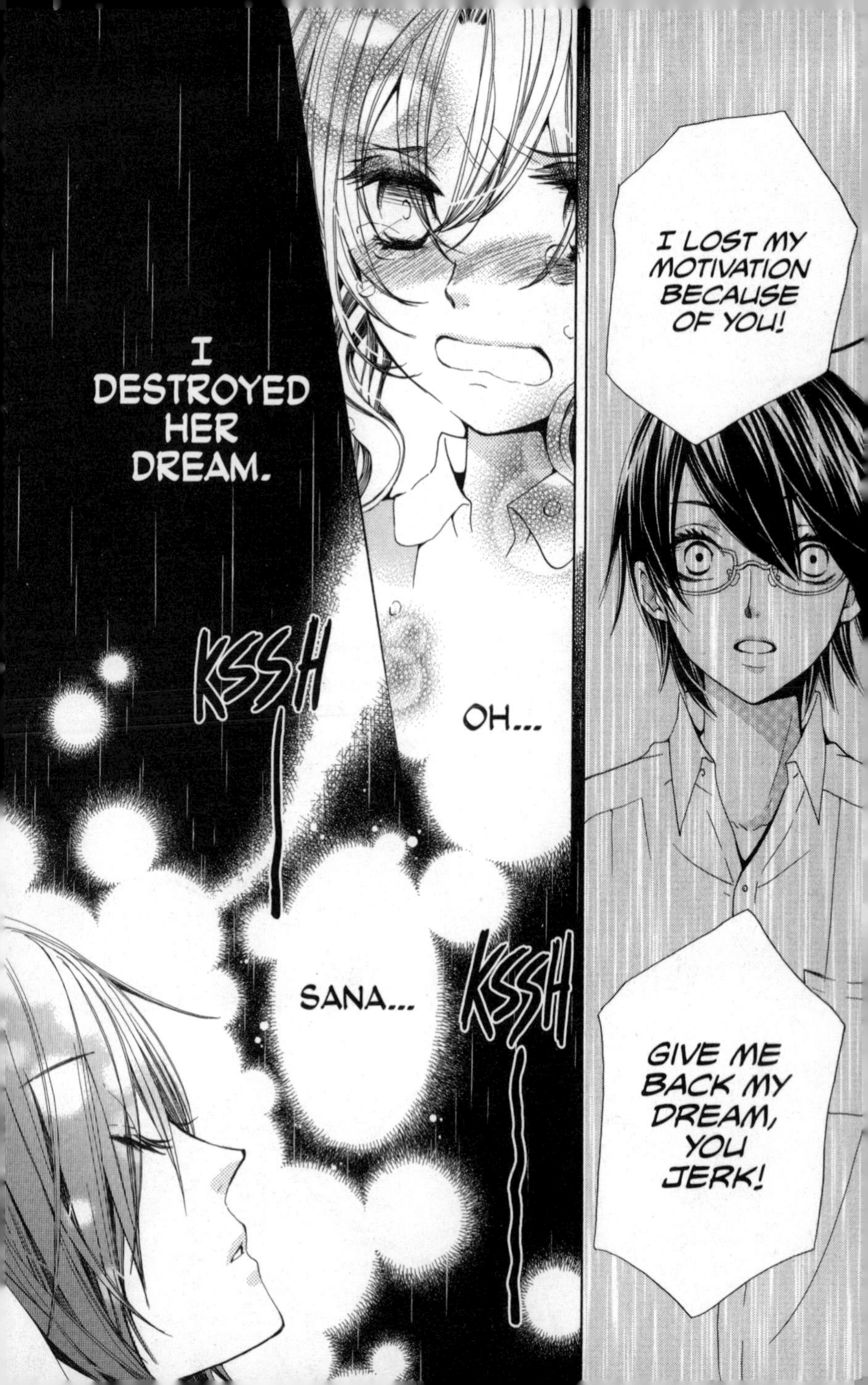
I LOST MY MOTIVATION BECAUSE OF YOU!
GIVE ME BACK MY DREAM, YOU JERK!
I DESTROYED HER DREAM.
KSSH
OH...
KSSH
SANA...

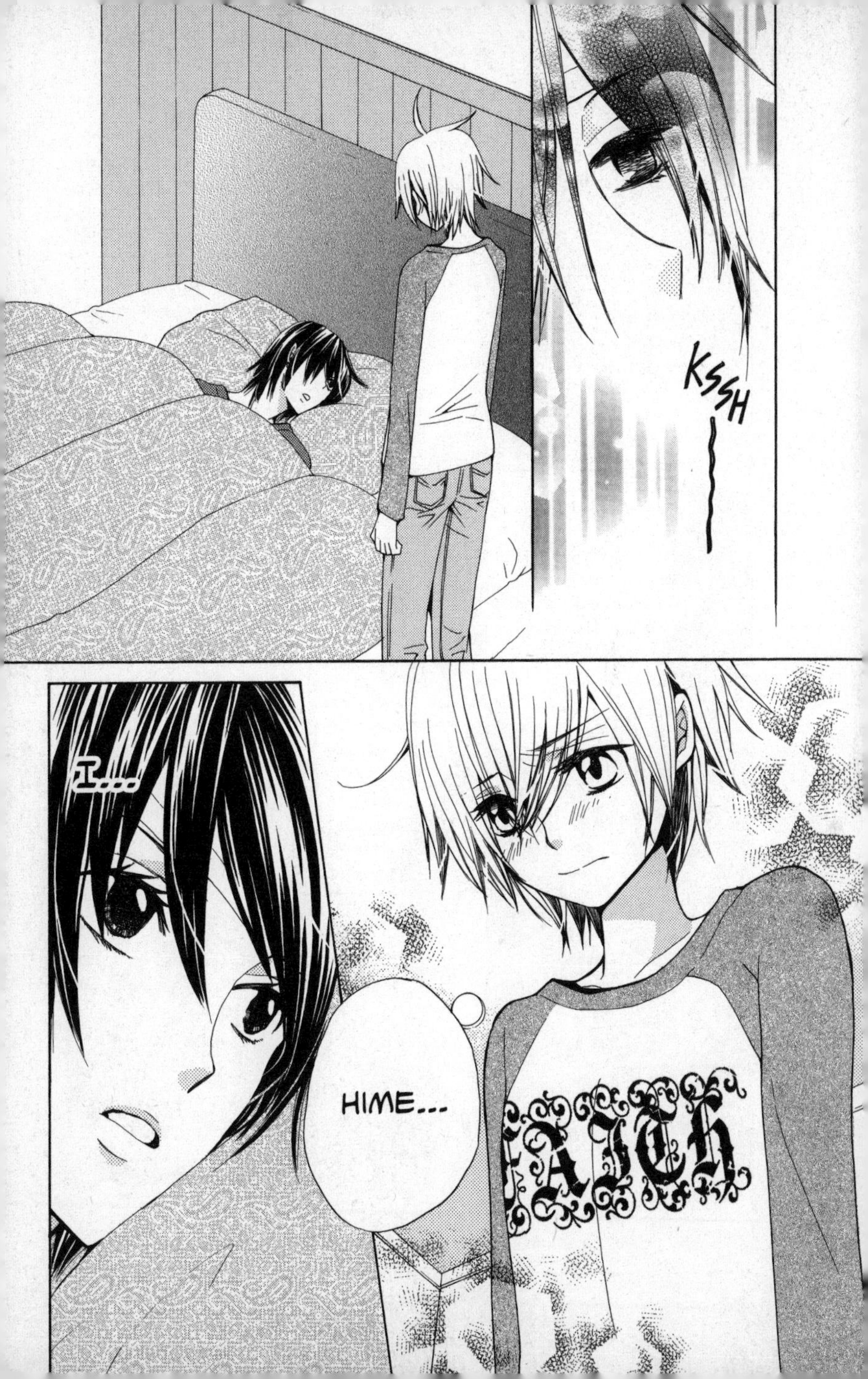
KSSH
I...
HIME...
FAITH

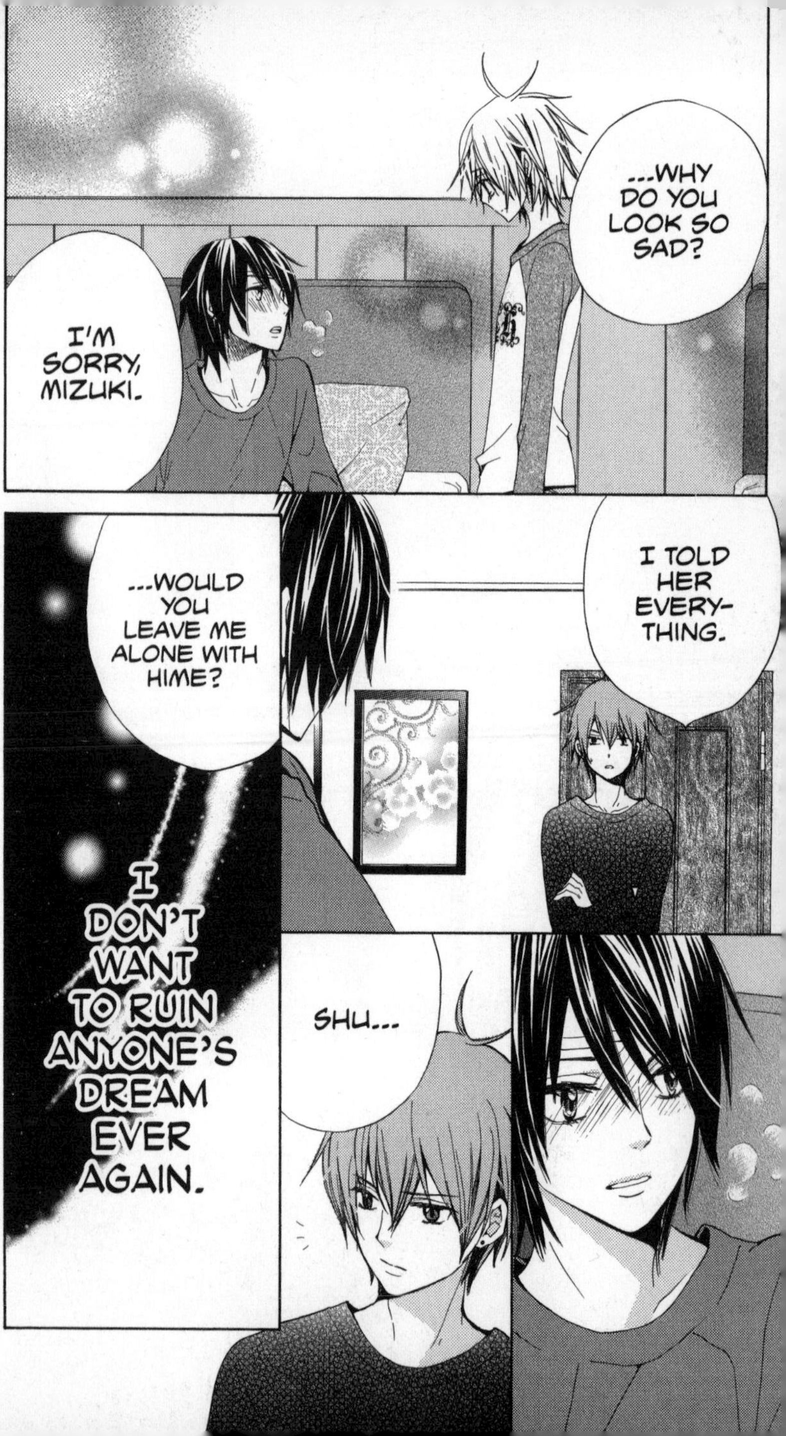
...WHY DO YOU LOOK SO SAD?
I'M SORRY, MIZUKI.
I TOLD HER EVERY-THING.
...WOULD YOU LEAVE ME ALONE WITH HIME?
SHU...
I DON'T WANT TO RUIN ANYONE'S DREAM EVER AGAIN.

Chapter 17

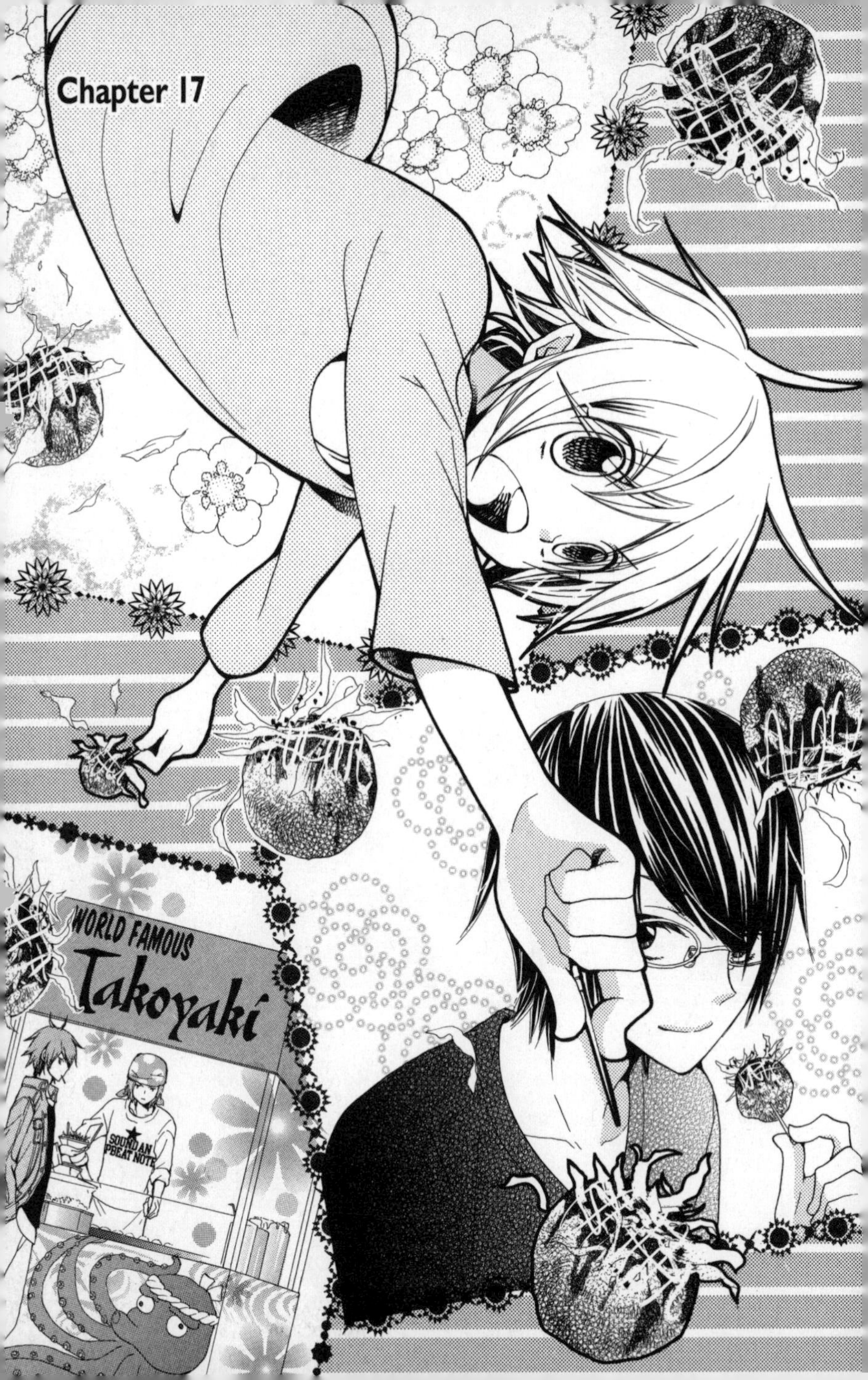
WORLD FAMOUS
Takoyaki
SOUND AN
PBEAT NOTE

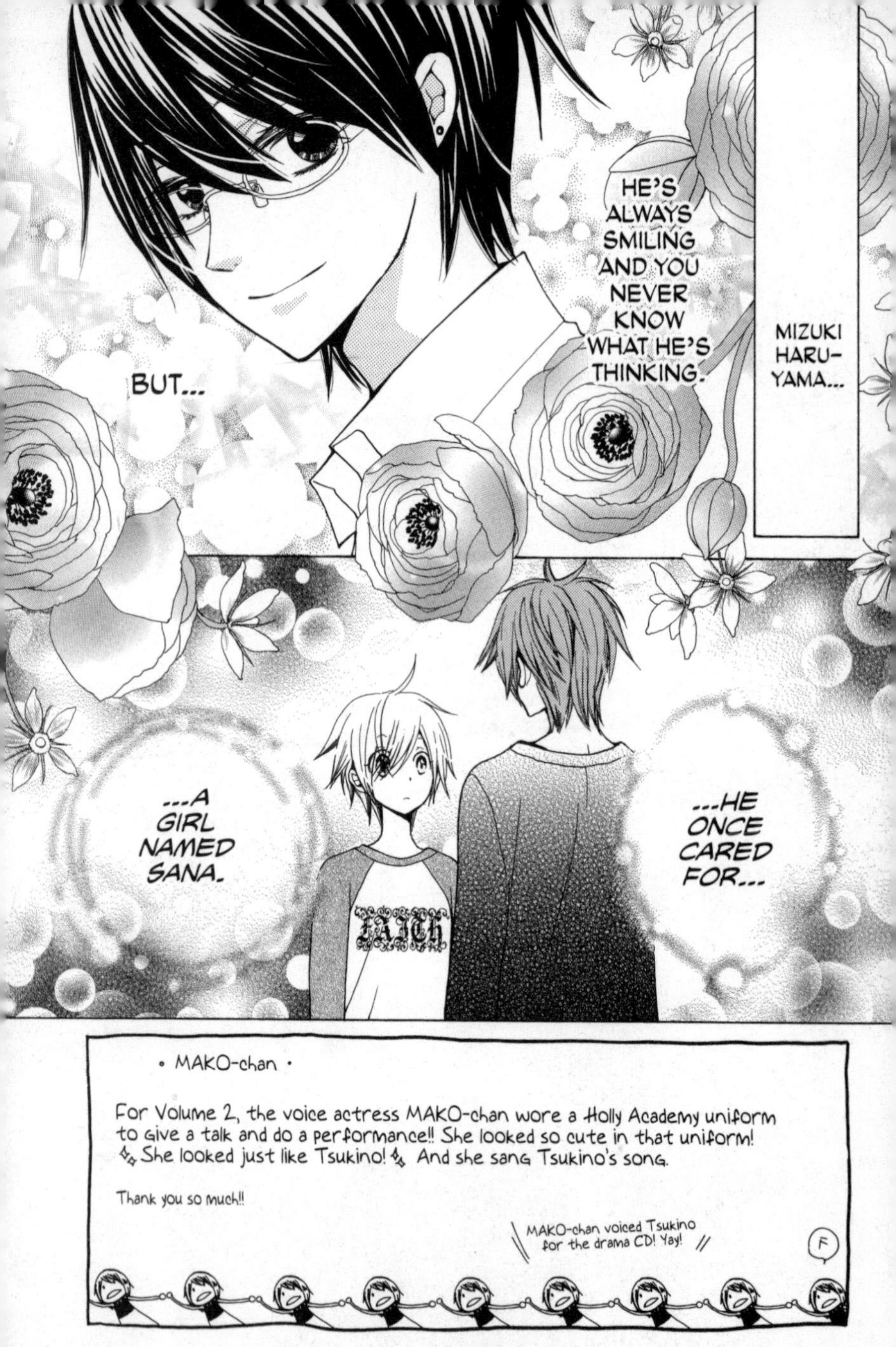
MIZUKI HARU-YAMA...
HE'S ALWAYS SMILING AND YOU NEVER KNOW WHAT HE'S THINKING.
BUT...
...HE ONCE CARED FOR...
...A GIRL NAMED SANA.

• MAKO-chan •

For Volume 2, the voice actress MAKO-chan wore a Holly Academy uniform to give a talk and do a performance!! She looked so cute in that uniform! ✧ She looked just like Tsukino! ✧ And she sang Tsukino's song.

Thank you so much!!

\\ MAKO-chan voiced Tsukino for the drama CD! Yay! //

F

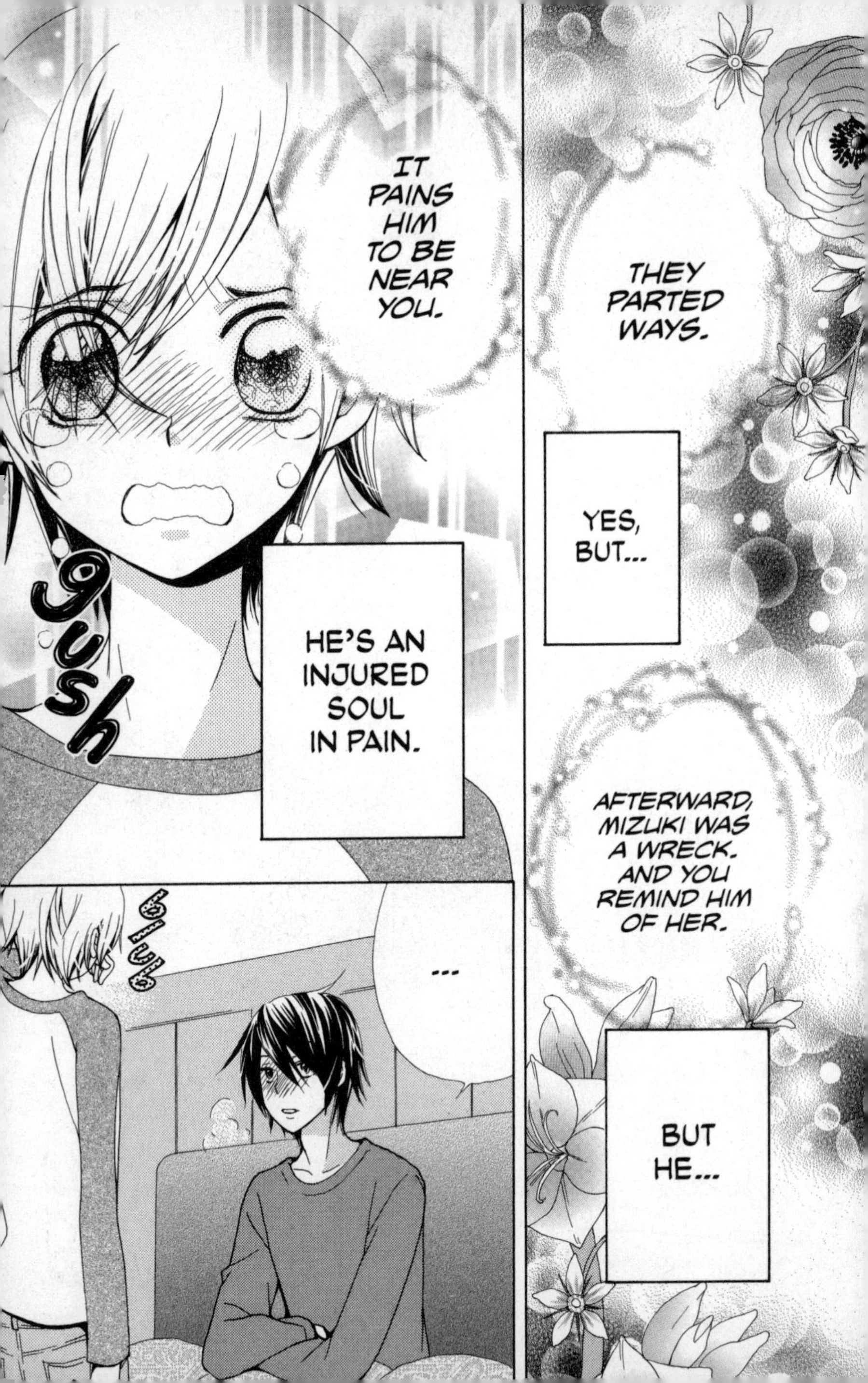
THEY PARTED WAYS.
YES, BUT...
AFTERWARD, MIZUKI WAS A WRECK. AND YOU REMIND HIM OF HER.
BUT HE...
IT PAINS HIM TO BE NEAR YOU.
HE'S AN INJURED SOUL IN PAIN.
gush
...
gush

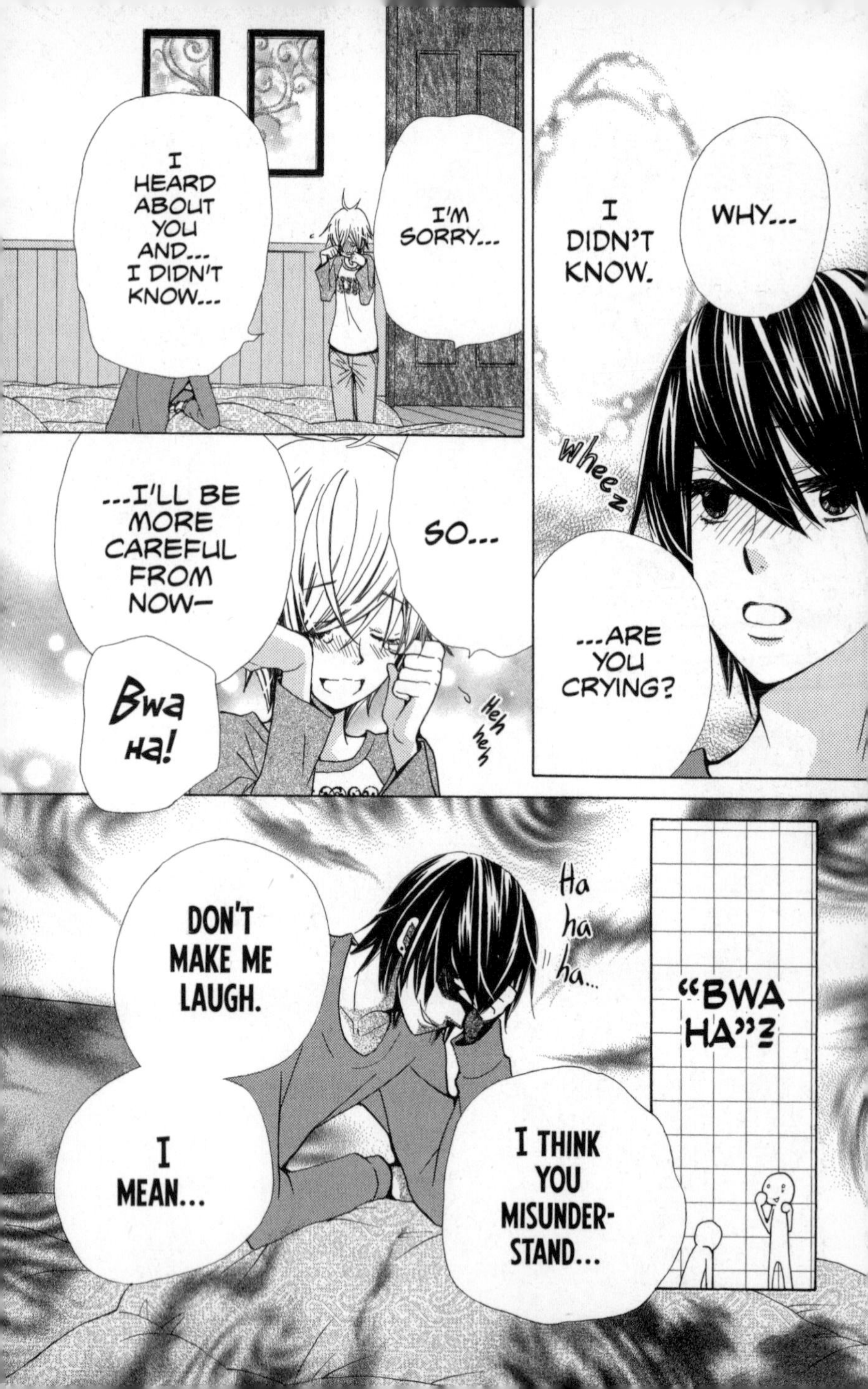
WHY...
I DIDN'T KNOW.
wheez
...ARE YOU CRYING?
I'M SORRY...
I HEARD ABOUT YOU AND... I DIDN'T KNOW...
SO...
...I'LL BE MORE CAREFUL FROM NOW—
Heh heh
Bwa ha!
"BWA HA"?
Ha ha ha...
DON'T MAKE ME LAUGH.
I THINK YOU MISUNDERSTAND...
I MEAN...

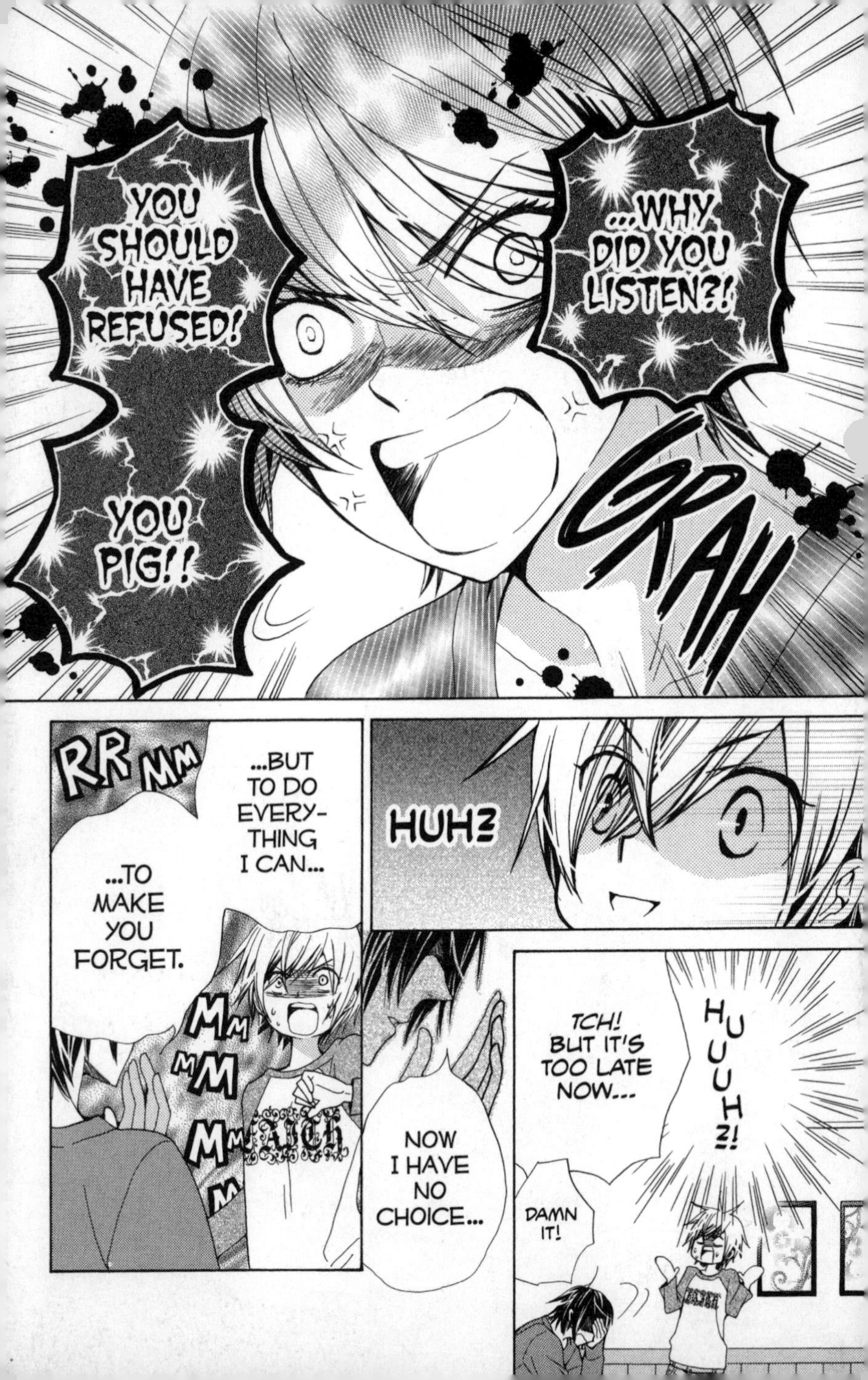
...WHY DID YOU LISTEN?!
YOU SHOULD HAVE REFUSED!
YOU PIG!!
GRAH
HUH?
HUUUH?!
TCH! BUT IT'S TOO LATE NOW...
DAMN IT!
NOW I HAVE NO CHOICE...
RRMM
...BUT TO DO EVERY-THING I CAN...
...TO MAKE YOU FORGET.
MMMMMMMM

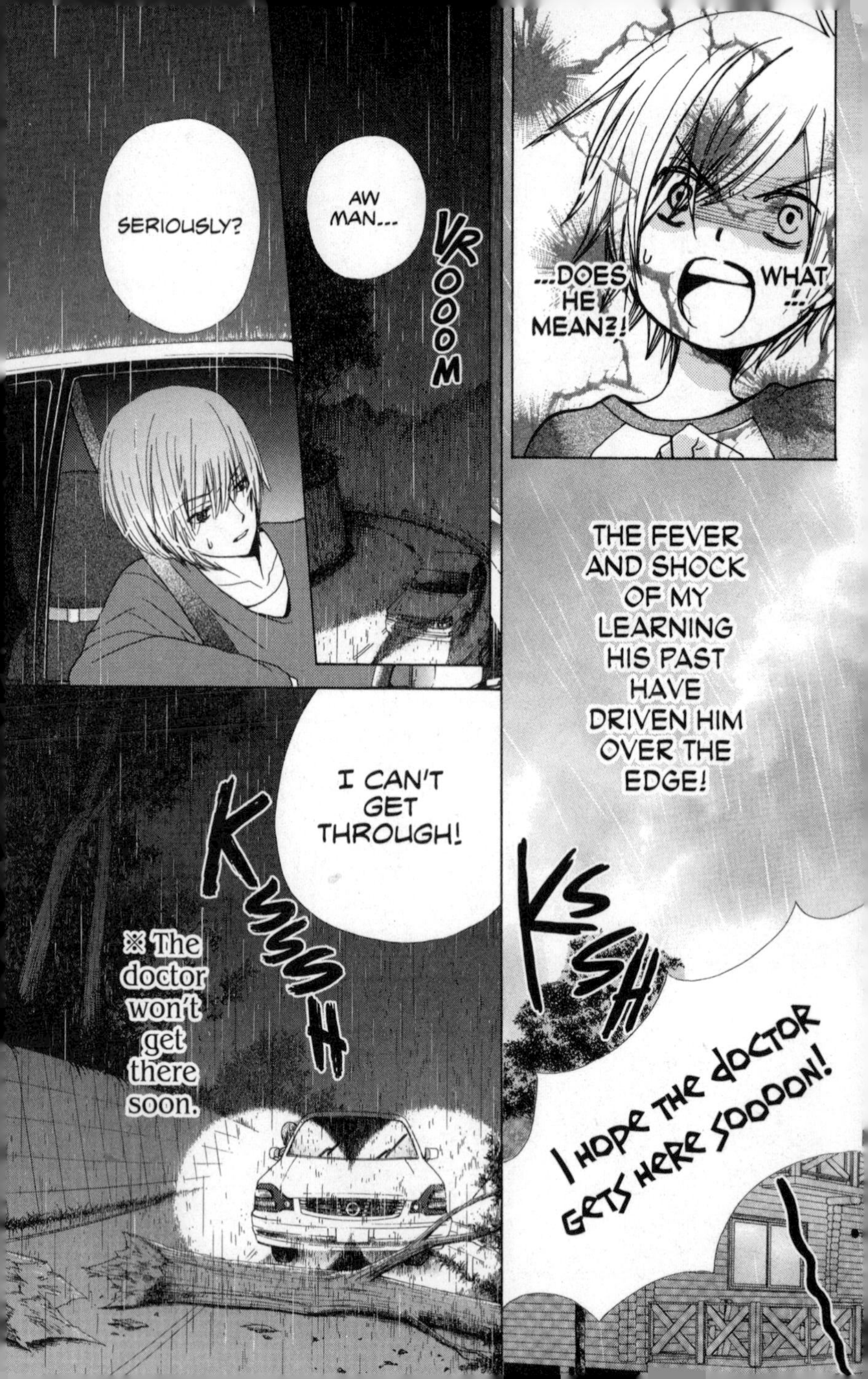
WHAT...
...DOES HE MEAN?!
THE FEVER AND SHOCK OF MY LEARNING HIS PAST HAVE DRIVEN HIM OVER THE EDGE!
KSSH
I HOPE THE DOCTOR GETS HERE SOOOON!
VROOOOM
AW MAN...
SERIOUSLY?
I CAN'T GET THROUGH!
KUSSSH
※ The doctor won't get there soon.

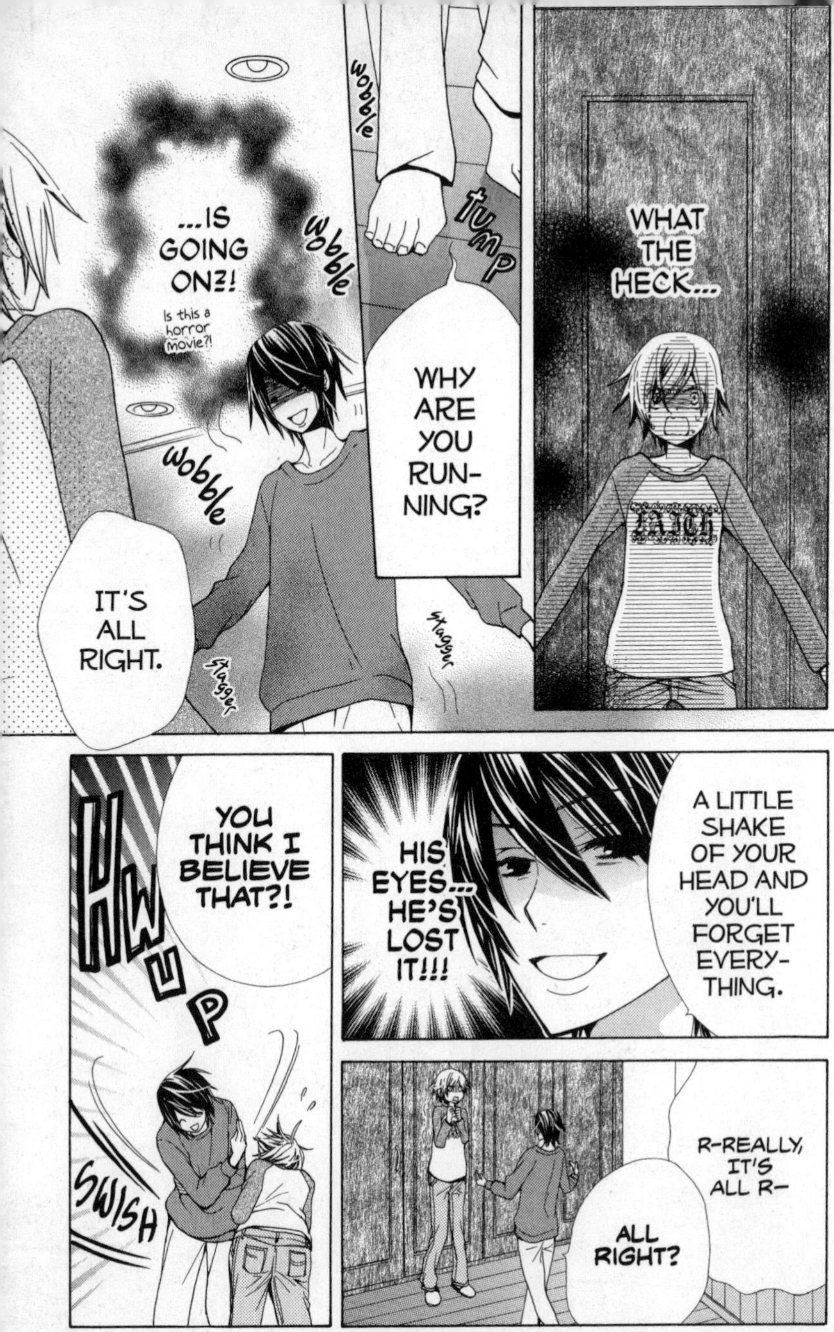
WHAT THE HECK...
wobble
tump
WHY ARE YOU RUN- NING?
...IS GOING ON?!
Is this a horror movie?!
wobble
wobble
stagger
IT'S ALL RIGHT.
stagger
A LITTLE SHAKE OF YOUR HEAD AND YOU'LL FORGET EVERY- THING.
HIS EYES... HE'S LOST IT!!!
R-REALLY, IT'S ALL R—
ALL RIGHT?
YOU THINK I BELIEVE THAT?!
HWUP
SWISH

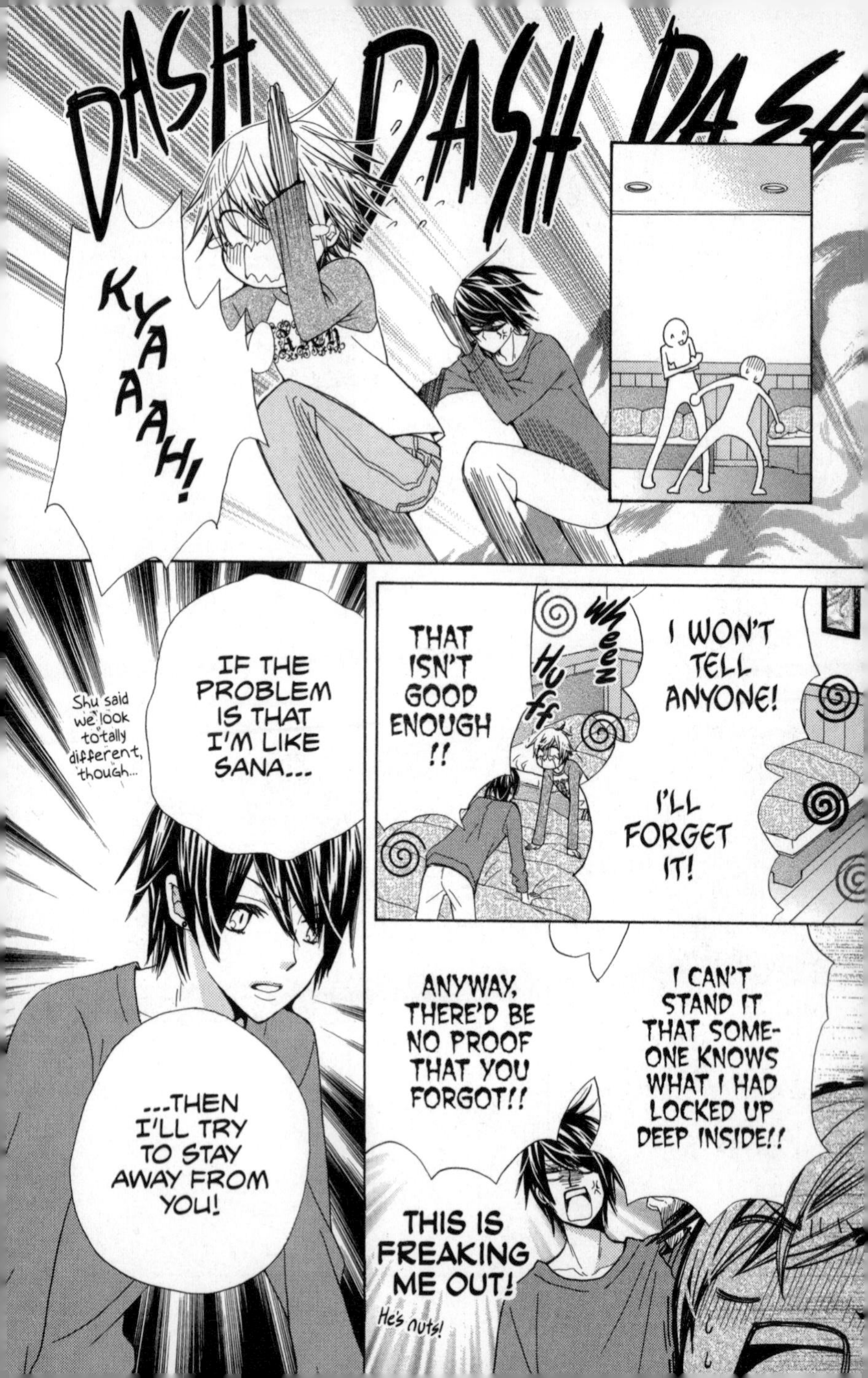
DASH
DASH
DASH
KYAAAAH!
I WON'T TELL ANYONE!
I'LL FORGET IT!
THAT ISN'T GOOD ENOUGH!!
Wheeze
Huff
I CAN'T STAND IT THAT SOME-ONE KNOWS WHAT I HAD LOCKED UP DEEP INSIDE!!
ANYWAY, THERE'D BE NO PROOF THAT YOU FORGOT!!
THIS IS FREAKING ME OUT!
He's nuts!
IF THE PROBLEM IS THAT I'M LIKE SANA...
Shu said we look totally different, though...
...THEN I'LL TRY TO STAY AWAY FROM YOU!

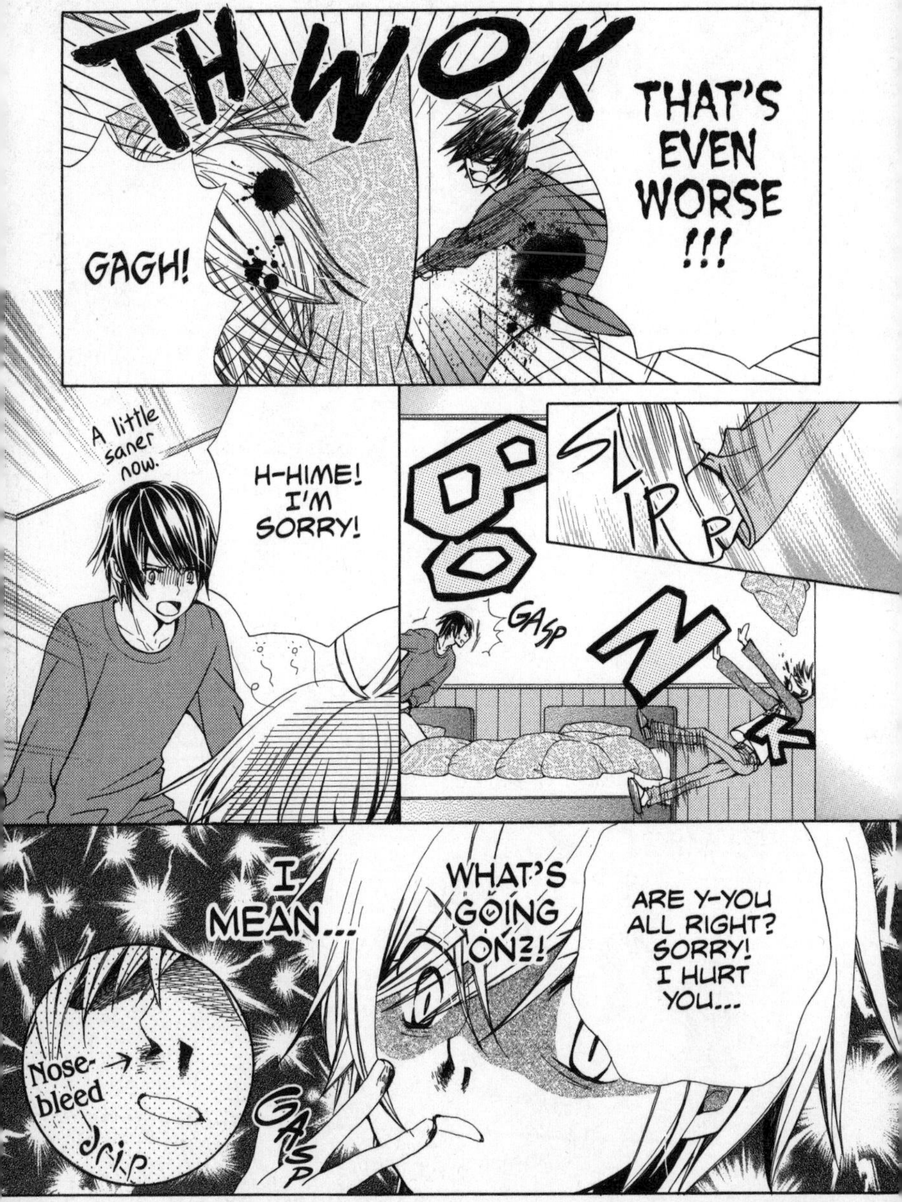
THWOK
THAT'S EVEN WORSE!!!
GAGH!
SLIPP
DOON
GASP
H-HIME! I'M SORRY!
A little saner now.
ARE Y-YOU ALL RIGHT? SORRY! I HURT YOU...
WHAT'S GOING ON?!
I MEAN...
GASP
Nose-bleed
drip

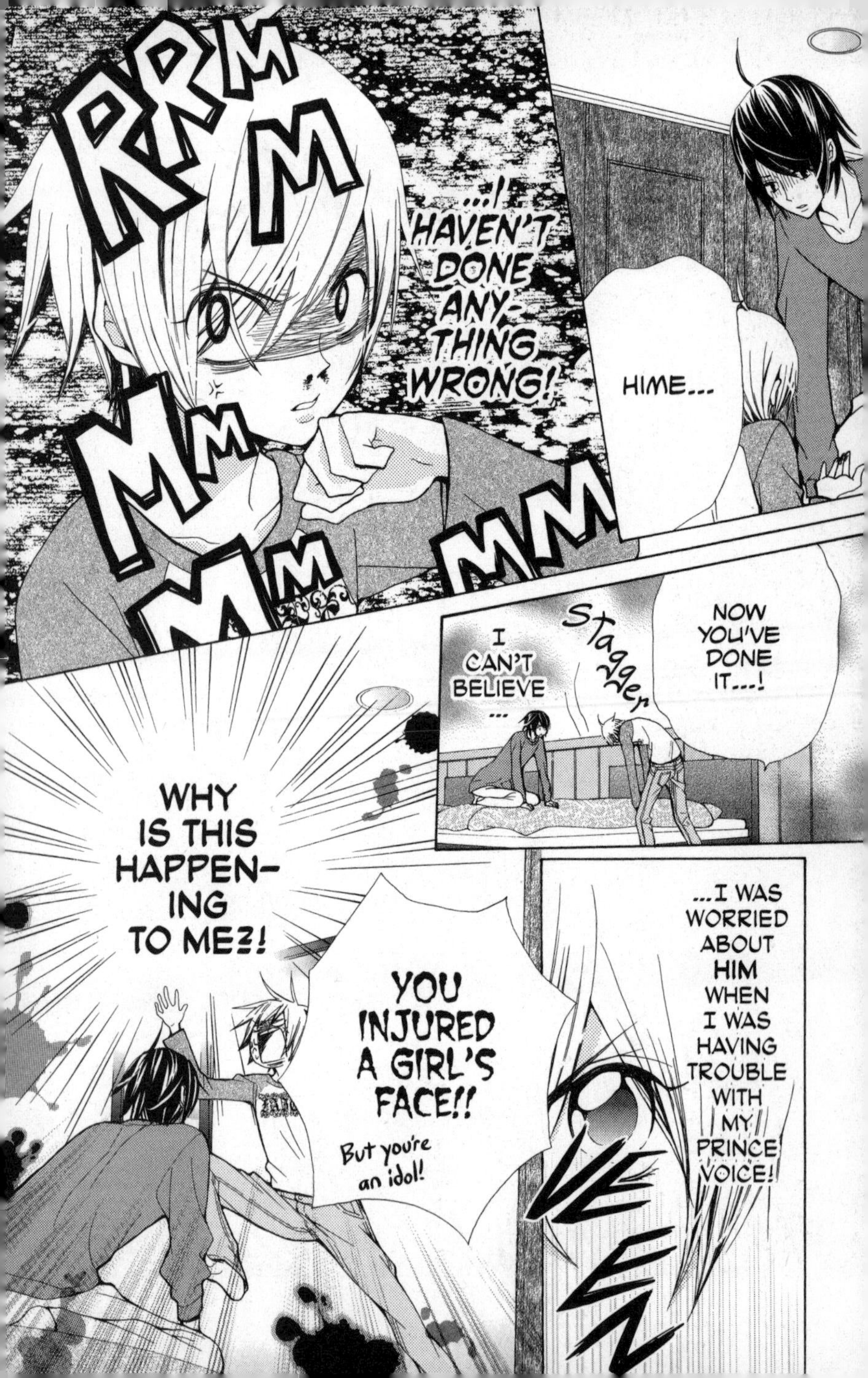
HIME...
RRMMM
...I HAVEN'T DONE ANY-THING WRONG!
MMM
MMMM
NOW YOU'VE DONE IT...!
Stagger
I CAN'T BELIEVE...
WHY IS THIS HAPPEN-ING TO ME?!
...I WAS WORRIED ABOUT HIM WHEN I WAS HAVING TROUBLE WITH MY PRINCE VOICE!
VEEN
YOU INJURED A GIRL'S FACE!!
But you're an idol!

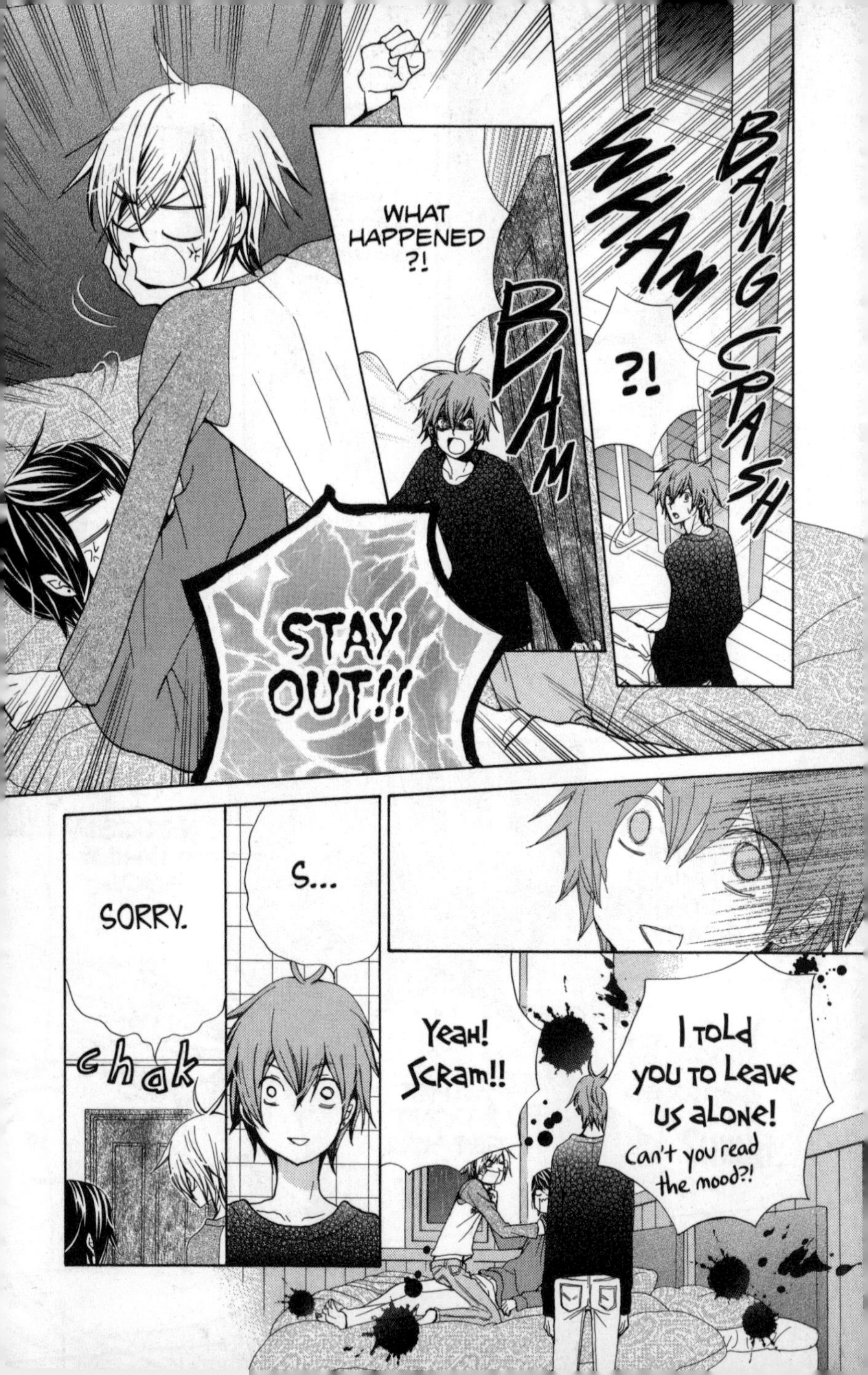
BANG CRASH
WHAM
?!
BAM
WHAT HAPPENED ?!
STAY OUT!!
S...
SORRY.
chak
I TOLD YOU TO LEAVE US ALONE! Can't you read the mood?!
Yeah! Scram!!

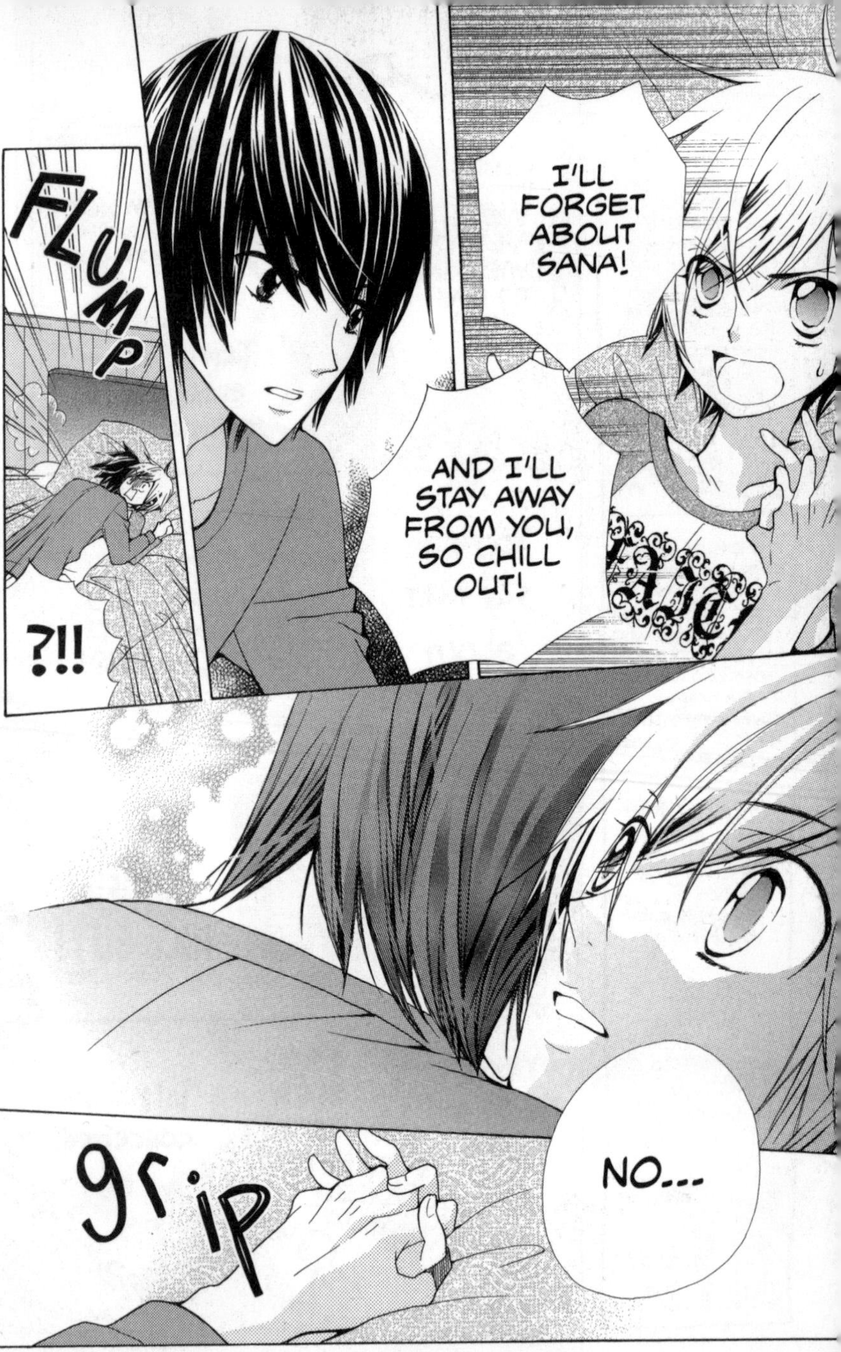
I'LL FORGET ABOUT SANA!
AND I'LL STAY AWAY FROM YOU, SO CHILL OUT!
FLUMP
?!!
NO...
grip

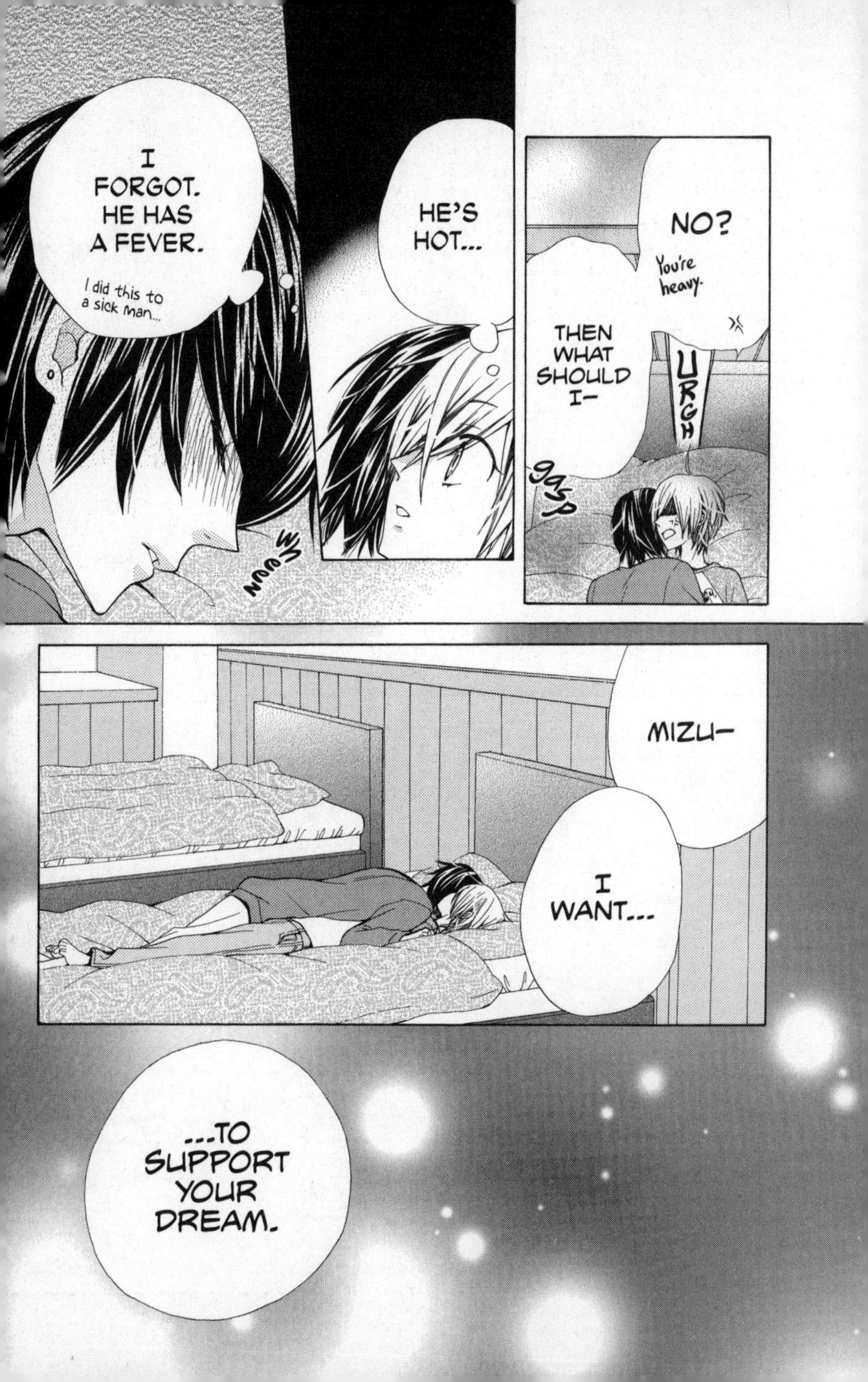
NO?
You're heavy.
URGH
THEN WHAT SHOULD I-
gasp
HE'S HOT...
I FORGOT. HE HAS A FEVER.
I did this to a sick man...
mween
MIZU-
I WANT...
...TO SUPPORT YOUR DREAM.

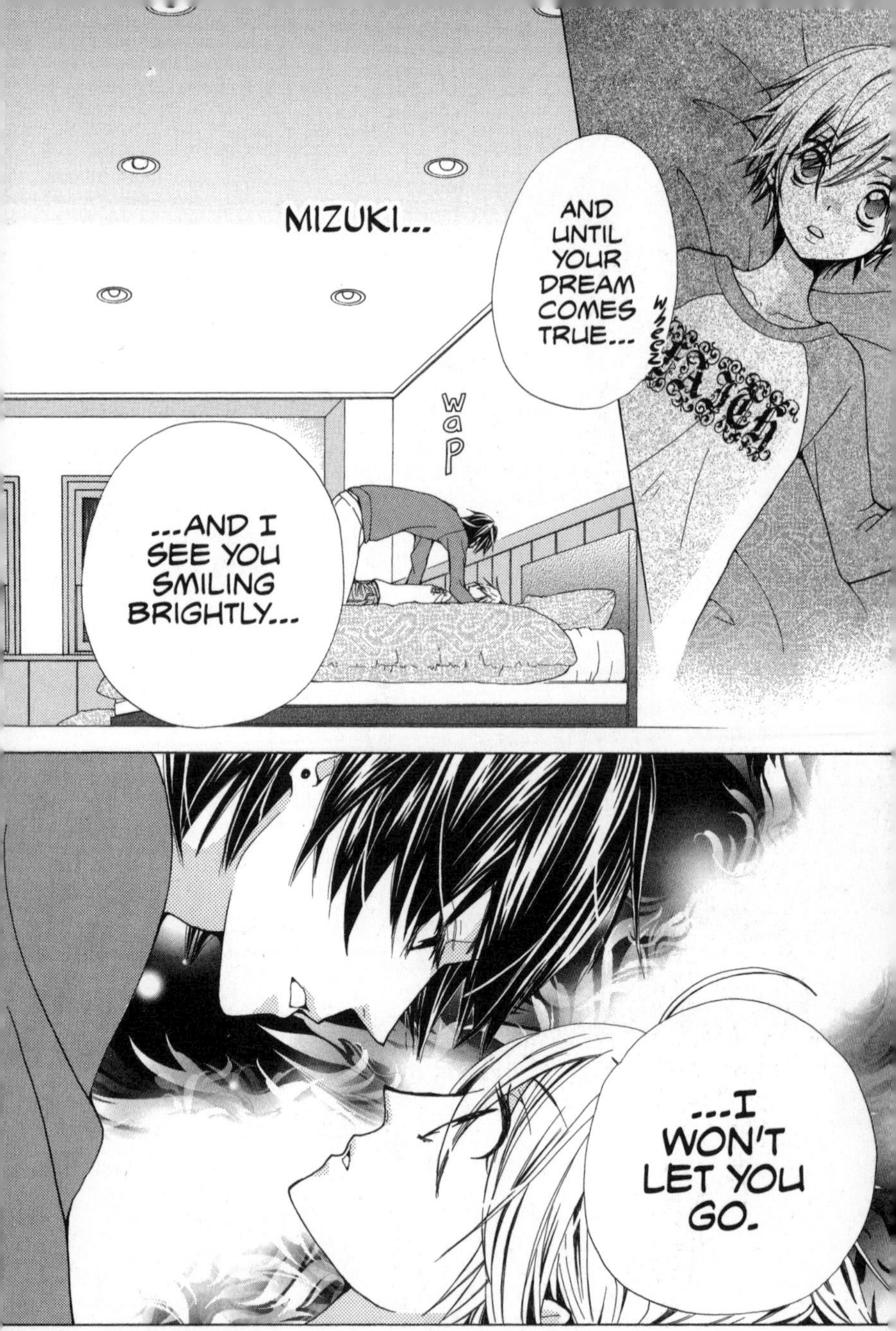
AND UNTIL YOUR DREAM COMES TRUE...
MIZUKI...
WAP
...AND I SEE YOU SMILING BRIGHTLY...
...I WON'T LET YOU GO.

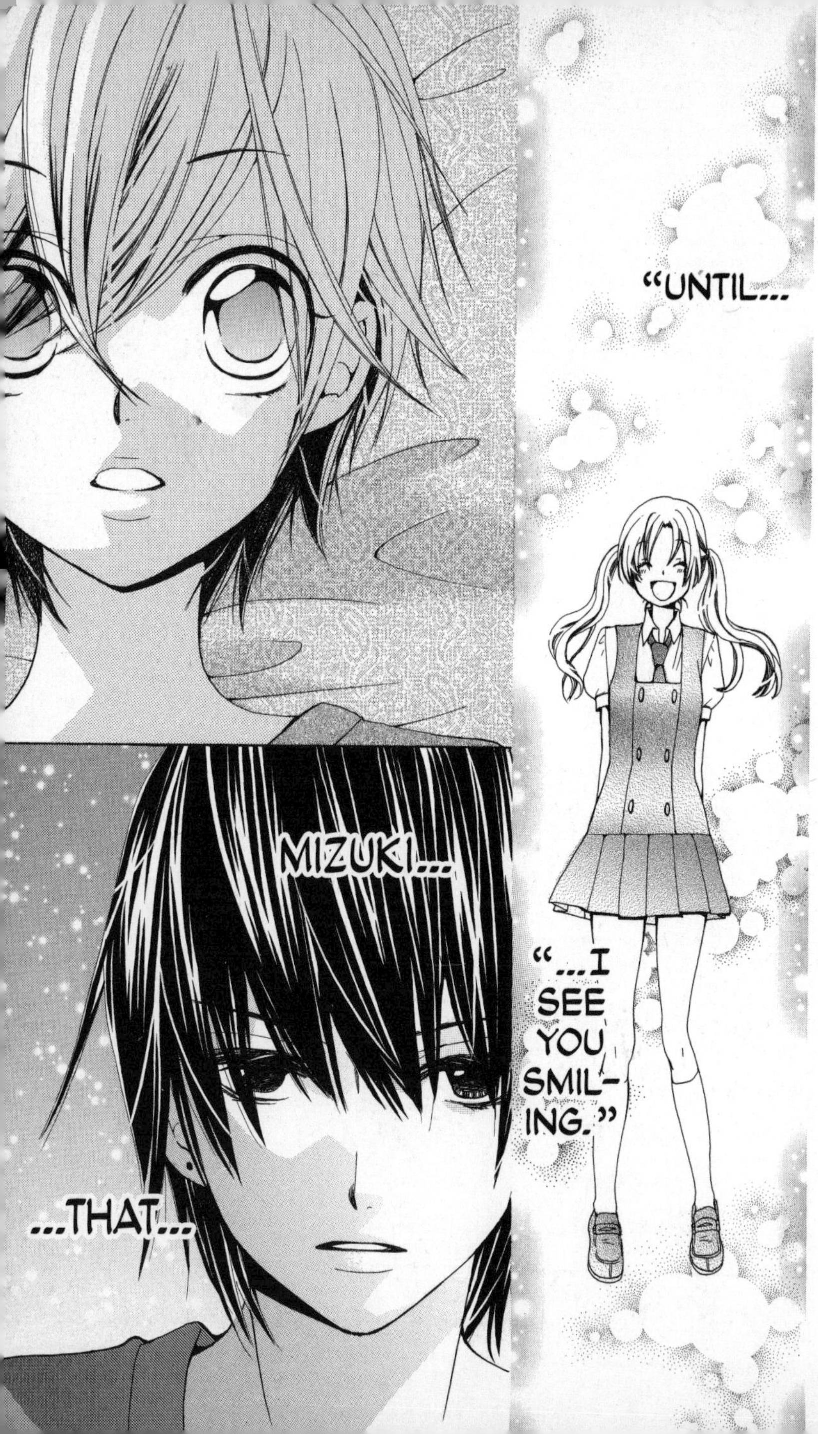
"UNTIL...
"...I SEE YOU SMILING."
MIZUKI...
...THAT...

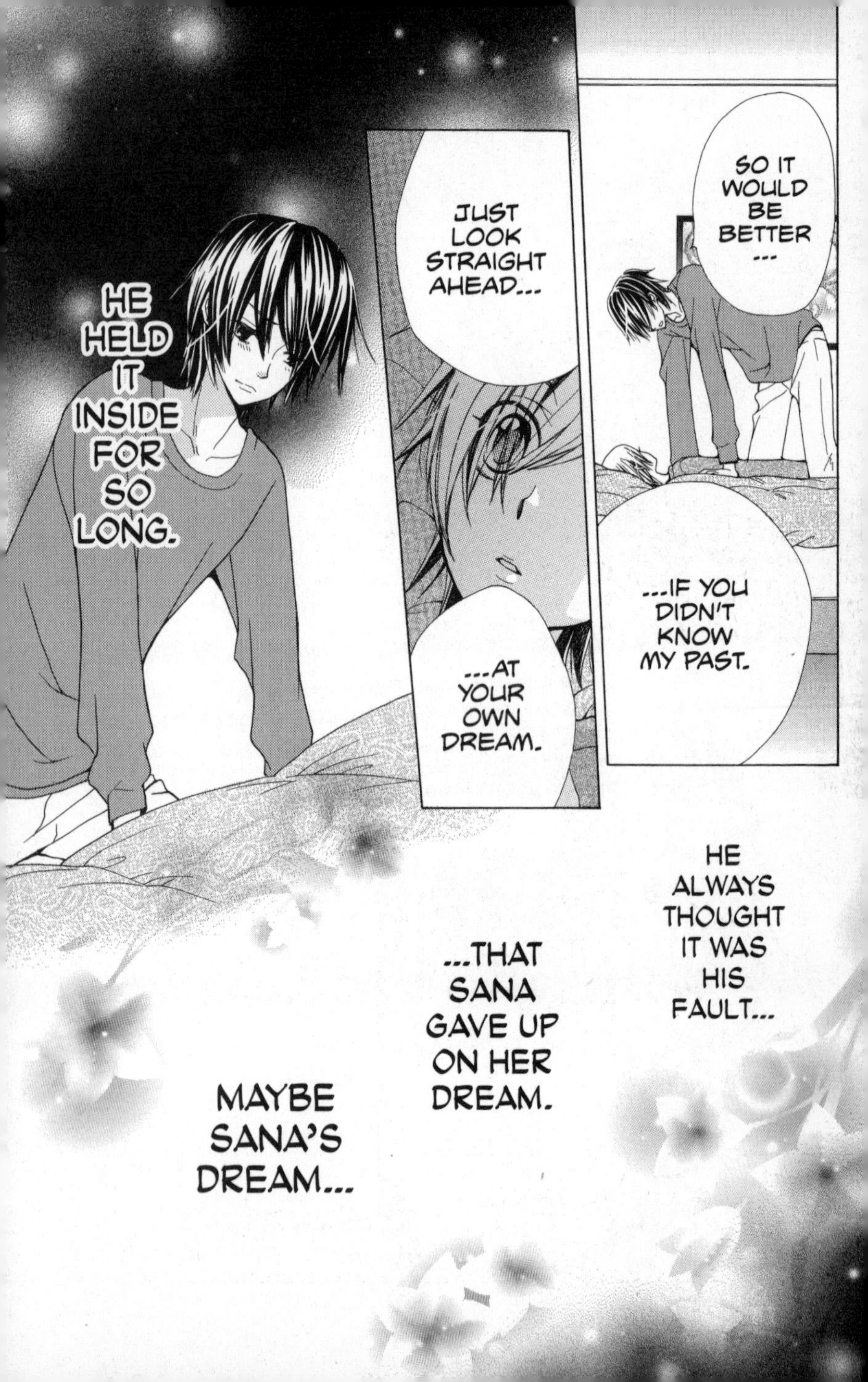
SO IT WOULD BE BETTER...
...IF YOU DIDN'T KNOW MY PAST.
JUST LOOK STRAIGHT AHEAD...
...AT YOUR OWN DREAM.
HE HELD IT INSIDE FOR SO LONG.
HE ALWAYS THOUGHT IT WAS HIS FAULT...
...THAT SANA GAVE UP ON HER DREAM.
MAYBE SANA'S DREAM...

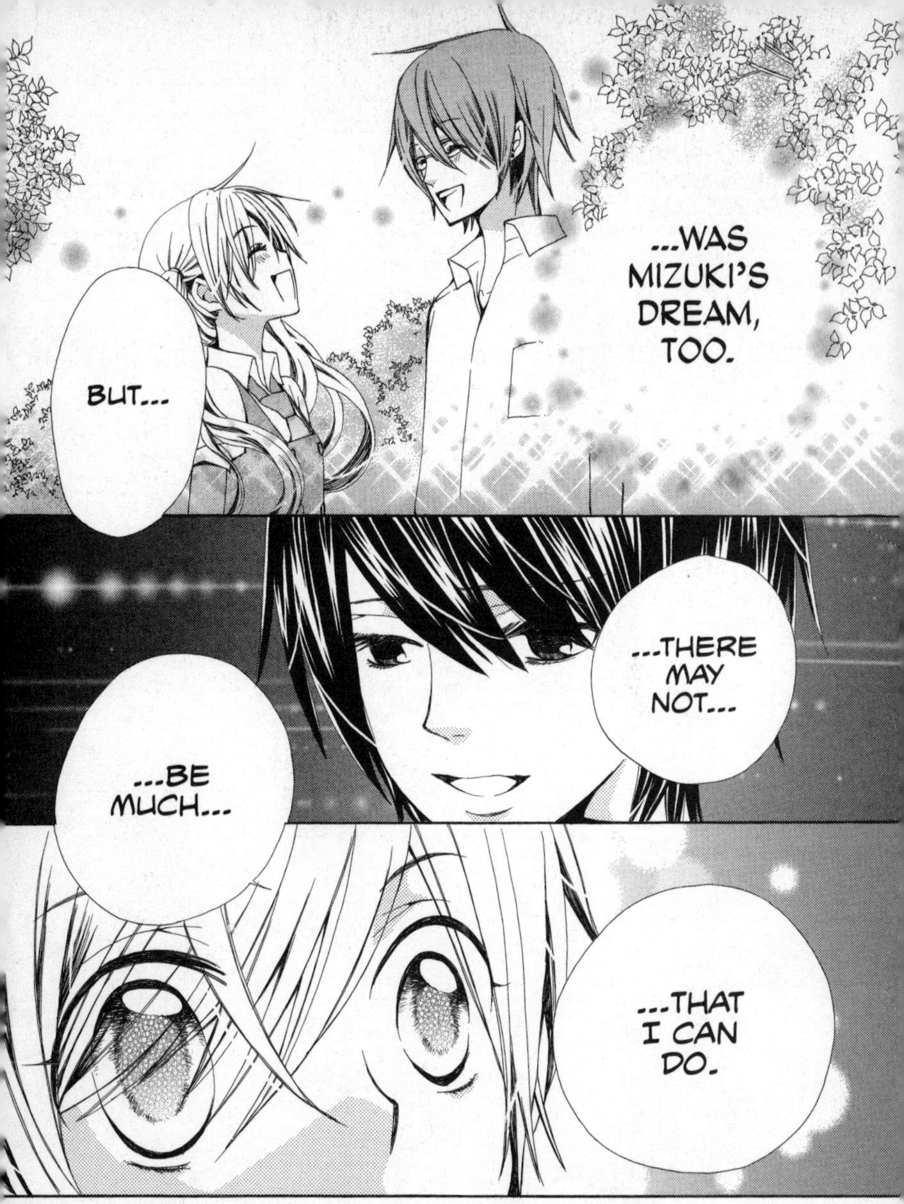
...WAS MIZUKI'S DREAM, TOO.
BUT...
...THERE MAY NOT...
...BE MUCH...
...THAT I CAN DO.

OH, LOVELY ♡ BLAZER...

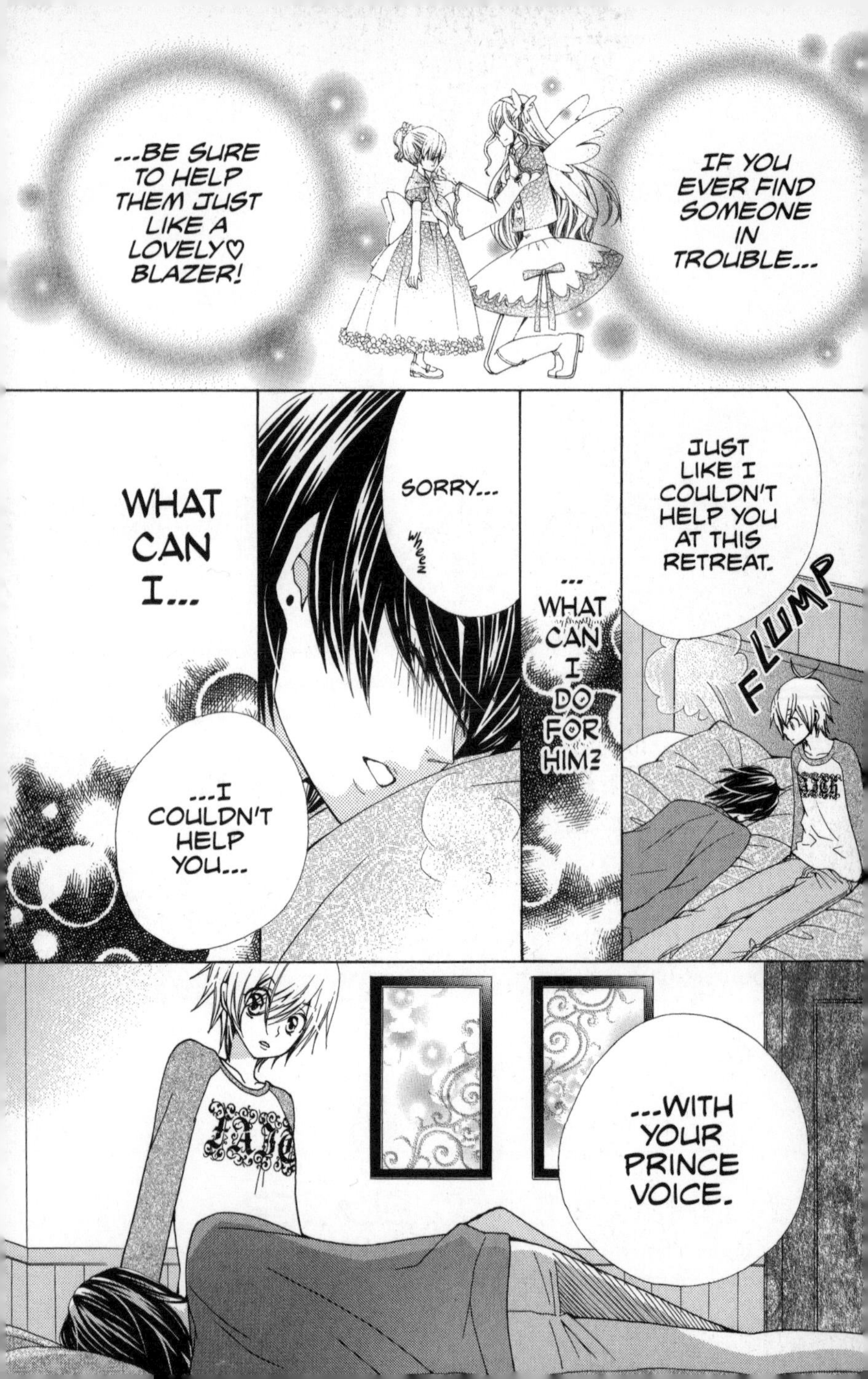
IF YOU EVER FIND SOMEONE IN TROUBLE...
...BE SURE TO HELP THEM JUST LIKE A LOVELY♡ BLAZER!
JUST LIKE I COULDN'T HELP YOU AT THIS RETREAT.
FLUMP
...WHAT CAN I DO FOR HIM?
SORRY...
...I COULDN'T HELP YOU...
WHAT CAN I...
...WITH YOUR PRINCE VOICE.

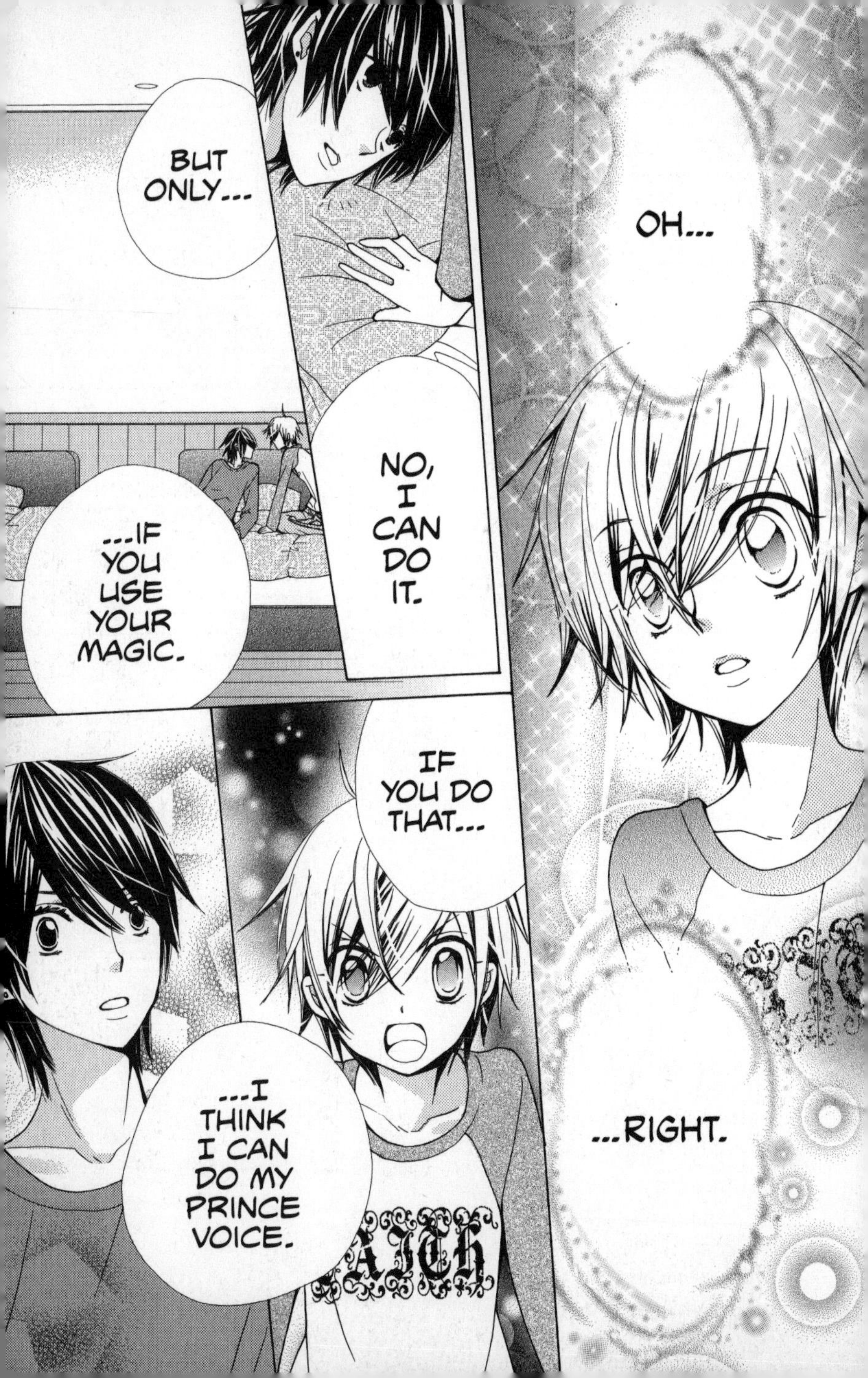
BUT ONLY...
...IF YOU USE YOUR MAGIC.
NO, I CAN DO IT.
IF YOU DO THAT...
...I THINK I CAN DO MY PRINCE VOICE.
OH...
...RIGHT.

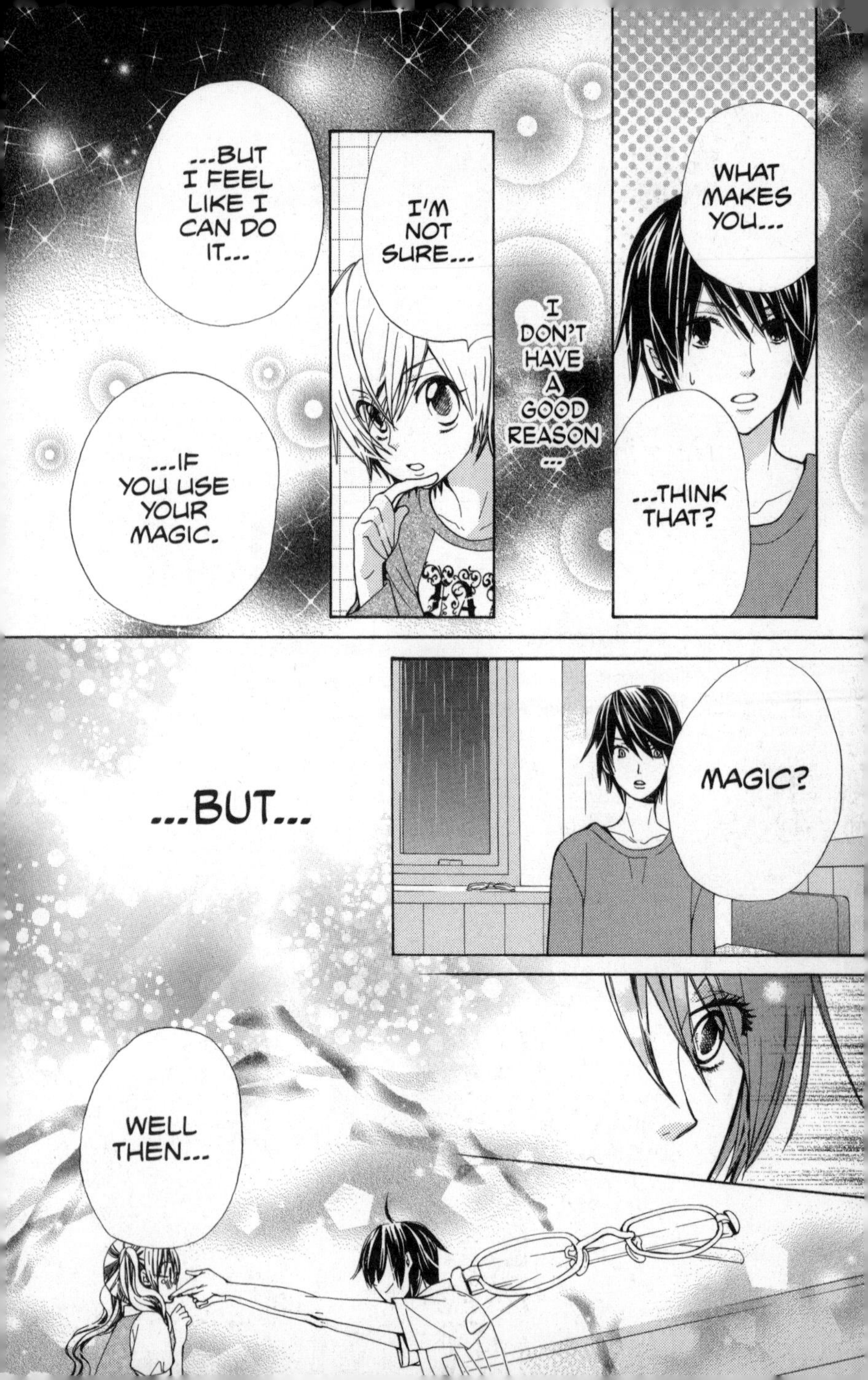
WHAT MAKES YOU...
...THINK THAT?
I DON'T HAVE A GOOD REASON ...
I'M NOT SURE...
...BUT I FEEL LIKE I CAN DO IT...
...IF YOU USE YOUR MAGIC.
MAGIC?
...BUT...
WELL THEN...

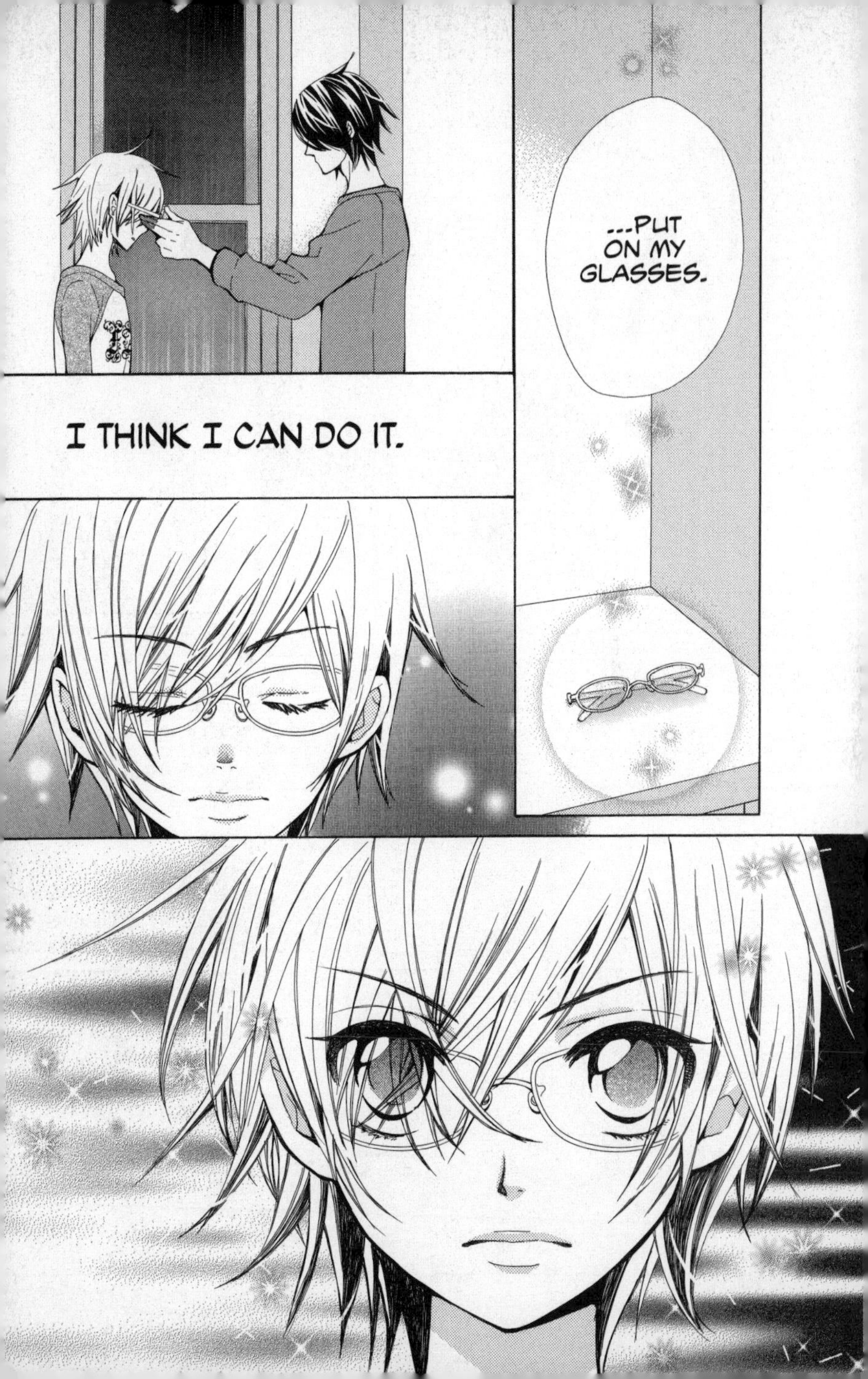
...PUT ON MY GLASSES.
I THINK I CAN DO IT.

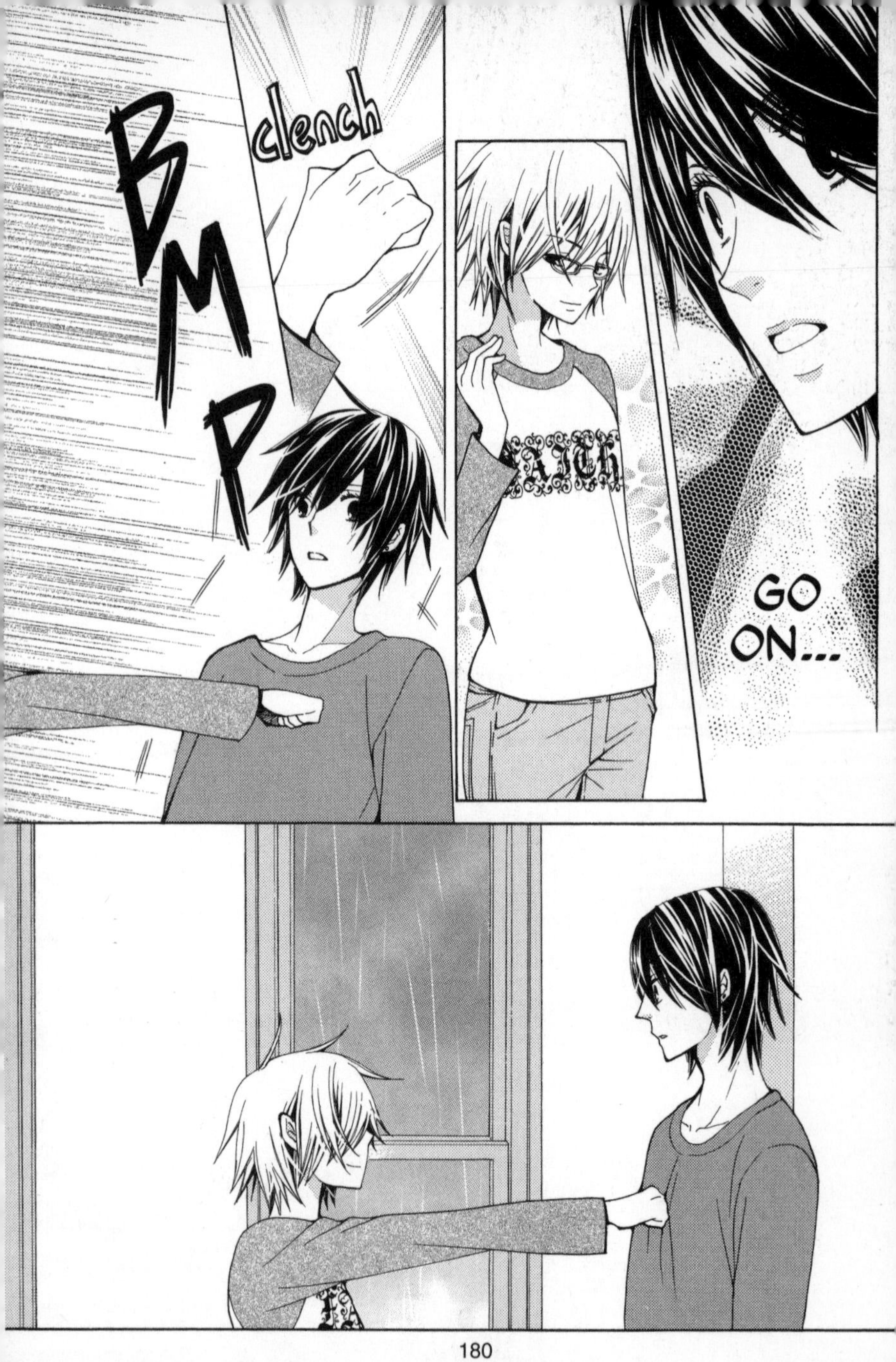
GO ON...
FAITH
clench
BMP

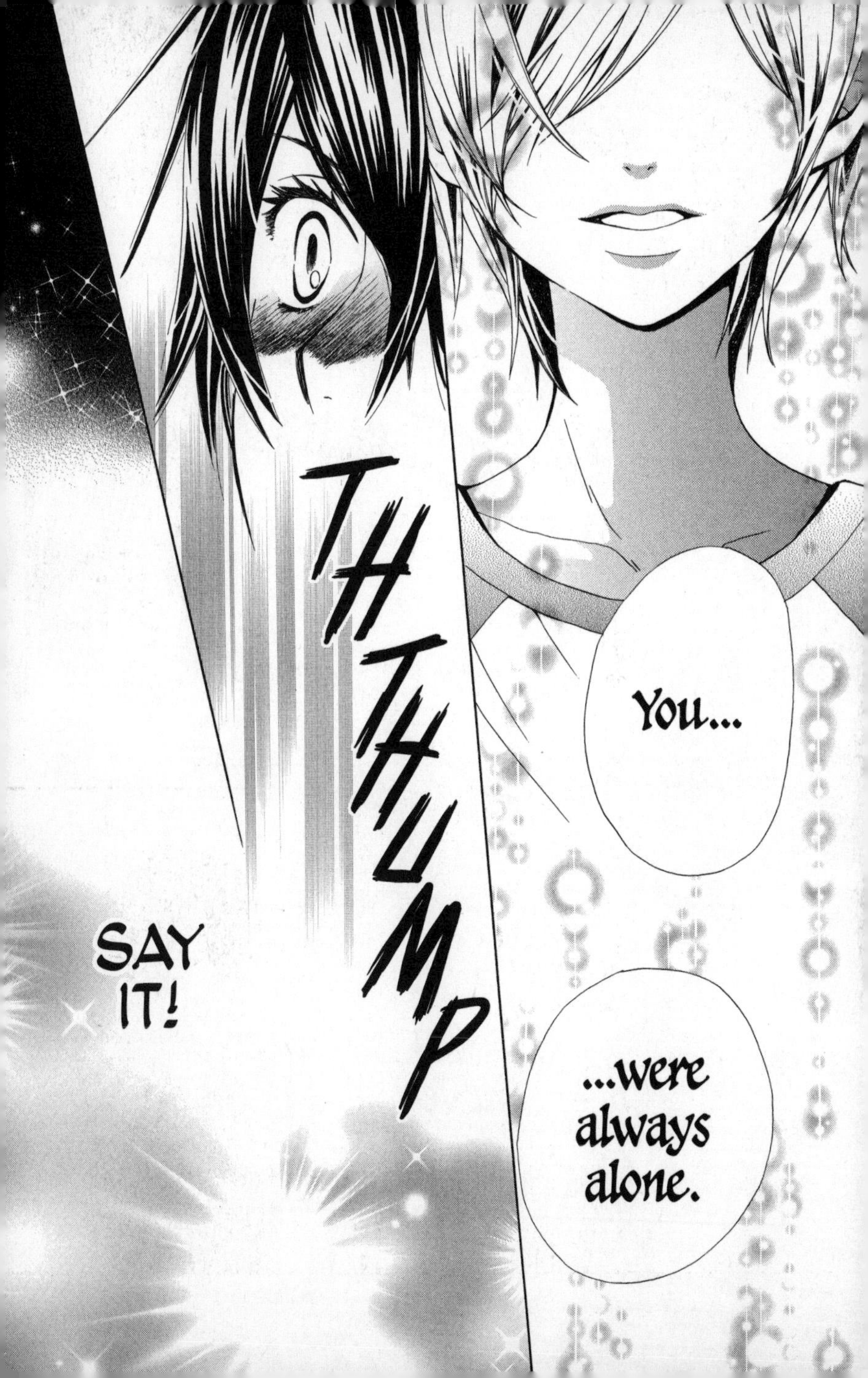
You...
...were always alone.
THTHUMP
SAY IT!

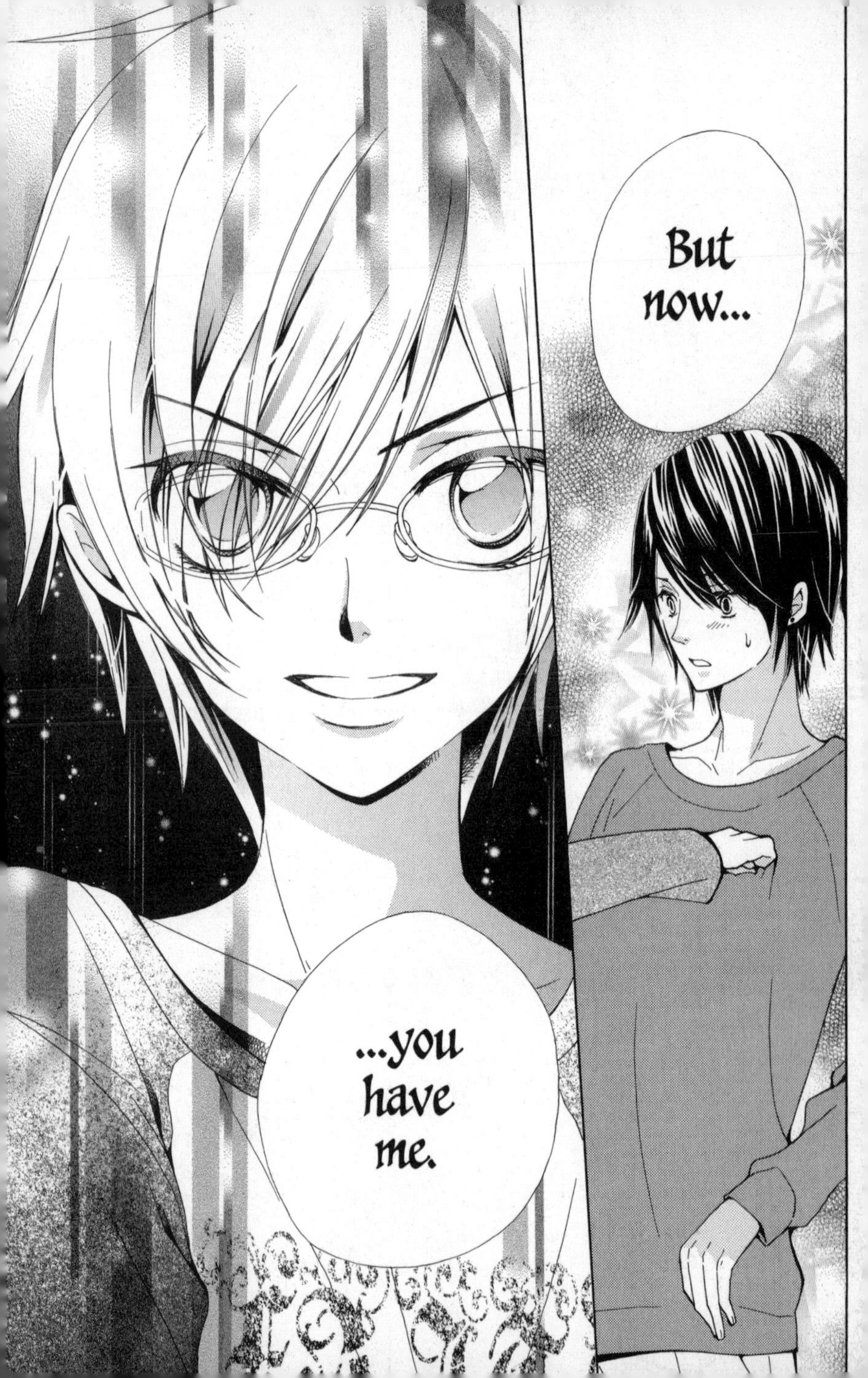
But now...
...you have me.

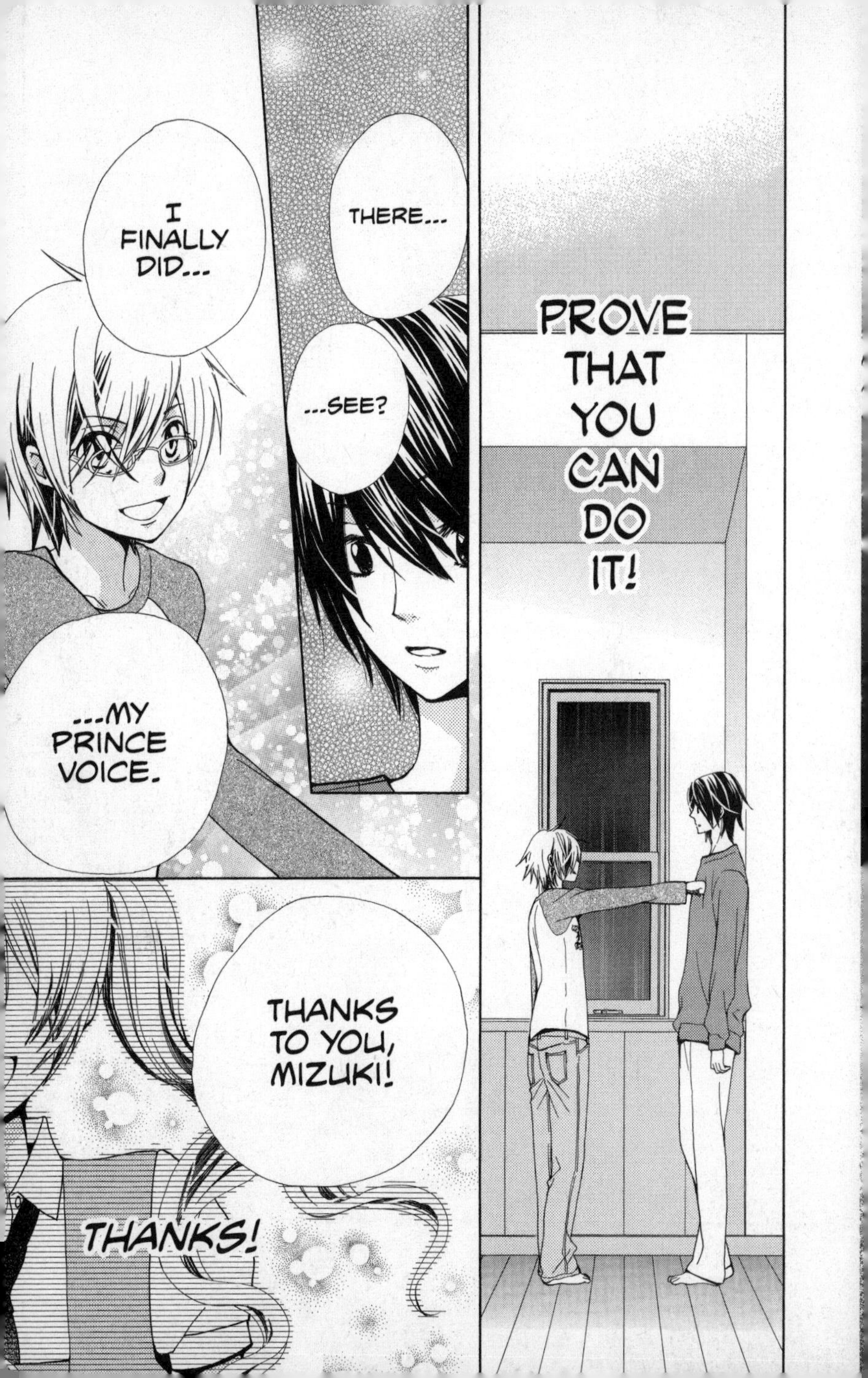
PROVE THAT YOU CAN DO IT!
THERE...
...SEE?
I FINALLY DID...
...MY PRINCE VOICE.
THANKS TO YOU, MIZUKI!
THANKS!

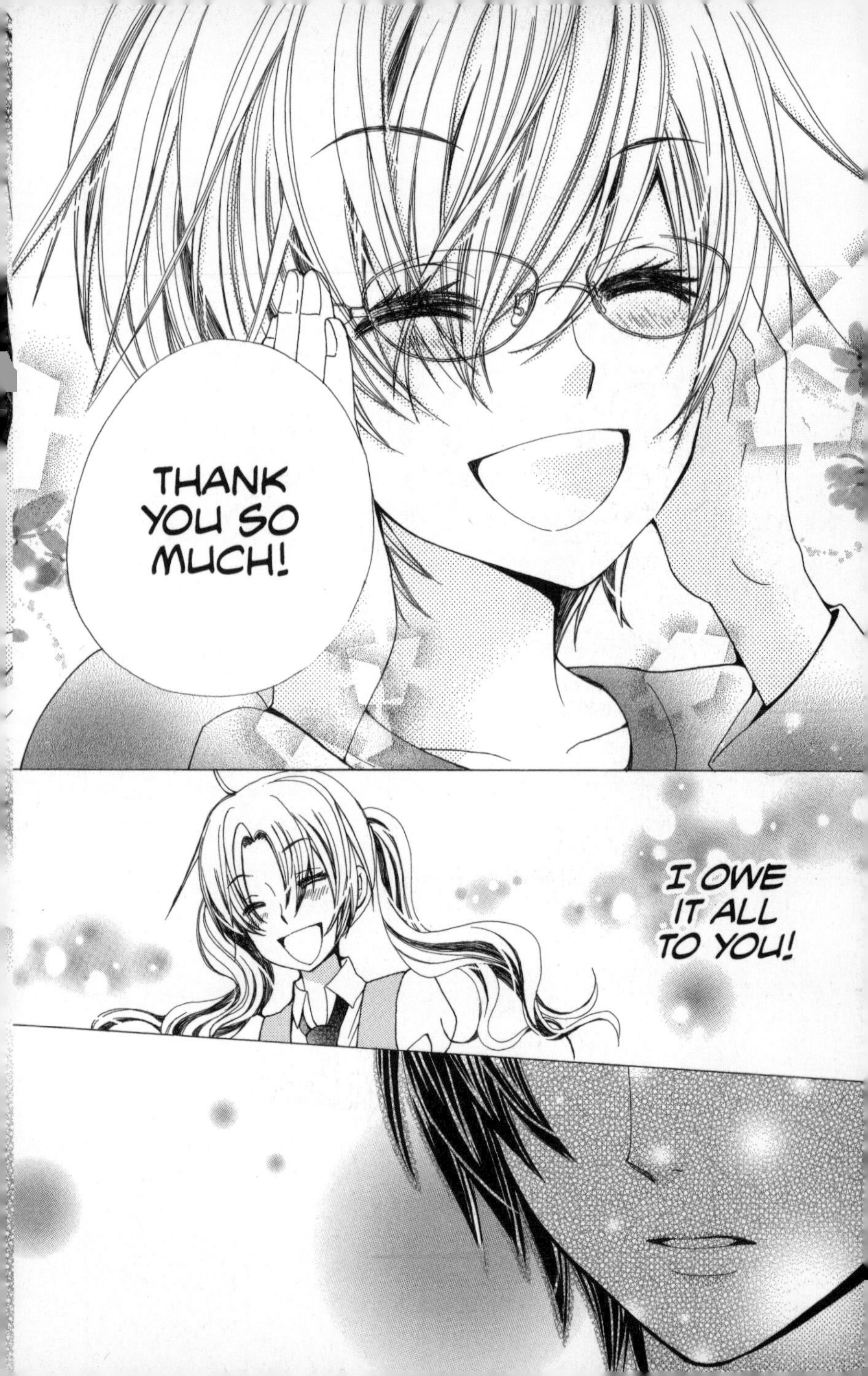
THANK YOU SO MUCH!
I OWE IT ALL TO YOU!

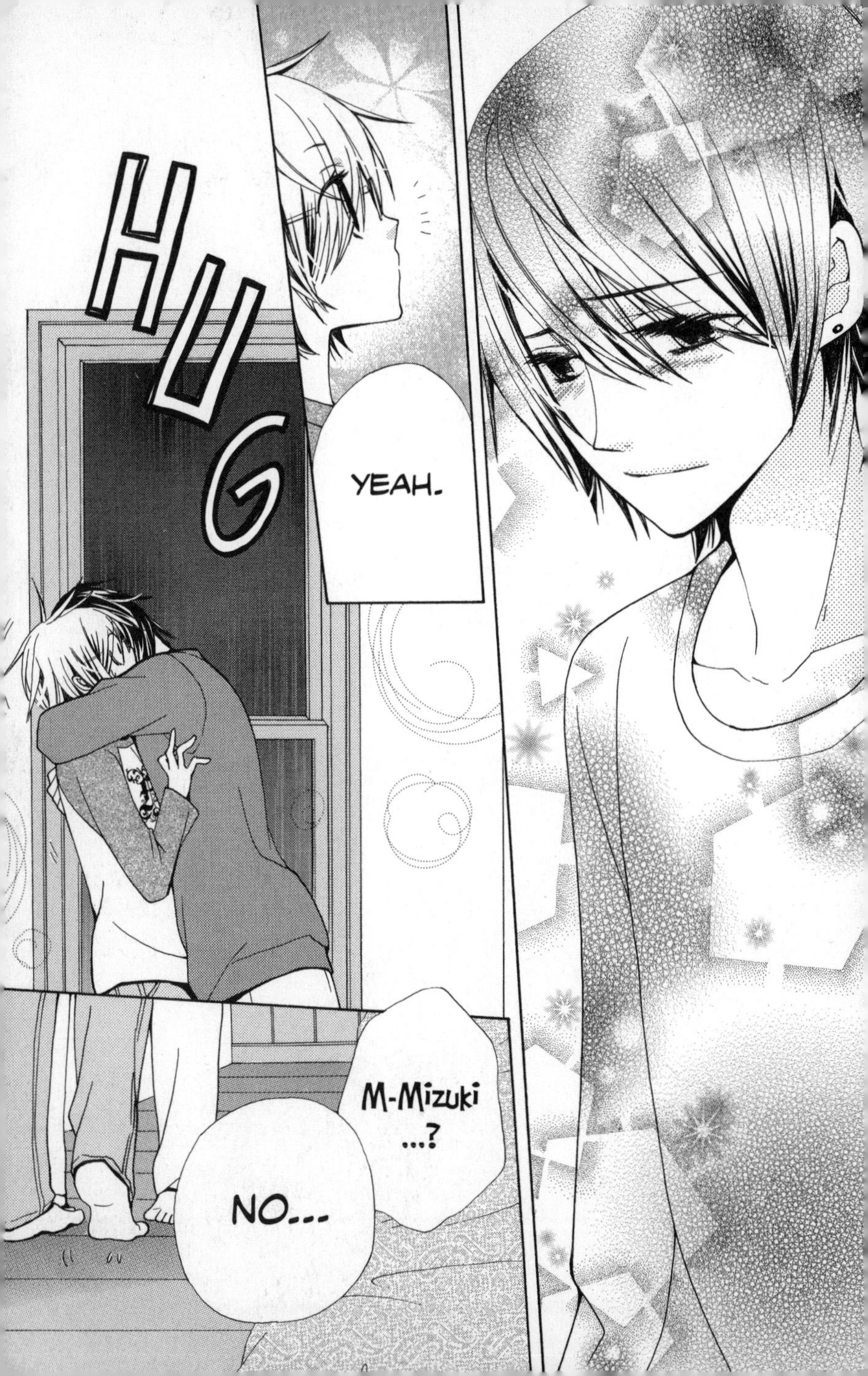
YEAH.
HUG
M-Mizuki ...?
NO...

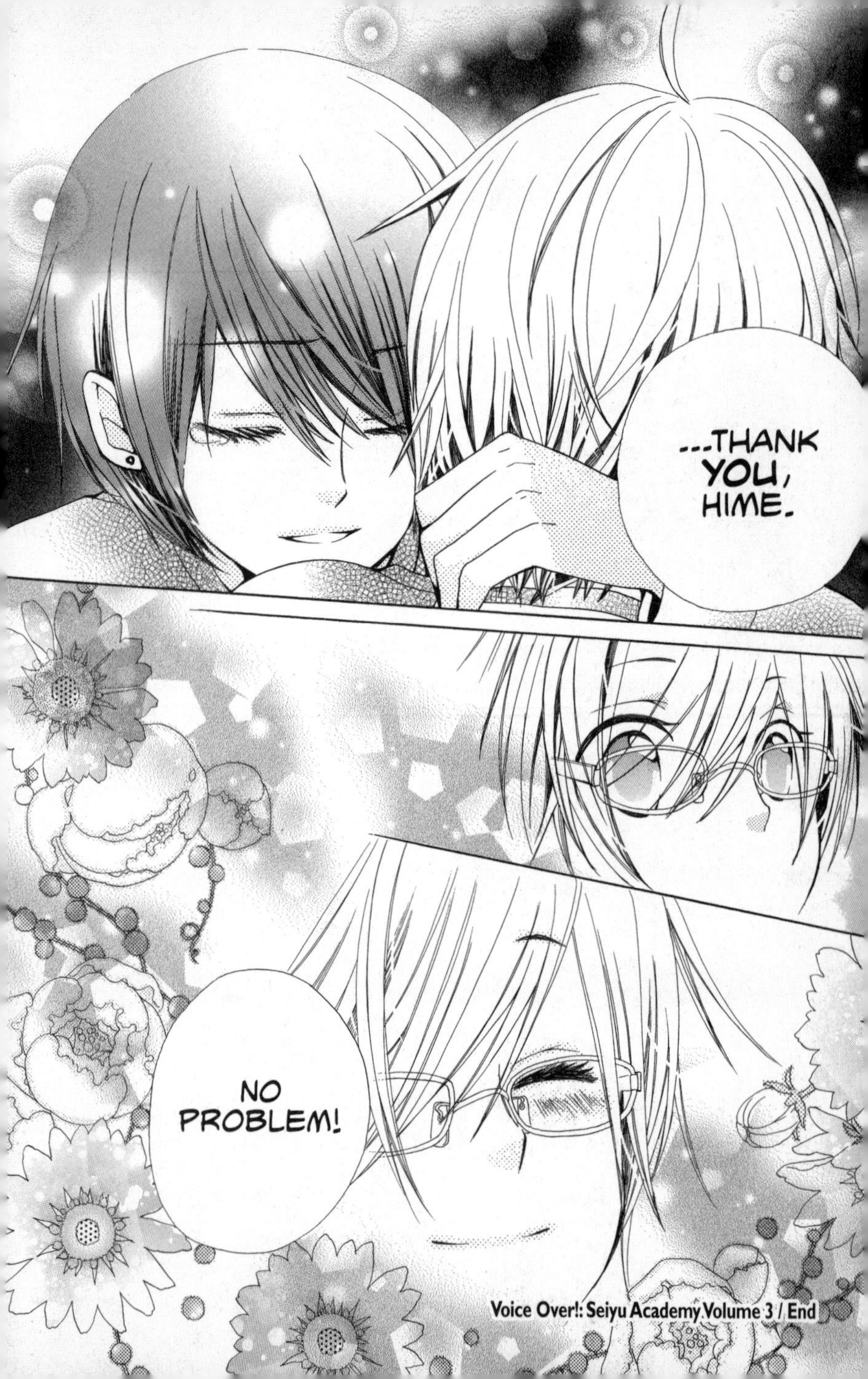
...THANK YOU, HIME.
NO PROBLEM!
Voice Over!: Seiyu Academy Volume 3 / End

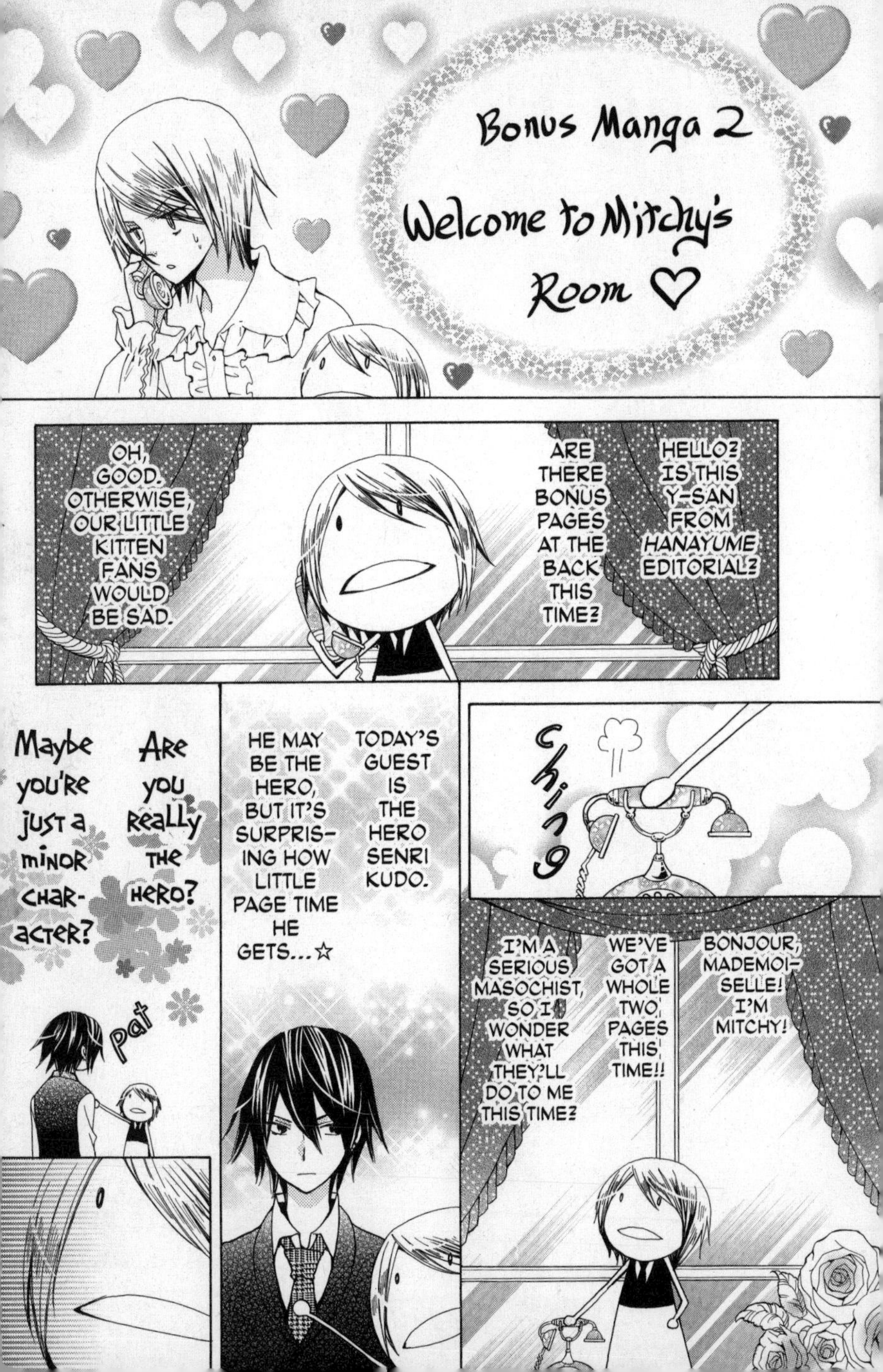
Bonus Manga 2
Welcome to Mitchy's Room ♡
HELLO? IS THIS Y-SAN FROM *HANAYUME* EDITORIAL?
ARE THERE BONUS PAGES AT THE BACK THIS TIME?
OH, GOOD. OTHERWISE, OUR LITTLE KITTEN FANS WOULD BE SAD.
ching
BONJOUR, MADEMOISELLE! I'M MITCHY!
WE'VE GOT A WHOLE TWO PAGES THIS TIME!!
I'M A SERIOUS MASOCHIST, SO I WONDER WHAT THEY'LL DO TO ME THIS TIME?
TODAY'S GUEST IS THE HERO SENRI KUDO.
HE MAY BE THE HERO, BUT IT'S SURPRISING HOW LITTLE PAGE TIME HE GETS...☆
Are you really the hero?
Maybe you're just a minor character?
pat

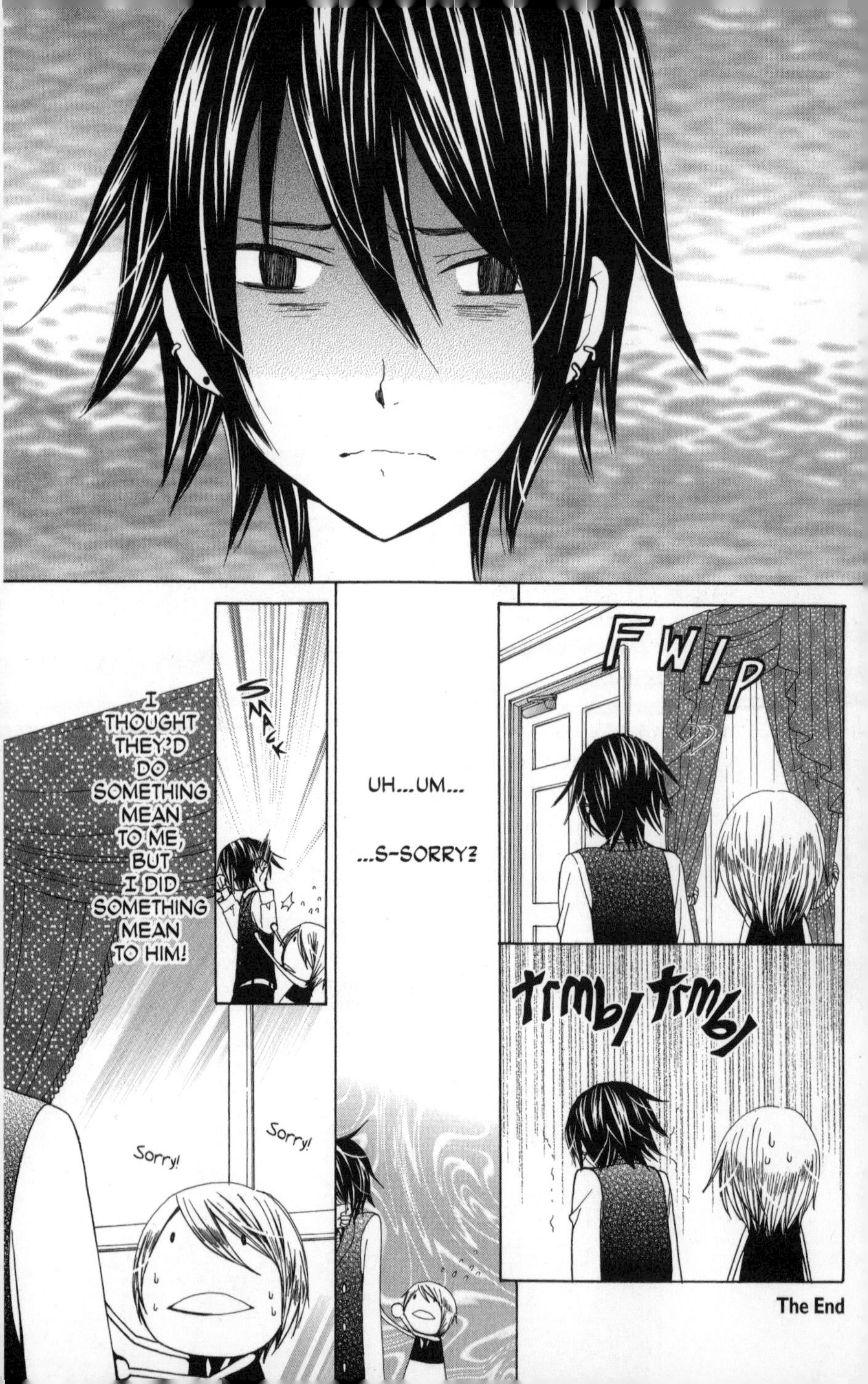
FWIP
trmbl trmbl
UH...UM...
...S-SORRY?
SMACK
I THOUGHT THEY'D DO SOMETHING MEAN TO ME, BUT I DID SOMETHING MEAN TO HIM!
Sorry!
Sorry!
The End

Voice Over! Seiyu Academy

End Notes

Page 73, side bar: Sensei
Sensei is a Japanese honorific used for doctors, professors, lawyers and other professionals. It is also used for people who have mastered an art form, such as manga creators, musicians, novelists and other artists.

Page 138, panel 3: Takoyaki
Dough balls with pieces of octopus in them. They are made using a hot plate and are often sold at Japanese festivals. *Tako* means "octopus" in Japanese.

Voice Acting Students Now!

The characters of *Voice Over!: Seiyu Academy* continue to show progress! But how do real students at a voice acting school spend their days? Let's talk to actual students from the voice talent department at Tokyo Animator College.

Reporter Y (R): Would you each please introduce yourselves?

Tsushima: I'm Yoshinori Tsushima. I turn 26 this year. I feel like I'm getting a late start because of my age, but I'm pretending it doesn't bother me.

Isobe: I'm Kazuhiro Isobe. I'm 19! I love *Gundam*! I entered this school because someday I want to be a Gundam!

R: Not a Gundam pilot, but a Gundam itself?

Isobe: Because I wanna be a Gundam! I wanna be a Gundam and shout like "Graaah!"

R: But Gundam suits don't shout like "Graaah." *(laughs)*

Everyone: *(laughs)*

Isobe: You know, maybe like venting air and stuff…

R: Oh, you want to express their emotion that way. So all you want to do in the future is spurt out air? *(laughs)*

Everyone: *(laughs)*

Okita: It's hard to go after Gundam…

Isobe: No, not at all!

Okita: And coming in third is me…Johnny Depp!

Everyone: *(laughs)*

Okita: I'm Takuya Okita! I'm 19. I love *One Piece*! Also, I have a flexible body. That doesn't come across through audio, but my shoulders are amazingly flexible! Watch this! *(Everyone applauds.)*

Okita: Thank you! My shoulder spins around and around!

Everyone: *(laughs)*

Okita: I also like to keep the conversation moving around and around!

Everyone: *(laughs)*

Hiraga: I'm Mie Hiraga! I'm 19, too! It's only been a year since I came to Tokyo, so I'm still having a lot of trouble shaking my Kansai dialect! I'm learning dance! I want to dance at events and stuff! That's all for me!

Matsumoto: I'm Rika Matsumoto! In junior high and high school, I was the vocalist in a band!

Everyone: Cool! *(laughs)*

Suzuki: I'm Asuka Suzuki! I'm 19. For eight years in elementary school, junior high and high school, I was in track and field events. I'm sort of built, so the other day my teacher asked me if I was putting something in my shirt to make my shoulders look bigger. But I'm not! *(laughs)* I'm also good at imitating things.

Sonehara: I'm Chihiro Sonehara. My favorite food is ice cream. My hobby is baking sweets. Nice to meet you!

R: What kind of classes do you usually take?

Hiraga: Dubbing, but sometimes we get handed the script right there and do it at first sight. They tell us to find out how many characters we can read in two minutes.

Isobe: There are a lot of practical training classes like dance and singing to improve our expressiveness.

Sonehara: Like short skits.

Tsushima: There's also free talking.

R: Because voice talents often get radio work. By the way, why did you enroll at Tokyo Animator College?

Sonehara: A big reason was that you can make your debut while here. I got to experience being in two anime and being a presenter. I work pretty hard among those at my level in school.

Hiraga: I thought I was doing relatively well at school, but this way I can get experience in different types of professional work.

Suzuki: Until high school, I didn't use my voice for expression through singing or plays and so forth, but this school teaches us everything from the very start, from fluency to vocalization. And being able to make your debut while in school is great.

Sonehara: I decided to try to become a voice actor because I like *Sakura Wars*. In the Imperial Assault Force, the voice actor performs a character, and then acts on top of that. I was impressed by how one person could do so much, and even cried. I decided to come here because Kumiko Nishihara, who voices Iris, teaches here.

Isobe: I decided to come here because Fuyumi Shiraishi, who was in *First Gundam*, is an instructor.

Suzuki: I was the youngest of three children, so my parents said, "We can't pay university fees for you." But you can choose to pay in installments here, and without any interest! Then my mom said, "How nice of them! Are you sure it isn't a trick?" I think it's all right, though. *(laughs)*

R: To finish up, I'd like to ask each of you to state what your dream is for half a year from now.

Tsushima: I hope work starts filtering in. If luck permits! Hopefully, I'll get to perform a named character and get to sing a character song!

Sonehara: People often tell me I can only do exaggerated performances and not subtle ones. I can already do something that jumps out at you, so pretty soon I want to do a performance in which some sort of passion is burning inside!

Matsumoto: I want to rapidly increase my ability to handle anything that arises, in work or elsewhere. And I'd like to get a little work now and then… *(laughs)* I want to do my best in my studies, too. Right now, we're practicing for the new student welcome party, and I'd like to handle every single thing like that so I don't have any regrets. That's about it.

Okita: It's like seizing something shiny and polishing up its character so it blooms!

R: What is character to you, Okita-kun?

Okita: It's being able to make people enjoy themselves and enjoying myself along with them. Having fun, but seriously! Shinier and shinier! I want a shine that others just don't have!

Isobe: I want to be someone others can rely on. I want to be the kind of person who, skill-wise and personality-wise, is relaxing to be around.

Hiraga: I want to be able to do all the things I can't do now. And I'd like to get a grasp of what my situation is and what type of character suits me. I'd also like to become more of an adult. I want to graduate after understanding that for myself.

Suzuki: Six months seems like a long time, but it is actually short, so during that time, I'd like to become aware of what I need to do, perfect my skills, be considerate, and become the kind of woman who can understand the situation and take resourceful action. I guess that's asking a lot *(laughs)*, but I want to graduate as the perfect Asuka Suzuki!

R: Thank you for your comments today, everyone! I'm looking forward to seeing you in six months!

Cooperation by: Tokyo Animator College http://www.tag.co.jp/

Maki Minami is from Saitama Prefecture in Japan. She debuted in 2001 with *Kanata no Ao* (Faraway Blue). Her other works include *Kimi wa Girlfriend* (You're My Girlfriend), *Mainichi ga Takaramono* (Every Day Is a Treasure), *Yuki Atataka* (Warm Winter) and *S•A*, which was published in English by VIZ Media.

VOICE OVER!
SEIYU ACADEMY
VOL. 3
Shojo Beat Edition

STORY AND ART BY
MAKI MINAMI

TECHNICAL ADVISORS
Yoichi Kato, Kaori Kagami, Ayumi Hashidate,
Ayako Harino and Touko Fujitani

Special Thanks
81produce
Tokyo Animator College
Tokyo Animation College

English Translation & Adaptation/John Werry
Touch-up Art & Lettering/Sabrina Heep
Design/Yukiko Whitley
Editor/Pancha Diaz

SEIYU KA! by Maki Minami
© Maki Minami 2010
All rights reserved.
First published in Japan in 2010 by HAKUSENSHA, Inc., Tokyo.
English language translation rights arranged with
HAKUSENSHA, Inc., Tokyo.

Printed in the U.S.A.

Published by VIZ Media, LLC
P.O. Box 77010
San Francisco, CA 94107

10 9 8 7 6 5 4 3 2 1
First printing, February 2014

www.viz.com   www.shojobeat.com

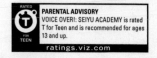

PARENTAL ADVISORY
VOICE OVER!: SEIYU ACADEMY is rated
T for Teen and is recommended for ages
13 and up.
ratings.viz.com

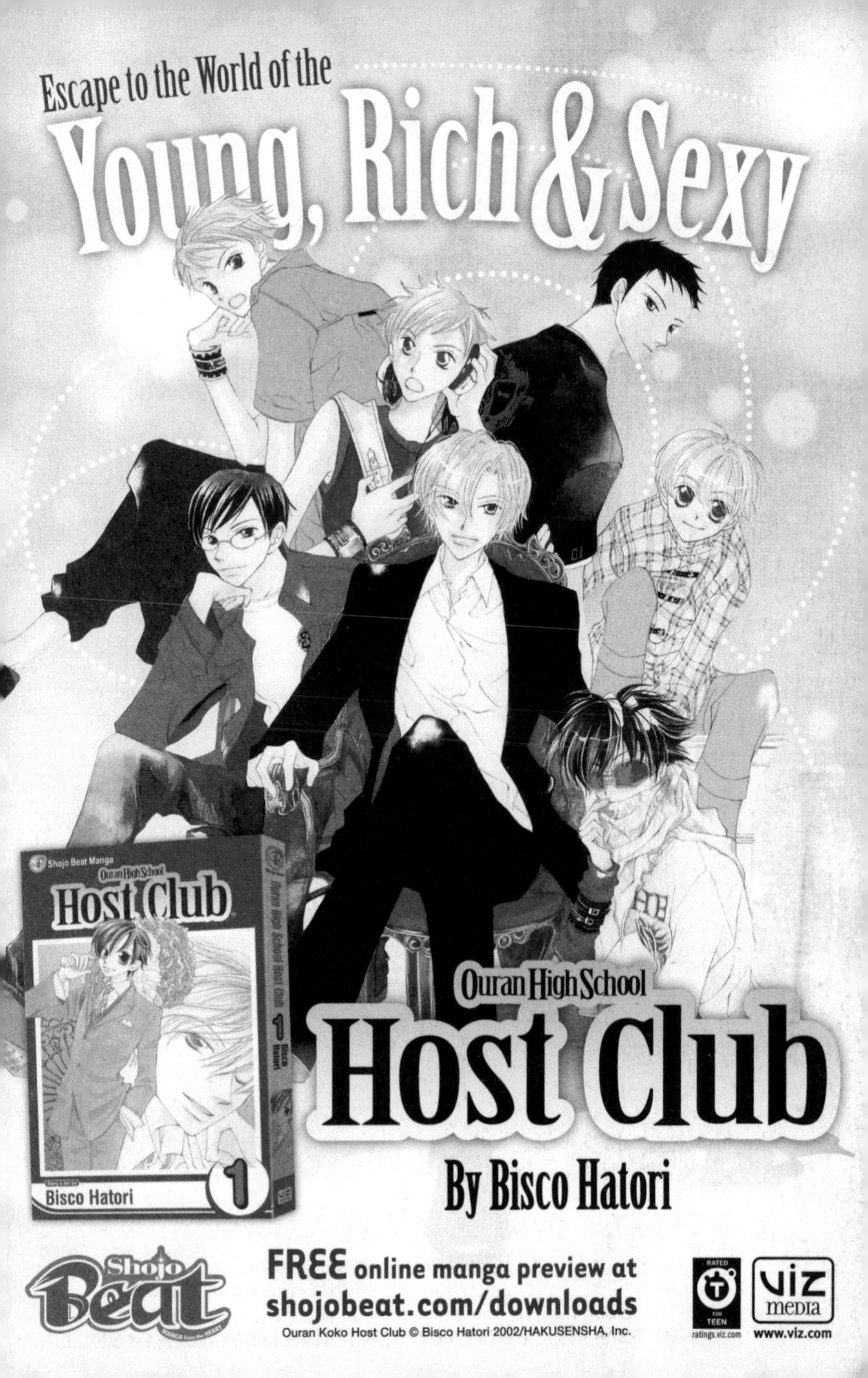
Escape to the World of the
Young, Rich & Sexy
Shojo Beat Manga
Ouran High School
Host Club
Ouran High School Host Club 1 Bisco Hatori
Story & Art by
Bisco Hatori
1
Ouran High School
Host Club
By Bisco Hatori
Shojo Beat
MANGA from the HEART
FREE online manga preview at
shojobeat.com/downloads
Ouran Koko Host Club © Bisco Hatori 2002/HAKUSENSHA, Inc.
RATED
T
FOR TEEN
ratings.viz.com
VIZ media
www.viz.com

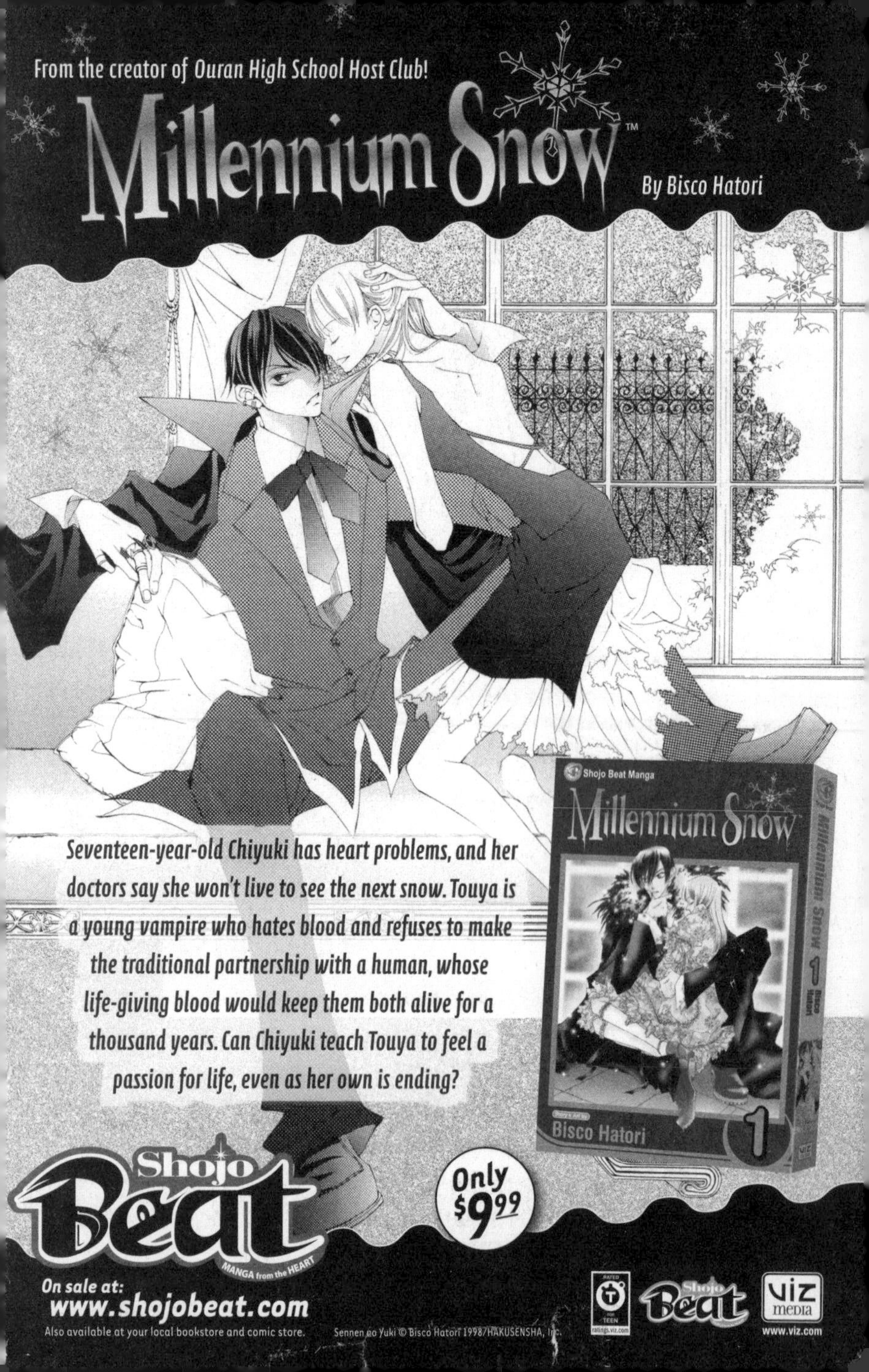
From the creator of Ouran High School Host Club!
Millennium Snow™
By Bisco Hatori
Seventeen-year-old Chiyuki has heart problems, and her doctors say she won't live to see the next snow. Touya is a young vampire who hates blood and refuses to make the traditional partnership with a human, whose life-giving blood would keep them both alive for a thousand years. Can Chiyuki teach Touya to feel a passion for life, even as her own is ending?
Shojo Beat Manga
Millennium Snow
Bisco Hatori
1
Shojo Beat
MANGA from the HEART
Only $9.99
On sale at:
www.shojobeat.com
Also available at your local bookstore and comic store.
Sennen no Yuki © Bisco Hatori 1998/HAKUSENSHA, Inc.
RATED T TEEN
ratings.viz.com
Shojo Beat
VIZ media
www.viz.com

This is the last page.

In keeping with the original Japanese comic format, this book reads from right to left—so action, sound effects, and word balloons are completely reversed. This preserves the orientation of the original artwork—plus, it's fun! Check out the diagram shown here to get the hang of things, and then turn to the other side of the book to get started!

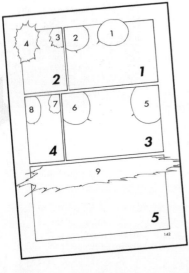